HOMELAND

HOME LAND

Oral Histories of Palestine and Palestinians

Edited by Staughton Lynd,
Sam Bahour and Alice Lynd

OLIVE
BRANCH
PRESS

An imprint of Interlink Publishing Group, Inc.
NEW YORK

First published in 1994 by
Olive Branch Press
An imprint of Interlink Publishing Group, Inc.
99 Seventh Avenue
Brooklyn, New York 11215

Library of Congress Cataloging-in-Publication Data

Homeland : oral histories of Palestine and Palestinians / edited by
    Staughton Lynd, Alice Lynd, and Sam Bahour.
        p.   cm.
    Includes bibliographical references and index.
    ISBN 1-56656-133-7 — ISBN 1-56656-132-9 (pbk.)
    1. Palestinian Arabs—Biography. 2. Jewish-Arab relations—1949–
I. Lynd, Staughton. II. Lynd, Alice. III. Bahour, Sam.
DS119.7.H67   1994
909'.049274'0922—dc20
[B]

Printed and bound in the United States of America
10 9 8 7 6 5 4 3 2 1

Our stories are not written in history.
People tell our stories on the long nights together.
So raise up your voices, raise them up!
— Marcel Khalifeh, "Aliha"

Contents

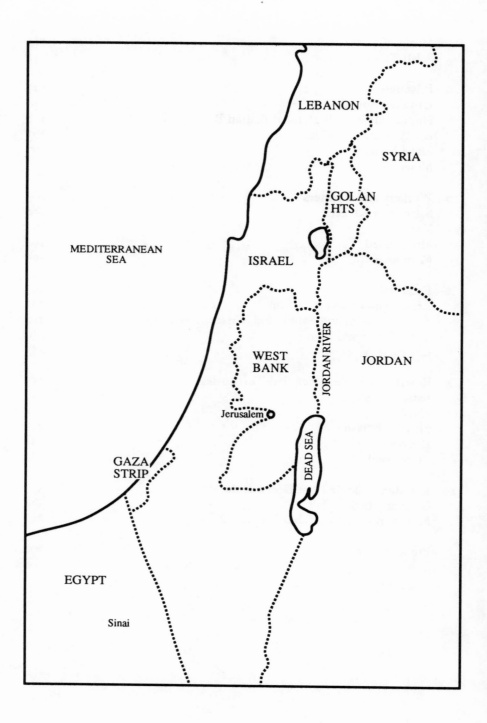

Introduction

Why This Oral History?

The Palestinian scholar Edward W. Said has suggested some of the difficulties Palestinians face in telling their history:

> [I]n the West Bank and Gaza, because people are so much in need of security, the Palestinians go from one day to the next and the last thing they want to do is tell their story. They just want to survive. That is true of the Palestinians in Lebanon and elsewhere where they're under assault. The problem of survival is so great that you don't think in terms of narration, just in terms of getting through to the next day. Internationally, whenever a Palestinian tries to tell a story, to put in a dramatic and realizable way the interrupted story of Palestine and its connection to the story of Israel, it's systematically attacked.[1]

Haidar Abdel-Shafi, spokesperson for the Palestinian delegation to the Madrid Peace Conference in October 1991, stated similarly in his opening remarks: "It is time for us to narrate our own story."[2]

For co-editor Sam Bahour, doing this history was a re-learning of the experience of his own people. As he wrote for an oral history workshop:[3]

> This lesson of history and of the Palestinian struggle came straight from the mouths and hearts of very beloved family and friends. For example, Husam Rafeedie is someone that I have been around since my childhood. I spent many nights hearing my elders speak about life in Palestine. Husam and my father would reminisce about their childhood days and discuss their political

1. David Barsamian, "An Interview with Edward W. Said," *Z Magazine* (Feb. 1992), p. 90.
2. "Madrid: Palestinians Tell Their Own Story," *The Middle East Justice Network* (Dec. 1991–Jan. 1992), p. 6.
3. "The Unheard Voices: Palestinians Speaking About Themselves," Oral History Association, 1992 Annual Meeting, Cleveland, Ohio, October 17, 1992.

convictions. But I never had the opportunity to hear Husam start from when he was a child and share his collective knowledge and feelings of the Palestinian plight. When I left Husam's home the evening of the interview I felt as if I had been introduced to a new person.

Likewise, many of the prisoners that we interviewed are close friends. I had known that they spent time in Israeli prisons, but I never received a full, first-hand account of their arrest and life in jail. . . .

During my activities in the General Union of Palestinian Students I spent hours upon hours working and organizing with two young men from "The Camp." But I was only faintly aware of the details of their upbringing. During their account I had my eyes opened to what they have lived through while living in a refugee camp in southern Lebanon and the extent of turmoil they have witnessed.

When we interviewed a family in the Gaza Strip I felt guilty to leave them in their predicament, knowing that in a few days we would be back in the States with all of our luxuries and comforts. When the family bid us farewell they asked for us to come back, knowing deep inside that most visitors to the Gaza Strip never return. When we did return the following summer I felt that our presence gave them hope in knowing that people abroad do care and are trying to explain their horrible diaspora. As we interviewed the mother of the family for the second time, she addressed a sentence to us and then two sentences to her children in an effort to make sure they also understood their mother's history.

Finally, when we went to interview my father I thought I had his account memorized. I was not expecting the interview process with my father to yield new stories. I thought I must have heard all that he had to say in my twenty-seven years.

I was mistaken. The initial interview did reiterate many stories that I had already heard. But to see my father tell them in sequence, and to detect the emotion that was being expressed, was priceless. After our oral history team transcribed the initial interview I took the responsibility to read it back to my father and make any corrections he saw fit. That next evening we did not get to making many corrections. Rather, my father gave me an account of his private life. If this book never would have become a reality, the making of that evening with my mother and father would have been worth all my efforts.

What Did We Do?

The idea for this book arose at an occasion in Youngstown, Ohio to celebrate the beginning of Ramadan in March 1991. Members of the Arab-American community and members of the Youngstown Coalition for Peace in the Middle East (including the three editors) gathered at the Arab Community Center. A representative of the Muslim mosque explained the meaning of Ramadan, and offered a prayer. In order to avoid Arab-Jewish or other confrontations, Sam Bahour asked people to speak only from their own personal experience of the crisis in the Middle East.

Among those who testified that night were Mazin and Abu Sam (whose accounts appear in this book). Jules Lobel, a professor of international law, said that his father's family had been part of the Jewish community in Palestine since the eighteenth century. On a recent visit to the area, he continued, during the day he inquired into human rights abuses, while in the evening he sought out relatives of his father who ranged from staunch supporters of Israeli expansion to a man who had refused service in the occupied areas and had been imprisoned.

After the Ramadan event, we began to tape record oral histories with Palestinian-Americans living in the Youngstown area or visiting in the United States. The fact that Salah Ta'amari conducts a summer youth camp a few miles from Youngstown gave us the opportunity to record his remarkable saga. Finally, on two visits to occupied Palestine and Israel in 1991 and 1992 many more persons told us their stories.

We were led from person to person by Palestinians wanting us to interview individuals who they knew had witnessed significant historical events such as the flights from Deir Yassin in 1948 and from Emwas in 1967. We sought diversity: thus the book includes representatives both of the mainstream Fatah tendency and of more radical groups, such as the Popular Front for the Liberation of Palestine. However, we do not pretend to represent every sector or point of view.

Some persons spoke in Arabic, others in English. When an individual spoke in Arabic, Sam Bahour translated on the spot and later compared a transcript of his translation with the tape. When possible, the person providing an account also reviewed the edited transcript. We apologize here for any mistakes or distortions that may have crept in.

We have identified some of those offering accounts by names that are not their own, lest they come to harm by contributing to this book.

Memory is not at its best in recalling dates, names, and numbers. While this book is not intended as a scholarly work, we have tried to verify the statements it contains. We sought corroborating information from other participants in events, and from public documents, newspapers, and secondary sources. Especially where the accounts deal with controversial themes, such as the treatment of Palestinian prisoners, we have found written sources and corroborating interviews which lead us to believe that the information presented is essentially accurate.

The editors have included footnotes of several kinds. Often the oral history was offered in the presence of other members of the family, friends, and colleagues. Comments and corrections by family members or friends who were present during interviews are included in some accounts. References to corroborating sources of information from scholarly studies and human rights investigations also appear in some cases.[4] And, in numerous accounts,

4. The United States is required by the Foreign Assistance Act and other legislation to consider human rights before approving various kinds of foreign aid. Except under extraordinary circumstances, no assistance is to be provided to any country whose government engages in a consistent pattern of gross violations of internationally recognized human rights, including torture or cruel, inhuman, or degrading treatment or punishment, prolonged detention without charges, etc. The U.S. State Department is required by law to send a report to Congress each year, considering relevant findings of international organizations such as the International Committee of the Red Cross and the International Commission of Jurists (of which Al-Haq is the West Bank affiliate). See 22 U.S.C. §

there are references to the Fourth Geneva Convention[5] and other sources of international law.

Historical Overview

These are narratives of individuals whose lives were shaped by history. For example, Lawahez was a seven-year-old girl at the time of the Six Day War in 1967. Thereafter, her father did not have work. This little girl saw the economic decline of her family under occupation and she responded by going on a demonstration. During her teens in the 1970s, she was arrested and imprisoned. As the result of her jailings, her mother's outlook and activities changed, and both parents came to respect her choices as a woman, including her choice of whom to marry. Many other mothers and fathers were at the same time being stretched by many other daughters and sons in prison. Such experiences create the limits of what a people regards as tolerable or admirable. We see the realignment of relationships under the hammer of history, within the family and within the larger society, through this one girl's story.

For those unfamiliar with this part of the world, it may be helpful to have an all-too-brief summary of its recent history.

Historic Palestine is bordered by Lebanon on the north, by Syria and Jordan on the east, by Egypt on the southwest, and on the west by the Mediterranean Sea.

For four centuries prior to World War I, this area was part of the Ottoman Empire. At the end of the war, the League of Nations asked Great Britain to govern the area in trust — as a "mandate" — until its people were deemed able to govern themselves. Arab spokespersons denounced the Palestine Mandate as a new form of colonialism. They invoked the "Fourteen Points" of United States President Woodrow Wilson, which included "the rejection of any territorial acquisition by conquest and the recognition of the right of self-determination of peoples."

Meantime, in 1917, British foreign secretary Arthur Balfour obtained cabinet approval for a statement that Great Britain viewed with favor "the establishment in Palestine of a national home for the Jewish people." The statement also said that "nothing shall be done which may prejudice the civil

---

262(d)(a)(1) and (e), § 2151n(a), and § 2304(a)(2) and (d)(1). These are the U.S. State Department, *Country Reports on Human Rights Practices*, from which some footnotes and headnotes are drawn to provide corroborating information from an independent, official source.

5. The Geneva Conventions of 12 August 1949, Commentary, published under the general editorship of Jean S. Pictet, *IV Geneva Convention Relative To The Protection Of Civilian Persons In Time Of War* (Geneva, Switzerland: International Committee of the Red Cross, 1958). The International Committee of the Red Cross published the Fourth Geneva Convention with commentary in hopes that its principles would become widely known and influential throughout the world. The State of Israel signed and ratified the Fourth Geneva Convention, but Israel has taken the position that the Fourth Geneva Convention does not apply within the West Bank and Gaza Strip. The Security Council of the United Nations has called on Israel to recognize the application of the Fourth Geneva Convention to the occupied Palestinian territories and to abide by its provisions. (Security Council Resolution 681.) Whether or not Israel is bound by the Fourth Geneva Convention within the Occupied Territories, Israel is still bound by the principles stated in the Fourth Geneva Convention insofar as they are statements of customary international law. (Article 158.)

and religious rights of existing non-Jewish communities in Palestine." This statement became known as "the Balfour Declaration."

Between World Wars I and II, continuing immigration of Jews to the area led to tension with Palestinians already resident there. Many older Palestinians told us of warm relations with their Jewish neighbors before the creation of the State of Israel. But there were also episodes of violent Palestinian resistance, in 1921, in 1929, and especially in 1936–39. The demands of the 1936–39 revolt were similar to the demands of Palestinians more than half a century later:

1. An end to Jewish immigration;
2. Prohibition of transfer of ownership of Arab lands to Jews;
3. Creation of a democratic government in which Arabs would share in proportion to their numbers.[6] (In 1936, according to Michael J. Cohen,[7] the Jewish population of Palestine was about 400,000, the Arab population about 940,000. A decade later, Jews were approximately a third of the total number of persons living in Palestine.)

In February 1947 the British government announced its intention to give up the Palestine Mandate. The newly-formed United Nations voted in November 1947 to partition Palestine into Jewish and Arab states. Jewish spokespersons like David Ben-Gurion accepted the U.N. plan, viewing it as a first step toward a Jewish state in all of Palestine.[8] Arab representatives rejected it. Jews proclaimed the State of Israel in May 1948. Both Arabs and Jews initiated military action. Jewish forces took control of an area larger than that envisioned by the U.N. plan.

The State of Israel as it emerged from war in 1949 included the Mediterranean coast except for the "Gaza Strip" next to Egypt; and the interior of Palestine except for the "West Bank" (a large, roughly rectangular, bloc of land running from Jenin and Nablus in the north to Hebron in the south on the western side of the Jordan River) and part of the city of Jerusalem, which was divided into Jewish West Jerusalem and Arab East Jerusalem. Egypt administered the Gaza Strip. Jordan administered the West Bank.

About half the Palestinians living in Palestine and perhaps five-sixths of the Palestinians living in what is now Israel became refugees during the 1948–49 war. Simha Flapan, an Israeli scholar, states: "Between 600,000 and 700,000 Palestinian Arabs were evicted or fled."[9] The first of the oral histories that follow describe the exodus. Two of the accounts recall the taking of Deir

---

6. Sami Hadawi, *Palestinian Rights and Losses in 1948: A Comprehensive Study* (London: Saqi Books, 1988), p. 73, quoting a joint memorandum presented to the British High Commissioner on November 25, 1935, by the leaders of the five Arab parties; Michael J. Cohen, *The Origins and Evolution of the Arab-Zionist Conflict* (Berkeley: University of California Press, 1987), p. 90.
7. Michael J. Cohen, op. cit., p. 90. Edward W. Said, *The Question of Palestine* (New York: Times Books, 1980), p. 11, gives similar figures for the Palestinian population in 1936: Jews 384,078, Arabs 982,614.
8. Simha Flapan, *The Birth of Israel: Myths and Realities* (New York: Pantheon Books, 1987), pp. 21–22, 30–33.
9. Simha Flapan, op. cit., p. 83. Other estimates for the number of Palestinians displaced in 1948 are 600–760,000, Benny Morris, "Debate on the 1948 Exodus," *Journal of Palestine Studies*, v. 21, no. 1 (Autumn 1991), p. 109, and 780,000, Said, op. cit., p. 14, and John Quigley, *Palestine and Israel: A Challenge to Justice* (Durham: Duke University Press, 1990), p. 86.

Yassin, an Arab village west of Jerusalem, on April 9, 1948, where an estimated 250 civilians were killed by Jewish irregular forces[10] under the command of Menachem Begin, later Israeli prime minister.

The Palestinian refugees found shelter in camps administered by the United Nations and located in the Gaza Strip (see the accounts of Mohammed Ibrahim Harb and Amal Deeb), the West Bank (as in the case of the two men from Jenin), Jordan, and southern Lebanon (where the refugee camp we have called "the Camp" is located).

In June 1967, Israel launched a preemptive strike in response to menacing military preparations by Egypt. In six days, Israeli forces took East Jerusalem, the West Bank, the Gaza Strip, that portion of Syria known as the Golan Heights, and the Egyptian Sinai Peninsula. East Jerusalem was annexed to Israel. In 1978 the Sinai Peninsula was returned to Egypt as a result of the Camp David Accords. The Gaza Strip and West Bank remain occupied territories, separated from Israel proper by an imaginary "green line" along the 1949–1967 Israeli frontier.

During the 1967 war an estimated 350,000 Palestinian Arabs were displaced from the West Bank and Gaza Strip, about a quarter of the total population of the two areas.[11] Whereas in 1948 the Israeli forces typically destroyed the villages they captured, and ordered the Arab population to leave (for an important exception, see Ghanem Habib-Allah's account of what happened in Nazareth and surrounding villages), in 1967 the destruction of villages was less common. Yet it happened, for example in Emwas and neighboring villages as described by Hikmat Deeb Ali, and throughout the Golan Heights.

In 1982 Israel invaded Lebanon. As narrated by Salah Ta'amari and Mazin, a huge internment facility was set up in southern Lebanon near Ansar. Somewhere between 9,000 and 15,000 males between the ages of 16 and 60[12] — 1,000 from "the Camp" alone[13] — were detained without charges in Ansar, some until November 1983. Israel withdrew from Lebanon in 1985, after declaring that a strip of land north of the Israeli border with Lebanon would be a "security zone" controlled by Israeli troops and Lebanese forces armed and trained by Israel.

From the beginning, as Israeli expansion proceeded a Palestinian resistance movement came into being. Inside occupied Palestine, what Amal Younis calls the "seeds" of resistance were planted. Outside Palestine, Fatah (an acronym for "the Palestine National Liberation Movement") was established in the late 1950s and early 1960s through the merger of nationalist networks "in the refugee camps, in diaspora groupings of Palestinian stu-

10. Quigley, op. cit., p. 58, citing *The New York Times*, Apr. 10, 1948, p. A6. To the same effect, see David McDowall, *Palestine and Israel: The Uprising and Beyond* (Berkeley: University of California Press, 1989), p. 194 and ch. 8, n. 44, citing numerous sources including the eyewitness account of a Red Cross delegate, the evidence of a Haganah intelligence officer who says he was denied permission to warn the inhabitants before the Irgun attacked, and Begin's memoirs.
11. Quigley, op. cit., p. 168.
12. U.S. State Department, *Country Reports on Human Rights Practices for 1982*, Lebanon, p. 1198.
13. Leila Richards, *The Hills of Sidon: Journal from South Lebanon 1983–85* (New York: Adama Books, 1988), p. 102.

dents, and in the embryo Palestinian communities of the emerging Arab Gulf states," and the Palestine Liberation Organization (PLO) was founded in 1964.[14] Um Sa'ad and Salah Ta'amari played a part in these events while university students in Cairo. In the late 1960s, Fatah and other Palestinian guerrilla groups became dominant in the PLO. First from refugee camps in Jordan, and then, after a break with King Hussein, from refugee camps in Lebanon, Palestinian guerrillas mounted small military incursions into Israel.

From the late 1970s onward, the center of gravity of the movement shifted toward those resisting Israel from within the Occupied Territories. Students, women, prisoners, and trade unionists — persons like Maha Nassar, Ali Mohammed Jiddah, Badran Bader Jaber, and Salah Abu Kteish — formed popular organizations linked by a vision of Palestinian nationality. The remarkable persistence of individual participants in these popular organizations (for example, the steadfast conduct of so many prisoners) is based in part on the mutual support of family members. Hence, in the section entitled "Families" we present narratives by persons belonging to different generations of the same families united in a common cause.

The Intifada or "Uprising" erupted in December 1987. The ongoing Intifada is a response to strategic realities such as the following:

> East Jerusalem . . . has been formally annexed to Israel;
>
> 120,000 Jews now live in East Jerusalem;
>
> 165 Israeli settlements have been established in the West Bank and Gaza Strip, with a total population of 93,000 Jews outside East Jerusalem;
>
> 55 per cent of the lands of the West Bank and 42 per cent of those of the Gaza Strip have been confiscated or otherwise alienated from Palestinian ownership;
>
> Palestinian construction is barred on 68 per cent of the West Bank;
>
> All the water resources of the occupied territories are under Israeli control — the bulk being diverted to the needs of Israel or of Israeli settlers in the occupied territories.[15]

Section 9 offers narratives of the Intifada by well-known public figures as well as by two obscure young men, one of them presently underground. All those whom we interviewed concur that the essence of Israeli occupation is the continuing process of Israeli settlement and Israeli confiscation of Palestinian land and water, and the heart of the resistance is the effort to reverse these Israeli-created "facts on the ground."

In a concluding section we catch glimpses of the less-well-known resistance activity of the perhaps 730,000 Palestinians who live within Israel as second-class citizens.

The independent State of Palestine was declared by the Palestine National

---

14. Helena Cobban, *The Palestine Liberation Organisation: People, Power, and Politics* (Cambridge: Cambridge University Press, 1984), pp. 6, 10.
15. Walid Khalidi, "The Palestine Problem: An Overview," *Journal of Palestine Studies*, v. 21, no. 1 (Autumn 1991), p. 10.

Council, the Palestinian parliament in exile, in November 1988. Implicitly recognizing the right of the State of Israel to exist, the declaration also affirmed that the State of Palestine "is the state of Palestinians wherever they may be." The right of Israel to exist was stated explicitly by the PLO Chairman one month later.

At this time the ratio of Jews and Arabs within Palestine is roughly the reverse of what it was in 1948. Then there were two Arabs for every Jew. Now there are more than three Jews for every two Arabs, distributed (very approximately) as follows:

Jews within Israel	4,250,000
Jews within the occupied territories	150,000
Arabs within Israel	730,000
Arabs within the Gaza Strip	715,000
Arabs within the West Bank including East Jerusalem	1,075,000[16]

More than three million Palestinians live in diaspora outside Palestine.[17]

Who We Are, Acknowledgments, Dedication

Sam Bahour is a Palestinian-American who was born and grew up in Youngstown, Ohio. He served as local President of the General Union of Palestinian Students from 1984 to 1988 and in several positions for the Arab Community Center of Youngstown, Ohio. In 1987, he was a co-founder of the Palestinian American Youth organization, and currently serves as its national coordinator. He has led trips to the occupied areas of Palestine annually for the last several years.

Alice and Staughton Lynd are Quakers (Religious Society of Friends), lawyers, and writers. Staughton Lynd was director of Freedom Schools in the Mississippi Summer Project of 1964 and chairperson of the first march on Washington against the war in Vietnam in April 1965. He taught history at Spelman College and Yale University before becoming a lawyer. Alice Lynd edited *We Won't Go: Personal Accounts of War Objectors*, and the Lynds jointly edited *Rank and File: Personal Histories by Working-Class Organizers*.

The editors give thanks to each of the contributors and their families and friends; to Phyllis Bennis whose encouragement and suggestions as an editor have made this a richer collection; to Jane Hallow for selecting from lengthy transcripts, focusing, and reviewing with Salah Ta'amari the material in his account of Ansar; to Jeff Vanik for helping to prepare the maps; and to others who helped to bring this book into being.

This book is dedicated to the late cartoonist, Naji Al Ali. Mr. Ali's parents fled from northern Palestine in 1948 and he grew up in the Ein El Hilweh

---

16. The Center for Policy Analysis on Palestine, *Facts And Figures About The Palestinians* (Washington, D.C.: 1992), p. 4.
17. Ibid.

refugee camp in southern Lebanon. He is the creator of the cartoon figure "Handallah," the little boy, with hair standing straight on end, who stands with his back to the viewer in Mr. Ali's cartoons. On a visit to Youngstown before his assassination, Mr. Ali said that Handallah was himself, a child who had never been able to grow up because of the terrifying things that he had been obliged to watch.

Sam Bahour, Alice and Staughton Lynd

The Contributors

Mohammed Ibrahim Harb is an elderly man. He spoke to us in English during August 1991 in a refugee camp where he now lives with his extended family in the Gaza Strip.

Amal Deeb lives with her extended family in the Rafah Refugee Camp in the Gaza Strip. She was a child when her family fled to Gaza in 1948. Several young members of the family were listening as she told her narrative in Arabic in August 1992. Her contribution to the women's section is based on a previous conversation with her in Arabic in August 1991.

Ahmad Ayesh Khalil is an elderly man. He spoke to us in Arabic at his home in Ramallah, West Bank, in August 1992.

Aiysha Jima Zidan was a young woman when she fled from Deir Yassin in 1948. She spoke to us in Arabic in Ramallah, West Bank, in August 1992.

Um Khalil was close to seventy years old when we interviewed her at her home in El Bireh, West Bank, in August 1992. After the years recounted here, Um Khalil established the Society of Ina'sh El-Usra, an organization that provides services to women and children who are in need, including a home for orphan girls, vocational and production centers, financial aid and cultural programs. She spoke to us in English.

Bashar and **Khaled** are men who came forward spontaneously to be interviewed at the Jenin Camp, West Bank, in August 1992. They spoke to us in Arabic.

Riyad is a young man who grew up in a refugee camp in southern Lebanon and came to the United States as a student. He was interviewed in English in May 1991.

Um Ossama lives with her husband and daughter in Ein El Hilweh refugee camp in southern Lebanon. She was interviewed in Arabic with her sons, **Ali** and **Mazin** (see below), in June 1992 when she came to the United States to visit.

Ali, son of **Um Ossama**, grew up in Ein El Hilweh refugee camp and came to the United States as a student. He spoke to us in English in May 1991 and June 1992.

Um Sa'ad was living in the United States when we interviewed her in 1991. She spoke to us in English in the presence of her mother and daughter.

Hikmat Deeb Ali was a young man in 1967 when he fled from Emwas. He has a collection of newspaper articles, photographs and other materials of historical interest related to Emwas. He spoke to us in Arabic at his home in Ramallah, West Bank, in the presence of his family and friends, in August 1992.

Husam Rafeedie lives in the United States with his wife, **Salwa** (see below), and four children. We interviewed Husam and Salwa in May 1991 in their home with their children eagerly listening, and again in April 1992 when **Zahwa Rafeedie** (see below) was visiting. Husam and Salwa spoke to us in English.

Salah Ta'amari was a young man at the time of the Six Day War in 1967. We interviewed him in English in July 1991 at a time when he was directing a summer camp for Arab-American children in Ohio, and in April 1992 at the home of a friend in Washington, D.C.

Lawahez Burgal is married to **Mohammed Burgal** (see below) and is the mother of three young children. We interviewed her in English at the home of her parents in East Jerusalem in August 1992.

Amal Younis was a young woman in the 1960s. She lives in the United States with her husband and children. We interviewed her in Arabic in her home together with other members of her family in January 1992.

Sarona is a woman in her twenties, now living in the United States with her husband and child. Although we spoke with her more than once, the material in this account was taken principally from an interview in Arabic in January 1992.

Maha Nassar lives in El Bireh, West Bank, with her husband and young children. This interview took place in her home in English in August 1992.

Mazin, son of **Um Ossama**, grew up in Ein El Hilweh refugee camp and came to the United States as a student. He spoke to us in English in May 1991 and June 1992.

Ali Mohammed Jiddah lives with his wife and young children in the Old City of East Jerusalem. Now a journalist, he learned on the day of this interview in August 1992 that the newspaper for which he was working (translating articles from the Hebrew press into Arabic) had just been shut down by Israeli authorities. He spoke with us in English.

Walid is a middle-aged man who was living in Nablus, West Bank, at the time we spoke with him in August 1991. He spoke to us in Arabic.

Badran Bader Jaber is a middle-aged man who lives in Hebron, West Bank. He spoke to us in English in August 1992.

Mousa is a young man from El Bireh, West Bank, now living in the United States. We interviewed him in Arabic in 1991.

Salah Abu Kteish is a man in his forties who lives with his wife and children in the Old City of Jerusalem. This interview took place in Arabic in August 1992.

Yacoub is a young man who was living in El Bireh, West Bank, at the time of the events narrated in this account. He spoke to us in Arabic at the home of a friend in the United States in 1991.

Mohammed is a young man who lives in the Jenin Camp, West Bank. We spoke with him in Arabic in August 1992.

Mamdouh is a middle-aged man who lives in a village in the Jordan Valley, north of Jericho. He spoke to us in Arabic in August 1991.

Leeka Bahour is a woman in her sixties who lives in Ramallah, West Bank. She is the aunt of **Abu Sam** (see below), and the great aunt of co-editor, Sam Bahour. We interviewed her in Arabic in her home in August 1992.

Abu Sam is a man in his fifties who now lives in the United States. He is the father of co-editor, Sam Bahour. We interviewed him in English in April 1991 and January 1992.

Zahwa, Husam (see above), **Salwa**, and **Wissam Rafeedie** are members of one family, some of whom are in the United States. **Zahwa Rafeedie** is the mother of Husam and Wissam. She lives in El Bireh, West Bank. She spoke with us in Arabic in April 1992. **Wissam** is in prison in Hebron, West Bank. Wissam's letters were written in Arabic. **Salwa**, from Birzeit, West Bank, is Husam's wife (see above).

Um Sa'alem and Family live in Jenin, West Bank. We spoke with them in Arabic in August 1991 and we returned for the family interview in August 1992. **Um Sa'alem** is the mother of **Sa'alem**, who is in his thirties, and **Ahmad**, who was thirteen at the time of the family interview. At that time also, **Fatmeh** was engaged to marry Sa'alem.

Um Elias is a woman in her sixties who lives in Beit Sahour, West Bank. She is the mother of **Elias Rishmawi** (see below). She spoke to us in English in August 1992.

Bassam Shaka'a, the last elected mayor of Nablus, now confined to a wheelchair, continues to live in Nablus, West Bank. He spoke to us in English in August 1991.

Nidal was a teenager living in a refugee camp in the Gaza Strip at the time of the events narrated. We interviewed him at the home of a friend when he was in the United States for medical treatment in 1992. He spoke to us in Arabic.

Hassan is a young man whom we interviewed at a refugee camp in the Gaza Strip in August 1992. He spoke to us in Arabic. Introduced to us as a "wanted man," he believed he might become the target of one of Israel's undercover units which allegedly kill rather than arrest individuals suspected of security violations.[1]

Elias Rishmawi is a man in his forties, son of **Um Elias** (see above), who lives and works as a pharmacist in Beit Sahour, West Bank. This account is based on an interview with him in English in August 1991, updated and revised by him a year later.

Riyad Malki teaches civil engineering at Birzeit University and lives in El Bireh, West Bank. He spoke to us in English in August 1991.

---

1. See Palestine Human Rights Information Center, *Targeting to Kill: Israel's Undercover Units* (Jerusalem: 1992). The U.S. State Department, *Country Reports on Human Rights Practices for 1991*, p. 1441, states: "In 1991 nonuniformed security personnel are known to have killed 27 Palestinians, many of whom were unarmed but were generally either wanted, masked, or fleeing from authorities after writing graffiti."

Ghanem Habib-Allah was thirty years old when we interviewed him in August 1992. He lives in the village of Ein Mahil, near Nazareth, within Israel. He spoke to us in English.

Mohammed Burgal grew up as an Arab living within the State of Israel. Material in this account was drawn from interviews with Mohammed and his wife, **Lawahez** (see above), in Lod, Israel where they were living in August 1991, and from an interview with Mohammed when he visited the United States in 1992. They spoke to us in English.

Glossary

Abu: father of [first son].

administrative detention: imprisonment without formal charges or trial.

Ansar: detention camp in southern Lebanon set up by Israelis in 1982.

Ansar 2: detention camp in Israeli-occupied Gaza Strip.

Ansar 3: [Ketziot] detention camp in Negev Desert, Israel, established during the Intifada.

Balfour Declaration: letter written in 1917 by Lord Balfour, British foreign secretary, to Lord Rothschild, head of the Zionist Federation in Britain, which stated that Britain viewed with favor the establishment in Palestine of a national home for the Jewish people.

DFLP: Democratic Front for the Liberation of Palestine.

dubka: traditional Palestinian dance.

dunum: approximately 1/4 acre.

Fatah: The "Palestine National Liberation Movement — FATAH" is the largest faction within the Palestine Liberation Organization.

fedayin: Palestinian guerrilla fighters.

green card: identification card given to a Palestinian who has been detained or arrested; bearer may not enter Israel or East Jerusalem.

Green Line: Israeli border as of 1948. "Inside" the Green Line is the area which became the State of Israel in 1948. The West Bank and Gaza Strip are outside the Green Line.

Hamas: Islamic Resistance Movement.

Hizballah: Party of God [Muslim].

ICRC: International Committee of the Red Cross.

Intifada: uprising; in particular, the popular protest against Israeli occupation which began in the Gaza Strip and West Bank on December 9, 1987.

kaffiyeh: Palestinian checkered headdress.

moukhtar: head of the village.

mujahadin: Palestinian guerrilla fighters.

PFLP: Popular Front for the Liberation of Palestine.

PLO: Palestine Liberation Organization.

Sabra and Shatila: Palestinian refugee camps in West Beirut, Lebanon where massacres took place in 1982.

shabeh: prisoner handcuffed to a chair or pole in a stressful position for hours, often while blindfolded or with a sack over the head, sometimes with feet also shackled.

sheikh: religious leader [Muslim].

shekel: Israeli unit of money; in 1992, 1.4 shekels = $1 U.S.

Shin Bet: General Security Services [Israeli].

Um: mother of [first son].

UNRWA: United Nations Relief and Works Agency.

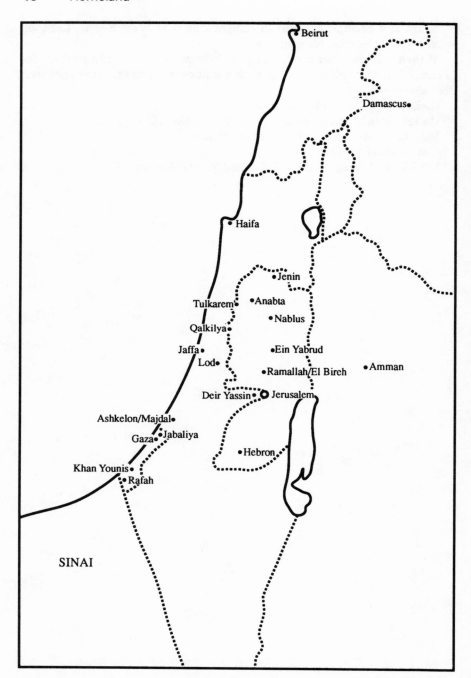

Beirut

Damascus•

Haifa

•Jenin

Tulkarem•   •Anabta

•Nablus

Qalkilya•

Jaffa•   •Ein Yabrud

Lod•   •Amman

•Ramallah/El Bireh

Deir Yassin• ◯ Jerusalem

Ashkelon/Majdal•

Gaza• •Jabaliya

•Hebron

Khan Younis•

•Rafah

SINAI

1

1948

As indicated in the Introduction, Israeli and Palestinian scholars estimate that at least 600,000 Palestinians living within what is now Israel fled in 1948. There is continuing debate as to the reasons for the exodus. Some believe that the flight of Palestine's Arabs was the result of a pre-planned, systematic Zionist policy of population transfer. Others emphasize the effect of Arab radio broadcasts. Israeli scholar Benny Morris, the leading student of the subject, concludes that "Jewish atrocities were a significant factor in propelling Palestine's Arabs into refugeedom, both directly, by affecting survivors, neighbors, and relatives and indirectly (usually via Arab media reports), by persuading Arabs farther afield that they might share the same fate if overrun by Jewish troops."[1]

Palestinians refer to the 1948 exodus as "al-naqba," a catastrophe or a disaster. Those who fled in 1948 have not been permitted to return.

★　　★　　★

Mohammed Ibrahim Harb

"He had been dead for two or three days when I found him."

I was born in Hamama, north of Ashkelon. The name of the town means "Peace Dove."

I grew up and married there. I washed dishes for a Christian family at the railroad station. I worked six and a half years for the British Army as a cook. I made twenty-one English pounds a month. I bought ten dunums of grape fields.

I worked for three years with a German Jew named Weiss. We slept together. We played football together. Why should we hate Jews? They are our brothers and cousins. Abraham is the father of us all.

---

1. Benny Morris, "Debate on the 1948 Exodus," *Journal of Palestine Studies*, v. 21, no. 1 (Autumn 1991), p. 108. See his major work, *The Birth of the Palestinian Refugee Problem, 1947–1949* (New York: Cambridge University Press, 1988).

In 1948, I took my mother, wife, brother and sister to the Jabaliya Refugee Camp in the Gaza Strip. My father remained in Hamama to watch our house. When I returned to get my father, he was dead. The door was broken down and he was bayoneted on the right side. He was blind and old. I think that when the Israeli soldiers knocked on the door, he didn't answer.

He had been dead for two or three days when I found him. A kitten was eating from his body. I buried him in a shallow grave and fled during the night. I took nothing from our home, not even our land certificates. I rode a donkey back to Gaza and told my mother.

Amal Deeb

"My family was the last pocket of resistance."

When we were exiled in 1948, we lived in Ikbebe. It was a small village near Lod. From there we came to Gaza.

In Ikbebe, we lived in houses similar to this but better. We had gardens. There was a very relaxed atmosphere. My grandfather used to tell us that half of the land in Ikbebe was his.

It was an agricultural area. We were farmers. We grew wheat, fava beans, oranges and grapefruits. Father, mother, and children, we used to plow and pick and do what farmers do. Also, we brought people to help us on our land.

The produce was sold to our village and to villages surrounding us through a market network of Palestinians. They used to come to our home and buy. We had storage facilities so we would take stuff in the summer and store it for winter. There was a continuous trade.

I had six sisters and three brothers. My older brother got an education. When he was not helping with the farm work he was going to school. All of my sisters studied except me. I was very young, so I didn't work and didn't go to school.

In an area by our village, people used to come from all over Palestine during the summer. They set up three-month summer camps for Palestinian children from Haifa and Jaffa and Lod. There was a religious shrine, a memorial for a sheikh who was old, well-known, and well-liked. People called him a prophet.

"We Slept in the Fields"

In 1948, when our people heard shooting in the next village, we left. We piled into cars. We took nothing with us. We had no time.

It was not a straight road. We left to the next village south. The following day, people didn't see a war so we went back to our village. When the shooting started again, we left for a second time. It was back and forth from village to village until finally we found ourselves on the border of Gaza without even knowing that we were coming here.

We slept in the fields. Those families who had friends or family in nearby villages would go and sleep with the people they knew. We had no relatives outside the village, so we ended up sleeping homeless.

My family was the last pocket of resistance that they found in Ikbebe. My two brothers and my father and my uncle and two friends stayed fourteen days fighting in Ikbebe until they finished all of their ammunition. When the last people left, my relatives left with them, and caught up with us.

We stayed in Majdal, which is now called Ashkelon, for three months. My uncle was a rich man in our village and made a deal for us to stay there.

From Majdal we came directly to Rafah. My father had a car. We were able to come here. But there were people who died from starvation in the streets, died from the heat, from walking too much. People dropped dead while they were trying to get down here. We had it easy.

Rafah Refugee Camp

When we came we found it all prickly pears. We cleaned up certain areas and we made tents. That was our home for the time being.

There were maybe twenty families here before we came. These were the original inhabitants of Rafah.

We didn't find in front of us any U.N. [United Nations], any UNRWA [United Nations Relief and Works Agency], or any kind of support mechanism. We built things up ourselves. A tent area of several families was an easy target, so whenever there was an airplane strike, we would move.

The people from Ikbebe did not stay together. We're here. We have family in Nablus. Some people went to Lod. Some people went to Khan Younis. They are spread out. Because it was a war zone, anywhere that we traveled we were trying to get away from trouble. If that took you to Rafah, you went to Rafah. If that took you to Lod, you went to Lod.

When we got this far there was not as much trouble as there had been on the way here. This is why we became residents of Rafah.

After things became calmer militarily, the U.N. came and started providing us with basic needs. They took a census of each area. Rafah was one area. They broke the areas up into how many families, how many individuals per family, how many tents were needed. The U.N. provided two kinds of tents, the hut type and the house type. If you had a small family, you took a hut type tent. If you had more than ten individuals, they would give you the house type tent. We were given a hut tent with straight sides.

If you look around the camp, wherever you find a house is where the tent for that family used to be. The second stage, after tents, was that the U.N. provided basic housing. The original house they gave us is still behind here, outside this window.

Many worked with the U.N. The U.N. was the only source of employment. If you worked, you didn't take money. You took a ration. If you were able to get an extra ration by working for them, you did. Otherwise, you took the hand-out ration, which was given to meet basic food needs.

My mother was a seamstress. After a while, when the U.N. started creating schools, they began to want school uniforms. They brought the material for uniforms to my mother. That was our income, other than the ration.

My brother worked with the volunteer committee. He was not educated enough to become a teacher in one of the schools. He volunteered his time for projects to build the camp. My father didn't work after he came here.

They brought us three water tanks for all of Rafah. Can you imagine the whole camp running after three tanks of water? It was a disaster.

My mother was so worried about her daughters being exposed to this bad situation, that she did not let any of her daughters go for water, except me. I made a fuss. I was eight or ten years old. I had to go. I wanted to help. So my mother would go with me and we would stand in the line to get water. We would carry the water on our heads in vases. We would have a drum here at the house. We would go there with little vases, back and forth until the drum was full, and that would be our water supply until it ran out.

[Continued below, Section 4, p. 94.]

Deir Yassin
I: Ahmad Ayesh Khalil

"Until this day, we don't know where they buried them."

I am seventy years old. We had a very nice house in Deir Yassin.

Before 1948, my father had a cement block factory. We also used to work on stone, breaking the stones.

We had much land before 1948. It was divided into plots. Some plots had olives. Other plots had fresh figs, almonds and grapes. One plot was where we used to work breaking the stones.

Deir Yassin was a small village outside Jerusalem. Before the massacre, we had 650 individuals from the youngest to the oldest. Deir Yassin was high and it was surrounded by valleys in which there were other villages. The Israelis came through the valleys from all sides and they surrounded Deir Yassin. They came with tanks and with automatic weapons.

You must understand what type of weapons we had. We had an Italian rifle, an old British rifle, and a German rifle. They were single shot. They could not defend a village. We asked the British government for better weapons. They gave us six British "parachute" rifles. The clip on each was ten bullets. What could ten bullets do?

About twenty of us from Deir Yassin were working as house servants for the British army at the Allenby Barracks, not more than two kilometers from Deir Yassin. We heard the news on the radio that the Zionists were attacking Deir Yassin. I, personally, went to the officer in charge of us and told him, "We have heard that the Jews have attacked our village. We're going." He said, "Goodbye. Go."

I went to a village, Ein Karem, that was in a valley below Deir Yassin. I found my uncle in Ein Karem and I asked him, "Where is my father?" He said my father was killed. "Where is my mother?" She was killed. "My brother?" He was killed also.

My sister was in her own house. She had six children. They did not see much because they were hiding at the time of the invasion. They were very, very scared. They came out at night from the lower floor and walked a few steps. The Israelis had already tied dogs to all the different corners of the village. As soon as the dogs saw them, they started barking. My sister and the children hid against the fence for a time. There was one narrow back road from Deir Yassin to Ein Karem that was left open, and so they were able to come to Ein Karem.

When the Israelis first came, the resistance that they found consisted of about one hundred young men. Those hundred young men were taken and shot. Until this day, we don't know where they buried them. Others whom they saw in the street were snipered down. They did not distinguish between pregnant and not pregnant, holding a boy or holding a girl: whoever came before them, they killed. The first people that heard the gunshots, if they were lucky, fled. Of the Zahran family — the mother, the father, the brother, the child, the entire family — not one part of their family tree remains.

After there was no more resistance in town, the Israelis brought buses and took the remaining residents of Deir Yassin and Ein Karem to a place in Jerusalem near the Italian Embassy, next to where the Russian Compound is today.

I found my wife in Jerusalem on the second day. She had her dress on. Except for that, she left as God brought her. I didn't have any idea where she was when I was coming to Jerusalem.

We went to Ein Yabrud, another village near Ramallah, where I had an uncle. We went from Jerusalem to Ein Yabrud in a car. At Shoufat, the Israelis were blocking off the road. A tank was blocking the street. We were escorted by British tanks to go through that area which the Israelis had blocked off as a "fire zone."

I had one child at that time. On the trip from Jerusalem to Ein Yabrud, I lost my daughter because of the bad health conditions: no food; no water like normal people should have. What could I have done?

When we got to Ein Yabrud, the United Nations began helping us by giving us essential foods: flour, bread and so forth. We stayed for more than one year in a storage facility that my uncle had in Ein Yabrud. Then work became available. They opened a road from Ramallah to Tibeah and we paved it.

I went back to see Deir Yassin a few years ago. The house of my family is still standing. In the fields next to our houses they have built a mental hospital for their mentally sick.

We have no notion where our parents were buried. The Israelis go to the Sinai and have a big operation to search for one of their dead, but my mother, my father, my sister, my brother, we don't know where they are. When an Israeli dies they build a memorial at the place and the whole world knows about it. We have one hundred young men from our village and, to this day, we still don't know where they were when they were killed.

Deir Yassin
II: Aiysha Jima Zidan

"It's not my village any more."

We were farmers. We had twenty-one grape vines. We used to have plums, wheat and olives.

Before 1948, my family worked in the stone business: breaking the stones, making the cement blocks. My uncle and my father worked together in this business. When I got married, my husband was employed by the British army at the King David Hotel in Jerusalem.

Abdul Kader Husseini, the Palestinian leader, was coming to Deir Yassin. On the way to Deir Yassin he was killed. Early the next morning they attacked Deir Yassin. I don't know why he and his troops were coming. I would guess that he was coming to talk to the men of the resistance in town but I don't know about politics.

For six months we had been seeing the Israelis right there in front of us, not far from us. We had security patrols. For example, if you had two men in your family, one would sleep and one would guard. Our patrols were at the outskirts of the village, watching.

Soon after midnight, those who were patrolling our village saw the Israelis come to us like rain. They flooded the village. They came from an entire circle surrounding us.

That night, my husband was working in the King David Hotel. I had my son, Mahmoud, four months old. In the adjacent house were my uncle and his wife. But in my house it was only myself and Mahmoud. I was seventeen or eighteen years old.

The attack began at about one o'clock in the morning. I was lying down and I was breast-feeding Mahmoud when I heard the tanks and rifles, and smelled the smoke. I saw them coming. Everybody was yelling to their neighbors, "If you know how to leave, leave!" Whoever had an uncle tried to get the uncle. Whoever had a wife tried to get the wife.

I held my baby in one arm, and I crawled on the floor against the wall until I could get down from the third floor and out of my house. I left with no shoes. I couldn't even get a blanket on my son. We fled the village. We were alone, but everybody was fleeing with us.

We got to Ein Karem. No one there resisted. They left in front of us. Most people had left by the time we arrived. We slept in Ein Karem. Those that remained in Ein Karem brought us a little water or bread or a piece of cheese, but not enough to feed the families.

At dawn, Arabic buses took us from Ein Karem to Jerusalem. When we got to Jerusalem, we found the other buses that came from Deir Yassin, and we started asking, where is this person, where is that person. "Where is your mother? Where is your father?" There was the mother who had lost her son, the boy that couldn't find his mother.

We began to understand exactly what had happened in the village. We found out that they had asked people in each house to come out with a white flag. When the door would open, they would enter the house. They would search the women and steal their jewelry, drag their kids out and put the women and children in buses. My uncle's wife was taken by the Israelis when they came. The males were killed on the spot.

These are old thoughts; this is hard for a woman.

Then, we began our own diaspora. We were spread out all over, some in Abu Deis, some in Ein Yabrud, some in Bireh, some in Ramallah. Until now, we are spread out.

We did not know what it meant to live away from our village. We would collect grass and weeds, and we would make a roof over our heads those nights.

We always used to be clean and neat. When we lived under these man-made roofs, I had to go to the well to get water. When I came back, I am embarrassed to say, I would find that my kids had urinated in their pants and they were dirty. But what could I do? I needed water. I had to go. We didn't know how to live like this.

We used to breast-feed our children. But, to be honest with you, my breasts dried up from everything we went through. There was an Arab committee that worked with the U.N. They brought us some flour here and some milk there.

We stayed in improvised huts for a long time. If you were lucky you left with a little ring or a bracelet that they didn't catch you with, and you would sell it and buy a barrel of oil or some bread or some flour, to enable you to continue.

Let me tell you how we made bread. We would find in the waste baskets a cylinder of metal. We would go to the fields and gather dead leaves and put them under the metal, light it, and we would make "scharash," the round bread that we eat in the morning. Then they opened up a bakery here in town. We didn't have any money so how could we go there? We would go to the field and gather two big baskets of dry straw, and trade the straw during the time it took to bake the bread.

Excuse me for saying it, but some of my own people used to go and beg. The beggars lived off of a piece of meat from this house and half a loaf of bread from that house. People lived; they are amazing! Should I lie to God? No, they did beg.

When we fled our village, we were too far from the King David Hotel for my husband to go there to work. Many workers who had been working there were no longer employed. They started working in stone. We needed to raise our kids and this was the only thing we thought of. We are still working in stone. This is our livelihood now.

After about a year and a half or two years, we sold all of our jewelry as a group — I and my uncles' wives and everybody — and we said that we wanted to build a house. We bought a piece of land in El Bireh. We dug, and every piece of stone that came out of the ground, we used for this house. It was a collective work. For example, this month, we worked on the part for your family. Then everybody came and finished the part for my family. This was a field here. Now it is a town.

Now, thank God, we are living and we have a house. But our houses in Deir Yassin are lost to us.

I went back after thirty-five years. My grandmother and uncles said, "We have to go back to Deir Yassin and see it thirty-five years later." I tried to convince them it was just going to open up bad memories. They said they wanted to go. They wanted me to show them which houses were whose.

The older houses were demolished but our house was still there. I told them, "This was my neighbor's house, this was my uncle's house, and this was my house." The individual living in our house now would not allow me to cut a rose from the garden. I told him, "This is my father's house. This is the house I was raised in. Let me just look inside." And he refused. He said that the house is now a home for mentally retarded persons.

I went to the cemetery. I was looking for my mother's grave. She died when she was thirty years old. I couldn't find it. Only three graves were showing out of the whole cemetery. The rest were all bulldozed. You couldn't tell whether there was a grave there or not.

Another individual who was with us went to the graves that were there. When he left in 1948, there were flowers around his family's grave, and it was taken care of. When he went back to see his family's grave, he didn't want to look at it.

My stomach is tight every time I talk about this. People go back every once in a while but I don't want to see it. They have changed the whole town. They've changed the landscape. It's not my village any more.

Um Khalil

"Why could they not return when the war was over?"

I was born in a village near Tulkarem called Anabta. We were a big family. My father was rich. He had lands and bees and he was mayor of Anabta for thirty-six years.

There were no schools for girls in Anabta at that time. So when I was five years old, my mother sent me to Nablus to have my education.

I lived in Nablus for two years with my aunt, the sister of my mother. I went to a Christian school for girls.

My father was a sheikh, a religious man. Every day when I was in the Christian school we used to pray, Christian praying, and we did it when the bell rang. My father would come and take me from the school to our village at vacation time. He came and I was with him in the car. When I heard the bell, I prayed. I said the Christian words, not the Muslim. My father, because he was a Muslim and a sheikh, said, "My daughter has changed her religion." He was old and he was close to his religion and he said, "I will not let her go back to the same school."

Then my mother convinced him to move from Anabta to Tulkarem, so that we could go on with our schooling. It was hard for my father to leave his town. He was the mayor of all the village, and to leave it was not good for him. But my mother convinced him and we moved to Tulkarem.

We stayed there until 1936. In that year there was a strike for six months. Everything was closed, the schools, the merchants, everything. So my family decided to move me here to Ramallah to be a boarder in the Friends Girls School and to go on with my studies. By now I was thirteen years old and my father believed that I would not leave my Muslim religion.

When I was in Tulkarem, I was with the young students in demonstrations. We would say, "Down with immigration. Down with Balfour." But I didn't know what Balfour was, or what was meant by immigration. I knew that Jews were coming and that we wanted to stop them and that we didn't want them to take our lands. But we used to say, and I don't believe in it now, that we wanted the British governor to help us solve that problem. So girls and boys went out into the street and shouted and sang these sayings.

I used to see the English people helping the Jews in the war. Our men, the Palestinians in the mountains, had to fight against both the British Army and the Jews. The Palestinians had little weapons, not strategic weapons, while the British and the Jews had good weapons. I remember, my mother used to tell me that nobody would give the Palestinians weapons. These men in the mountains had to get their guns from the people. Every family had to collect money and buy a gun for them.

These mujahadin, the fighters, would come to a village for a week. The whole village would give them food, cook for them, and clean their weapons for them. When the fighters were in the mountains, someone from the village would go up to the mountains carrying a white flag. This flag would be pointed to the right or to the left and would tell the fedayin whether to stay or to leave. Sometimes while they were eating, the flag would tell them to leave. They would leave the food and flee. This was the life that my people used to live.

Before 1948, we never felt that the Jews were our enemies. My cousin married a Jewish girl. She was very gentle. She used to come to our house with her children. We used to love them, sleep with them, eat with them, share presents. But these were the Jews before they started to swallow our lands.

My mother and my neighbors used to go to the houses of the Jews and light candles for them on Saturday, because their religion told them that you mustn't light a candle or a primus on the Sabbath. The Muslim families would go to their Jewish neighbors and light the candles. The Jews would come and do things for us. We never thought that they were enemies. We were friends together.

During the strike, my father was one of the committee that collected dry food, wheat, and gave it to the poor whose work stopped during the strike. Once, I remember, British soldiers pushed their way into the house and made a long line to take bags of flour and throw them in the well. My father started to shout, because we used the water. We had no water except from the rain at that time. He shouted. They went on with what they were doing and my father, a huge man, fell to the floor. I and my sister started to shout and the neighbors came and they carried him to his bed and we called the doctor. It won't go from my eyes. Until now, I can't forget.

When I went to the Friends Girls School, I thought that everyone who spoke English was English. So I would not look the American Quakers in the face. Sometimes I did not speak to them in a polite way, because I thought that they were dangerous. The teachers would tell the pupils that American visitors were coming and the teachers would say to me, "Please, don't attend. Leave the class until the visitors have gone." I led the girls to be against them. I didn't want them to come. The teachers would tell me and try to convince me, "They are not English. They are American." But I would not believe it.

I stayed there until before the tenth year. In the tenth year at the Friends Girls School, boys and girls were in class together. So my father said, "I will not let her be with the boys." They took me out of school and they told me, "Don't go back to the Friends Girls School. Study at home. We will bring you teachers." At that time, the father would say and the girls would obey. The husband would say and the wife would obey. Not like these days.

Marriage and War

While I was studying for the high school examination, I found the house was crowded. I asked, Why? They said a man had come. They told me, "This man is educated and he wants you." I started to weep. I wanted to go on with my studies. But this was their order. I was married in 1940 when I was seventeen years old.

My husband was from a village in the same district where I was born. We moved to Qalqilya, near Tulkarem. My husband was the principal of a secondary school. I was happy with my husband.

In 1944, the British moved my husband to Majdal, which is now Ashkelon, near Gaza. The Qalqilya school went only to the first year of secondary school. In Majdal my husband became principal for a full secondary school. So this was a higher position. We had our two sons in Majdal.

In 1948 the war came. I had given birth to a third child, a girl. And my husband said, "Our daughter is delicate. Take the children and go to Tulkarem until we see what is happening with the war." I took the children in a truck; there were no taxis because of the war.

After a few months, my husband wrote to me and said, "The Egyptian army has entered Gaza district and is ruling the district and everything is good. I will come and take you back with the children." He came and took us. We went from Tulkarem to Nablus to Jerusalem to Hebron, to go back to Majdal. When we reached Hebron, we couldn't go on because there was a battle. So we stayed in Hebron.

I was pregnant with our fourth child. It was due in one month. I was very tired. We were staying with friends. After three days I told my husband, "Let us go in *any* way to our house in Majdal."

We rented a car. To go to Majdal we had to pass through Gaza. So we went there. We looked at the city. There was nobody at all in the streets. Everybody was in hiding, waiting for airplanes to drop bombs. We saw a man there. He had a cart. We told him, "Please. Take us to Majdal." He said,

"Are you mad? All the people are living under trees. Nobody is living in Majdal, nobody. Every five minutes there are airplanes that come to kill the people. I will not take you. You should search for a place in Gaza."

We remembered that there was a cousin of my husband's in Gaza. My husband knew the house. We went there. We found it full of people. We stayed there waiting for the war to let up.

During this time, every day there were girls knocking on the door, beautiful girls, twenty or twenty-five years old, carrying their bracelets. They would say, "Please. Buy it. I, myself, wore it for my husband. I have no money. I am starting to sell my jewels."

I told them, "I am myself selling my jewels." But these girls would say, "The bracelet that cost fifty dinars, please, take it for twenty. Take it for ten. For five." And they shouted, weeping, "We want milk for the children. They are dying from hunger. Please." I couldn't do anything, but this would make sadness that collected in my heart.

Every day people would come. I would see groups of people, carrying their children, carrying their precious things, singing sad songs, and weeping, living mostly under trees, in the churches, in the schools; no shelter, no food, nothing! And the airplanes dropping bombs.

I had my shelter. They gave us a small room. I was living in a room which was kitchen, sitting room, bedroom, everything. They didn't help with many things. We stayed in a very, very bad situation.

When the war was coming to an end, I took my last bracelet and gave it to my husband. I said, "Please sell this bracelet, go and rent a car, bring us some clothing from our house in Majdal and find out how we can return."

He went. I waited and I was so worried about him, and at night he came late. He looked very sad. I said, "What's the matter? Where's the clothing? Where are the things?" He said, "I'm sorry. The soldier told me: 'Go back. It is *not* your house.'" And I was very, very sad about that.

When the war was over the Egyptians asked my husband to return to his work, to be an assistant in the field of education. We left to the south. There was nothing in the rooms. I put two blocks here and two blocks there and I put a piece of wood on them and we had a bed. We covered it. And we used to sit on the board and to sleep six, four children and mother and father, on one bed.

I started to save our money from the Egyptians. I started to buy glasses, forks, things that were very necessary. Every month we saved a little money to buy the things that were most needed. And we stayed in Gaza until 1952.

In that time, I used to help my husband by going to the houses to convince the girls, educated girls, to be teachers for the refugees and take them grapes, dry food, butter, and flour. I told them that we must help our students, we don't want them to be without schools. The government schools under the Egyptians couldn't help all the people that came from around Gaza into villages like Khan Younis and Rafah. These people had been pushed into Gaza because the Israelis took all the surrounding land.

Till 1952 we didn't see anybody from our family. We didn't know. No telephone. No letters. It was closed between Gaza and the West Bank until

1967. We didn't know whether they were alive or not.

We found that we would have to live without any piasters three months and a half to cover the trip. We would have to take the train from Gaza to Cairo and the airplane from Cairo to the airport near Jerusalem. We had a fifth child, so we were seven. If we could collect three and a half months of salaries, it would cover the trip. We couldn't. If we spent all our income to travel, how were we to eat?

So we dared — it was a very dangerous dare — to get a boat with two oars, and two men to row the boat, and to take it from the shore of Gaza to the shore of Beirut. Imagine how dangerous it was. Every two days, the rower would shout: "Oh people. Raise your hand to God so that he will help you. You are near the shore of Israel. Maybe they will shoot you." The children would start to weep and we would be afraid. Another time, he'd say: "Raise your hand to God. A big wind is coming. The water will come and the boat will go down." We didn't see anything except the heaven and the sea. We blamed ourselves: why had we gone on this dangerous trip?

It took about one week. We ate very little the whole trip. All the time we were dizzy and our hearts were thumping, loud. I could not have imagined how bad this trip would be. Then we reached Beirut.

We drove from Beirut to Damascus to Amman to Jerusalem to Nablus and then to Tulkarem. I found students in the garden when I reached my father's house. I thought, "Did they die?" I was so afraid. I went from the car to the neighbors. They said, "Hello! You came!" I said, "What's happened? Please, tell me. Where are my father and mother and sister?" They said, "They left. All their good lands were taken by the Israelis."

We found them living in two small rooms. It was very tight. Once I went to my father's room. I saw him weeping. Seventy years old, weeping. I said, "What's the matter, Father?" He said, "Oh, you came after six or five years and I didn't do a party for you and you are buying the milk for your children from your own pocket. How shameful for me."

I told him, "Why? Why should you be ashamed? I am writing down every piaster. Would you like us to go back? Should I take your grandchildren from you twice?" He started to laugh and to cry at the same time. I told him, "Abdul Nasser is a strong man and a brave man. He will return your lands to you." From that time on, he would always say to me, "Come on, Samiha, where is Abdul Nasser? Is he nearer to us? Is he going to return my lands? Am I going back to my house?" And I told him, "Yes." I said things to put him at rest, so he would not be angry.

Our relatives said, "Please, don't go back to Gaza. There is work here in the West Bank. Gaza is under the rule of Egypt. Here we are under the rule of Jordan." Many people tried to convince my husband to work for the Jordanian government or with the UNRWA.

We preferred the UNRWA because the pay was much better. We took a house here in El Bireh.

And I found again here what I had seen in Gaza: people living under the trees. The first time I went to the markets I saw in front of the UNRWA office a long line of my people, men and women, everyone getting a bag, waiting to take dry food. I lost my mind. I started to shout: "What UNRWA! What United Nations!"

The United Nations was established to give people peace after two big wars. The first point in their rules is: The land that anyone is living in now is his own land. Britain for the British. France for the French. And Palestine for the Palestinians, from the Mediterranean to the River Jordan. It is by the rules of the United Nations. It is *our* land.

And they put another point: Nobody can take a land from the other by force. So under the rules of the United Nations, legally, it is our Palestine. Palestine is for us.

I shouted: "Why doesn't the UNRWA help us to return to our land, to our fields, to my house that is full of furniture?" I had things new, I didn't use them. Why should they have been taken? People came to live with other people, but why could they not return when the war was over?

So, I was blaming the UNRWA, the United Nations, and telling the people to throw this flour away, because we don't want it. But how could I say this when they were hungry?

Two Men from the Jenin Camp
1. Bashar

"I want you to feel for the Palestinians, feel for the destruction, for the oppression, for the loss of dignity: just to feel."

I was born in 1932 in a little village next to Haifa. I did not know my father. He died before I was aware that I had a father. There were three girls and two boys in my family. My mother was the one who raised us. We lived in a two-room house. It was my father's home.

Everyone had a parcel of land at that time. We ourselves had four dunums. We raised wheat, lentil beans, and hummus beans (chick peas). That was our livelihood.

In 1948, I was a high school student. There was a war. We left when there was bombing from planes and bombardment from the sea. We went inland because we thought that was the only place where we could be safe. We came here to Jenin, walking from Haifa, wearing our pants and our shoes and carrying our clothes. That's all we had with us.

The strongest of the village left first. The ones who had less strength left next. Those that were not able to make it were taken in vehicles and dropped in Jenin. I came with my mother and brothers. We left at 6:00 at night. We got here at ten o'clock the following morning, walking.

We had no relation to anyone here. When we arrived we found the Iraqi army. They were using the houses of the people who had fled from Jenin. The British Mandate was finished and the British had evacuated the area. The people in Jenin were evacuated before the people from Haifa came.

It was summer. We stayed in one of two places: under trees, or in the mosque.

The Red Cross came and passed out clothes and food. They distributed three kilograms of flour per family. There was an American lady named Theresa. I worked with her. I used to earn three dinars passing out milk. I carried milk on my shoulders from the Red Cross office to the refugees. The Red Cross helped us until the U.N. came.

When the U.N. came, they made a census of the area and passed out ID cards. We began to get rations.

The Jenin Camp was built on empty land that had been British territory until then. There was no distribution of land. Whoever found the barracks of the British army used the barracks. Other than that, anybody who came to any piece of land started to build on it. Wherever we found ourselves, we claimed that part of the camp. We started bringing rocks or whatever, trying to build some kind of makeshift housing. This is how the camp began to be built.

After the Red Cross left, I was yet a boy. I learned how to make and repair the kerosene heaters on which we used to cook. I worked at fixing and maintaining them for people in the camp. I used to work for five kroosh per day, which was nothing, just a few pennies. We would take some of that money and buy the dried milk available to refugees. We dipped bread into the milk and ate that.

I have not moved from here since 1948. In 1954, I got married. I had three boys and five girls. My brother died in 1949 so I also raised my brother's nine children. We would buy the bad tomatoes, crush them, mix them with some water and some bread and eat that as our food.

I went back to our village after the '67 war. I found that they had made the four dunums that we used for growing crops into cow stalls. When I went back a few years later, the house that was still standing in 1967 as well as the cow stalls were all demolished. There was an Israeli housing settlement there.

I want you to feel for the Palestinians, feel for the destruction, for the oppression, for the loss of dignity: just to feel.

2. Khaled

"I brought back some dirt and I let my kids step on the dirt so that they can be tied to the land."

I come from Jaffa, a coastal city near Tel Aviv. Before 1948 it was the largest port in Palestine. I was a baby in 1948 but I will tell you what my father told me.

My father left with the hope of returning soon. He had chickens. When he left he covered the chickens because he thought he could keep them warm for seven days. He thought he would be back. But his hopes were empty.

I work as a manual laborer, both inside the '48 area and here. There are special places where you can go and get work if you have the right papers. When we work inside Israel, the rights that we get as workers are nowhere near the rights that the Israeli workers get and we do a lot more difficult work than they do. We receive about 30 shekels from a 50 shekel job.

In 1969 I was arrested. I received my certification as a teacher during the nine months I was in prison. But it is in my file that I was a prisoner, so I have not been able to teach ever since.

My wife is from Jordan. She was required to return to Jordan when our first child was 40 days old. For eight years she had to go back and forth in this way. We had a marriage by mail.

I returned to my village after the '67 war. A military base prevented us from getting close to it. I brought back some dirt and I let my kids step on the dirt so that they can be tied to the land.

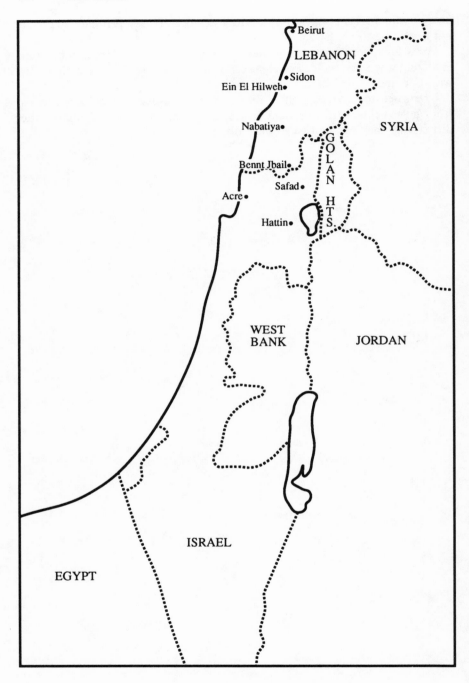

Beirut
LEBANON
Sidon
Ein El Hilweh
SYRIA
Nabatiya
G O L A N H T S.
Bennt Jbail
Safad
Acre
Hattin
WEST BANK
JORDAN
ISRAEL
EGYPT

2

The Camp

Since 1948 ever-increasing numbers of Palestinians have lived in refugee camps, administered by the United Nations Relief and Works Agency (UNRWA). The largest of these camps, such as Jabaliya and Rafah in the Gaza Strip, are now communities of over 50,000. The number and distribution of refugees in 1950 and 1990–91 as indicated by UNRWA figures are as follows:

Country	1950[1]	1990–91[2]
Lebanon	127,600	331,757
Syrian Arab Republic	82,194	301,744
Jordan	506,200	1,824,179
West Bank	[part of Jordan]	430,083
Gaza Strip	198,227	528,684
Total	914,221	3,416,447

The refugee camps described by Riyad, Um Ossama and Ali are located in Southern Lebanon.

★   ★   ★

Riyad

"I used to stand in southern Lebanon and at night I could see the lights in northern Palestine."

I was born in 1961 in the Camp. My family originated in the northern part of Palestine in a village called Hattin. Hattin is a famous name because an historic battle happened there.

My family had to leave in 1948 because of the establishment of the Israeli

1. David McDowall, *Palestine and Israel: The Uprising and Beyond* (Berkeley: University of California Press, 1989), p. 79.
2. The Center for Policy Analysis on Palestine, *Facts And Figures About The Palestinians* (Washington, D.C.: 1992), p. 17, citing *Map of UNRWA's Area of Operations*, June 30, 1991.

35

state. The south of Lebanon was the closest place to northern Palestine. At first they resided in a place on the border between Palestine and Lebanon which is called Bennt Jbail. But they didn't stay there long. It seems that the Lebanese government arranged with the United Nations for an influx of refugees from Palestine, and the United Nations prepared for it. My dad told me: "As soon as we got to Lebanon we found the camps there. All the aid and food and stuff was waiting for us there, as if everything was arranged."

In Palestine my family were peasants. They worked their own land. My dad and his four brothers owned about 700 acres. We still have the deeds. They used to hire a lot of people from other areas to work for them. They grew oranges, olives, wheat, and all kinds of vegetables, plus they raised all kinds of animals like cows and horses.

So when they came from Palestine to Lebanon there was no other job for them except to do the same thing. They weren't skilled or well-educated people. They started working for the Lebanese landlords. All they wanted was to survive, to go on with their lives. The United Nations provided basic services, like health and education.

In the Camp

At the Camp people started living in tents and later began to build concrete walls. People from the same village in Palestine lived in the same section of the camp. So you could say, "This is the Hattin area." Up to the present time, it is easy to find any person in the camp without having his address. All you have to do is ask which village he is from in Palestine. You say, "He's from Hattin." "OK, this is the Hattin neighborhood."

When I was born, between fifty and sixty thousand people lived in the Camp. The Camp first expanded horizontally, up to certain limits. The land on which the Camp is located was leased by UNRWA from the Lebanese government for ninety-nine years.

Families got bigger and bigger. People could not afford to go and buy houses in the city unless they were working and making good money, which very few were doing. Most of the people had to use the area on which they already lived to accommodate additional children. So they changed the corrugated ceilings into concrete roofs and built another story. Now some houses have three stories. You can see parents living on the first floor of a house, and their children and grandchildren on the other floors.

Facilities in the Camp improved through the years. Now we have a hospital, clinics, pharmacies, bookstores. These things were not there twenty years ago. If I wanted my picture taken, I had to go to the city. Now I can do it in the Camp. All of these improvements are due to the presence of the PLO [Palestine Liberation Organization] in the Camp.

The infrastructure was all planned by the United Nations. But it's not great. In the winter the sewage pipes are flooded all the time. The streets are filled with water. Most of the time you are walking in mud. In the summer, water is scarce. Drinking water comes just to the lower level of the homes.

"Capital Was Education"

My dad worked hard to raise the family and to educate myself and my brothers, to send us to schools and colleges. In Palestine, all their capital was the land. But in Lebanon, where there was no land, he thought capital was education. This was the only thing you could depend on as a Palestinian. A very high percentage of Palestinians are well-educated.

The United Nations provided elementary education. My older brothers had to go to school in tents. There were no paved streets and no cars to take them back and forth to school. They had to walk in the mud. Forty or fifty students sat in one tent. The teachers and school administrators were Palestinian. The planners and organizers of the whole educational system were from foreign countries, mostly from Scandinavian countries at that time.

The United Nations provided textbooks. All the textbooks were by the Lebanese government. Arabic was the first language of instruction. English is the major second language in Lebanon. Science and math and such subjects are taught in English.

I personally studied in the Camp for six years of elementary education and four years of what we call "intermediate." After that you have to take a governmental examination. If you pass it you go on to the secondary stage. At the secondary stage the family has to provide for their kids' education.

We learned Palestinian history from our families, from our parents, and from our own personal research. Palestinian history was not required as a subject at school or for exams. So we had to do our own study to learn our own history.

We didn't live a happy life like other children in the world with toys and vacations and all the things that kids look forward to. The minute I started to grow up and to see the world around myself, I began to see war. The Israelis bombed the Camp from the air two or three times a month. The Lebanese civil war erupted in 1975. It was at the beginning of my adolescence. Instead of starting to live a different life as a teenager, I had to live in a war situation.

Our schooling was interrupted many times because of the war. We had to stay out of the schools for months at a time. The war created refugees and they came to the area where we lived and they stayed in the schools because they had no other place to stay. So the schools closed for one or two months.

I went to the first, second, and third years of secondary school in the city near the Camp. My family provided it. In the second year you take another Lebanese government examination, which was called the "baccalaureate, part one," and in the third year, "baccalaureate, part two." I passed both of them.

After that, I was planning to go to the American University in Beirut, but my family could not afford to send me there. I had to go to a two-year vocational college run by the United Nations. This college trains students for mechanics and other trades and for business. So I went to the business school there and graduated in 1983.

The PLO in the Camp

Before the early 1970s, security was provided by the Lebanese police. There was a police station in the Camp. There was Lebanese intelligence also. Civilian life — health, education — was ruled at that time by the United Nations. This was by agreement between the Lebanese government and the United Nations.

Up to the present time, some civilian services, such as travel documents and birth certificates, are done by the Lebanese government. On our ID cards the word "refugee" appears five times. Even though we were born in Lebanon, we have no citizenship.

After 1970, when the PLO came to Lebanon, the camps were ruled by the PLO. There was an agreement (the Cairo agreement) between the Lebanese government and the PLO that the PLO would take care of the Palestinian refugees. That remained in place until 1982 when the Israelis came and ruled with their collaborators until 1985. In 1985, the PLO took over again.

It used to be that you could get first aid in the Camp, but if you needed a hospital you had to go to the city. Now the PLO has started a hospital with X-ray equipment and all medical facilities.

After 1985, the PLO started a secondary school in the Camp. There are about 2,000 students in it. The PLO also provides scholarships for students to go to the American University in Beirut and overseas.

They have sewing and embroidery factories. These factories represent a major economic force. They employ hundreds of people. Their products are sold all over the world, not just in Lebanon or other Arab states. They make dresses, pants, shirts, even shoes.

We have bakeries established by the PLO. If you want to go to the private sector, to the city, to buy 24 loaves of pita bread, you pay 500 lira. If you buy it in the refugee camp, which is financed by the PLO, you pay 150. The bakeries have been destroyed many times. We had about five of them. Now I think we have only one. Clinics established by the PLO have also been bombed.

Shelling

If I were to explain any day of the shelling, it would be the day that I was wounded in 1985. There was heavy artillery shelling of the Camp from the Israeli border by Lebanese forces. It was haphazard, random shelling. For this reason, it scared people more than bombing from the air. All you could hear was the screaming of women and children running to the shelters and the sirens of the ambulances.

When I got injured, I was sitting at my uncle's house. The shell fell on the roof of the house. The whole room collapsed. I was knocked onto my stomach. Rocks fell on my back. I was injured on my chin and head.

The Future

My father is still alive, the only survivor of the five brothers. He is about eighty years old. He is still in Lebanon. I spent a month with him in the

Camp. He had surgery on his hip and he is not doing very well.

The economic situation is awful. There is no way I could afford to rent an apartment in the city, so I will return to the Camp. My brother is teaching for UNRWA. He has been teaching for twenty years and he has two degrees. His salary is $280 a month. An apartment in the city is $100 or $150 a month. The only way I could live is with my family, by building another story on the house. Also, I wouldn't feel safe anywhere but where my family lives.

My dream is to go to where my father and my grandfather lived in Palestine and just see it. I have never seen it. I used to stand in southern Lebanon and at night I could see the lights in northern Palestine. The whole area would light up. I used to stand and look at it and say, "That used to be our homeland, way back."

Um Ossama

"Our goal in life is to go back home."

Forced Out

I am from Deir El-Assi, a village next to Acre, which is in northern Israel not far from the border of Lebanon.

My family had a lot of land. We used to grow tomatoes, beans, wheat, tobacco, corn and feed for the animals. Everyone had livestock. Whatever we grew, we bagged or wrapped it and took it to the market.

When I was ten years old, we were forced out. I am not sure what year it was; I am illiterate. I am fifty-five now.

The news of the town was that planes were coming to hit us. I was with my mother and father. We fled to a wooded area that was outside of town. Someone told us to wait there because a mediator was coming to make up between the Jewish people and the Palestinians so we could go back.

As time went on, no one came, and no one said that there was any possibility of going back. It was the opposite. It became a more and more tense situation.

So we went to Ermaysh, a village to the north of us on the border inside South Lebanon. We stayed in the olive groves for days. We had no food, no clothes, not one thing in our hands from our house. The villagers of Ermaysh brought us cheese and bread and the essentials, and that's how we survived. Some of our people were able to bring money with them. They were able to live a little easier. Others, like my family, had not been able to get back to the house so we ended up there with nothing. I was young and stayed close by my father.

The next thing that I remember, some committee — I think now it was probably the U.N. but I did not know at that time — came and made a census of who was there. They divided up the people and put them on buses to refugee camps in different parts of Lebanon. They said: "You are a Palestinian refugee. We can take you any place we want." People went to Beirut, to Tal Al-Zattar, to Sidon, and to several villages. My destination was Ein El Hilweh Refugee Camp.

In the areas where they took us, people set up tent camps and that was our home. There were bread trucks that would come around daily to pass out bread. For every two individuals, we would get one loaf of bread. The line would be further than your eye could see.

Those who were able to work, a minority, did go and work and that's how they raised their families. Others who weren't able to work would wait for the rations to come. The rations became less and less every time.

We suffered. Our whole life is suffering. We are refugees. We are homeless. We are nationless. We are the lost people, and there is no one asking about us. There is no decent human respect for us.

Marriage

I was sixteen years old when I got married. It was an arranged marriage. For Palestinians it is traditional that the girl has no say-so. The family would look for a nice guy. If the guy was nice and the family was nice, it would be agreed. And the girl would end up in that predicament, not because she wanted to but rather because the family had arranged it for her.

We lived in a tent. There were two rows of restrooms in the camp, one for the men and one for the women. That was what we had of your high technology. There was no running water. We were very dense, living very close together.

When we were first there we were foreigners. We did not know what to do, where to go, or how to get work. Now, people know how to get work if there is work and people have become accustomed and have assimilated to living in Lebanon. So life has become easier compared to when we first came.

It was not that we didn't want to live better but we didn't have the opportunity to live better. At the beginning, if we wanted to pour concrete to start building some kind of foundation, the Lebanese authorities would not let us because they were not looking for anybody from outside of the country to become permanent residents.

I had three kids while I was living in a tent. First a son, then twins, one of whom died at seven months of sudden death syndrome. The next was Ahmed, and I had six more after Ahmed.

When we had Ahmed, we had already put aluminum on top of our home. We turned the tent upside down and we made a roof of molded aluminum. They didn't say anything was wrong with putting up aluminum with a foundation at the corners to hold it up. That was the beginning of a house. In the winter time it was so cold and in the summer time it was boiling hot. But it wasn't just a tent any more.

There was a Lebanese vocational school in Sidon. I had 19 liras of gold that my father had given me. I sold the gold so that my husband could go to school to learn how to paint cars and do body shop work. He opened up a shop on the same street as the gas station. He worked and he did well. And from that we were able to raise our children.

The mother's role was to make the bread and to clean and to wash. You'd need water for all your day's work. To get water we had to walk about half a mile. To have enough water to work with for the whole day, I would go early in the morning and I would carry twelve loads of water on my head. Each container contained five gallons. Twelve trips, five gallons each trip.

Civil War in Lebanon

Before the civil war in Lebanon, Palestinians had become accepted as workers. We were accepted as people who were in a crisis and we were not looked upon any more as total foreigners or complete strangers. Even the villages were very receptive to the concerns of our communities.

When the Palestinian resistance movement came into Lebanon from Jordan, and they began to implant their Palestinian thoughts, there came about a conflict between the Palestinian resistance movement and the Lebanese community. A tense situation developed.

We were very pleased that these people in the Palestinian resistance movement came. Our goal in life was to go back home. This was the road to go back home. Someone had to stand up for our right and it was these people.

For the next fifteen years it was us against the Lebanese government and the Lebanese government against us. And, to make it even worse, Israeli planes came in every so often — sometimes daily, sometimes weekly — and hit us. The bombing began after the resistance movement entered Lebanon.

We knew they were coming when we heard the air raid sirens go off. We would go outside of the house into the field or wilderness area, and we would wait. We would see a plane. It would be high. Then all of a sudden it would come low and it would raid the camp and go back. You could see some of the planes flying far away, resting, while other ones would come and hit us. They would take turns. There would be continuous hitting.

Then we would return to our homes. The person who had his home demolished would fix it. The person who didn't have his home demolished would continue where he left off before he left the house.

During the civil war, because the government had collapsed, we started building houses with concrete foundations. We still did not have permission to build but the government didn't have the ability to stop us.

Our house was next to the shelter. As soon as anything would happen, everybody would go to the shelter. I would move a portable oven into the shelter. I would put thyme and oil onto pita bread and cook it. I would feed as many as I could.

We cooked for the fedayin, the commandos, and we helped house them. When there was water, I would have guys come in: "Shower here. There's water for drinking here. There's food." I was very active.

[Continued below, Section 5, p. 102.]

Ali

"I thought the bombs were doves."

"I Never Had a Childhood"

I was born in 1957. My mother told me the story of how my family was driven out of their homeland. Planes attacked their village.

My father used to be a shepherd in Palestine. His village was near Safad. My uncle's wife went down and visited my grandfather's house in 1982. Nobody was living in it but the house was still standing. A pomegranate tree was still alive.

In 1954 or 1955, my family moved to Ein El Hilweh refugee camp. At that time we were not allowed to build anything without the Lebanese government's permission. It was next to impossible to get approval to build anything, even a bathroom. So we had public bathrooms. If you wanted to go to the bathroom in the middle of the night, you had to get out of your bed and walk about half a mile to the bathroom and come back. There were no doors. It was not clean. And outside these public bathrooms was where garbage was dumped. There were open sewer lines.

In those days, the walls of the houses might be made of canvas or hay mixed with clay. Eleven of us lived in one room and a kitchen: nine kids, my mother and my father. I remember very clearly, we used to sleep with my mother in the middle with four or five kids on one side and four or five kids on the other side, and my dad slept outside under the tree.

There was not enough of anything. There was not enough food. If you bought a pair of shoes, it was worn by five kids. There would be 45 kids in one classroom.

There was no electricity in the house. I used to use a kerosene light. If I had an exam to study for, I would sit at the table with the kerosene light. At seven or eight o'clock in the evening, the Lebanese security forces would be going around. When they saw the light, they'd tell you with an "f" word like "mother f", "Why are you still up? You're supposed to be asleep. Go to sleep!" This was a Lebanese curfew in 1967, 1968.

On April 29, 1969, before the PLO came to Lebanon, we went on a peaceful demonstration to improve our system of education. The Lebanese forces started shooting indiscriminately. From our refugee camp there were six people killed and fifteen injured. I was twelve years old and I was carrying a stone in my shirt when one of the soldiers caught me and said, "Where are you going?" I said, "I'm going to throw a stone at you guys."

There was a playground near our house. We used to play baseball and soccer, barefoot, no shoes. I got cut almost every day. There was broken glass. Nobody came to clean it up. It was a rough life.

In the sixties, our favorite game was a war game. We would split into two teams, Israelis and Palestinians, and we fought each other. We shot at each other by making noises with our mouths, "b-r-r-r-r-r-r-r-r." We chased each other from corner to corner. I'd shoot you. Then I'd say, "You're dead, you're dead, you're dead."

I never had a childhood. The first time I saw an airplane bombing the camp, I thought the bombs were doves. I was looking at the airplane and things fell down. I was talking to my friends and I said, "Look at the birds!" Suddenly we saw the smoke coming out, and we heard the loud noise. After a while we knew what it was.

The kids became experts. A kid could tell you, "The MK airplane was here this morning," or "That was a 14.5 millimeter." We could discriminate between the noises and we could tell if the shell was coming toward us or when it passed.

Air Raids

I witnessed an air raid in the Nabatiya refugee camp in 1977 or 1978. The driver of an ambulance did not know the way to Nabatiya and he wanted somebody to go with him. We drove about eight miles under shelling. A shell struck each intersection every two or three minutes. The roads were blocked so you couldn't take the injured people to the hospital. I went to check on a friend of mine who they told me had died. I found him alive.

The Nabatiya camp was destroyed one hundred per cent.[3] The only thing left standing was a section of an elementary school. Everything else was demolished. I stood by the church, which was caving in, and I watched the Israeli tanks close by in the open fields and on the hills.

I witnessed the cluster bombs. I carried them in two pieces after they exploded. We put the pieces on the side of the road at the entrance to the refugee camp when [U.N. Secretary General] Kurt Waldheim came to tour the area. These cluster bombs were made in the United States; they were stamped, "USA." Under United Nations resolutions, nobody was allowed to use these cluster bombs. They were used in Vietnam. They were used in Lebanon. If you have the power, you can do anything you want.

Air raids came and went. After 1978, Israeli air raids started increasing — daily — so the PLO decided to build an air raid shelter in every neighborhood. The shelters were good for shrapnel or rocks, but they could not protect against a direct hit. They were made of concrete, underground, like a basement.

In 1982, the Israelis destroyed all the shelters. Those that were not destroyed by the shelling, they put explosives inside them and blew them up so that no one could use them again.

By about 1985 or 1986, people had kind of gotten used to the air raids. They didn't care any more. The Israelis would come and hit the camp. You would hear the sirens. An hour later, life would be normal again. Before that, the schools would close for a week, the people would run away, the area

3. As Ali later explained, Nabatiya, the camp (not the town), was 100 per cent destroyed in 1976. The camp was rebuilt about 70–80 per cent when in the 1982 war it was once again 100 per cent destroyed. Today there is no longer a Nabatiya camp.

would be deserted. But this kind of war became part of people's lives. It's sad but that's what happened.

In two of the air raids I witnessed, I saw an Israeli airplane get hit. The last time was in 1986, before I came to the United States. The plane came in low and a Palestinian fighter hit it with a SAM 2 missile, like what they call a "Stinger." It was a direct hit. I was standing on the roof, watching the bombing, and I saw the airplane explode.

Our house in the camp was destroyed twice. During the invasion of 1982, there was indiscriminate shelling and one of the shells hit our house. By that time we had two rooms, a kitchen and a bathroom. The shell destroyed two rooms and left the kitchen and the bathroom.

Then the Israelis wanted to widen the roads in the camp so they could move quickly between the houses. They destroyed our house with a bulldozer. They took the whole thing down. So we had to build it again.

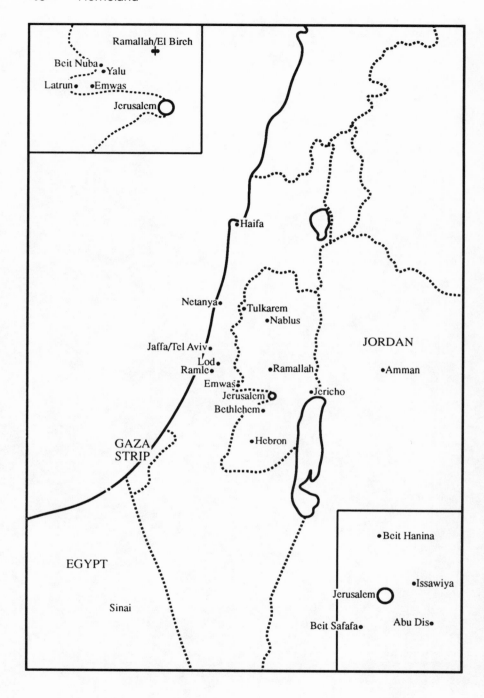

3

1967

"The lands known as 'the occupied territories' (the West Bank, Gaza Strip, Golan Heights, and East Jerusalem) were occupied by Israel in 1967 and have been under military occupation since then."[1]

When the Israeli army attacked their localities in 1967, as Um Sa'ad and Husam Rafeedie relate, "some residents fled in fear, recalling the 1948 killings. . . . The Jordanian army's rapid retreat contributed to the fear. . . ."[2] The Israeli army "blew up the entire villages of Emmaus [Emwas], Yalu, and Beit Nuba,"[3] as narrated by Hikmat Deeb Ali.

It is estimated that one-fourth of the Palestinian population was abroad during the 1967 war.[4] Like Salah Ta'amari, most such persons were not permitted to return and cannot reside in the Occupied Territories. For Palestinians who remained in the Occupied Territories, Lawahez Burgal and others indicate that economic circumstances worsened after 1967.

★   ★   ★

Um Sa'ad

"At that moment, I remembered Deir Yassin."

Childhood, 1936–1956

Jerusalem is everything to me. I was born there in April 1936, just at the time the six-month general strike began. I grew up there. Whenever I want to think of something I like, I remember Jerusalem. I hope to go and die there.

My mother and father came from a wealthy family. They used to call the house that I was born in "the mansion." Almost the whole hill belonged to

---

1. U.S. State Department, *Country Reports on Human Rights Practices for 1991*, p. 1440.
2. John Quigley, *Palestine and Israel: A Challenge to Justice* (Durham: Duke University Press, 1990), p. 168.
3. Ibid.
4. U.S. State Department, *Country Reports on Human Rights Practices for 1992*, Occupied Territories, Sec. 2(d).

our family. The fields we used to play in were filled with fruits and olive trees. I grew up there until 1948.

The Jews started building the Hebrew University before I was born. They took a piece of land near our house. I used to see the Jews sitting on their balconies or going or coming, and to me they were just normal people. I never felt scared of them. I never felt that I had to hide from them. They used to talk Arabic and we used to talk to them as we did to any other Arabs.

In the beginning of 1947, I started to feel that there was an enemy that was trying to take part of our land. I remember hearing my family talking about how the Zionists took the top of a mountain so as to build a settlement. The Hadassah Hospital is on top of a hill and they wanted to enlarge it. They took part of the village of Issawiya.

Then the war started. I remember when houses were demolished close to our home. The Israelis were in the Hebrew University on top of the hill. They came from the Hebrew University to those houses at night. I think it was around two in the morning. They set off explosives under the first and second houses, and started digging to demolish the third house. The whole area was awakened and people started screaming and crying. The houses collapsed on the families while they were sleeping. Nobody was in a shelter. I will never forget the scene as they carried the children on stretchers. One of the children on the stretchers was dead.

The whole area was frightened that their turn was coming. I didn't understand it when I was young. Now I can imagine that this was their way of terrifying people, because it happened in other villages. They would, for instance, attack two or three or five houses at the entrance of the village. But the whole village would leave their houses out of fear, so as to escape and not to be killed.

After that, my family and I left our house and we went to a house in a village outside Jerusalem, Abu Deis. We felt that it was safer for us. We used to take a bus from the village to our school. I was twelve years old at that time and my sister was nine years old. When we went to school and came back, sometimes we were afraid that one of us would be killed. When we got home, I remember, we used to feel happy that we were safe.

We didn't take all of the things from our house in Jerusalem. The school was not far away from our house. If we needed anything, my mother would tell us, go to the house, get us something. So we used to pass by the house, take what we needed, and then go to the village.

One day we were leaving the house to go back to the village. There was a villager who had produce on his donkey so as to sell it to people who wanted to buy fruits. I was looking at him and thinking, shall I buy something from him? Suddenly a bullet came into his head and he fell. He died in front of me!

Then school closed and we had to stay at home, waiting for my father to go to work and come back. His many lands had all been taken, so he opened a grocery store. He would travel to Jerusalem and back.

We stayed in the village around ten months. In villages they used to have a guest house. The villagers gave us the guest house, and said we were welcome to stay there as long as we wanted. It was really very hard. All of us — my mother, my father, and five children, including a newborn baby — lived in two rooms.

We were not used to living in a village. Everything was different. There was no running water. You had to get the water from the well. There were no indoor toilets. There were no stoves. You had to burn wood outside the house. Our life was reduced to only the minimum necessities.

We learned the way they made the white cheese. And, of course, we used to look at them when they took the milk from the cow or the milk from the goat or the sheep. Before, I never knew how to do that. So we lost something and we learned something.

I helped my mother. One of my brothers was born when we were in Abu Deis. At that time, we didn't have diapers. My mother bought material for the newborn baby. Because we didn't have a sewing machine, she taught me how to sew the diapers for my brother by hand.

While we were in the village, a Palestinian leader named Abdul Kader Husseini was killed by the Israelis. We didn't have an army at that time. All we had was a few fighters who would protect their village or protect a street with very minimal weapons. We didn't have tanks. We didn't have airplanes. The British Mandate made it very hard for the Palestinians. The Palestinians were not supposed to have weapons. If anybody had a weapon, he was supposed to give it to the British.

Our fighters used to live in the mountains. In the village we saw families who had their son, or the woman her husband, with the fighters. He had to come at night to see his family and then before the dawn he had to leave and go back to the mountains.

The women's share at that time was getting food for the fighters, cooking for them, or helping the husband or the son to go. Sometimes the men would want to hide. They would go to a house and the women would hide them.

Deir Yassin is a village that was attacked by the Israelis, or by the Zionists, on the ninth of April, 1948. Husseini died on the eighth of April. The day after his death, they attacked Deir Yassin. Most of the men were with Abdul Kader Husseini, fighting.

You would meet people who would tell you, "This is what happened at Deir Yassin," because they were there. I met a woman who said that they brought her son and they asked her to put him on her lap and they killed him. They used knives, bayonets. It was really slaughtering, not fighting. There was nobody to fight. They were mostly women and children. Many, many people were massacred at that village.

This massacre scared the *whole* population of Palestine. Everyone talked about the massacre in Deir Yassin.

In 1948 they divided Palestine. School opened and life went back to almost normal. We went back to Jerusalem, not to our old house but to a rented house, and everything settled down a little bit. We lost a year of schooling. I went back to fifth grade.

Jerusalem was divided into two. We couldn't get to the other part of Jerusalem. We couldn't visit there. I remember a village, also a suburb of Jerusalem, called Beit Safafa. It was divided into two. If they had a wedding in that village, part of the family would go from one side and the other part of the family would go from the other side. There was a wire fence in between and they had to celebrate the wedding on both sides of the fence.

1948 taught Palestinians to get as much education as they could. It started in the camps. I remember a student who went to Egypt to study. He told me that the first time he sat on a chair was when he went to Egypt to college. If you didn't have a degree you would not be able to leave the camps and you would have to stay in the camps all your life. So the lesson of 1948 for Palestinians was that if you wanted to clothe yourself, if you wanted to get somewhere, you should be educated.

At that time, we didn't have universities in Palestine or Jordan. Anyone who wanted higher education had to go to Lebanon or to Egypt. If you went to Lebanon you had to go to the American University and the tuition was high. It was cheaper to go to college in Egypt because there was public education in Egypt. If you had good grades you would be accepted in any college you wanted.

College in Egypt, 1956–1960

I graduated from high school and I went to Egypt on a scholarship from 1956 until 1960. I was excellent in math. But because I had to take a scholarship from the Jordanian government, and because the country needed it, I had to go into physical and health education. I was the first person in Jordan to get a degree in physical and health education.

Leaving Jerusalem and going to Cairo on my own was a kind of liberation for me. My mother was my first supporter. She used to push us, saying, "You should be on your own" and "What you believe in, you should do!" Of course, there was the culture that said we had to stay within a certain circle. I couldn't go outside of that circle. But at the same time, I would fight for what I believed. I met many that believed the same way I did. If I think of the students that I was with in Cairo, they are now leaders all over.

Most of the women students were active with certain groups: some of them with the Socialists; some with the Muslim Brotherhood. If you belonged to some group, as a woman you could be as active as a man. The women's movement had been there for generations. I remember we met Nawal Sa'adawi. She was a writer and one of the leaders of the women's movement in Egypt.

In Palestine, my aunt was one of the leaders of the women's movement. She started the Union of Palestinian Women in Jerusalem in 1921, and then it spread all over Palestine. They called for demonstrations against Zionism, against the British, against the Balfour Declaration. They had clinics to help the wounded in 1948. They had schools. They helped the refugees. Liberated women would join those movements. Later, I worked with them.

In 1956 there was the tripartite attack on Egypt by Israel, France and England. Refugees came from the Sinai. They were brought in trains to Port Said. We students volunteered to help them. We helped them get off the train and we would take them somewhere to live. We used to make sandwiches for them.

The General Union of Palestinian Students started in Egypt. The PLO chairman and the whole leadership of the PLO were in that Union. I remember one time there was an election for president of the Union, and Yasir Arafat was running for president. I was one of the people who elected him. So he was our president while he was a student and now he is the PLO chairman. We want him to be president of our government, too.

Some of the young men who were studying in college came from Gaza. For instance, Abu Jihad and Abu Iyad came from Gaza. Abu Jihad grew up in one of the camps. He was from Ramle which was occupied in 1948. Abu Iyad lived with his family in Jaffa and then in Gaza. Those who came from the camps to college remembered whence they had come. They started talking about the liberation of Palestine. Of course, it was a top secret thing.

Gamel Abdul Nasser, the president of Egypt at that time, was calling everybody to be under the Arab umbrella. "Don't say that you are Palestinian. Don't say that you are Syrian. Don't say that you are Lebanese. Say that 'I am an Arab'." This nationalism joined most of the thinkers and most of the educated people in the Arab world. Some of the governments started fighting it. In Syria they fought it. In Saudi Arabia they fought it. In Jordan they fought it. But we were the believers. We believed in the unity of the Arab world.

Jerusalem, 1960–1967

After I graduated, I went back to Jerusalem. A teachers' training college had been started in Ramallah in 1952. It was the first two-year college in Palestine or Jordan. In 1960, I became a teacher of health and physical education in that college. I enjoyed teaching. I taught there until 1967.

My husband was a student in Cairo when I was there. My husband's family left Jerusalem in 1948 and went to Cairo, so he grew up there. He was around twelve when he left Jerusalem. There are only twelve days between us in age.

I met my husband back in Jerusalem at the beginning of 1960. We started a club for university graduates and we met in that club. Then we got to know each other better. I fell in love with my husband and we dated before we got married, according to our tradition. We would sit, take coffee or dinner or lunch, spend an evening with each other, and talk and make decisions for the future. There were certain things that we agreed on together: being Palestinians whose homeland was divided and taken over was something that we had in common.

We got married in 1964. In 1965, I had my first child, Sa'ad. When Sa'ad was two months old, one night after midnight soldiers came to our door. They were Jordanian soldiers who wanted to search the house. We were not supposed to have certain books or anything that was against security in Jordan. My husband opened the door. They came into the house and they started searching everything. As a teacher, I used to have stacks of papers. They looked all over my papers, the books, everything. They took my husband with them. I had to stay at home alone with my son.

I didn't know where they had taken my husband. The next morning I ran to the mayor of Jerusalem, Rohie Khatib. I told him that they had taken my husband after midnight and I didn't know where he was. So he immediately contacted the prime minister of Jordan. The prime minister's answer was, "It's good that he is still alive."

My husband spent, I think, ten days in prison. They brought him once to get some papers from the house. I looked at him and didn't know that he was my husband. His face was very disfigured and swollen. He didn't have a lace in his shoes and his head was wrapped with a kaffiyeh. When you see something like this you get furious, and you want to fight whoever is your enemy. "Who is my enemy?," I wanted to know. "Who is my enemy?"

The West Bank was joined with Jordan, and Amman was the capital for both. We Palestinians were sixty, seventy, eighty per cent of the population, because so many Palestinians fled to Jordan in 1948. But we were treated as second-class citizens by the Jordanians. They didn't want Palestinians to be active so they put them in jail. If we talked, if we moved, if we did anything, we were under a microscope. We had to work. We had to do something. But at the same time we were crippled.

1967

We stayed in Jerusalem until 1967. My husband was an engineer. He and his partner had a successful construction company. He had those big, big machines all over Jerusalem and the surrounding areas. When the 1967 war started, the Israelis took them and used them to bulldoze Palestinian houses.

I remember when they entered Jerusalem. We were at home when they came. We used to live near the Jerusalem airport, between the airport and the highway. The Israelis came from the back of the airport toward the highway. They had to pass by where we lived. When I saw a Jordanian soldier running in *my* back yard with a gun, shooting, I felt that they were very close. At that moment, I remembered Deir Yassin. I thought, "they will come now, kill my husband, kill my son and give me sorrow to live with all my life." We fled our house because I didn't want to be massacred, or have somebody kill my child or my husband in front of my eyes.

We learned later that the Israelis attacked each other. Some were coming from the airport and some were coming from Beit Hanina. The Israelis coming from the airport thought that those who were coming from Beit Hanina were Jordanians or Iraqis, so they started shooting at each other. When they retreated from our area, that gave us a way to escape.

We went to Ramallah and we stayed with my mother and my brothers. That night we didn't have the chance even to close our eyes because of the shooting, the bombing, the tanks, everything. We stayed in Ramallah the whole six days.

After the war was ended, somebody came and told me, "We saw your doors wide open." I didn't know what to say. I lost everything in that house. I found a couch that was slashed all up and down, no draperies, nothing in the house that you could use. Our wedding pictures were just stabbed. They left clothes under the bed or under the table. And there was a curfew.

Nobody could leave his house to steal or to do something like this. It had to be Israeli soldiers who did it.

We left that house and moved to a more crowded area, Beit Hanina. During the summer we went all over Palestine. We visited Haifa and Jaffa, Lod and Ramle, Tel Aviv, Netanya, and the Gaza Strip. I had never been to Gaza before.

I remember Haifa. It's the most beautiful city. You sit on Mount Carmel, and in front of you is the Mediterranean Sea, the clear water, the beautiful weather. All of this, why did we have to lose it? It's ours, our land.

My husband wanted to visit land that belonged to his father and his uncles before 1948. They used to have what in Arabic we call *bayara*, an area of land where you plant fruit trees. It was a very big piece of land in Ramle that was filled with fruits. My husband wanted to visit where he used to enjoy playing. So we went.

He knew the way. He still remembered the gate to the bayara. He remembered the metal house where the water was and the trees. The house was up there and we were thinking of reaching the house. Suddenly we found ourselves faced with an area as big as a football field filled with army. We thought that we were going through the driveway to the house, and there was a camp or training area filled with Israeli soldiers! We were so scared, we backed out and left and never went there again.

One of my husband's uncles went to Gaza after 1948. Some of his children are still in Gaza. They went and asked if they could take part of the land they used to own, because it's theirs, it's their father's. They were refused, and they will never get it because it is not theirs any more.

Here is one more story about my husband's family. In Jerusalem, their house was in Sheikh Jarrah, exactly on the line with the Israelis. In 1948, the Jordanian army took it as a place to see the enemy. In 1967, the first thing the Israelis did was to demolish it because it was used by the Jordanian army. I remember my sister-in-law standing in front of that house crying, crying, because they had demolished it.

In September 1967, my husband had to leave Jerusalem and go to Jordan, just for a short trip to meet somebody. When he left he told me, "If I don't come back in fifteen days, you follow me."

After he left for Jordan, I went one day to Ramallah and I met one of his friends. We were talking and he said, "Tomorrow I'm leaving for Jordan. If you want me to give anything to your husband, tell me." I told him, "Yes. I forgot to give him his ties. So I'll just wrap them up for you to take to him." He told me, "I'll pass by the house at six in the evening." So I told him, "OK, I'll be at home." That was at noon. Six, seven, eight went by, nobody showed up. The next day, his name appeared in the paper. The Israelis had arrested him and put him in jail.

After that my husband sent a message to me, "Bring Sa'ad and come to Amman." I knew that he must not be able to come back. He had learned from somewhere that the Israelis were after him. He said that at a certain hour, "I will be waiting for you on the other side of the bridge in Jordan."

I took my son and we left. You had to go through checkpoints — the first checkpoint, the second checkpoint, the third checkpoint — until you reached the bridge to cross the Jordan River.

Before I got to Jericho there was a checkpoint. The Israeli army stopped the car. I had to leave the car while they searched it.

At that time, whenever someone was leaving from Jerusalem and going to Jordan, anybody who knew you who wanted to send something to Jordan would come and ask you, "Please can you take this letter?" "Can you take this message?" "Can you take this thing?" Sometimes they would give you something and you didn't know what was inside.

One of my husband's friends had come to me and given me a letter and told me, "Please give this to" somebody, he mentioned the name. "Give it to your husband and your husband knows to whom he can give the letter." So I carried the letter. Just to be safe, I wore a girdle and I put that letter in the girdle. You couldn't pass with a letter or a picture or even perfume. They would take it from you. If it was lipstick, they had to take it out and break it and see if there was anything inside.

So I got out of the car. I was carrying my son because he was less than a year old. They started searching everything.

Leaving from Jerusalem and going to Amman meant that I had to take whatever I could take because I could not come back. I remember filling my bags for the whole night. In each bag I put a big towel or a bedspread or something to wrap all my things in. If the bag opened, the cloth would hold them. It was part of my way of keeping it all neat. So what the Israeli soldier did was to pull the bedspread so that everything in the bag was scattered all over.

I remembered that when I used to look at refugees coming out of their towns or villages and carrying a cloth or plastic bag, I used to say to myself, "Don't they have decent luggage to put their things in?" And I thought, "Oh my God! This is the situation I am in. I am going to carry these things because I can't fit my clothes back into that bag in a minute or two minutes. I have to carry these things in my hand." So now when I see refugees looking as if they didn't have the time to take care of things, it's not that they don't know anything better. It's because they were forced to go like this.

As I passed the bridge, my tears were streaming down my face. I couldn't believe it. How humiliating this was, every minute and every second of it! I was leaving my town, my country, going to another country, and for how long, I didn't know.

I arrived on the bridge very late because of the checkpoints. I didn't find my husband who had waited from eight o'clock in the morning until almost five in the evening. He thought that I was not coming. He left, and he left me a message: "If you come, there is a cab waiting for you. He knows the way. Just come."

So I took the cab and went to the address he gave me. We went into a hotel for a couple of days. Then we rented a furnished apartment.

Whenever anybody asked my husband, "When are we going home?," he would say, "Oh, I think in not more than fifteen days we will be back in Jerusalem." He always had the hope that we would go back after a short

period of time. We lived all our lives thinking that "this time is coming." But when is it coming? We don't know. Or we said, "If we are not going there, our children may go there." I don't know. We are waiting to see.
[Continued below, Section 5, p. 98.]

Hikmat Deeb Ali

"The answer was, 'If anyone remains you will die'."

I am from Emwas (Emmaus). I left Emwas on June 6, 1967. I left without anything but my children.

Emwas was occupied twice: once in 1948, when we lost most of our land; and a second time when they destroyed the entire village in 1967.

Before occupation, the population of Emwas was about 4,000. The majority lived from farming. There were about 45,000 dunum of fertile land for agricultural purposes.

My father was the sheikh, the religious leader, and the moukhtar, the head of the village. He died in 1941. The person who took his position was my older brother, Ahmad Deeb Ali.

There were two seasons, winter and summer. In the winter months the crops were beans and hummus and wheat. In the summer months we grew white corn and sesame seed. Before 1948, there was no mechanical equipment to plow the land. We used an ox with a single metal plow blade. Remember, this was a small village.

Every one had land. If you had 100 dunums, you were thought to have little land. The majority had 500 or 1,000 or 1,500 dunums.

Education in the villages was almost unheard of. My father had a high regard for education but his financial situation did not allow him to educate more than one son at a time. My older brother went to a school that took only the brightest kids and he continued in a British college for two years. My brother died when he was twenty-three so he did not get to use his education. My father then educated a second son. He finished medical training in Egypt.

1948

I was twenty-one years old in 1948. I won't tell you what my father said; I will tell you because I was there.

The Arab armies attempted to defend Emwas in 1948 when the Israelis attacked. It was not a clash between equals. The Israelis proceeded on the offensive and the Arab armies were in the defensive position. We lost forty persons. Of those forty deaths, one house was struck with a shell that went through the center of the house and killed the family. Other than that, homes were not destroyed.

Families did not flee. We stayed in the village. Emwas was on the Green Line between east and west, on the road between Jerusalem and Tel Aviv. In 1948, a buffer zone or no man's land four kilometers wide was created west of the village. We lost 40,000 dunums of land. What was left to the village to farm was five to six thousand dunums.

Those who had land that was not taken from them remained the owners of that land. Those who had land taken from them became landless. This is the reason why after 1948 we had a lot of people working as laborers. There was not enough land for all the farmers to continue farming, so many had to become laborers in order to make a living. About half the people continued to work within Emwas itself. The other half would go outside of the village to work in Jerusalem or in Ramallah. When I began working, I worked as a laborer.

1967

After 1948, for four or five years there was no work at all. I began working in different things, mostly construction — two-day job here, one-day job there — until 1962 when I was hired by a company in Jerusalem that made cement blocks.

I got married in 1958. I had five children by 1967.

I took my family to Amman for three years during that period, from 1959 to 1962. I opened my own block factory. My brother and I thought we could create this factory but it didn't work out. If you have funding, any project works. If you don't have funding, as we did not have the proper capital to start a factory, you have only your own labor and you hope for the best and that's not enough.

I returned to this area and found work in Jerusalem in a factory owned by the Nuseibeh family. There were about six workers. A union was not allowed. I used to live in Emwas and work in Jerusalem.

In 1967, I was working for the Nuseibeh family on the Jerusalem Electric Company building. Until now it's not done completely. When they said there was a war, every one of us left our work as it was and went back home. I went back to Emwas.

I found people looking at each other. They were waiting. There was no sense of what was next.

In the region of Emwas, there was a sixty-member force from the Arab armies. At midnight exactly, I and my brother, who was the moukhtar at that time, were standing on the street. Our house was on the main road. We heard two cars in front of the house. Somebody got out and yelled, "Abu Deeb, Abu Deeb" (which was my brother). It was the captain of the Arab forces in the area. He said, "Abu Deeb, we are withdrawing. Take care of yourselves."

We had a bus in Emwas. We put everyone we could in the bus to go to the Latrun parish house. Abu Deeb suggested the bus. I said that it was only a half a kilometer away, so I would walk and leave room for someone else to go in the bus. Just before we got to where we were going, the shelling started. Those who were in the bus left the bus and fled on foot.

I and my two cousins went into a church. There was not one Christian in our village. But Emwas is a holy place. In the New Testament it is called

Emmaus.[5] The church was built in order that people would come and visit this holy place. There was one priest there.

That's where we hid. The way the church was built, the view that you saw was the entire west, exactly where the Israelis were coming in from.

The first thing we saw was Israeli tanks coming into the village. They struck the physical center of the village, where forty or sixty soldiers had been about ten minutes earlier. The Israelis were shelling a place when no one was any longer there. I saw this very directly. Nothing was obstructing our view.

The places they were hitting were deserted. There is a little saying that you would hear an echo because there were no humans to hear.

Next came machine gun fire. It started in the same place, where they thought there were going to be soldiers. That was the first building they opened fire on after the shelling. Still there was no one in that building. It was a waste.

We heard the soldiers get out of their vehicles and begin dancing and singing. Then they moved to the castle or fort. We saw them all gather there. They did exactly what they had done in the center of the village: they shelled it, they opened fire on it, and they entered with army personnel.

By that time, it was becoming daylight. They entered into the residential area of Emwas. Their maneuvering within the residential area was very precise. Everywhere where they thought there was an Arab soldier guarding, they would pass it, find no one there, turn around and go to the next security point. In the residential area not one shot was fired. There was no need to, because there was not one shot fired at them.

They proceeded to go to the main road, the Emwas-Ramallah road. Right there they found a bus that was blocking the road. It was just a regular service bus. A tank came up beside it, moving very slowly, and knocked it over the side of the road. From there they continued.

I had a pillow in that bus which I used when I would go to work. A soldier looked in the bus after they knocked it over. The soldier saw the pillow. He put his hand in and pulled the pillow out because the Israelis think that we Arabs keep our gold and money in pillow cases. So he took it.

On the Road

At the end of town there are two roads. One goes from Emwas to Yalu, the other goes from Emwas to Ramallah. The Israelis divided into two groups. One took the Ramallah road, the other the Yalu road.

By this time it was total daylight and you could see from far away. The road was packed tight with army vehicles and personnel for at least four kilometers.

---

5. The Gospel according to St. Luke, Chapter 24, begins with the discovery that the stone was rolled away from the sepulchre and Jesus' body was not to be found. Two of the disciples "went that same day to a village called Emmaus, which was from Jerusalem about threescore furlongs" (Luke 24:13). It was in Emmaus that Jesus first appeared to his disciples after being crucified.

A special patrol unit came to the parish house where all the people were that had run from that bus. My family was in the parish house and told me later what happened. One of the soldiers told the people, "You have one road to leave. It's the Ramallah road. We don't want to see one of you pass by your home. You leave from here." There was an older gentleman who asked the soldier, "I want to go by my house only to pick up my shoes," because he had left shoeless. And the soldier told him, "If you stop home, you will die. You should take Ramallah. It's better off."

All of this happened while I was still in the church. I could see my own family walking between the columns of soldiers, leaving on the Ramallah road. My wife had just had a child, one week old. She had five children with her when she left.

When I saw everyone finish leaving, I and my two cousins who were in the church said, "Now, it must be safe. Let's go see what happened to the house." We got into our home. There was nobody in it. We saw patrols going from house to house. The one that stopped at our house yelled from outside, "Bring any children you have and come out." We didn't have any children. We were only three adults. We then left ourselves.

When we got to the outskirts of town, to where the gardens and farms were, we saw hell: young children, elderly, medically ill, handicapped, kids that couldn't walk, an old lady, all being accompanied out. Every time I think of it I want to lose my mind. Everyone left as is: pajamas, suit, anything you had on, that's the way you left.

The oldest of the old in the village went to the soldiers and said, "Why us? A government came and a government left. We're not soldiers. The same way we lived under the first government, we will live under this government. Why leave?" And the answer was, "If anyone remains, you will die." I heard it. I was right there.

From there we walked. If you were able to walk or you were not, you walked. I found my family at Beit Ur.

From Beit Ur, I walked with my family into Ramallah. At El Tira the army stopped us and said, "You can't go any further. Ramallah has not yet fallen." So we stopped there.

The first house we found was a closed house that had a window open. The kids crawled through the window and opened the door. About 100 people, women and children, slept in the house. We men slept in the yard outside. When I put my head into the house just to see how the kids were doing, it was as if I were putting my head into an oven. At eight o'clock, the soldiers that took us out of Emwas told us to leave that house.

From there we walked to Beituniya, the next village. In Beituniya, we were stopped and they took all of the men away and told the women to keep on going. They took twenty-five young men from our village. I had a kid in each hand and one sitting around my neck. The two soldiers in front of me got into an argument with each other. One said, "Leave him alone. He's with the kids." The other one said, "No, take him." Luckily, I was rejected. I passed by.

I had a brother in Beituniya. We went to his home. We found that he was in Amman at that time. We broke the door down and that night about eighty people stayed at my brother's house. For two days we hadn't eaten. When we got to this house we finally found food. The soldiers who took us out of Emwas, who took us out of El Tira, took us out of Beituniya. They told us to leave my brother's house.

We reached Ramallah. By the time we got there, there was a ceasefire ordered. This was about the thirteenth or fourteenth of June.

Nadim Al-Zarrou, who was the mayor of Ramallah and the military administrator of the town, announced that everybody should return to their homes. Everyone asked, "Do you mean Emwas?" They said, "Yes. Emwas, Beit Nuba, Yalu, you are all to go back to those villages." Those that heard this communique went running back home. When they got to Beit Nuba, which is one village before Emwas, they found a column of tanks and were told not to pass or they would be shot.

I was not one of those who went back. I was not able to walk back with five children. I was too tired to walk back. We heard what the mayor said. We said, "Fine. If the village is now under our control, we will rest and go back tomorrow." So we did not rush back the same day. I had a brother in Ramallah (he is now in Egypt), and the family stayed in his house. I continued my work with the Nuseibeh family's cement block company.

Those that went back hoping they would enter the town again were not able to come back as easily as they went. They got stuck in the village of Beit Liqia, which is on the outskirts of Emwas. They viewed the destruction of the town. When they did get back, they told us what happened.

The construction or demolition companies that destroyed the homes hired Israeli workers with Israeli trucks to take the rubble away. The people who picked up the rocks were just workers. They acted as messengers to the villagers about what was happening. When we went to see what they were dumping we saw half a car, a bed, a crib, all our stuff being dumped in pieces.

We have a committee of Emwas, calling for the return of Emwas to be a village. We have pictures of the demolition from the soldiers themselves, pictures that the soldiers took when they were overseeing the exiting of the people from the village and the village's destruction. The stones were taken by the Israeli workers because they thought the stones were things of value, whereas the personal possessions, the beds, the tables, the pictures, the clothing, were used for landfill.[6]

6. A Special Committee established by the United Nations General Assembly in 1968 to investigate whether there had been contraventions of the Geneva Convention of 1949, reported as follows: "The Special Committee recalls the mass destruction of the three villages in the Latrun area — Yalu, Emwas, and Beit Nuba — which were completely razed to the ground and whose inhabitants were dispersed. The Government of Israel is said to have offered alternative accommodation to the inhabitants of these villages in another area, but the Special Committee has not been able to verify these reports. The Special Committee acknowledges that these reports, if correct, show that the Israeli authorities are aware of the problem created by this destruction. It strongly urges that these villages be rebuilt and that the inhabitants be allowed to return to their homes. . . . Destruction of property is prohibited by article 53 of the Fourth Geneva Convention. Certain . . . exceptions are based on considerations of military necessity. The Special Committee is of the opinion that there is no question that with regard to the destruction of these three villages, refuge cannot be taken behind these exceptions. . . . The Special Committee considers that in the case of the three villages of Yalu, Beit Nuba and Emwas, Israel had 'unscrupulous recourse' to military necessity in carrying out this wanton destruction." (UN Document A/8089, 5 October 1970, paras. 124, 126, 129, 131; quoted in

Husam Rafeedie

"We were kept in the dark."

Family Background

I was born in 1951. We were the only Christian family in town.

My great grandpa was from Rafeedia, which is a town north of Nablus. Stories tell us that there was a fight. They shot somebody and the family had to leave town. They came to Ramallah, which is the only Christian town in that area. Families in Ramallah didn't want to bother with them because somebody might be looking for them. They said, "We can't protect you so you go find someplace else."

So, they came to El Bireh. They explained what happened, and someone asked, "Well, what can you do?" "We crochet. We make clothes. We make carpets. We make anything. You give us the wool and we'll make everything for you." They tried my great grandpa and he could do the work. So they said, "You'll stay here and we'll take care of you."

Grandma lived with us throughout my childhood. Grandpa passed away in the early forties. I did not know him. He was one of the best educated people in town. If anything would happen that had to do with something written, any letters from overseas, they came to my grandfather's house so he could read it for them. He was one of the very few in town that knew how to read.

My father owned the only flour mill in the West Bank at that time. It's been in business for better than a hundred years and it's still at the same place. My father took it over from my grandpa and his brothers. In the back of the mill, there is the bakery that we built.

People from all the small towns and villages would plant and cultivate the land and then bring the wheat over to my dad. My dad would clean it. Then he'd send it through a big machine with a couple of stones turning opposite ways, the old fashioned way, and the flour would come down. People would take the flour home and make dough, mostly flat round bread. (They started making the modern pita bread maybe in the early fifties.) They would bring the dough back to the bakery and we would bake it.

We used diesel fuel but we called it "solar." We had a small motor and then in 1948, right before they declared the State of Israel, my dad made a deal with one of the British companies and imported a big 78 horsepower motor from Britain. It was around the first of May when they were bringing it from the port in Jaffa, and there were planes dropping bombs.

That motor has been in business through the years up until now. I worked on it and I cleaned it many times. We all helped my dad in the business. That's what he knew how to do. He supported the twelve of us and we lived happily. My oldest brother, Mousa, is running the business now.[7] He's the

The Question of the Observance of the Fourth Geneva Convention of 1949 in Gaza and the West Bank including Jerusalem Occupied by Israel in June 1967, prepared for and under the guidance of the Committee on the Exercise of the Inalienable Rights of the Palestinian People [New York: United Nations, 1979], pp. 14, 34).

7. Deceased, January 1992.

third generation and he still has the same motor, the same stones, and the same bakery.

Before my father got married, he was in the United States. His mother's family had a business in New York City. My father wound up in Youngstown, Ohio as a salesman who went door to door. It was during the Depression. He stood on the soup line. He wanted to get married in the States but, being the only son in his family, they wouldn't allow it. They sent a telegram to his cousins in New York (his cousins were his suppliers). The cousins told him to come back to New York: "We need you for something." They put him on a boat and shipped him back home.

Because we were Christian, my dad had to marry a Christian. He got married in 1939. [See Zahwa Rafeedie, Section 8, p. 218.]

School Days

I went to a Catholic school until I was about halfway through high school. I was very active with the Boy Scouts in Ramallah, and I used to be one of the captains of the soccer team. I was in high school in 1964–1966. In 1967 or 1968, the Catholic schools started mixing boys and girls in high school only. The government schools were not mixed. They had one school for girls and another school for boys.

We were kept in the dark about our own problem, Palestine. From kindergarten through high school, there was not one single lesson taught on how Israel became a state, or how the land was taken. None of that was ever brought up in school.

We would read about the American Revolution. We would read about the French Revolution. We would read about the Germans. We would read about the Islamic revolutions. We read just about everything you could think of about the Bolshevik Revolution, about Russia. We were very informed concerning history and geography. But when it came to what had happened to our brothers and sisters and our families in Palestine, believe me, there wasn't one lesson taught, at our Catholic school or at the government school either.

I believe the reason for this was that we were under Jordanian rule — King Hussein and his father and his whole family — and their job was to protect the Zionist organization in Israel and to see that we stayed dumb.

Any time you opened your mouth about the Zionist organization or about the Jordanian government, the next morning you were in jail. If we said, "We'll go to jail because we are asking for freedom," some of us would go for six months and nobody would know where we were. If they caught you with a fishing knife in your pocket, that was against the law.

You didn't live in fear as long as you did not open your mouth, and were not a member or supporter of any Arab group, especially a Communist group or Hizballah.

About six months or seven months before the Six Day War started in 1967, the newspapers and the radios informed us that Gamel Abdul Nasser, who was the president of Egypt, said that we ought to take back by force whatever had been taken from us.

Then just before the war started, they called all the high school kids together and they said, "We're going to teach you how to protect yourselves because war is coming." They brought in a couple of lieutenants from the Jordanian army. They came into the high school and they showed us how to march left and right and how to salute.

They told us that as soon as the war broke out, which was going to happen, "Such-and-such are the places where the weapons are going to be. All you have to do is go and get the weapons. They will give them to you in order to protect your neighborhood." They showed us what to do if we got injured.

We went through three months of practice. The guy would come and say, "Today we're going to show you how to shoot with a rifle." The rifles that they gave us were made in 1919 or 1917. We'd take the rifle and we'd go out on the range, and fire a bullet. It would land right in front of us. That's how bad they were. Each one of us was allowed to fire only five bullets. Then they gave us a small sub-machine gun. We weren't allowed to fire that one. There wasn't enough ammunition, they said. Then they showed us pictures of hand grenades.

We were led to believe that if the war came, we could go to such-and-such a place and with respect to anything we needed, "You'll find it there. They will give it to you."

Six Day War

I remember the last week before June 5, 1967. We were so busy in the flour mill with my dad that we worked almost twelve hours, day and night. People were lined up outside waiting because everybody knew the war was going to happen. We had a couple of radios on.

I used to go to school with the son of the lieutenant who ran the Jordanian army in the West Bank. Headquarters for the Jordanian army were in Beit El about two miles from my house. The son used to come in a Landrover. He had a chauffeur because his father was the commander of the whole West Bank unit. He'd come right by the door of my house, beep the horn, and I would ride with him to school.

Thursday or Friday, he didn't come. Saturday, I walked up there. There was nobody at the central command of the Jordanian army in the West Bank, that was supposed to protect us, or to be on the front line! All the trucks, the jeeps, tanks or whatever they had, were gone. The place was completely empty.

There were a couple of guards in front of the building. I asked, "Where is Muhammed Saleem?" That was his name. "Can I talk to Muhammed Saleem? He's my friend. We go to school together. Two days he hasn't made it. What happened?" I was worried about his family.

Later on, we found out from the neighbors that Thursday and Friday orders came in from His Majesty King Hussein to pull all the troops back beyond the Jordan River.

The war started on a Monday morning. We listened to the Jordanian and Egyptian radio. They would say, "Our troops have moved half way into

Jerusalem." "Our troops have moved in on the mountain of so-and-so in Jerusalem." They would come up with a bulletin: "Our planes have demolished so-and-so."

I was watching the motor in the mill and handling the oil because it was working so fast and so hot all night long. And every time I would hear something on the news, I'd go tell my dad: "Dad, I just heard this and this and that." He said, "Good. Pretty soon we'll be in Tel Aviv." "Dad, they just announced that the Jordanian army moved in from Nablus," from the north. "If they've done that, the Jordanian army is a good army! Very soon we'll be in Tel Aviv." We didn't know much at the time. It makes me cry.

On Monday morning we saw a few F-14s and F-15s coming over. There was only one cop left in the police station. He would go out with his English rifle, which was made in the forties, and start firing at the Phantoms. He said, "I'll kill them myself." I said, "You've got to be crazy. These pilots can see everything on the ground. If they see you firing at them, they might come back." And believe me, they did come back. When they came back the second time, they dropped a couple of bombs about two blocks up the road in the soccer field that belonged to one of the American schools, the Friends Boys School.

When you sit on the roof of our house, you can see almost to Jerusalem, about eight miles away. We watched all night long. Smoke! You do not know how much smoke there was in that mountain where Jerusalem sits. And all you heard was the heavy, heavy "BANG!" It was like thundering. You'd look and you'd see big thick smoke. We kept telling ourselves, "There is nothing left in Jerusalem. They must have demolished the whole city."

Early Tuesday morning, we woke up and went to the main street. We saw a column of tanks coming from Jerusalem. In order to fight your enemy, I suppose, you have to know your enemy. I'm going to tell you how much we were in the dark. We did not know what the flag of the Jewish State looked like. We thought that Jews were a little different from ourselves, but we did not know what they looked like.

Tanks started coming. When they came close, we could see that they had pictures of King Hussein, of Gamel Abdul Nasser, of the Syrian leader, and the soldiers were talking our language. We thought that they were part of the Arab force that, from what we heard, was supposed to come in case of war.

We started talking to them and they talked back to us. We gave them water. We gave them cigarettes. And we kept telling them, "God be with you. I hope you will be victorious." And they kept telling us, "Don't worry. Everything's under control."

Then an ambulance came. On the ambulance there was an Israeli flag. The soldiers stopped talking to us and started talking to the men in the ambulance. We were myself and two or three brothers, two or three other guys from the neighborhood, and this guy who was maybe in his thirties. I was seventeen. "You stupid so-and-so's," he told us, "Those are Jews! Those are Israeli soldiers!"

They heard what he was saying. All of a sudden, they opened the top of the tank and we saw a machine gun. They could have gotten rid of us [clap, clap] just like that. They started shooting up in the air. We ran like hell!

We couldn't believe it. "What the hell were they doing here? What happened?" We began to realize that we had been cheated by the Jordanian government. After we saw the tanks, the column of the Israelis, we tried to go to some of the places where we had been told by the Jordanians we would find weapons. The doors were locked with big locks. There was nothing there. Nobody was in there. There were weapons at one place in the Old City of Jerusalem where there were supposed to be some weapons, but nobody was there to give them away. They were all locked up. On Friday morning, the Israeli army brought in a couple of semis and hauled away everything that was in there. Everything was in brand new boxes and they just took it away.

I have a cousin that was a major in the outfit that was supposed to be behind Hadassah Hospital. He told us that orders came from Jordan to pull out and to go back to the Dead Sea beyond the river.

Some of the soldiers refused orders to withdraw. A few soldiers remained on top of a hospital in Jerusalem and decided to defend that part of the city. They were Palestinians in the Jordanian army. For eight hours they prevented the Israeli army from coming in from that direction. They were on top of the hospital. The Israeli army thought that there were a whole lot of them up there. They dropped paratroopers in order to find out what was going on. Soon they found out that there were only three of them. I think they captured one and they killed one and one ran. The reason I know that story is because one of my very good friends worked in the hospital in the lab, and he was there when the paratroopers came.

The same thing happened towards Nablus. Two or three of the lieutenants, who were Palestinians, decided not to withdraw and put up a good battle. Until now, if you go towards Nablus or Tulkarem, you'll see some remaining parts of the tanks that were burned and are sitting on the side of the road. There were a few pockets that resisted the order to go back to the River.

My wife's uncle was a first lieutenant with the Jordanian army. He buried the weapons he had in the ground before the Israelis moved in.

When the first bus rolled into Jerusalem on Friday morning, I was on it. There was a lady from Ramallah who left her home in Ramle right before 1948, and she had a key for the house. I went to school with her kid. He was my buddy.

He said, "Husam, you want to come with me?" I said, "Where are we going?" He said, "We're going to go to Jerusalem. My mom is going to go inside West Jerusalem, and she is going to try to see about our house." I said, "You've got to be crazy." He said, "I am telling you, here's my mom." I didn't believe him. So I asked her and she said, "Yeah," she says, "I'm going to go to West Jerusalem and if there is a way to get through . . ." I said to myself, "If I go tell my dad, there ain't no way he's going to let me go." But I wanted to go. I didn't say anything to my dad. I went on the bus. I wanted to go see what it looked like.

I had been to East Jerusalem many times. We went shopping in East Jerusalem. The Old City of Jerusalem was considered the Arab section. But we weren't allowed in West Jerusalem. That was in the hands of the Israelis. There was a four-lane highway. We used to go one way and then turn left, and that was our part. And on the right, there was a wall and we never saw what was behind that wall.

So we got on the bus and we went. The wall was already down. The war started on a Monday, so they had Monday, Tuesday, Wednesday, Thursday, and I suppose they moved some of their troops along the main drag into the Old City of Jerusalem. We got in.

We got off the bus and walked on the street. Nobody said a thing to us. She knew her way. She left in 1948 — this is 1967 — and she still remembered everything about Jerusalem. That was her country.

We got on the bus to Ramle. She spoke the Jewish language. I didn't know Hebrew. She paid something and we went. She had the key for the house in her purse. We went in to Ramle, which is maybe forty-five minutes on the bus. We got off at the street and you'd think you were in a Western country. We didn't have that type of decoration. And she said, "Husam, that's the house." I said, "You've got to be kidding me." She said, "That's our house. This is where I used to do this and I used to do that. They must have just changed a little bit up here. Come on."

She knocked on the door. A woman and a man came out. "Can I help you?" They looked at us and they started talking Hebrew to each other. She jumped in. She told them, "I used to live in this house. And this house is mine. Do you mind if I go inside and take a look?" They told her, "If you don't leave immediately, we will contact the police." She begged them! She cried. I'll never forget that. And they refused. So we backed off. We got back in the bus and we went home.

And let me tell you what else the Israelis did. They demolished three villages. One was named Emwas, one was named Yalu, and one was named Beit Nuba. They came into those villages and they chased everybody out. As soon as the people left, they blew up all the houses. They completely demolished those three towns.

They made a park there named Canada Park. I went there in 1983. In our country, on the top of the door you put a big stone and you write, "This house belongs to Mr. So-and-So, and it was built in such-and-such a year." They used some of those lintel stones to build some of the fences that are in Canada Park. One says on it, which is well-known in our language, "There is no God but one God." And, "This house belonged to one person, his name is Muhammad."

Those people came towards Ramallah and El Bireh. They told us that the Jews had come in and demolished everything and they didn't have anything left. A lot of people decided to get out before the Israelis reached us.

Israeli Occupation

My dad used to tell us that under the Jordanians, at the end of the year my dad would tell the tax collector, "I made twenty thousand dollars." "How many do you have in your family?" They had a schedule. You paid so much to the Jordanian government and that was it. Most of that money was kept in the municipalities. They'd blacktop streets, they took care of sewers, just like anybody anywhere else.

When the Israelis came in, I believe there were six different taxes that they imposed.

We started seeing merchandise that we had never seen before. Everything was manufactured in the State of Israel. This is what you had to buy. They would not allow us to bring in stuff from any other Arab country. Before the Six Day War there was nothing whatsoever in the market that said Israel on it.

Here's an example of how things went sour. My wife's father was a blacksmith. He made furniture: chairs, tables, mostly beds with springs. He had a shop and about twenty-one people working for him. He made an honest living. When you bought a bed from him, that bed was going to be there for you and for your kids! He used to sell it for, let's say, two dinars, which is Jordanian money. He used to get the raw materials through Jordanian officials.

Now, when the Six Day War came, he had to go through the Israelis. First, they doubled the price of raw materials. Second, they gave him second class material. Third, the market was flooded with manufactured goods. A lot of the guys that were working with him wanted more money and he couldn't come up with it, so they started leaving, one after the other, until he wound up doing all the work himself. When I met him, he used to put in twelve hours a day just to buy bread for his kids. They had a family of ten.

If he did make something, people didn't have money to buy it. And if they bought it, he couldn't sell it for enough to buy more raw materials. He told me that United Nations people came to him and wanted fifty-four folding cots. He made them. They paid for them. When he tried to get more material to replace what he had used, it cost him more than he had made from the sale. He went into debt and finally he decided to retire, close the shop, and move all his equipment to the house. It's still there rusting.

Two of my brothers left one month after the war. My dad had a business but there were seven of us. How much were you going to make? The other thing was, you needed to get higher education. If you didn't go to college, let's face it, where were you going to work? There weren't any GM factories. If you didn't have a piece of property you couldn't even plant a crop. There was nothing, really, for a boy with only a high school education to do. From what we heard about the American way of life, the dollars, the work, the opportunities, why not go and educate yourself over in the United States?
[Continued below, Section 8, p. 222.]

Salah Ta'amari

"I wanted to be a teacher in a place called 'The Wilderness.'"

My history is the history of my generation. You cannot separate the "I" and the "we." My experience is not more unique than the experience of hundreds of thousands of Palestinians; the difference is like between one thumb print and another.

Early Memories in Bethlehem

My earliest memory was when I was five years old. We heard the sound of explosions and we were scared. We asked what was going on. The name of a family's house was mentioned, the Hadwa house, in the suburbs of Bethlehem, where some Palestinian fighters were resisting the Zionist organization's attack. It must have been early 1948.

Another early memory was in the mid-1950s. The Israelis attacked the village of Hassan on the road between Bethlehem and Hebron. As kids, we went there out of curiosity. I still remember the armored vehicles. I still remember a Jordanian jeep that was burnt up by the Israelis. I still remember a rock which was studded with bullets, and a track of blood. I can even recall the sensations of burnt tires and flesh. That was a very vivid memory.

When I was a kid I used to go and help my father who worked in the canteen in the police station. That police station was built by the British with a large gate, stables on the left, then a yard, and a corridor with offices on both sides, the canteen, the court, and then a cage where people would be kept as detainees. At that time the police were Jordanian.

I saw what they did to detainees. As a boy I would just go anywhere, unnoticed. One day I heard screaming. I followed the sheep that were coming out of the stable. Then I saw two young men. One was lying on his back; the other man was lifting his feet up. A soldier was whipping the feet of the man. The whip was the shoot of a pomegranate tree. Then the young man who was lying on the floor was forced to stand up and the guy who was lifting his feet was forced to lie down.

There was an elderly couple watching. The woman was half-covering her face with her head cover. The man was carrying his prayer beads. Each time the whip slashed the feet, I could see the muscles of the face of the man twitch, as if they were beating him.

It was appalling and confusing. I felt a mixture of fear, resentment and rage. I went to my father in the canteen. I told him what I had seen. He said, "Those are the parents of the two young men."

One day I went to the canteen and my father wasn't there. I asked the policeman who was gentle and friendly with my father, "Where's my father?" He said, "He's in the cage." It was an iron cage. Even the ceiling had bars.

I walked across the corridor and turned right to the other corridor and I could see his silhouette. I couldn't bear it. My father was put in the cage because he offered a cigarette to one of the detainees. They kept him one or two days.

My mother had to care for fourteen children. Four of the children died. Ten survived. This was not a bad percentage. That was accepted as part of life. God gave; God took away. This conviction enabled our people to go on, despite all the trauma which is alien to us. The conviction is the belief and faith in God and in destiny, but not in a submissive way.

We worked together to make a living, especially when my father, like the rest of his generation, went to Kuwait. They couldn't afford a visa so they had to cross the desert. My father, along with about ten of his colleagues, was lost for several months. Some never made it there; some never made it back. My father died in Kuwait.

I went to a government school, a public school. There were dozens of private schools in Bethlehem, but there were many Muslims and Christians who could not afford private school and who went to the public school which was almost free.

In Bethlehem and in Palestine generally, you couldn't draw a line between Muslims and Christians. They had the same reverence for places of worship. The best place where we used to socialize on Sundays, or on Christmas, was the Church of the Nativity. You'd find more Muslims there than Christians.

Jews were a part of this indistinguishable group of people. My grandfather's generation never spoke ill of Jews; they almost spoke of a good relationship. The European Zionists changed the course of things. The Jewish immigration was planned, premeditated and was part of a British colonial policy to create a state to protect the Suez Canal.

We should draw a line between the Jewishness of those people who started coming to Palestine and their new status as occupiers. Occupation is bad. I don't care who the occupier is, be it Muslim, be it Christian, or be it Jewish. Occupiers are bad if they happen to be Muslims or they happen to be Christians or they happen to be Jews.

Even if the Jews came to our country as saints — they thought it was empty, they thought it was theirs — then they were confronted with a situation where they found a population. Those saints needed to control the population. After a while, they resorted to the same means that others before them resorted to: divide and rule; the stick and the carrot; collective punishment. Then, after a while, they were no longer saints.

December 19, 1955

My whole generation was baptized in fire. It was a purgatory.

Our school was adjacent to the Church of the Nativity in Bethlehem. If you were facing the little gate of the Church of the Nativity, our school was on the left. Across the street was the police station and then the mosque.

When I was almost thirteen, on December 19, 1955, the older students were shouting slogans. We kids followed them out of the school. As we went into the yard, the army opened fire. Four were killed. The oldest among those who were killed was fifteen.

Right after that demonstration there were demonstrations all over the place. In a few days it was normal to see little groups of kids, each group planning an organization, with whatever names occurred to them: "The Black Palm"; "The Green Palm." Mine was the Pinks, simply because every other color was used.

Student in Egypt

I went to Cairo University, as many did. On the West Bank we didn't have universities at that time, so after school you would go to Kuwait or to the Gulf to take a job, or go to Syria or Egypt or the United States to acquire higher education. I went in 1963.

I wanted to be a teacher in an elementary school with a small piece of land in a place called "the Wilderness." In Arabic it is called "Berea" which means wilderness. It is to the east of the Shepherds' Field, between Beit Sahour and the Dead Sea, in a semi-desert area. That was my dream.

I had an uncle who went to Panama in 1930 and another who went there in the early fifties. They wanted me to go to Panama. I refused. I knew what I wanted. I told them, "I don't want to leave here. I love it. I just want to get a degree and stay here."

I was one of those who adored Nasser. Egypt was a sort of Mecca for those who believed in Arabism, who believed in progress, who believed in the justice of our cause, who wanted to feel free. We all went to Egypt.

I remember that when I arrived at the airport we thought we would just sail through immigration. Our passports were collected and we were asked to stand aside. I could see Americans, British, every other nationality, just sailing through and we were waiting for almost one hour! We thought that was trivial and we should ignore it. We still believed in Nasser.

I remember there was a shortage of salt: Egypt, that lies on two seas, had a shortage of salt! We all believed that there was an imperialist conspiracy against Egypt.

A week after my arrival I enrolled in the General Union of Palestinian Students (GUPS). I studied English literature.

I joined Fatah in 1965. Fatah was on the rise but we were underground. The major movement at that time was the Arab nationalists and they were in control of the Union. We ran for election as independents — we could never say we were Fatah at that time — and we won. I belonged to the military branch of Fatah although we were students and didn't have any kind of military activity.

In 1966, after my election as the Secretary General of GUPS in Cairo, I was detained in Jordan for three days. Everything was banned in Jordan. It was not unusual to detain somebody, especially coming from Cairo. They took me from the immigration desk. The bad thing about it was that my brothers were waiting for me at the airport in the West Bank.

I was supposed to graduate in 1967 but the war broke out in June 1967. We were listening to the radio. The number of Israeli planes shot down, according to the Egyptian announcer on the radio, was more than all the NATO countries put together could have had! The first retreating Egyptian soldier reached Cairo, barefooted, while the announcer was still talking about knocking down Israeli planes and tanks.

We rushed to the GUPS office. We had had military training a few years before so we volunteered. Before we got into the trucks and buses, the war was over, but they didn't tell us that.

I went back to my apartment. Another tenant in the building was a retired civilian pilot who always listened to the BBC and Voice of America. His apartment was next to mine with a little balcony. He was sitting on the balcony. I could hear the voice of Moshe Dayan in an interview. I heard him saying, "We are here and we are not intending to go out. The Wailing Wall is ours." That meant they were in Jerusalem! It just pierced my soul.

If the war had occurred two months later, I would have graduated and I would have been on that piece of land near Bethlehem. In fact, I was shattered. I wanted to reach that piece of land. That fixation is still a fixation and it does not mellow as time passes by.

[Continued below, Section 5, p. 106.]

Lawahez Burgal

"This was the first thing that led me to think about what was going on."

1967

I was born in Jerusalem in the Old City. We are part of the Jaberi family from Hebron. It's a bourgeois family and the biggest family in that city. The mayor of the municipality until ten years ago was from the Jaberi family. His name is Mohammed Al Jaberi. He was one of the men who made an agreement in Jericho when the Israelis occupied the country. He was part of the Jordanian system. You can't even say he's Palestinian.

Under the British Mandate my father was in the fedayin, and a big hero. He worked as head chef in a hotel. Before the 1967 war we were in a good situation.

I remember the war. I was about seven years old at that time, but I still remember everything: the destruction of houses, and how my family escaped from one house to another, and bodies on the street. My mother was holding one or two children in her arms and shouting and praying.

My father wasn't with us. For twelve days, we didn't know where my father was.

We were right here in East Jerusalem. Our house was destroyed at that time. Along with many other people in the Old City, we went to live in a cave. It was very small. I remember that a Jordanian soldier came to that cave and said, "Please, keep me here." Some of the women took his uniform and gave him a woman's dress; they also took his gun, broke it down, and hid it.

The only thing we had to eat was bread. The women had flour and they cooked bread for the children.

One other thing I still remember is that my mother took care that because we were girls no man would sleep beside us. She put our bags and clothes between us and the others. After twelve days, my father came.

The war brought a big change in our lives. I started to hear inside my family that my father no longer had money. He couldn't work. Why? Because of "Israelis," because of "the Jewish." These were the words I was hearing as a kid.

Before the war, my father always used to bring us gifts, games for the children, nice presents. If you saw our photographs you would see that we were living well then. But after the war, the economic situation in our house became very bad because my father no longer had a job. And why? Not because my father was a political man, or fought in the war. No, it was because he was a Palestinian.

This was the first thing that led me to think about what was going on. I didn't know anything about the Palestinian problem at that time. No one told us why the Israelis came and occupied us. We didn't know this. But the war led us as children to think that something big was happening. I started to feel as a Palestinian.

The Big Change

Between the ages of seven and eleven, I started to hear on the radio about the fedayin, the commandos, Palestinian organizations. I started to hear that there had been demonstrations. I didn't know why. But I started to hear these words — commandos, demonstrations, shooting, prison — from radio, from TV, from people who knew these things.

When I was eleven years old, I took part in a demonstration for the first time in my life. Some men came to our school and said that eight persons from the West Bank were going to be exiled out of the country. So we shared in the demonstration.

At that time, I felt that I was going to do something because my father was suffering: because my father was starting to say, "I'm poor, I have no job." We didn't have gifts. We didn't have clothes. And I was shouting in the demonstration because something had happened to me as a person and to my family.

They caught me in that demonstration. When one of the security men came to arrest me I made some movement with my hand and my nails entered into his eye somehow and he started bleeding. I spent one week in Moscobiyya Central Prison under interrogation. I was eleven years old.

For the first time in my life I started to think as an Arab. I began to feel that I was one of the whole society, that I was part of the problem. I was in prison, not because I was Lawahez and my father's name was Abed, but because I was a Palestinian. There was a big problem. I had to think about it.

The only thing I was scared about at that time was that maybe my father was going to beat me when I was released. I didn't care about what the security men might do to me, only about my father.

It brought a change in our home that a girl from this conservative family had gone to prison. My family was angry. "Why did she do it? She's a girl!" This is what they were scared about. "She's a girl. She's going to spend one week?"

The newspapers wrote about this case and that I beat the security man and he was bleeding. When they released me, all the neighbors came. They brought chocolates with them to my mother and they said, "She is a hero." My mother started to see that Palestinian society was also thinking about the women who entered prison and was proud of them.

After my release I wanted really to be involved in the Palestinian problem, to study, to hear in person. I began to discuss events in our house. "Did you hear about the fedayin who killed an Israeli?" "Did you read in the newspaper . . .?" "Did you see this book . . .?" I started to know about Marx and Lenin. I expressed concepts about the economic situation, about big cultural and political problems. This was something that they weren't used to hearing from a young girl!

My father knew that I was changing and that I was going to do something. He didn't want to believe it, but he couldn't stop it, because he himself was a nationalist. He had educated us to love our homeland and our people. He was always telling us stories about the British Mandate, and also about the Jordanians when they were here. So he couldn't stop me; and besides, he didn't know for sure whether I had yet joined an organization.

[Continued below, Section 6, p. 148.]

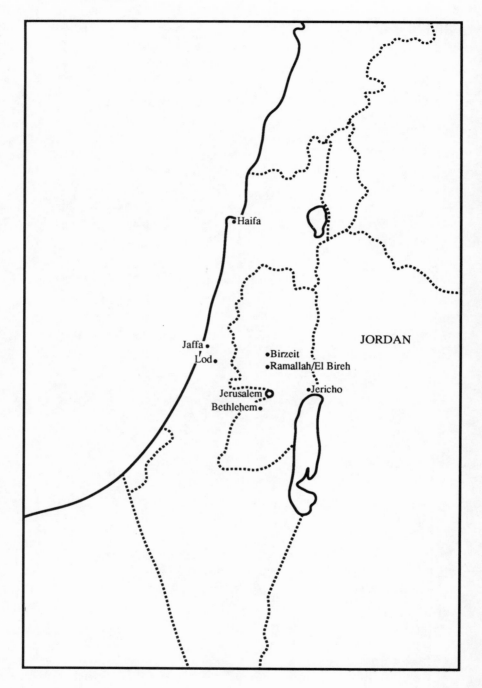

4

Women

The status of women in the Occupied Territories reflects traditional Palestinian values and practices. Arranged marriage was the norm until recent years. However, the proportion of females in schools and colleges grew steadily after 1967, so that twenty years later 45 per cent of students in primary and secondary school and 30 to 45 per cent of students at coeducational West Bank colleges and universities, were women. Unfranchised under the Jordanian law in force before 1967, women were permitted to vote in the Israeli-sponsored municipal elections of 1976 (the results of which were overturned by the Israeli military occupation authorities soon after). Most Palestinian women holding jobs outside their homes live in urban areas, and are employed in service industries, education, and health care. Even before the Intifada there was a wide range of women's cooperative groups for health care, child care, handicraft production, vocational training, and other services.[1]

The women in this section describe some of the changes that came about and that they helped to bring about under Israeli occupation.

★   ★   ★

Amal Younis

"We were the seed of the women's movement on the West Bank."

Childhood

I was born in 1945 in the town of El Bireh. My name, Amal, means "hope." I have two sisters and two brothers.

My father had a small store where he would market wheat, grain and raw materials. My uncles were in the United States so my father was the head of the household, looking over the family of one of my uncles as well as my

---

1. U.S. State Department, *Country Reports on Human Rights Practices for 1982*, p. 1175; *Country Reports on Human Rights Practices for 1987*, p. 1199.

family. He was the one to take care of the land, to make sure paperwork was done, and to make sure the family had food.

We used to depend on income from abroad more than from local industry or business. I never really knew my uncles. They left the country in 1924 and they had grocery stores in Youngstown, Ohio.

My family and my uncle's family lived in the same house until I was about ten years old. At times there would be about twenty people living in that one home. When I was sixteen years old, one of my uncles retired, took a pension, and came back home. That was the first time I met him.

I went to a preschool. I remember my teacher. In King Hussein's time, before Israel, a child had to be seven years old to go to government school.

I remember that from when I first became conscious, we were told that King Hussein would not provide our society with anything. He was an enemy. That is what I learned when I was small and didn't know anything about him. As an example, when a light industry would open in Ramallah or El Bireh, the Jordanian government would relocate that industry to the south or into an area within Jordan. My feelings were, and the society's feelings were, that the Jordanian government was always pushing to shift whatever good the Palestinian community had to the interests of the Jordanian government.

We demonstrated against Jordan. I was there. I was one of the demonstrators, not just watching. I remember demonstrating when I was about ten years old, during the mid-fifties. Many times we were faced with armed police and shootings. They would shoot first into the air to scare us. Most of the time we would flee, but we would find ourselves regrouping and starting our demonstration over again. Many people were injured. Many people were in jail and subjected to torture. I remember one jail under Jordanian rule, Jafr, was well-known for its torture.

I went to the girls' school in El Bireh. I finished high school there in 1965. In 1964 Algeria was liberated. I was planning to go to a girls' teachers' college and I had signed a contract to go to Ramallah College. Many of my friends were going into education and a lot of my friends had also signed up at Ramallah College. But I wanted to go to Algeria!

Algeria

I had friends who had been to Algeria and they told me it was a great place to live: the work was stable and very well paid, and the people were kind. I became very enthusiastic, which made me brave enough to go and ask my father. I said, "I have been nineteen years living in the house with you and I have been good and I have done everything you wanted me to do. Would it not be a good idea if I were able to go out and become conscious of what is outside this house?" I brought some of the letters that my friends had sent back home to try to convince him. "Look at all the girls who went and say it is a nice country. It's safe. There are no problems. It's good work." My father agreed to let me go.

The person who did not agree was my youngest brother who did not want to see me go off alone. He refused to bid me farewell when I left.

In 1965, we were still under Jordanian rule. I went to the Algerian Embassy in Amman, Jordan. I showed them the contract that I had to go to Ramallah College, and I requested that I be able to go teach in Algeria. They needed teachers in the Arabic language at that time because Algeria had been under French occupation and instruction had been in French.

I and two other students from my high school in El Bireh went to Algeria and registered to teach. In addition to officials from the Algerian government, some Palestinians came and met us. They said to go to one of the smaller villages: "They need you more." Another reason we were persuaded to go to smaller villages was that there were still pockets of French counter-revolutionaries in the larger cities and clashes were still happening, so it was safer to go to the small villages.

Three of us were picked to go to a village called Saeida. We did not know anyone there. Each of us stayed with a separate family. One went to an Egyptian home and one to a Syrian home. I stayed with an Iraqi family and they treated me very well. We felt that the community received us more warmly than they received our host families because we were Palestinian. The people were very nationalistic and they were very helpful.

A normal day would be to get up, have breakfast, and go to the school until three o'clock in the afternoon. The children I taught were ten years old. The Algerians had a rule that required the teachers to speak classical Arabic, as it is written, not slang. It was a difficult job but I loved it.

During the Algerian resistance, women played a very distinct role. For example, women would take food to the resistance movement and they would themselves be exposed to the French when they were going and coming. One woman I met had been caught by a French patrol and she was burned by cigarettes as punishment for taking food to the resistance. I think the Algerian women played a very critical role in the liberation of Algeria — not only liberating Algeria, but liberating themselves.

The resistance was not finished and over when I arrived. It was still happening while I was there. I saw that the woman was equal to the man. Of course, there were some incidents of repression because of the religious backwardness of some people, and some cultural changes that the women's movement was proposing that did not become widespread. But changes did take place in the society as a whole.

The person who was in charge of the school where I taught was a woman. Previous to this in the Arab world, you did not find a woman in charge of a school. There would have been a male schoolmaster. This is an example that women were playing the roles of the male or were equal. I saw that in the cities there was a greater opportunity for women to come and go and interact with other people and to have more freedom. But a woman was in charge of the school in a small village, which should have been even more backward than in the city, and I saw this. During the time I was there I saw them moving forward.

One thing that surprised me was that everybody wore a gown that covered the whole body including the face. Those who were "liberated" would have their faces showing, whereas others had only their eyes showing. These people were moving forward in society and yet they were covered. I felt this was awkward. It was not a total change.

The Algerian women would ask us simple questions like, "What is the geography or landscape of Palestine? Is it mountainous or hilly? How is life?" They did not know anything about physical Palestine or what our struggle was all about.

A Turning Point

The PLO was initiated in 1964. In 1965, there was a conference in Algeria. I was there. That was a turning point for me. After the formation of the PLO, I began to take politics more seriously and to look for a role that I, myself, could play in the movement.

I was conscious enough of the living conditions when I left Palestine in 1965 to feel that there was a need for people, especially women, to become involved. That is one of the reasons why I was motivated to become politically inclined.

It was not much different from what's happening now. Today it may be on a different scale. But the same things that motivated me to become involved are happening today and are motivating people now to become involved politically.

My role then was soliciting funds. It was made easier for us because the people who were in support of the Algerian president at that time were helping us and giving us all the resources we needed to go out into the community and raise money.

I stayed in Algeria for one school year, about nine months. During the summer break I came back to Palestine. I went to Ramallah and got a job as an administrative secretary. I worked one year until the occupation took place in 1967.

Occupation

After the Israelis entered the West Bank in 1967, I changed my whole life and what I wanted to do. I became involved in how to change reality. Some of my friends encouraged me to join a group of women who would meet regularly — we called it a "cell" — and I did.

We lived in a religious society. The Islamic religion does not promote women and men meeting together. At that time we were not against this idea because we thought we could open up and possibly be more frank with each other as a group of women. We were raised not to open up, not to be frank in our discussions, if a male were there. Once in a while, in my group, a male would come and give a lecture.

At the beginning we would read books about politics and people would explain to this group of women what the books meant. I remember we read a book called "The Palestinian Cause." Most of the education was about how the Palestinian movement came about, from 1936 on, and also about the

Zionist movement and how the Jews put themselves together from all around the world to come to Palestine.

After a time, there came responsibilities. We were asked to go and do something, whether in the streets or in the community.

I remember being involved in several demonstrations. I remember the Israelis squirting some sort of acid water on us. I remember people being hit with billy clubs.

We would go to the mosques and hold sit-ins. I remember when they wanted to deport the elected mayor of El Bireh, Abdul Jawad Saleh, we held an event in the mosque. The army came into the mosque and there was a clash within the grounds of the mosque.

At this time, the martyrs became more apparent in our society. One of the roles we would play was to visit the families of the martyrs and to try to raise money to help the families of those who had been killed or those who were in jail.

A woman from one of the cells in town was caught by the Israelis. She gave the name of the leader of the group and this leader got a lifetime sentence.

This leader was one of the first in the women's movement to get a lifetime sentence. They demolished her home (where her parents, her brother, and her sister also lived).

Another woman was caught at the same time and also got a lifetime sentence. These two women were exposed through the organization that they created. One of them, together with my group, had opened up a girl scout group to provide day-care for young girls. The authorities found out that this organization was politically inclined and, therefore, the two people who were running it were exposed and caught.

We became scared. One of the other women came to me and asked me, "What are we going to do if they come for us? They have taken two people who were most active in the women's groups." We were not prepared to take a decision on our own, but we were faced with that decision. We agreed, if they came and took us, we were not going to confess to anything. "We will not resist going with them. We will go with them but we will not confess."

It was not two days later when the Israelis came to my house. (This was in 1968.) They knocked on the door. My mother answered the door. She had just gotten up and did not have on her regular clothes. My mother said I had gone to my aunt's house. That would give at least enough time to get dressed. They left.

Somehow they found out where my father's store was. They went to the store and came back to the house with my father. At this point I was ready to go. I told them, "Come on in. We have nothing to hide."

The first thing they told me was that I was accused of being involved with — and they named the individuals they had already arrested. I denied having any relationship with any of these individuals. They told me they had to take me to the central military command post for interrogation.

We arrived at the police station at about 9:00 a.m. I stayed until 4:00 p.m. They kept asking me questions and trying to make me talk. I didn't. The two main questions were, what were my relationships with the individuals who were imprisoned, and why I left the country to go to Algeria.

I attempted to deny everything to the point where I made myself look as if I didn't know anything about anything. I thought that if I acted crazy I would not be exposed to what I heard had happened to my friends who were in prison for life. We heard that they were tortured — that one lost her virginity and the other was paralyzed from her legs down — so I wanted to avoid this.

Another woman was arrested and was being interrogated at the same time I was. I knew her by name but I did not have any relationship with her, or I would have been scared that she would tell about my activities. We only knew the three other people in our cell. We didn't know details about anyone else. So I was lucky I did not know this other person.

Later I heard about this girl who was arrested that I did not know, that they were playing with her eye as part of the interrogation. Today she has a glass eye, an artificial eye.

At about four or five o'clock, the interrogators left to go eat and they left me in a room. This was probably the most frightening time for me because I did not know what was going to happen. Then someone came in and said that they were going to get my father so he could bail me out.

This bail had a string attached. Somebody had to sign to say that I would not be involved. I didn't sign but they got my father to sign. Unfortunately, because of all the stress and pressure, my father signed the paper to get me out.

A new thing that we noticed in our community at that time was that there started to be great numbers of collaborators. The Palestinian movement began to concentrate on dealing with the collaborators. First a warning would be sent to the individual. Then they were sent two or three written things. Then, if they continued — at that time there were no guns on the West Bank — they would be dealt with in a physical manner, by poison in something that they would eat, or by actually visiting and killing them. The financial aspect was a tremendous incentive to be a collaborator.

We were very, very scared during this period. People were talking about what happened to the women at the Deir Yassin massacre, and the Kafr Qasim massacre, and other massacres that took place. Now I was in a position where I could be exposed to the same thing. We were deeply frightened by this.

My father recommended that I leave and come to see my brother in the United States. Word was getting around that they were treating women very badly in jail. My two friends were examples. My father asked me to leave and I did.

We were the seed of the women's movement on the West Bank. We didn't have any experience behind us at which to look. Basically we were playing by ear.

Sarona

"The Intifada didn't just happen."

I was born in 1968, a year after the 1967 war.

In 1948, my mother was not yet born and my father was very small. My father came from Raas Abu Ammar which is one of the villages in the Bethlehem area, and my mother is from a town called Malha near Jerusalem.

Most of my information about the situation before 1948 came from what my grandfather on my father's side used to tell me. I do not know as much about the people in my mother's hometown.

The pre-1948 history that my grandfather gave me was not a history of tragedy. It was a history of how well we were doing in the land, how much we loved our land. He would talk about how he had horses that worked the land. Palestine at that time had an almost feudalistic agricultural lifestyle. My grandfather spoke of having Jewish individuals working for the Arab population because the Jews were a minority at that time and they were poor and therefore they were looking for work as hired labor with the Arab farmers.

My grandfather described the difference in living conditions and living styles after 1948 and he explained the tragedy that happened to him as well as many others. The village that my grandfather and my father came from was completely destroyed in the first phase of the establishment of the State of Israel. That village was wiped off the map and it became agricultural ground for a new Israeli village. When my grandfather fled he took nothing: no land, no money, no personal belongings.

After 1948, my grandfather went to Jordan for a while, but then he came back and lived the rest of his life in Dahaisha Refugee Camp in Bethlehem. Like any refugee in Dahaisha at that time, he was living in U.N. housing. His living conditions were terrible. During the winter we would bring my grandfather to live in our house in Ramallah because there was a constant leak in the ceiling of his house when it was raining. But he would always rather stay in his own house, even if it was in a refugee camp. While he was living in the refugee camp, he spoke constantly of how life was before, and he died in his memories of what was going on before his Dahaisha time.

I have one uncle that lives in Aida Refugee Camp near Dahaisha. My oldest uncle lives in El Baka Camp in Jordan and another uncle died in a city in Jordan. My parents were lucky. We never lived in refugee camps.

The life of my mother was very different from the life of my father. My mother came from a more wealthy family. After 1948 her parents went to Jordan and they were well-to-do in Jordan. From there they went to America which made them even more well-to-do.

Mama began losing her eyesight when she was very young and she used to go to the Helen Keller School for the Blind. My father was a student at the Lutheran School. Both of them went to the same church. Two friends on my father's side married two friends on my mother's side. That is how they got to see each other. While they were in school they would meet at the church. But they were married in the Islamic way.

My mother and father never really understood each other because one came from a poor family and the other came from a wealthy family. She teaches music and English. My father sells things in a store.

School Years

I was involved in the activities of the women's movement from the time I was eight or nine years old. My older sister was politically active and when she was a student she spent a lot of volunteer time with the trade union movement. She introduced me to the women's movement.

The trade union movement was not just men. The primary activities were meetings for the purpose of education — male and female. Much of the grassroots activity was volunteer work in different small factories, in construction, or going to Jericho during the harvesting season. The Palestinian landowners did not have enough capital to hire people during the harvest season to pick all of the tomatoes. Therefore, instead of allowing half of the tomatoes to go bad and depending on Israeli tomatoes to fill the vacuum in the market, they would take people — from old men to young women — to harvest as volunteers in order to supply the market with Palestinian products rather than Israeli products. This was in the late '70s. I was real small.

My sister's future husband was very political and he helped to develop my sister's radical thoughts. My sister implanted in me nationalistic views but she gave me no basis, no foundation to build upon.

Then I was introduced to an older man who was in the Palestinian Communist Party. He spent a lot of time discussing politics with me. He was like my godfather. It wasn't an intimate relationship. He was a wise struggler. He is the one who implanted a foundation on the basis of which I could start making decisions about what I wanted to do. He gave me books, political direction, and the motivation to get involved.

The first demonstrations that I joined were funerals. A boy named Khalil Al-Liftawi was killed. They burned the Israeli and American flags. Later, a young man called Ibrahim was going to the mill to get wheat ground for his mother. A settler shot him in the head and killed him. I joined the funeral demonstration.

Then came the Women's Day celebration on March 8, 1981. It was organized by the student movement, which was boys and girls, and, of course, by women's organizations, and by everybody. This was the first time I was arrested. Following this experience, my life became a lot more focused.

It was winter and we were outside. The army encircled us with barbed wire. They made the circle around us so tight that if one of us moved the wire would puncture her skin. I was the youngest. Because I talked to another girl, the soldier made both of us put our hands on the wall and he whipped us on our fingers. This was the first time I was hit by an Israeli soldier. It was so painful! I didn't cry at the time. I don't know why. But I felt so much hate! I felt, "What right does this man have to beat me?" Because I was below the legal age, I stayed only two days in detention. My parents bailed me out.

This incident changed my personality. My life was no longer to be spent having a good time. There were more important things to do.

After my first arrest I became close to a woman who was an activist in town. My sister gave me an emotional kind of support. My "godfather" gave me an ideological sense of where I stood. But the woman that I met gave me a programmatic outlook, something that I was lacking and to which I became very attracted. Before I met her, we would go out to a demonstration or to a volunteer activity but I never saw any linkage among all of those activities. After meeting this woman and becoming involved with her, I started to see a linkage. This was the most critical period of my development. I was almost fourteen years old.

Two things allowed me to become more active with this woman. One was that her group was proposing a democratic secular state in the whole of what used to be Palestine, not a two-state solution. Ever since I was very small, I felt something was wrong with the idea of two states. I could not justify in my own mind a State called Israel being built on land that was stolen.

Second, I was introduced to a theory that allowed me to feel that, being a woman, I was a part of society, and that I was part of the human race and the human race was part of me. In the group, there was not the level of discrimination that the society around me practiced.

What I was hearing was one school of thought saying, "Me, period," and another school of thought saying, "You and I." "You and I" made a lot more sense. Both my "godfather" and this woman were proposing the "We," whereas the society around me was teaching everybody the "Me, period." I had learned from my "godfather" role model about the collectiveness of the work. And I felt that this woman was educating me on the collectiveness of the society, rather than the male role or the dominance of one sector of society.

Another reason I moved toward this trend of thought was that the Communist Party literature said one thing while the individuals were doing something different. This caused me to start thinking critically. In a demonstration, the Communist Party would pick up a red flag — they thought that had priority over picking up a Palestinian flag. The Palestinian Communist Party also proposed a relationship with the Israeli parliament. We viewed that as taking Lenin's statements on working to change the system from within — taking an experience in the Soviet Union — and implanting it onto a completely different experience in the West Bank and Israel. The Communist Party dealt with Israel as if our history began in 1948. We had a pre-1948 history! The Israeli parliament is not an innocent body.

My mother put me in private schools when I was little. I left private school after intermediate school and I went to a public high school. During the time I was in high school, our neighborhood was in turmoil. Our upstairs neighbors had two children in detention. Our next door neighbor had one child detained in Israeli prisons. My brother had been detained and released a number of times, and the neighbor living in front of us was also detained. Other families had children who were severely beaten by the army. When we got older, the army started entering our homes by force. People were close to each other in the neighborhood. We used to stay up late at night discussing the issues. These troubles gave me a sense of belonging.

In the political trend I was involved in, there were several spheres of work. I was a student so I became most involved in the student movement. If I were a worker I would have become involved in the trade union movement. If I were an agriculturalist, I would have become involved in that part of the work. If I were an activist housewife, I would have been actively involved in the women's movement.

In the student movement, I began by being introduced to activities through weekly meetings for educational purposes, and through going on field trips. These field trips introduced us to the geography and the richness of our culture in Palestine. There are valleys, mountains and plains all in the same country. Many people do not know the religious meanings of all the artifacts and historical places. The trips were to introduce us to our own land. Also there was a very active group to teach the dubka (national folkloric dance).

There were also various activities to unite us with students in other villages or cities. We became involved in sports events, joint field trips, joint meetings or lectures. This helped us to develop a sense of oneness, a united movement, rather than a movement fragmented according to where you lived.

Our week was full with meetings and our school work, demonstrations and political activities. One day a week we would go outside of Ramallah to one of the villages to introduce people to the student movement. I would go and get to know other people. We would find people who were not able to pay the tuition for schooling and try to help them solve that social problem. If someone did not have enough clothing or did not have sufficient shelter, we would either volunteer our time to help or find funding for that individual. Those that knew about medical problems would give health education lectures in the surrounding areas.

After I completed high school my time was divided, half for the movement and half for the Palestinian Popular Folklore Troupe, El-Fanoon. I was a dance member of the troupe.

That troupe was not created only to allow us to dance and sing. Its role was to educate us in the importance of our culture, whether through teaching us customs or teaching us music and dance in the historical context of our culture. We studied the poems of Palestinians, and from those poems we created dubkas or songs, and that in itself was teaching us about our own identity. (The dubka is a style of dancing that traditionally had seven to ten steps in it. But that also, like society, develops. There is one step that means "forward." Now we have "forward" and "new forward," "sideways" and "new sideways.") The El-Fanoon troupe went back and dug up a story about a British soldier, before 1948, when British soldiers were in Palestine, and created a production around this story. This introduced us to a part of our history that we would never have known because it was not in our textbooks. Knowing that literature, knowing that identity, knowing those old customs that made us what we are today, made us feel more tied to the land and more tied to our people.

When I am doing the dubka or doing Palestinian song and dance, I feel that I am expressing my identity as a Palestinian. Even when I am in America, I feel that I am being an ambassador for my people through this dance.

I entered college on October 2, 1987. Between October 2 and October 25, there were two demonstrations which caused the college to close those two days. We were demonstrating for the liberation of Palestine and the right of Palestinian refugees to return. When there was a third demonstration on October 25, the Israelis closed the college for good.

The Intifada and the Women's Committees

The Intifada (Uprising) began in December 1987. The Intifada didn't just happen instantaneously. It came into being because there was a movement building towards it, even though we did not know what it was.

During school I was only introduced to the work that students were able to do. Once I finished school I entered into the women's committee. This gave me more of a birds-eye look at society and the social problems that society was facing.

We took on several projects. Many women did not know how to read and write. That affected their children's education also because they could not help their children with schoolwork. So one project was to combat illiteracy.

Another activity of the women's committees was making social visits, having in mind a topic they wanted to discuss with the woman of the household. Our society has been brought up in such a traditional way that women would accept oppression or repression in the household rather than even think or talk about liberating themselves as women. We would attempt to take these women to other areas, to be introduced to many other people. One of the downfalls of a traditional household is that the woman is between four walls. She doesn't see much other than her own experience. So if she were able to go out and see women in other villages, how women who were more developed were working and taking a role in society, this would give her some hope or new insight on what she could possibly become.

The overall strategy of working with women involved two things: first, becoming involved in the social life of the woman, and second, through the involvement in that relationship building a politically conscious woman. The first of these was the primary goal. Women were facing real problems. And we felt, if we wanted to be active and to gain the confidence of the masses, we needed to make those problems our problems.

Those women who lived on the same street and were active in the women's movement would meet on a regular basis. But the following month, those women would meet with the women on the next street. The goal was that these individuals see themselves as part of a movement of individuals who were related to each other, not to think that the whole movement was themselves. Twice a year there was a conference or a convention of the entire women's movement when we all got together.

The idea of meetings on a regular basis was there before I even became conscious of it. There was a movement in place before I came into being. Proof of that is that some of the educational materials we used were materials that came from meetings before I was born. We took the old movement and developed it for the new circumstances that we faced in our generation.

When the old movement first began, like anything that starts new it had no knowledge of any previous movement. What they put forth as a program and as a strategy may have been correct but because of their lack of organizing experience and because of their lack of clearly defined goals, first they fell into organizational problems that they could not solve, and second, they did not view the whole spectrum of problems.

One pitfall may have been the degree of centralism in their activities. We believed that our opening up chapters in various villages was more effective than expecting people to come to a city and become involved in a central activity. If we had a committee in Ramallah and we were able to open one in Jerusalem, after a couple of years the Jerusalem one might be able to open one in Bethlehem, and so forth. This pyramid shape of organization left a wide base in which the majority of people could work.

Another problem that we had in the past was that we viewed the social aspect as separated from the political aspect. At the beginning, the movement primarily interacted socially with the woman. However, because we were living in the West Bank, we became political beings and the social aspect and the political aspect became one.

We came into the movement in a better situation than the women who went before us because we had their experience and we could see more of the problem. In ten years, the movement will look at what we did, see what we learned, and widen its horizon.

Before the Intifada, the organizing was not as intense as it is now. Pre-Intifada there might have been one meeting a month. After the Intifada, everything became weekly. That was the major change, pre- and post-Intifada.

The style of organizing did not change. Before the Intifada, we were organizing for a mass movement. We didn't call it "Intifada," but it was organizing for a mass movement. So when the mass movement came about, there was a higher intensity of organizing, but the style itself did not change.

From 1967 until the Intifada (December 1987), we were under occupation but there were many opportunities for employment. Even though they were weak opportunities, people were able to put bread on the table. After the Intifada, work in Israel got cut off, it was harder to find work within the West Bank, and it became more expensive to live. You could see in the neighborhood women whose husbands could not find work. We had a neighbor whose husband could not work. They had children so she started working. We had another neighbor whose husband was in prison and she had to work to feed her children. There were also women whose husbands were working outside Palestine but the money from outside was not reaching them. So these women started to become involved in work that brought in money.

Before the Intifada, the woman was not accepted in the workplace to the degree she is today for two reasons: first, custom; and second, practically, she didn't have a degree, she didn't have vocational training, and so forth. Post-Intifada she was required to work in order to keep the family going.

After the Intifada, one of the main aspects of organizing that was not there before was home economics. We tried to educate and help people to plant their own gardens and to keep some livestock at home in order that the home economy could become an alternative during curfews and other hard times. If people did not have seeds, we would bring them seeds. If people were not farmers and just did not know how to grow, we would take someone that did know how to grow and teach the committee on that street or that household how to grow at home. Pre-Intifada you never saw an agricultural leaflet. Post-Intifada there is a leaflet on how to grow a home garden.

Creating an alternative economy became an organizing task of the entire community. But the women played a major role in it because of their place naturally being in the home. The work was both male and female, collectively. If a household could not afford a tractor and they had a parcel of land that they wanted to plow, we would volunteer and go out and plow the land. That was one of the work tasks on strike days. The strike days were not meant for people just to stay home and watch TV, but rather to use those days to build another block in the struggle. Our block was building home gardens and home economies.

The women's committees had to face the problem of providing food for families. We would collectively bake bread in bulk to distribute. At times we would have donation drives when we would go to the store owners for contributions and we would make relief bags to go to homes that could not provide food for their own families.

There were two other projects. Everyone knew how to cook. So we would do canning and reselling. That was very popular because it allowed the woman to work and at the same time to work within her household because of the children being home. If a parent could produce enough of a product at home — sweaters or whatever — that could be sold through the women's committees, that would be 50 shekels that she could not get by any other means. The women started cooperatives to sell their products and then share the profits.

Bringing bread into the household was only one aspect of it. The woman also had to be the child-rearer and she was responsible for the educating of her children. This was even more of a role after the closing of the schools.

The Intifada touched every life, not just the lives of one class of people. The Palestinian woman knows that she can't count on the presence of a man. He may die as a martyr, be imprisoned, be exiled, live underground or just disappear in struggle. The women were holding things together in the home and in the neighborhood. The woman had to play the male role as well as the female role.

There were also changes in activism. Women stopped playing a passive role. In the past when they saw the Israeli army entering a home forcefully, they closed their doors and did nothing. After the Intifada started, women started going out of their homes to support the people affected. Pre-Intifada, you rarely saw a woman being part of a demonstration. Post-Intifada you would see demonstrations created solely for women to take part in them. This was to encourage women to understand that they could play a role. Pre-Intifada they had a barrier of fear because they saw what was happening to the males. And they had a mental barrier, thinking that there was no way a woman could face a soldier. We proved just the opposite: not only could we face the soldier but we could defeat a soldier. For the first time, women played a role in securing the villages and cities by being guards all night long. Women did other things that used to be roles of males only like going out and writing slogans or passing leaflets at night.

Day of the Child

As soon as someone gets imprisoned, the entire life of the family and its way of thinking changes. My oldest brother was detained many times by the Israelis. One time he was taken when an Israeli army bus was hit with rocks and they indiscriminately collected people from the street. Most of his detentions were for short periods of time — one or two months at a time. We used to visit him in prison.

Prior to the Intifada he worked for a wholesale storage company. But later, he was wanted by Israeli intelligence. He stopped working — because if he worked they would have been able to find him — and he went into hiding for three years. Then he was captured and he is still in prison. I do not know what his sentence will be or when he will come out.

My younger brother was fourteen and a half the first time he was detained. Imagine what it can do to a fourteen year old boy and his family if he is detained and his family does not know where he is until five months later!

In 1988 I got a job as a secretary in a research institute. I enjoyed working there and I made good money. But I was detained within a few months of taking this job.

On June 3, 1988 the children at the Qadorah Refugee Camp were celebrating the Day of the Child and it became a riot. The children were carrying posters. Most of the children were not older than nine. The army surrounded the entire area and the soldiers started hitting the children. You could hear nothing but cries and screams.

One of the children ran behind me for protection from a soldier with a billy club. The child was my neighbor. He knew me and that's why he came to me for protection. The soldier then tried to grab the child from behind me and I would not let him. The soldier screamed at me and wanted to hold me responsible for organizing the riot. Then the soldier hit me. In retaliation, a group of young men standing on a hill started throwing stones at the soldier. I grabbed the young boy and ran home.

Three days later, on June 6, 1988, as I was walking along the street with a friend, a Molotov bomb exploded in the produce market in Ramallah. The army immediately surrounded the adjacent area. My friend said there was a soldier pointing at her. I told her to run and I would follow her. As soon as she started running, I felt the hands of a soldier grab me and I panicked. I did not recognize the soldier until he took off the barred helmet that covered his face. Then I recognized him: he was the one who wanted to blame me for the riot three days earlier at the refugee camp.

As soon as he grabbed me, six more soldiers appeared and started hitting me. They dumped me into a jeep and I fell onto the driver. The driver handcuffed me and put me on the seat near him. All the way to the detention center the driver was spitting on my face and pulling my hair.

As soon as I got to the detention center they took off the metal handcuffs and replaced them with plastic. The plastic handcuffs caused me much pain. My hands turned blue. Eventually they changed the handcuffs but my hands remained inflamed for at least a month afterwards.

Then I was taken into the interrogation room. The interrogator was accusing me: "You organized a riot for 100 young men." In three days the children had become men and they had grown in number to 100. He added, "You hit the soldier on his head with a bottle. You insulted a symbol of the State." My attempt to protect my young neighbor from beating with a billy club had become a criminal act that insulted the State of Israel. They had six criminal counts against me.

Actually, the women's movement *was* solely responsible for creating the Day of the Child event. The leadership of that event was the women's movement.

Maha Nassar

"The voluntary work committee, two or three different theater groups, labor unions, womens' committees, came to be perceived as different aspects of a single movement."

I was born in the Old City of Jerusalem in the year 1954. I belong to a Christian Greek Orthodox family, considered to be middle-class. My father was the chief fire officer of Jerusalem.

My father had been one of the people involved in political life before 1948. When he was young, he had the enthusiasm to confront the Israeli movement at a time when there was no Israel, it was all Palestine. Before 1948 he belonged to a small troop called the Wounded Struggler. They had only very simple weapons during the British Mandate. The good weapons were given to the Zionists. My father almost died in one of their conflicts with the Jewish gangs.

When I was young my father used to teach us ideas and ways of living. He used to tell us how to feel with the poor people, how to help poor people, how to help the neighbors. He was very good among the neighborhood. Everybody respected him. And he was good during the oppression of Palestinian students by Jordan, for example when my sister took part in a demonstration calling for the unity of Jordan with Egypt and got a bullet in her leg from the Jordanians. He was good when the Israelis attacked villages on the borders.

So my family was a nationalist family. But my parents were afraid for their daughters and for their sons.

Our family consists of three daughters and four sons. Most of them are graduates of universities. I didn't suffer from being a woman because my family did not elevate men over women, even in education. It is true that my brothers took the money for their education from my father whereas we, the daughters, worked hard for our certificates. But still, my family was progressive from this point of view.

I myself graduated from Birzeit University with a B.S. degree in physics. Except for that I think my childhood was just like the childhood of many other Palestinian women.

I was in a government school, which made an impression on my home life. I was not educated in private schools that express a high standard of living for the bourgeoisie. Government schools gave me a way to meet our poor people and the common people.

Boys and girls were not together in the government schools. After 1967, I was in a school where there was coeducation. Then I went back to government schools.

I shared the suffering of my people through this experience. Originally, when I was young, I could express that in some religious beliefs.

When I went to the university, my political life started. I was in the first elected committee for voluntary work at Birzeit University. Our committee started with the proposal that voluntary work should be a prerequisite for graduation from the university. It was about 1973.

We were the first people to come to the university with enthusiasm after 1967. After 1967, there was a very large calm. The Palestinian people were shocked and depressed after the defeat of 1967. We were shocked by the civilization of the Israeli State, and we were shocked to be the inferior. We were confronted with the facts that the Arab regimes were deserting us or deceiving us by saying that Israel was a small country which could easily be defeated. After 1967, we faced the question of what to do to end the occupation; the question of what to do about our dreams of getting back or liberating Palestine, when now all of Palestine was under occupation. Many people had lived from 1948 to 1967 dreaming of the day they could return to their homelands in Jaffa and Haifa and Lod.

So, in 1970, students and professors at the universities began discussing these problems on an intellectual level. Why had we as Palestinians suffered so much? What required us to have such experiences? How could we get rid of them? Where was our identity as Palestinians, as a nation? This movement started with intellectuals.

Then, to revive our society again, such discussions took place in many fields. People who were interested in folklore started talking about Palestinian folklore and asking, how was it oppressed by the Jordanians, by the English, and now by the Israelis? What about our problems as Palestinian women? What about unions of workers, laborers and so on?

I remember the first theater movement, the first student movement, the first voluntary work movement to help the poor. Such movements rose up under the leadership of intellectuals. You could see how political attitudes were formed through these committees or through these discussions. We had weekly meetings, for example, in libraries, where we used to come and sit together and talk about everything. We started it in the El Bireh library and the Ramallah library, the only places outside the university where we could meet together, and inside the university as well.

Out of this emerged a semi-organized movement. And, of course, women's issues were expressed in direct ways, and women started seeking access to each other and discussing how they could do something for other women. Women's issues were raised together with other issues. It was a kind of revival.

It was the end of the '70s, around 1978, when such discussions came to be understood as mutually supportive. The voluntary work committee, two or three different theater groups, labor unions, women's committees, came to be perceived as different aspects of a single movement.

In Birzeit we started this movement among students. Some political streams accepted it and other political streams rejected it. But in the end, it was viewed as a significant movement. We wanted to legitimate this movement by struggling for it within the student movement. We talked about this to all of the students.

We started convincing them. In the summer we went to the refugee camps and started building cement barriers between the houses, because all through the winter water would get into the houses. We picked olives with peasants. We made a playground, a very big playground in Jericho for a refugee school. And when we started in Birzeit to put this forward as a political line, rejecting the classical model of revolutionary political action, it was to an extent refused by other political streams which thought that confrontation with Israel meant army to army confrontation. We thought that such confrontation would never lead to any kind of victory for Palestinians.

So in Birzeit we started this and the university administration said, OK, you can go into elections and you can make a committee for the voluntary work. I was among nine persons who were proposed for these elections. And I was one of the five who got the most votes.

After the election, we organized more and more voluntary work until the university started to be convinced by what we were doing. We used to organize students in groups. We took them by buses to villages and refugee camps and so on. So, a year after that, the university said that every student should work 120 voluntary work hours in order to graduate.

A very interesting thing is that the beginning of this movement was led by bourgeois intellectuals and it ended up in two years to be representing only the poor. The middle-class students and intellectuals started to tire. They dropped away. They could not take more suffering. And then came the poor students, from villages and refugee camps, who eventually became the officers and went on with the work in a better way.

This experience involved me, for the first time, in the common ways of our people. Being directly inside a village or a refugee camp made you closer to them, to their reality.

And after that I was involved in the women's movement. In 1980 we held the first conference for our union of Palestinian women's committees. Since then we have been developing programs about how to answer the needs of women and how to help the woman to be self-dependent and to share in solving her own problems and the problems of her society, in order to be active, to have a political role, to have a role in the production process.

In the first years of our work as a women's movement we came to the conclusion that we should jump over the classical Palestinian women's movement that was concentrating on charitable work. We discussed that direct charity to women left their consciousness at a certain level and did not develop it. The leap was to realize that women in our society lie under many kinds of oppression: the political, the national, the economic, and the social. And you cannot deal with one without dealing with the others. This means that when women are politically independent, when women are economically independent, then they will be socially independent, as well.

Arrests

I was arrested in 1975 after I was elected to be the vice president of the student council. The army came to our house about eleven o'clock at night. I was arrested twice from my father's house. This was the first time.

They came to the house and talked with my father. They told him, "Your daughter is involved in politics and she should confess whatever she knows before we destroy the house." And they said, "You are Christians and you should not be involved in the national struggle because the majority here are Islam and you are suffering for nothing, for a people to oppress you in the future." Of course, they do not understand the feeling of nationalism.

Then I spent fifteen days in jail under interrogation. I was not put in a cell. I was treated as a young student. I was beaten. I was threatened in a way that I did not experience in my other detention periods when I was known to the international media and so on.

For my family it was very difficult to say in front of the society, "Our daughter is in jail for being involved in political life." They were ashamed that I was in jail. They called me stubborn. They tried to forbid me from going out, forbid me from talking about politics, even though I did not stop doing these things. Finally they came to a point where they saw that it was useless to talk this way.

The second time that they arrested me from my father's house it was a tearful occasion for my parents but they behaved very normally, because they knew that one day I was going to be in jail again. The second time was very short. It was for five days. They suspected me of hiding a wanted person and that I knew where he was. That was in 1978. They released me because they didn't have a charge against me and at that time I had a Jerusalem identity card, and I could not be kept in jail unless I was brought in front of a judge within 48 hours. (Later, when they arrested me from my own house, although I still held the Jerusalem identity card they considered that my activities were in the West Bank and they tried me as a West Banker.)

Marriage

I met my husband in 1973. He was out of jail after being imprisoned for five years. He was arrested in 1967 and given a life sentence, then because he was very young the sentence was reduced to seven years, and after Black September in Jordan he was one of those released after five years in jail. I met him after that as a man involved in organized political life.

Then he disappeared for a while. He was arrested another time in 1976. He got out of jail in 1978.

We had some contact while he was in jail. His family used to see me sometimes in the street and they would say, "He says 'hi' to you, and he is asking how you are." Sometimes he was asking whether I was still involved in politics or not. And when he got out of jail, we started thinking about getting engaged.

My husband was wanted for several months because he was involved in the National Front. In that period, the National Front consisted of representatives of different Palestinian political organizations that were spokespersons for the PLO here. One of them was Karim Khalef, who lost a foot in an attempt on his life and who later died. Another was Ibrahim Tawil, who they also tried to kill. Others were Bassam Shaka'a [see below, Section 9, p. 256], who had his legs cut off by a bomb, and Raja Boud, who was killed after that in Amman. My husband was working with them. He had to disappear for a while. That postponed our marriage.

Of course, my family was not pleased with this in the beginning. But in the end, they said, "It's better for us to let her marry whoever she wants because not every man in this society would agree to be married to a woman who is politically active. A classical man or a traditional man or a reactionary man would not accept her. So if this man will accept her life as it is, let her go. Have him hold her troubles. Why do we have to hold her troubles?"

They started becoming more comfortable with my fiancé at that time. They liked him very much. During the time when he had to disappear they were willing to protect him and to give him any help they could. He helped my family to accept what we were doing and to realize what the benefit of it was.

We were married in 1981. The same week, we had a confrontation. We married Sunday. On Monday, Rabbi Kahane came to the municipality of Ramallah and tried to take over the place because he considered Ramallah to be for the Israelis.

During the years since then, our political thinking changed. Our will to confront changed. The Intifada gave us a new life. Our feminist ideas started growing up.

We have started to activate women in their homes. Now in the year 1992, we have begun to think about how to change the civil laws concerning women. Now we are making studies to prove how religion was an obstacle in the progress of women and to show the origins of the existing laws about marriage, about inheritance, and so on. We have women's centers now. In the past it was very difficult to get inside the village and talk about women's problems, because they said that in doing this you were agitating women to revolt against their husbands.

After the Intifada some committees started and some committees vanished. Neighborhood committees came with the Intifada. Cooperatives came with the Intifada. But with the Intifada we no longer need a committee for family visits. The visits are part of the neighborhood work. Production turned from income-generating projects to cooperative projects, but now, because many women have lost the financial support of their husbands who are in jail or unemployed, we are turning again to income-generating projects.

I was arrested three times after the Intifada began. Besides that, our house was attacked by soldiers just to search for confidential materials nine times during the Intifada.

My husband was arrested and held in administrative detention for six months in Ansar 3 at the beginning of the Intifada. And while he was in jail, I was arrested at the same time. [See Section 6.]

I had a miscarriage during the March 8 Women's Day in 1989. I was pregnant and I had a miscarriage from tear gas. I was two and a half months pregnant. I was skeptical of people who were saying that we lose our babies because of the tear gas. At that time, my friends and everybody around me told me, "You should not take the risk and go into the demonstration." And I said, "No, I can't do that. I cannot see my friends and my people going into the demonstration, the eighth of March, the Women's Day and me staying at home," so I went.

We were not shouting. We were not even raising Palestinian flags. We were just walking in a peaceful march and then, all of a sudden, a tear gas bomb. The moment I smelled the tear gas I fell down unconsciously. I didn't know what happened to me. Some people took me to the house and from the house to the hospital. I had a check-up and the baby was still good. The next week I went for another time on the ultrasound and the doctor said that the baby was no longer alive.

[Continued below, Section 6, p. 167.]

Amal Deeb

"I can't eat in my house if I know my neighbor's child is hungry."

I have five children. Two are in jail. One got out of jail two days ago. The other two are smaller. I am raising not only my own family but the family of my son who is in jail.

My husband worked as a laborer in Israel. He lost his job due to the Gulf War. Then my sons were arrested and my husband could not go back to work in Israel. Now he works for the Rafah municipality. He makes 400 shekels a month. Seventy shekels are taken out for our electricity, and our son's phone and electricity are also deducted. My husband's take-home pay is about 200 shekels a month [approximately $140].

During the Gulf War, life stopped for four months. The U.N. brought some bread, and the popular committees brought some. I have relatives in Riyadh, Saudi Arabia, and they sent me money for a pilgrimage, but I said I would keep it for my children's education. Without the help of relatives we could not have made it. No one went outside her front door, not even to the courtyard where we are sitting now. There is no money from outside now.

When my daughter married, we looked for an apartment to rent on the outskirts of the camp. It was too expensive.

Before the Intifada, I made a visit to my uncle in Nablus. Except for that I have always been in the camp. Recently I tried to get a permit to visit him for just one day, not even for the night, but it was refused.

I haven't slept through the night since two years before the Intifada, because that is when my first son went to jail.

My son who is thirteen years old was beaten with boots on his knee and required an operation. He won U.N. scholarships to France and Germany, but the government refused permission for him to go because his brothers are in prison. He will study computer at the U.N. school.

Only one of my children finished school. The others were bright but their schooling was interrupted by detention. One was jailed for two years, got out, graduated from school, applied to Birzeit University and was admitted to study science. Then he was jailed again. He is in the Gaza Central Jail. There are no visits, no charges, and no lawyer. We have an Israeli lawyer but they will not let her in.

My seventeen-year-old son, who just got out of prison, took the [high school equivalency] test. Now it's a question of what country they will let him go to college in. Right now, they won't let him leave the Gaza Strip.

Once, when four of my children were in jail at the same time, the little one was crying, "Mom, help!" I called to my son to shout so that people would come out. A pregnant woman came out next door. Soldiers hit her in the stomach. I said that an ambulance was needed. When I tried to approach, the soldiers beat me back with rifle butts. Finally the kids burned tires and the soldiers went away.

I take part in the women's committee, visiting the families of prisoners, comforting the families of neighbors. Each neighborhood does this. We are all together. We are serving the people.

The woman now has respect because she is carrying on the family. The man's role is to go to prison. The woman's role is to keep the family going.

My daughter doesn't wear the veil. Her husband, who is in jail, does not mind and her brothers say, "If anyone bothers you, you let us know and we'll take care of it!"

The Intifada exploded here unbelievably. We act as one. We share. If I have bread, I know my neighbor does also. I can't eat in my house if my neighbor's child is hungry. We are in solidarity with each other.

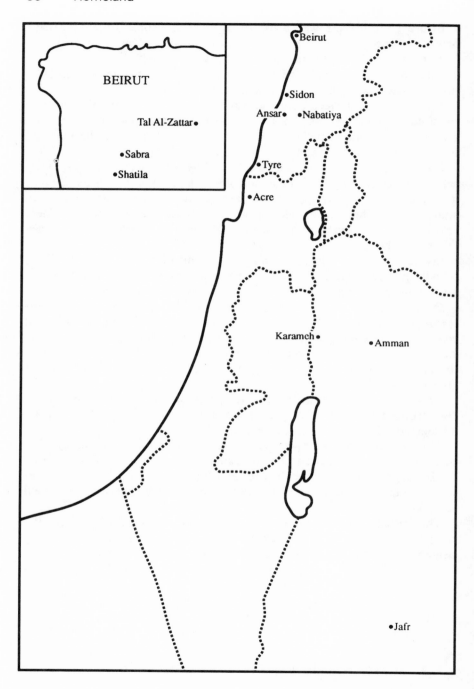

5

Jordan and Lebanon

As a result of the 1948 and 1967 wars, several hundred thousand Palestinian refugees fled to Jordan, and the PLO initially made Jordan its principal base of operations. Edward Said writes of the battle in March 1968 (mentioned by Um Sa'ad) at a Palestinian town called Karameh inside Jordan:

> [Karameh] marked the first post-1967 and post-1948 battle between regular Israeli forces . . . and Palestinian irregular forces. . . . Not only did the Karameh defenders stay and fight; they inflicted much damage and many casualties on the Israeli armed columns, who until that time had been accustomed . . . to amble in with impunity, destroy property, kill Arabs and leave pretty much unscathed.[1]

Hostilities between the government of Jordan and the PLO in 1970 caused the PLO to move its operations to Lebanon. During the Lebanon years in what was called "Fatah-land," the PLO consolidated its political and organizational structures, including popular organizations of women, students, and others. But by the mid-1970s, PLO militants like Salah Ta'amari found themselves embroiled in a civil war among different political and religious factions.

During Israel's invasion and subsequent occupation of southern Lebanon and Beirut in 1982, thousands of persons were detained without charge by the Israelis at the Ansar internment camp. On November 24, 1983, a prisoner exchange was arranged involving Israel and the PLO. Approximately 4,500 prisoners, predominantly Palestinians and Lebanese from the Ansar Camp, were exchanged for six Israelis.

*   *   *

1. Edward W. Said, *The Question of Palestine* (New York: Times Books, 1980), p. 158.

Um Sa'ad

"Most of us lived in fear."

After leaving the West Bank, I went to work in Amman, Jordan, as an inspector in the Board of Education. I used to visit schools. One school, Jabal Hussein (Jabal means mountain), was close to a Palestinian refugee camp. I would say 98 per cent of the students were Palestinians. Two of the teachers in the high school were from a Jordanian background, and the rest were Palestinians. So I lived in a Palestinian community and felt that I was among family, but at the same time I was not able to live with my family in Palestine.

In Jordan I had my daughter, Sue, and the PLO started their war.

The PLO struggle started in 1964, but it was under cover. Now, in Jordan, they started the revolution. They had camps to train what we called fedayin, or freedom-fighters. Wherever you went you could see freedom-fighters coming here and going there with their weapons. The Israelis knew that there were freedom-fighters in camps on the Jordanian bank of the River Jordan, and every now and then there was an attack on Jordan.

The Karameh battle was the first battle between the Palestinians and the Israelis outside Palestine. The Palestinians fought with small guns and machine guns, and the Israelis attacked with tanks and airplanes. Karameh was the first victory for the Arabs after 1967. Some Israeli tanks were unable to go back. They found Israeli soldiers, dead in the tanks. I saw this with my own eyes after the Karameh battle. Everybody went there and saw it.

The PLO started with maybe a thousand men. After that battle they reached twenty thousand. I remember, my brother left Kuwait and came to join the freedom-fighters. Palestinians, Jordanians, Egyptians, Algerians, came from all over the Arab world, to join the Palestinian struggle. It was all on Jordanian soil.

As in any revolution, there were factions within the PLO. Sometimes they agreed. Sometimes one faction would agree on something, and the other faction would not agree. This led in 1970 to what we called Black September, when the Jordanian army got into a fight with the Palestinian revolution.

It was so hard for the Palestinians *and* for the Jordanians. Half of the Jordanian army were Palestinians. Most of the leaders or the commanders in the Jordanian army were Palestinians. Half of the ministers in the government were Palestinians. It was as if you were putting two brothers to fight each other — one with the army and one with the revolution — and they had orders to attack each other and to kill each other. Everybody there had somebody in the revolution and somebody in the army. Until that moment, I think that was the worst that had happened that I saw.

I was living in Amman as a Palestinian, but as a Jordanian too because I had a Jordanian passport. Sue was two years old. Sa'ad was five years old. My husband was not at the house. The city was divided. My husband was on the PLO side of the city and I was on the Jordanian side, and I could see the Jordanian troops moving their tanks towards where my husband was. Things were boiling. You couldn't talk, because you didn't know to whom you were talking. Were you talking to a friend or were you talking to an enemy? We didn't know who was going to kill us, the Israelis, the Jordanians, who? Who our enemy was, we didn't know.

After Black September, I went to school one day and a teacher from a Jordanian background said to me, "Are you still here?" I told her, "Why? Where should I go?" She said, "I thought that you were going to leave here," as if she was telling me, "You have to leave Amman." I said, "OK. I'll think about it." Really, this is the way we started to think about leaving.

We stayed in Jordan until the assassination of Wasfi el Tel. Wasfi el Tel was the prime minister of Jordan. He was visiting in Egypt, and he was killed by Palestinians.

After that, I remember, there was a family who I knew very well. They took the man and put him in prison. They took the brother also, and put him in prison. Of course, the woman had to stay home. She didn't know in which prison they were. She didn't know whether her husband was alive or dead. She didn't know what to do. After several days she learned that they took her brother to a place in the desert called Jafr. But for thirty days, she didn't know exactly where her husband was. It was horrible. Time went by and he was freed.

Almost all Palestinians living in Jordan came to feel that they couldn't take it any more, to be under pressure from the government for so long. They left Jordan. We left Jordan too and we went to Lebanon.

Lebanon, 1972–1978

It was 1972. In Lebanon we started living in a hotel, then in a furnished apartment for another year, and then we moved to a house. On the tenth of April, 1973, the Israelis attacked three leaders in one night: Kamal Udwan, Yussef al-Najjar, and Kamal Nasir.[2] That night we had a telephone call from Kamal Udwan's wife. She was my best friend when we were in Amman and they came to Lebanon before us. They attacked her husband while he was sitting in his dining room doing some paperwork. They killed Yussef al-Najjar while he was sleeping with his wife in their bed. Kamal Nasir lived in the same building with Kamal Udwan, and they attacked him while he was writing. Four of them were killed — the three leaders and the wife of one of them — in their homes, in front of their children and their families.

Those three leaders had guards at the doors of their building. One of the Mossad [Israeli secret police], a woman, came and lived in that building for almost a whole year. She reported the times that they were at home. Verdan, the area where they lived, was very close to the command center for the Lebanese army. It was the best street in Beirut, and the busiest area in

2. See Helena Cobban, *The Palestine Liberation Organisation: People, Power, and Politics* (Cambridge: Cambridge University Press, 1984), p. 55: "In April 1973, the Israelis were able to bring off a significant coup when their commandos landed by night on a Beirut beach and drove to the apartments of Fateh/PLO leaders Kamal Udwan and Muhammed Youssef al-Najjar (Abu Youssef, then serving as the PLO's 'Foreign Minister'), killing them along with the Palestinian poet Kamal Nasir, who was then the PLO spokesman."

Beirut. The assassins came to that area by sea. They went more than half a mile inside the city of Beirut. They killed the guards and then went to the apartments. They knew exactly where each one of them was. They killed them and they escaped. Nobody knew until after they left.

I knew two of the men very well, and I knew their wives.

After that we lived in fear. Every moment I felt that we were threatened. After Yussef al-Najjar and his wife were killed in their bed, as a husband and a wife, I felt that somebody was going to come and kill us the same way. We were so scared, not even to, what shall I say, to live as a husband and a wife. Until I came to the United States, I lived my life scared that they would come and kill me with my husband.

You didn't know when they were going to attack you or pick you up. For instance, when they killed Abu Jihad, they killed him in his house in Tunis in front of his wife and his children. I had been to his home. It too was in a very busy area of Tunis, and there were guards and servants at the house. They just killed the person who they wanted to kill and left as if nothing had happened. This gave us the feeling that every Palestinian is threatened in one way or another, wherever we might go.

I remember when we moved into our house in Ramleh el Bayda. There was the dining room, the living room, a big hall, and then there was a corridor for the bedrooms. The first thing we did, my husband and I, was to see which would be our bedroom. We didn't want to put our children in rooms between us and the entrance of the home. If somebody was coming to get us, let him get us first, not our children.

One day we were told that our names were on the Israelis' list. It was said that at so-and-so hour and so-and-so date they will come and attack you. This was one night out of hundreds that we stayed all night long waiting for somebody to come and knock at the door. We used to have our bag ready so we could put ourselves in the car and just run to the mountains somewhere. But later on, we felt that it was something that we couldn't do all the time. You can't expect to stay all night long waiting so that nobody will come and take your life while you are understrength. We had to settle down a little bit; we had to wait and see.

After Verdan, the Lebanese government asked all the PLO leaders to protect themselves, because it was not the Lebanese government's responsibility to guard them or to stop the killing. So each one of the leaders in the PLO had to assign somebody to guard his house or the building where he lived so as not to be assassinated.

For instance, when we lived in Bourj abu Heydar [a section of Beirut], my husband, like everybody else, had guards at the door of the building. One of the women who lived on the tenth floor of that building was Lebanese. She had children. They were my children's age. It happened that they had lived in an area where there was shooting most of the time. On the first day we lived in that house, when their children were coming out of the car they saw the guards at the door with guns. They went to their father, scared. The woman came to me demanding that this end because her children were scared. I was friendly with her. I told her, "We are like you. It's not guarding only us. It's guarding the whole building and it's safer for everybody in the building. We don't want anybody to be subjected to an attack." After that we got to be very close friends. But at the time, I felt that she was kicking me out of the building where I was living.

The civil war started in 1975. It started between Palestinians and Lebanese. The Syrians came into the scene, the Lebanese army and, of course, the Israelis. There were factions: Christian against Muslim, Palestinians against Palestinians. Lebanon started to self-destruct.

That same year I had my last son. The doctor told me, "You have fifteen days." That meant that any time I might have labor and have to go to the hospital. If there was shooting, I might not be able to go there. So the minute I felt that I had a little bit of pain — it may be I ate something that gave me gas — I felt that this was the time. So I went to the hospital. They told me, "No, you are still early." So I went back home. After two or three days, I thought, "This time it is true." So I went. My husband was standing with me. He told me, "Listen, if he tells you 'Go home,' tell him, 'I'm not going home till I have my baby.' Even if it goes fifteen days, you have to stay at the hospital." So they examined me. They said, "I don't know, it's still . . ." I told them, "OK. I'm sitting here till I have my baby." I was there one day before my son was born.

After that, the Israelis attacked. They came to the seashore and they started bombarding the camp in Sour [Tyre]. Nobody in that camp could get out without injury. Those who could flee, where could they go? They had to settle somewhere and they needed help and cover. I was a member of the General Union of Palestinian Women. We started collecting blankets, food, things like that, and sending them to those who were safe, wherever they were.

The camps in Lebanon were not only for Palestinians. They were mixed, Lebanese with Palestinians. Some of the Lebanese who were attacked by the Israelis in southern Lebanon left and started living in the camps with the Palestinians. Or if they had relatives they would go to the mountains or somewhere in Beirut. But they started leaving their houses and land and going somewhere else because the Israelis occupied part of southern Lebanon.

I would like to tell about an incident. I think it was in 1974. There was a bus that came from Tal Al-Zattar, a camp. It was in an area where most of the people were Palestinian. Suddenly the bus stopped at a bus stop. Several men came into the bus. One man was carrying a tomato and he started asking each one of the people in the bus, "What is this?" Palestinians say, "Bandura."[3] Anybody who was Lebanese would say "Banadura." The man would tell him, "Get out of the bus." Of course, nobody knew why they were saying that. After they took all the Lebanese off the bus, they started shooting everybody in the bus with machine guns. Forty people in that bus were killed and all of them were Palestinians.

3. According to Um Sa'ad's daughter: It's like saying "tomayto" and "tomahto". Lebanese have one accent, Palestinians have another accent, and that's how they distinguished if you were Palestinian or Lebanese.

During the civil war, the Syrians started attacking Palestinian camps, helping the Phalangists against the Palestinians. The Phalangists are a Christian militia group in Lebanon [with whom Israel was in alliance]. They shelled Tal Al-Zattar and then they took it.

After the bus incident took place, and the civil war started, all the Palestinians who lived in the Christian areas, or who were in the areas that were close to where the Lebanese were threatening the Palestinians, had to move.

Every time you moved you thought, "Why? Why am I moving? If I were on my land, in my home, Palestine, would I be suffering this way? Am I going to be threatened every day this way?" It was not only myself; it was hundreds of thousands who were living either the way I was living or worse than that. I would look at myself. I had a house. I had children. I had work and things that I could afford. Some of the families didn't have anything.

We decided to leave Lebanon in 1978. We felt that from 1974 until 1978 we were under bombardment. I remember the last incident. In Lebanon they use open balconies a lot because the weather is so nice in the evening; you can sit on the balcony and feel the fresh air from the sea. It was eleven in the morning and one of my neighbors came and brought her kids with her. So Sa'ad and Sue (my older children), and another two kids (my neighbor's kids), were playing and they went on the balcony. Sam (my youngest) was still very young; he was asleep at that time. We were on the third floor. The children were playing and we were sitting just taking coffee and cake. Sue came and said, "I want to go to the bathroom," and she ran to the bathroom. Sa'ad and the kids went in to get toys. At that exact moment, a bomb exploded on the street under our balcony. Six people were killed on the spot and many injured. My daughter ran from the bathroom with her underwear down — "What is happening?" We were so scared! On the first floor, they had a balcony with glass windows. All the windows were down. Shrapnel from the bomb went into the buildings and those shreds were on the balcony where my children had been playing. At that moment I prayed. "My God," I prayed, "How can He help me so much that they were not on the open balcony at that moment!"

Three of my brothers were in the United States and they called me and said, "Just bring the children for a visit, at least for the summer." So we applied for a visa from the American Embassy and I brought the three children to the United States.

Um Ossama

"My home is in Palestine."

Israeli Invasion

In 1982, Israel decided to invade Lebanon. And not only did we have the air raids to worry about, but from the sea they hit, from the gunships they hit, from the rockets they hit, from the tanks they hit.

I have a daughter who had polio and cannot walk. So I stayed in the camp until the Israelis surrounded it. I thought, "If I leave, I'm committing homicide to my daughter." I would have had to leave her in the house — which I could not do. But when the Israelis surrounded the camp I had to leave. There were no cars. We were in a war.

I found a safe house for my daughter in a Lebanese home. Once I made sure she was safe in a Lebanese home, we went to the town of Abra.

A few days later, I went back to the house where I had left my daughter to get her and take her with me, and I found she wasn't there. The Israelis saw me and stopped us. I asked them, "What happened to my daughter?" The Israelis told me, "Are you looking for someone that doesn't know how to walk?" I said, "Yes." The soldier told me that the Lebanese guy took my daughter to Sidon.

My daughter was lost for ten days. We did not know where she was. After ten days, I found that a Palestinian had taken her to his house and kept her there, waiting. We were looking for her and he was looking for us. He found us before we found them.

A time came when they called on a loudspeaker to the people outside the refugee camp and told them, if they want to go back to their homes in the refugee camps, they could do it.

Israeli Occupation

We responded and we went back. God will believe me, it was a disaster. We went to homes with no doors, no windows. They had bulldozed our home with all its contents. We had nothing to wear except what was on our backs. We found an uncle whose house was not demolished and we slept at my uncle's home. The water distribution system itself was bulldozed with our homes.

No one knew where the other one was. I tried my best to get my family back together. I was not able.

The males of the camp were all arrested at that time. You have probably heard that they were arresting and detaining commandos, fighters. It's a lie. They arrested any male from anywhere in the street. You didn't have to have anything to do with what was going on. If you were a male within the ages they were looking for, you would be arrested. They would take any male individual outside his home, put his hands above his head, arrest him, blindfold him, hit him or shoot him. There was no authority to say "No."

They took Abu Ossama, my husband. I had small kids and all of my older children were gone. They took my husband to the Ansar detention camp in southern Lebanon and blinded one of his eyes from the beating. When he was no longer able to see, they brought him home. My husband explained to me how he felt after the blow on the side of his head that caused him to lose his vision. He felt as if fire came out of his eyes.

They charged all of them, including my husband, with being part of the resistance movement. He was not part of the resistance movement. He had a paint shop. He was working. That doesn't mean he wasn't helping. This is our people. This is our struggle. We're taking part in our struggle.

The soldiers continuously told people, "We're going to search your house." I went to a soldier and told him, "What are you doing to us? We sleep on the ground. We have no food, no resources. You took all of our males. What do you think we are hiding in our house? God help you if you continue. What are you trying to do to us?"

The soldier responded to me, "Are you serious? You don't have any water to drink?" The soldier went and got a tank of water. They called on the loudspeaker that there was water at a certain building. We used to go every day: that was our water supply. We would go get one gallon of water to use for the day.

I would send my youngest son, Ibrahim, to get bread, hoping that they would give bread to a younger person, and that the Lebanese would not refuse to give him bread "because you are Palestinian."

After I and others made a big fuss that there was no bread for Palestinians, we told the Israeli soldiers, "The Lebanese tell us to go. They don't want us here any more. We are in the camp under your bombardment. We have no bread. We are stuck. What are we going to do?" After this conversation, they made two lines to the bakery: one was the Lebanese line, and one was the Palestinian line. And for every one loaf or one package of bread that would go to Lebanese, they would give one to Palestinians.

This time it was the Israelis who set up tents for us. But this time they found that the kids would burn the tents down because we weren't about to go back in our history. We would stay outside of the camp. At one point, the Israelis came to donate food to us. We refused. After what they did to us, are we going to eat out of their hands?

We didn't want handouts. The community pooled its resources within itself along with anyone who had resources outside, in the Gulf, in the United States, wherever. We recommended to ourselves that rather than live under the conditions that we were experiencing, we might as well die holding some of our values and traditions.

The Israeli soldiers started asking individuals for their ID cards. When they came to me, asking for my ID card, I told the soldier, "You bulldozed it with my home." The soldier told me, "Go to the military administration. They are issuing papers to anyone who lost an ID card."

I went to the officer in the military administration and asked for permission to go to Beirut. I told him, "I want a travel document to go to Beirut, and I don't have my ID card because it was bulldozed."

So he started asking me questions. "Are you going to get paid?" In other words, was I going to the PLO to get some money? I got very uptight and I said, "You have destroyed my home. You have arrested my children. Now I'm coming here and I'm asking for permission to go to Beirut. You don't have the right to ask me one other question. Give me an answer. I want one thing. I want permission to go to Beirut." The guy said, "OK, I'll give you permission. Where do you want to go exactly?" because people were going to the villages around Beirut. I said, "I want to go directly inside Beirut." He said, "No one is going directly inside Beirut. What are you going for?" I said, "I'm going to the UNRWA Medical Center because I'm sick. I want to see a doctor." He asked me, "Is Yasir Arafat paying for it?"

I became very frustrated with him. I got permission but when I left the room his face turned yellow because he did not want to talk to me any more. I was a thorn in his side.

When my son, Mazin, was arrested for the second time and I was looking for my son, I went back to that same officer. I asked him, "Why did you take my son from the street? What did he do to make him get arrested?" The soldier started asking me questions about myself, where I was from. I said, "I'm Palestinian." He started joking with me and saying, "Where in Palestine are you from?" I said, "I'm from one of the villages around Acre." He laughed and said, "Oh, the fish in Acre are this big!" I told him, "I hope you get full on the fish that you have in Palestine. You are laughing at me. But not one of you should open your mouth and laugh at me or my family. I am a mother asking for my son. Would you like to see my son doing the same thing to your mother?"

There were several of us women who went together to look for our sons and family members. Once when the soldiers stopped us at a checkpoint, the soldiers started asking us where we were from. We were from different camps. One said, "I'm from Nabatiya." Another said, "I'm from Miya Miya." When they came to me, they asked, "Where are you from?" I said, "I'm from Palestine." "What do you mean, you're from Palestine?" My blood was boiling! I said, "I am a resident of Ein El Hilweh, but my home is in Palestine!"

Our Right to Return

There were no shelters after the invasion in 1982. The Israelis destroyed the shelters. Even when we had those shelters, they could not take a direct hit. If you can just imagine, a family of twenty-five could be sitting in a room under a zinc or aluminum roof. If the bomb hit your house, you and your family would be gone. Every raid, there were twenty or twenty-five wounded or killed.

One of my brothers died in an air raid on Ein El Hilweh in 1984. He was walking on the street when it happened. The bomb hit by chance. It didn't pick and choose. My brother was one of many.

When the Intifada started up inside Palestine, the Israelis responded by hitting Lebanon. Until today, they come and bomb the camps. The Lebanese army is on one side of the camp and the Israelis are making their little missions above us every week. It is very tense.

After the Israeli invasion, the PLO built wells and they gave water to different parts of the camp for two hours a day. A year ago, the Lebanese government came and cut off the water supply and food from outside. They wanted to rid the camp of arms and ammunition. Now the Lebanese are controlling the wells inside the camp and they give us water for an hour a day.

Our family is scattered. I have a son in Abu Dhabi. I have brothers in Libya. I have sons in America. I have to travel to see my kids. When I am in Lebanon, I can't stop thinking about what's happening to my kids in America. The day

I get to America and see my kids, I start thinking, how are they doing back in Lebanon? I don't find anybody with anyone else any more.

Living in Palestine, we were living in our home with our family, with our house. I was living and working with what was mine, what we inherited or what we as a family worked to get. It is different to live as a nomad, with no resources and no wealth.

When I see another Palestinian, wherever they are, there is a mutual understanding, a mutual respect. It is one people, one tradition, one culture. Everyone likes the place where they were born and brought up. That's just human nature.

Where we are is a matter of history, not a matter of choice. An Israeli soldier asked me, "What are you?" I said, "Palestinian." He said, "Say you're Israeli and maybe life will be better." I said, "I will never tell you I am an Israeli. I am Palestinian and I'm proud to be Palestinian." They get mad at us, but we will tell them: "We are Palestinian. Our land is Palestine. If you don't like it, too bad."

This is our right in life — to return to Palestine. If we don't make it back, the next generation or my kids' kids' kids will make it. Don't worry.

Salah Ta'amari

"It was only when I thought of others that I stood up."

Fighting Outside Palestine

I arrived in Syria in June 1967. Fatah had a military base in the suburbs of Damascus. It happened that in Jordan there was a division of the Iraqi army, the commander of which was sympathetic to us. He offered us uniforms. We put on Iraqi uniforms and crossed from Syria into Jordan. When we reached the Jordan Valley we spent a few nights there for reconnaisance before we crossed the Jordan River into the West Bank, and then went on to Gaza. It was a long, long, long way.

Members of our group came from Egypt, from Kuwait, from you-name-it. A member of the first group that accompanied me was half-Jewish. We were joined by some Palestinian and Arab officers who belonged to other Arab armies. They deserted and joined us.

Those who could afford it and had the documents went directly to the Occupied Territories. I didn't have the documents at that time.

Later I was put in charge of a refugee camp in the Jordan Valley called Karameh. The Israelis attacked Karameh in 1968. That was the first time ever that the Israelis left tanks behind. Leaving the bodies of soldiers — that was something unheard of — and they left a total of seven.

After that we moved to the Sault hills and I, myself, moved to the south of Jordan where I stayed for two years. Then I moved to Amman, a couple of days before the civil war started in Jordan, to reinforce our troops in Amman.

I remained in Amman after the Arab League decided that we had to leave Amman. The field leaders had a meeting. I think I was the only one among the twelve who said, "No, I'm not leaving." And I didn't. I stayed in a refugee camp in central Amman and we reconstructed the camp again.

Then a joint resolution was reached by the PLO central committee and the farmers of Jordan that I should be gotten out of Amman, by force if necessary. They sent a senior colleague to me and he escorted me in his car to Syria. It was six or seven months after the end of the civil war in Jordan.

I was offered the options of going to Europe or to the United States. I said, "No, I'll go to the south of Lebanon."

We were really in bad shape, licking our wounds, regrouping. It was very tough, very hard. We were alone. But it took us only a few months to build up again, to maintain the faith, maintain the morale.

The Israelis attacked after a few months. It was a major attack. Then the Lebanese attacked. They besieged us in Beirut. [Civil war in Lebanon began in 1975.]

Civil War in Lebanon

If war is ugly, which it is, then civil war is the ugliest war. Civil war is similar to suicide at the individual level. It's one's bitterness internalized. We fought because we had to, not because it was our choice. So you forced yourself.

There came a time when you could not be understood by either your friends or your enemies. You could no longer categorize people by who was on your side and who was on your enemy's side. Brutality was committed by both sides. The question was, who is brutal on this side and who is not brutal on this side? One could not get away because that would be deserting, abandoning so many people on both sides who might need your help.

You manage: to see people killed in cold blood and not be able to stop it; sometimes to be forced to pull the trigger yourself at some of your people, supposedly your men, to stop them from burning a church or stealing; to confront your colleagues and ask them not to execute a prisoner of war but to send him back to his family; to face a situation where you see seventy people gathered in a church but it's already laden and charged with explosives, to be blown up, and you can't do anything about it. And yet you have to do something about it and you do.

You cannot always draw a line between good and bad from the point of view that the person who is with me is good and the person who is against me is bad. Sometimes you draw a line between the oppressed and the oppressor — many who are your colleagues, your friends, or supposedly in your front. You drag yourself on. You cannot quit. The rate of change is so minimal. It's like marching through a barbed wire that snatches bits and pieces of your flesh at every inch you cover. There's hardly anything left in you other than the spark that may, or may not, rekindle your anger.

Many made it. Others were defeated. They became bitter, lost faith in humanity, lost faith in the inevitability of history.

Amongst our people, we talk more about our love for our land than we talk about our hatred of our enemy. That is significant. That means our motive is love, even if we are not aware of it. In our stories and songs we hardly mention our enemies, and when we mention our enemies it's always after we mention our country with love. So the motive is love. It stems from your love for your family, your love for your village, your love for your country, then your love for the people. I think if we become bitter we distort our love for our country, we distort our love to humanity, because you cannot love your country heartily without loving humanity. Bitterness and love cannot coexist. Bitterness destroys. Bitterness is utter defeat.

What I learned from the civil war is that the ugliest acts are not necessarily triggered by viciousness. The worst acts are triggered by fear, not viciousness. That's why minorities can be so brutal, for they are so much afraid. Never go and check a military post that is manned by a new recruit. He would be afraid of any sound and he would fire until he emptied his magazine although it could be the sound of the wind against the leaves of a tree. It's fear. It's not even hatred.

Apply the same thing to the acts of the Israelis. Sometimes it's fear, whether this fear is justified or not. That was a lesson I learned from the civil war.

I think anger is the noblest feeling. I'm not talking about hate; I'm talking about anger. Anger is like steam. The more it is confined, channeled, the more able it is to move a vehicle. Do you think Christ was not an angry person? How can you make the world a more decent place to live in if you don't get angry at injustice? I'm not talking about breaking down walls. No. I'm talking about the driving force, the inner force, that keeps you strong and maintains a forcefulness to change. If you don't get angry, how can you change?

The Invasion of Lebanon

When the Israelis invaded Lebanon in 1982, I was in Beirut. I was writing the last issue of the youth magazine when a colleague of mine phoned me and told me, "You are late." "Late for what?" I had been invited by a family in the Shatila camp to come for a visit. "Well, you promised the kids to come for lunch and it's almost three o'clock." I packed my papers rapidly and went down the dirt road to Shatila.

His wife had cooked. I was sitting in the living room, playing with his kids as usual, when the whole world shook as if it were an earthquake. It was an air raid. We didn't even touch the food. We just got the kids to the shelter.

After the raid when I went back to my office, not a window was standing. The center of the attack was the stadium, not more than two hundred yards away. The next day I went down to Sidon.

Beirut took the limelight, but in fact Sidon was under severe attack. I remember seeing a nine-story building split in two, down to the shelter. No one survived in the shelter. The climax was when the Israelis hit the government hospital. They attacked from the air and from the sea.

I had a group of young fighters at the entrance to Sidon. The tanks landed north of Sidon, but instead of coming in where we were entrenched, they went north and east. My estimate was that they were encircling Sidon so I moved and people just followed me. I told them, "They may come down this way so we better leave the post." There was no leadership left.

Our house in Sidon happened to be on the crossroads, between that section of Sidon which is Shi'ite and the Maronite section, and the Sunni and then the refugee camp of Ein El Hilweh which is Palestinian. Our neighbors on the right were two Shi'ite families, on the left a Sunni family, and right in front of the house was a Maronite who was in the Lebanese army. That illustrated the whole situation. During the 1982 war, they all ended up in our house for refuge. Our house was at the front line.

I could have made it out of Sidon. Many came to take me out of Sidon, including a Maronite priest. I said, "No." The least I could do was to share with people what they went through. I wouldn't have forgiven myself if I had not done that, whether other people did or not. Maybe it's because I'm the eldest amongst the survivors in my family. There's a need to take care of people. I think it's deeper. Maybe, instinctively, I wanted to engage with the enemy at a different level.

I was betrayed in Sidon. I thought I would spend the night at a place where they welcomed me, but after ten minutes they changed their minds. They told me, "You go out to the Israelis or we bring them in." So I had to negotiate with that person for the safety of my sister who was with me and I would turn myself in. That's what happened.

Sometimes at certain junctures in our lives the decision that we make could not have been made five minutes later or five minutes earlier. It was like the ball in the roulette.

Sometimes it is easier to die than to survive. Sometimes it is immoral to die and it is courageous to survive. Sometimes life teases one or mocks at one. You throw yourself into the heart of danger and you survive when you never meant to survive.

Solitary Confinement

I was put in solitary confinement for three and a half months. Solitary was hell. Others went through worse conditions than mine. Some didn't survive it. Because I was alone I had to be strong.

I experienced what it means to be deprived of sleep for a month.

Anything they used was based on their knowledge of human nature. First, they didn't allow you to know the time. You were time-disoriented. You didn't know the place. You were place-disoriented. You ended up with self-disorientation.

When you reach the bottom, you have only two options: to rest at the bottom and give up, or to touch down and spring up to reality again. It all depended on what we were, what was at the core of us. When I reached the bottom, when I thought of myself I gave in. It was only when I thought of others that I stood up.

I couldn't tell the time because it was always bright. The lights were on twenty-four hours a day. I couldn't sneak a look at the guards' watches. I couldn't tell the time by the meals because they were the same kind of food and several times they missed a meal.

It was my culture that rescued me. I remembered that in our culture, time is the morning star, sunrise, noon, afternoon, and evening. It's not divided into seconds and minutes and hours. But how was I to know when it was dawn or noon or night? It would not kill me not to know whether it was nine or ten or seven, but I needed to know whether it was day or night.

It was the twittering of the birds coupled with the roar of cars on a far-away highway that told me. Their escalation meant that it was morning. The twittering of birds with the roaring of cars dying out, that meant it was evening.

The place could have been anywhere — Lebanon, Nazareth, Bethlehem. I didn't know. I thought to myself, "Let me know what the place itself looks like." After two weeks they took me outside for five minutes to have fresh air. I was blindfolded, but I rubbed my back against the wall. I thought, "When they take me back to the cell I can at least see what color is on my shirt." The color was white. That was a huge piece of information.

I convinced myself that if I concentrated on the wall of the cell I could see the concrete melting down and I could see the guard room, the showers: "Those are trees, these are paths, that is the grass." It was a figment of my imagination. I loved it.

What made me look for time and place was the moment when I found myself asking the question, "Who am I?" I didn't know who I was. I found this finger which I had hurt in a demonstration in 1955, which I always hid because I was embarrassed to show it. That was my anchor. I hung on to it. That was me. Then I built the place and the time.

I could not stretch my limbs in the cell. It was too short or too narrow. The handcuffs and chains confined my movements. So I had to lean against the corner of the two walls.

One night or one day — I don't know whether it was night or day — I spilled the water that was in the plastic water jar. I was thirsty. I learned very fast not to ask for anything because they never tell you "Yes" or "No." They'd say, "We'll see." And they would keep you waiting until you became a nervous wreck.

When the two guards came and saw that I didn't have water, they asked me, "Do you want water?" I said, "Yes." They took the plastic jar and came back with a stainless steel jug. I could see the drops of water on its outer side. It was boiling hot. The moment they offered it, I grabbed it and threw it away. I never wished to kill anybody in my life as I wished to kill that person!

Every night I heard dogs barking and human beings screaming in pain — night after night after night. I said to myself, this must be sound effects. It was demoralizing.

Then one day they asked me to come and they took me to an interrogation room. I sat on a bench. All of a sudden a huge German shepherd dog stepped in. It was very frightening. It was not a sound effect. It stood right in front of me with a guard standing next to it. I didn't move. I just gazed at the dog, transmitting to him all my love. I love dogs. I had a German shepherd that was maybe one-fifth the size of that dog. I knew that dogs have a melancholic look in their eyes, and this dog was no exception. I swear to God I was talking to that dog through my eyes. I don't know how long it lasted — two minutes, three minutes, five minutes. Finally the dog went out, followed by the warden. I remember that I stayed in that position without moving for maybe five minutes after the dog left.

Nice things also happened. I knew that somebody was listening behind the door of my cell. I could sense it. I did not know who it was. It came to me that if I spilled some water under the door, I could see the reflection. The reflection would not give me a complete picture, but at least I would know what kind of shoes the person was wearing. In the morning, when I saw their shoes, I could tell who was behind my door.

When I insisted on singing, they insisted that I shouldn't. They brought plaster and applied it to my mouth. I loved singing because it generated inner power, and I wanted to communicate with others. I used to sing and change the words so as to get information from other prisoners.

The man in charge wanted to play chess with me. When I wanted fresh air, when I wanted to see the sky, he wanted to play chess. I couldn't afford to lose. I checkmated him. I was so tired, all I wanted to do was to go back to my cell.

We developed dependency as prisoners. We looked forward to the sound of the key in the lock. One of the vicious things that they did quite often was at the time when the meal was supposed to come, they would put the key in the lock and turn it, but they wouldn't open the door. They would say, "We lost the key. It's not the right key." One had to control one's fear, one's agony, and say, "Never mind. I don't want to eat."

Survival was not the issue. The question was how to move to the counter-attack?

I had to be in control. To be in control in such a situation had to be at my own expense. If I was allowed ten minutes of fresh air, I asked them to take me back to my cell after six or seven minutes. I never ate all the food that they brought me although I was hungry.

But the solitary served the purpose. Unless you go through the solitary, you do not comprehend fully what it means not to have another human being with whom you can communicate. Being in solitary sharpened my sense of justice, of beauty, in exactly the same way that the earth sharpens the plough. The huge, tremendous fight in the solitary made me become able to act and respond quickly at Ansar.

[Continued below, this Section, p. 122.]

Mazin

"Here there is no God."

I went to school when I was six years old. I did well in school. My mother told me, "You're not going to work at manual labor. That's why you have to do well — to get you out of this situation."

We had a teacher in the Camp who presented a special program in the summer. Before we went to the second class, in the summer he taught us what was in the second class. My family would pay him $1 for the whole summer. In that summer program, I remember, we didn't have desks. We used to sit on the floor. We used to get boards and put them in our laps and take notes.

I remember the smells of the sanitation outside. It wasn't covered. The Lebanese women would say: "We take good care of our kids. They don't go and play in the garbage, and they get sick all the time. Look at these Palestinian kids! They play in the garbage all day with no clothes on, and they never get sick." We used to say that we got immune to the viruses because we played with the viruses all the time.

I used to see all these poor people in the streets, and I thought that I should become a doctor, in the future, to help all of these people. That was my dream when I was about seven years old, to become a doctor and come back to the Camp and treat all of these people. I remember the hardship in which people lived.

I used to work with my father. Because he was Palestinian, he was not allowed to have his own business. It was under a Lebanese man. My father bought all the fixtures for the body shop. He'd do his own business and then give the Lebanese man fifteen per cent of the profit, just because that man would let him do business under his name.

When I graduated from intermediate school, I went to secondary school. We didn't have enough money, so one time I went down to the city and I sold my blood. I sold it to our neighbor. I would have given it to him for free but he was snobbish about the fact that he had some money. So I told our neighbor that I would give him sixteen ounces of blood if he would give me 500 Lebanese pounds, because I needed it to buy books and I wanted to pay the rest of my tuition. In our culture it is shameful to give blood for money, so I gave them another name instead of my name at the hospital. That was in the 1970s.

I graduated from high school. We didn't have enough money for me to go to college. I was thinking of going to Romania or somewhere for medical school. But I had two brothers who were going to school in the United States and two sisters in school in Lebanon, and the whole family was collecting money to support them. At the time I graduated my father told me that I had to wait. He said that when my brothers graduated, they would get jobs and help me. So I went to a Lebanese university, studying psychology, and at the same time I was going to a United Nations college taking business courses. This was in 1981.

In 1982, the Israelis invaded Lebanon and everything changed. They destroyed the whole Camp. I didn't know what had happened to my family. For fifteen days I lost them and they lost me. I stayed in the camp, looking for them, while they were outside.

The Palestinian people who lived in the Camp were afraid to stay there. Many took shelter in the Lebanese government hospital. The Israelis bombed that hospital. Hundreds of people were killed.

A lot of dead bodies were laid in the back yard of the hospital. A friend of mine said, "Let's go and check and see if our families are among these people." We couldn't get in during the day because a sniper would have shot us. The Israelis were on the hills to the south and east of the Camp. They could have seen us had we gone to the Lebanese government hospital during the day.

We waited until eleven o'clock or midnight. I had a flashlight. I went there. I walked between all the bodies. I think there were more than 400. There were a lot of wounded people on the ground. Nobody could help them because the Israelis had bombed all the hospitals.

I found one of my friends who was dying. I said, "What do you want?" He said, "Just give me some water." We had been taught that if you give a wounded person water, he will die. But I knew he was going to die and I thought, "If he dies, having had some water, it's better." I gave him some water and he died.

I found another friend. He was a mental case. He used to live near our house. I could see blood all over his body. I gave him water.

There was another man. He was from the Camp, but I didn't know him. He had lost his hand but he was in good shape; he could walk. We helped him. We took him back to the Camp. But in the Camp we had nothing. We were surrounded by the Israelis. We were mostly young men. We were afraid that if we surrendered the Israelis would kill us. We put the wounded man in a shelter and gave him antibiotics. But after about three days, he died.

After the war ended, his mother came to me. There were rumors in the Camp that he was still alive, that the Israelis had taken him to Israel, and so on. Some people were telling his mother these stories to make it easier for her. But I told her the truth.

When the Israelis occupied the Camp they destroyed all the shelters. There were a lot of bodies in the shelters. They stayed under the ground. Nobody found them.

First Arrest

After about fifteen days I used my underwear to make a white flag so that we could leave the Camp. Between the Camp and the city there was just a street. After we crossed the street we knew that we were not safe but we would not be killed.

The Israelis said through megaphones that civilians would be safe if they went to certain areas. They used an area east of the city. We went there. Because we were afraid that the Israelis would arrest us, we stayed in a building and did not go out. We slept on the floor. We had nothing to eat for four days.

Then the Israelis used their megaphones and said that all men between 16 and 60 should leave that area and go down to the coast. We went down there at eight o'clock in the morning. We stayed there in the sun the whole day with no food and no water. It was so hot.

The Israelis had some collaborators. These were people who, under beating and so on (they call it "physical duress" in the United States) said that they knew some people who worked for the PLO. They wore masks. They were in jeeps. The jeeps had lights. You had to pass in front of four jeeps. If one of the collaborators sounded the horn of a jeep, they would put you in prison right away, without interrogation.

I was lucky. I passed the first jeep. There was no horn. I passed the second one. I passed the third one. I passed the fourth one. Nobody said anything about me. They stamped my ID that I had passed by the collaborators.

My aunt lives in the city. She has a lot of money. She has five sons and they are all engineers, in Saudi Arabia and Kuwait. She took me into her house. I stayed in her house two or three weeks.

I still had no idea what had happened to my family. On the coast I met one of my sisters and I said to her, "Don't worry. You are not my sister now, OK? You don't know me. Don't talk to me."

After three weeks I found that the Israelis had arrested my father. My mother was living in the city at the edge of the Camp without any money. I told my mother not to worry. I worked collecting garbage and I sent money to my mother. I worked for two weeks. The next week the Israelis came and knocked on the door and they arrested me.

They took me to an interrogation center for seven days. The center was a factory south of the city. It was very cold at night and very hot during the day. We had hardly any food. I was really sick. They put five, six hundred people in a yard behind the factory. If you wanted to go to the bathroom, you had to shit in front of everybody.

A man was going to the bathroom and I was smiling. (I always smile.) A soldier said, "Why are you smiling? What's funny?" I said, "Nothing." He started beating me because I was smiling, without even asking me any questions. He hit me in the abdomen so that I couldn't pee. My abdomen would swell up instead.

I remember the Israeli doctor whose name was Abraham. He was both nice and not so nice. This doctor, Abraham, gave me shots so that I could pee. But I also saw this doctor beating a guy really badly. It was savage. They were kicking him, up and down, and accusing him of being in the PLO. He was so young, about nineteen years old. Dr. Abraham said to me, "You did not see anything. If you say anything outside about what you saw in here, I'm going to do the same thing to you." Yet he was so nice to me. At night he gave me a blanket.

There were some soldiers who stole property from the prisoners. One of us found the courage to complain to an Israeli officer. The officer reprimanded a soldier and made him return a gold chain.

For the first three days, they gave us one tomato and one piece of bread a day. For seven days they didn't ask me any questions. After seven days, they asked me, "Are you a member of the PLO?" I said, "No. I am just a student."

Again I had to pass in front of collaborators. In the factory they were sitting behind boxes with small windows. They had masks on their faces. I passed by four of them. Nobody said anything. You were at their mercy. If one of these collaborators says, "He is," that's it: you will be in prison; you will be beaten. It was at this factory that, according to many of my friends, an

Israeli peace activist in the army put on civilian clothes, and passed in front of the collaborators, and one of them said he was a member of the PLO.

They let me go, and I went back to my aunt's. My relatives put me in the hospital because you could see bruises all over. Then I went back to work and, later, to school.

"Here There Is No God"

I didn't return to the Lebanese university. I went back to the college because it was under United Nations protection and, unless they took down the United Nations flag, the Israelis could not come in. The Israelis used to come, but they could not bother anybody, because if they did there would be a protest in the United Nations. One time they took one of the teachers for three days. The United Nations made a big deal of it and the Israelis let him come back.

I stayed there for a while. My brother was able to send some money to my mother to rebuild our house in the Camp. This is part of our culture. But my brother wired the money under my name. Nobody could touch the money except me. I had to come down to the city to release the money for my mother. I went to the Arab bank and took the money to my mom.

My mother sent my sister to the college to tell me not to visit the Camp. She said, "Don't go there. If you go there they will arrest you." I had not seen the Camp since the Israeli invasion and I wanted to take a look at it.

I went to the Camp and I could not recognize where our house used to be. We used to have a big tree. My father planted that tree when he came from Palestine. It was a fig tree. We used to feed the whole neighborhood from that tree. I could not find it. They had bulldozed the whole camp.

There was a school in what used to be an orchard near our house. I saw the kids. It was in January and it was raining that day. When I saw the kids with their umbrellas going into tents in the mud, it reminded me of the sixties. When I was a little kid, we had umbrellas and boots — the same thing.

After I saw the school, I decided to visit my grandmother. It was about four o'clock in the evening. The sun goes down at five. I decided that before the sun went down I would take a taxi back to the city and then go back to school.

I visited with my grandmother. I went to get a taxi. I was standing on the street, motioning for a taxi to come. A car with four guys stopped. They were collaborators. I knew one of them. They pulled two pistols, an AK-47, and an Uzi sub-machine gun, and said, "Get into the car." I said, "What am I doing?" I got into the car. They took me to the interrogation center.

For the first three days they didn't ask me any questions. I was handcuffed and blindfolded. They put a bag over my head and face. They use the same technique in the West Bank and Gaza Strip.

One of the soldiers peeed on my face. Then he put the bag on. For three days I could smell it. It was their psychological torture, that after three days you would be exhausted and say, "OK, just leave me alone."

I didn't know where I was. I heard some voices and I felt safe that I wasn't only by myself. When I said, "I want to go to the bathroom," the soldiers said, "We don't have a bathroom here." The soldiers spoke Arabic with a Palestinian accent.

After three days, two men interrogated me. One of them was about six foot five inches. He said, "We have intelligence information that you are a member of the PLO. You've been working for the PLO since this-and-this-and-this. And you have four AK-47s in your house. Your father is a big officer in the PLO." I said, "No, I'm not." And then one of the soldiers knocked me in the face. I lost three of my teeth. I felt blood in my mouth. With my tongue, I went, "one, two, three . . ."

I denied everything. One of them pretended that he was nice. He said, "If you say that you *were* with the PLO, and if you know some people who are in the PLO, officers and so on, then we will let you go home." One of them was going to torture and beat me and one of them was so nice, but he was worse than the other. This is the technique they use.

I remember, they said, "This guy's very stubborn." They put me for two more days with the bag over my head and my hands handcuffed behind my back.

The interrogator called me a liar. He said, "All the Palestinians are liars." I said, "I swear to God." He said, "Well, here there is no God." He opened the drawer of his desk and said, "The God you believe in is in here." And he closed the drawer and locked it. He said, "Don't say, 'I swear to God.' We do not believe in God here." That's what he told me. I said, "We are all human beings. We are the servants of God." He said, "Shut up."

Then they took me to another room with five people. They were collaborators with the Israelis. They said things like, "What faction do you belong to?" I knew these guys. They were from the Camp. They had mattresses in that room. I said, "I haven't slept in five days. I think I'll take a good night's sleep."

They took me again to the interrogators' office. They used bad techniques. They used pliers on my genitals. (Later I told the International Red Cross.) Still they could not get anything from me. So finally the interrogator said, "I think I'm going to give you a visa." That meant I was going to Ansar.

Ansar

They put the bag over my head again, handcuffed me, and put me in a jeep with other guys. I didn't know who they were. But when they took the bag off, I found that two of them were neighbors.

They took me to Section 11 in Ansar. My father was in Section 13. He used to send us letters and he put his address as "Section 13." That's how I knew where he was.

This is how my father found out that I was there. At the time I arrived, a man was moving from Section 11 to Section 13. That guy said to my father, "You know, when I was leaving Section 11, they brought in a guy and he was smiling. He had a huge smile on his face." "That's my son!" my father said. (Later I was moved to the same section as my father.)

In each section of Ansar there were eight tents, and a ninth tent as a kitchen. There were twenty-four prisoners in each tent. You had a small mattress and slept on the earth floor. They gave each of us two blankets. They gave us prisoners' clothes. I used my boots as a pillow.

They fed us one cup of tea, some bread, and a piece of cheese every morning. At midday there were so many spoonfuls of rice and beans, in the evening either a boiled egg or seven pieces of olive or one teaspoonful of jam. You had one loaf of bread for the whole day. It was an Israeli bread, not like pita bread. I was hungry for the whole time I was there. I used to imagine that the stones in the floor were loaves of bread.

As far as "bathrooms" are concerned, what the Israelis used to do was to dig a hole. They covered it with a piece of wood and made holes in the wood. When you shit you had to do it in front of 350 or 400 people. Some people used water to clean their asses, so when you shit there was a whole lot of water in the hole and it splashed up. The smell was awful.

In wintertime I went three months without a shower. Hot water was never provided.[4] So in wintertime I would not shower because I was afraid that if I showered outside with cold water I would get sick. I got skin diseases, rashes. They took me to an Israeli doctor outside the prison who didn't know the conditions. He gave me medication. He said, "You have to take a shower before you put it on." I asked him for alcohol. He gave me some.

They moved people from section to section for psychological reasons. You had to take your mattress and your two blankets and carry them like a soldier. The purpose was not to let you feel that you had settled down in a particular section.

There was a street between each section and the next. At night tanks ran up and down the streets, so you couldn't sleep. Outdoor lights were kept on constantly so you could not see the night. One time there was an electricity failure and I was so happy because I could see the stars. Inside each tent there was one kerosene light.

During the first several months that Ansar was in operation, you had to stay in your tent most of the time. You had to have permission to go to the bathroom. If you had diarrhea and went outside without permission, you would be punished. I remember one of my friends went outside without permission. They put him in a tank, outside in the hot sun, with zinc walls to reflect the heat.

Medical care was inadequate. You could see people vomiting or with diabetes or arthritis. Diseases developed because of the stress. I witnessed a prisoner with ulcers who was vomiting blood.

One time I got sick. I started vomiting. We had some doctors who were prisoners. They said my blood pressure was dangerously low. They called the Israeli officer. He called an ambulance. When I woke up on the second day, I was in a hospital in Israel. I met a Palestinian doctor. He was an Israeli citizen. He said, "Don't tell anybody. I'll give you some vitamins." He gave

---

4. The U.S. State Department, *Country Reports on Human Rights Practices for 1983*, Lebanon, p. 1329, states that at Ansar Camp, "only cold water outside showers were available."

me about 200 vitamin tablets. When they took me back I split them up and shared them with other prisoners inside Ansar. I said an Israeli doctor gave them to me.

We had a lot of intifada. Some people got killed. We would demonstrate to improve our situation. When the International Red Cross came, we would shout and so on. After several months we gained some freedom. We could go to the bathroom any time we wanted to.

Every day you had to wake up at six o'clock in the morning and clean your mattress. First the Israelis counted everyone to make sure we were still there. Then they gave us breakfast. After breakfast, some people would use pencils and paper that the International Red Cross provided. The Red Cross provided Qu'rans, Bibles, chess, cards, everything. Once in a while the Israelis provided us with newspapers. That's how we learned when the Marine barracks were blown up in Beirut.

I wrote things down day by day in a diary. When I left, one of the Israeli soldiers took it away from me. I cried. I had written over 600 pages in almost a year.

Basically what we used to do was play cards for three hours after breakfast. Before lunch, I would write in my diary. In the afternoon we played chess. Then, after five o'clock in the evening, we had a speaker. We had well-informed prisoners, intellectual people, who would give us lectures about Christianity, about Islam, about communism. Anybody who had an idea about a certain topic would talk and we would sit and discuss it. It might be about Israel or the PLO, or the situation we were living in. We met together outside the tents. Sometimes the soldiers would listen.

I gave lectures about values. I said that whatever religion we are is due to our heritage. I am Muslim because my family is Muslim. What any religion teaches us is values. "Be an honest person." "Don't cheat." "Don't kill."

There was a guy who had a Ph.D. in French. He came back to Lebanon in 1982 to visit his family and he ended up in Ansar. When Sabra and Shatila happened, we didn't know the details. The International Red Cross provided us a book in French. That guy translated the whole book into Arabic, night by night, chapter by chapter.

We had electrical engineers, doctors, Lebanese lawyers, a radiologist. You could meet all kinds of people. There were alcoholics who were always cracking jokes. They asked one man what type of blood he had and he answered "Toma," a kind of wine. There were prisoners who had ten kids. They would wonder what was going on with their kids and sometimes they would cry, especially on the feast days. There were families with the father, three or four sons, and cousins, all in Ansar.

There were about thirty-five women who were kept in Nabatiya, about ten miles from Ansar. The mother of one of the prisoners was there.

There was a committee made up of top PLO officials from different factions. The chairman was Salah Ta'amari. [See below, this Section, p. 122.] There was a Lebanese lawyer, Nami Jumaa, who belonged to the Ba'ath party. The radiologist, Dr. Nabil, belonged to the PFLP. There was a man named Abu Leila from the DFLP. The committee was established to fight for the prisoners' rights. The committee said sick prisoners should go home, old people and young people should go home, and so on.

The PLO had captured six Israeli soldiers in 1982. It was proposed to release them in exchange for 1,000 prisoners from the West Bank and Gaza, the 4,500 prisoners at Ansar,[5] and the materials the Israelis seized when they captured the Palestine Research Center in Beirut. One of the conditions the PLO put on the exchange of prisoners was that the committee from Ansar should be a negotiating partner with the Israelis. Salah went to Jerusalem and negotiated with the Israelis through the International Red Cross.

This committee was very effective. They did a good, good job. They improved our situation. One time the Israelis arrested them and put them in cells. The people in Ansar started making more and more demonstrations, big intifada, and the Israelis were forced to release this committee and send the members back to Ansar.

One time the prisoners were protesting and burned all the tents.[6] The Israelis said, "OK, you burned the tents. We're not going to give you any more." It was summertime. We created small tents for three or four people with our blankets. Because we were protesting, the Israelis were not able to count the prisoners. We could visit back and forth between sections and at night come back to our section.

While I was there the prisoners dug a tunnel. A Palestinian engineer designed it. The tunnel was dug in Section 8. Across the street from Section 8 was a hill with barbed wire at the top. They dug the tunnel under the street. Then the prisoners pretended to have a party. They were doing the dubka. The soldiers were paying attention to the dubka. And one after another, more than seventy prisoners went into the tunnel.

It was very organized. The purpose of the first ten men was to go to the Bekaa Valley and to inform the PLO of conditions inside Ansar. The rest just wanted to get out of Ansar.

The last man out of the tunnel was arrested. Before we burned the tents, he had made a canvas bag out of some of the tent material. He had the bag on his back. When he was leaving the tunnel, his bag got caught on the barbed wire. The barbed wire shook back and forth, and the Israeli soldiers became aware that something was going on.

Most of the people who went into the tunnel escaped. They went into the tunnel at about eight o'clock and the Israelis did not find out until two-thirty in the morning. You could see the flares and the helicopters. The people they arrested were put in cells for something like two months.

Of those who escaped, some were from the Camp. They could not return to the Camp until the Israelis withdrew from Lebanon in 1985. Then they went back.

5. The U.S. State Department, *Country Reports on Human Rights Practices for 1983*, Lebanon, p. 1328, states: "Approximately 4,500 (mostly Palestinian) detainees held by the Israelis in Ansar Camp in southern Lebanon were released on November 24 [1983] as part of a prisoner exchange arranged by the ICRC between Israel and the PLO."
6. The U.S. State Department, *Country Reports on Human Rights Practices for 1983*, p. 1328, states: "Living conditions at the camp were poor. Some prisoners protesting the conditions burned their tents, and consequently the only shelter available was strung-together blankets."

After the tunnel, they moved us to the "Valley of Hell." They moved about 3,000 prisoners. We spent about two months there. All you could see was the sky. The guards were very tough, like Marines.

Then they rebuilt Ansar. This time there was asphalt on the floor of the tents. They did it not because they like us but because with asphalt floors we could not dig any more tunnels. They built little walls around the tents so the water would not flood inside the tents. They were nice the second time.

"We Became Good Friends"

I had some friends among the guards. One of them was from Germany. I played a trick on him. I said, "If you give me some cigarettes and a lighter, I'll make a necklace for your girlfriend." The International Red Cross used to provide us with beads from which we could make necklaces. He gave me two packs of cigarettes.

The second day he asked me, "What is your name?" I told him my name and I said, "In the morning, you call my name. Then I'll give you the necklace." He called me to give him the necklace. I went outside the tent. He said, "Where's the necklace?" I said, "Take this." I gave him the finger. I said, "You took our homeland. If I take two packs of cigarettes from you, do you think that's too much?"

He started talking to me. He said, "What do you do?" I said, "I am a student." He said, "You are not a PLO guerrilla? You were not fighting when they arrested you?" I said, "Hell, no. I was on my way back to school." And he said, "Are you serious?" Even the soldier doesn't know.

I said that my mother and father were born in what was now called Israel, and that they were kicked out. I said, "You were born in Germany and you came back here. How about my family?" He understood that. Then he started saying that it was the Zionist dream for all the Jews to live in Palestine.

We became good friends. To tell you the truth, I trusted him and he trusted me. He came from four to six to guard us. We were not allowed to talk to the guards. But when he came, he called and then we talked. He spoke a little bit in Arabic, a little bit in English, a little bit in Hebrew. We could communicate.

He gave me his telephone number in Germany. He was not going to stay in Israel. He was going back to West Germany. He said, "If you ever have a chance to call me, call me." I threw his telephone number away. I was in the middle. The PLO was saying — you know what I mean? — that I am a collaborator. And it would cause a problem for him too. But if I were to see him now I could recognize him from among 200 people. He was a nice guy.

One time he even provided us with bananas. We never had bananas at Ansar. He threw three bananas to me. It was a big deal. I divided them into six and shared them with my friends.

Most of the soldiers were awful. They looked at us as terrorists and killers. They told us, "Palestinians are killers." Some of them said they wouldn't talk to Palestinians, to "troublemakers." While I was there, one of the soldiers opened fire on the prisoners indiscriminately. Several people were killed and wounded. We protested. The International Red Cross said he was drunk.

One of the soldiers at Ansar committed suicide. He could not stand what was going on. He said, "What we are doing to the Palestinians right now is what happened to us in the past."

When we burned the tents, they brought in a lot of soldiers. I teased one of the soldiers. I told him I saw his picture in the Sabra and Shatila camps. He said, "Not me!" He got excited and said, "I was not in Sabra and Shatila! I didn't kill children!"[7]

One day the International Red Cross came and said we were leaving. They provided us with sweat pants to look nice and good, good tennis shoes — Nikes. We Palestinians from Lebanon had a choice to go back to our families in Lebanon or to go to Algeria. The Palestinians from the West Bank and Gaza Strip had to go to France, and from France to Algeria. Some of my friends decided to go to Algeria because they were afraid that the Israelis would release us for a while and then they would arrest us again.

The reporters asked us, "How did they treat you?" We said, "Very good." We were afraid that if we said anything else they would arrest us again.

My father was released about six months before me because he got sick. The Israelis beat him with a shovel and injured his eyes. He had difficulty seeing and I had to help him go to the bathroom. I was relieved when he was released.

The first day home I took a shower. It was the first time I had hot water in almost a year. My mother prepared a big meal. It was a celebration. Everybody was happy that I came back. Then I left the house.

After about five days, the Israelis came back and asked about me. They re-arrested a lot of my friends. I slept in ten different houses during the year and a half after I was released from prison.

It wasn't easy to live under occupation. I give credit to Palestinians who live in the West Bank and Gaza Strip. I lived one and a half years under the Israeli occupation. It was like fifteen years.

What Did It Mean?

When I lived in the Camp, I never met a Jew, I never met an Israeli. The propaganda was that they were all killers. The first time they bombed the Camp, I was eleven years old. It was 1972. They destroyed a lot of houses. They killed a lot of my friends. What would you expect me to feel about Israelis? I felt that they were killers, that they had taken our land, and so on. I never felt that they were human beings.

When I went to prison, I met some Israelis. I changed my attitude. When we heard that that Israeli killed himself because he could not stand the

---

7. The U.S. State Department, *Country Reports on Human Rights Practices for 1982*, Lebanon, pp. 1196–97, states: "[After the Israeli invasion of West Beirut,] Lebanese militiamen, in an operation coordinated with the Israelis, entered the Palestinian refugee camps of Sabra and Shatila in West Beirut. The militiamen perpetrated a massacre of hundreds of civilians. The Government found the bodies of 328 victims of the massacre; several hundred more probably remain unlocated. . . ."

situation and was very sympathetic with us, and when I met that friend — he was really a nice person! He was a human being! I started distinguishing between one person and another.

Before, I had an attitude that came from living through all the hardship and shelling, living from one invasion to another, having our house completely destroyed by the Israelis. But violence breeds violence. I had some friends in Ansar who attacked Israelis after their release to get revenge. They are all dead now.

I changed my mind about how a human being can torture another human being. Now I don't have the heart to torture another human being, because I know how it feels. Even the person who tortured me, if I should meet him one day, I would never torture him because I know how it feels. That's how it changed my attitude.

I made good friends there. It was a good experience. It makes me very humble. I appreciate everything. I remember how I used to fight with my mother about food all the time. Afterwards, whatever she cooked, I ate. Can you believe, we had no Pepsi and no orange juice in Ansar? No coffee the whole time? I started appreciating life more. Whatever I have, I feel that I have more than I need. That's how I changed.

Palestinians are treated by other Arabs the way Europeans treated Jews. Palestinians and Jews are more educated. They are considered aggressive, greedy. I would like to start a school for Palestinians and Jews so they could learn to love one another.

We as people have to make the change. Sometimes, like when I am driving by myself for three hours, it hits me — memories come back. Sometimes I cry. Why can't people live together? Why do we have to torture each other?

Salah Ta'amari

"Imprisonment was simply a new arena in which the human being had to continue his struggle."

Arrival at Ansar

Handcuffs and shackles fill my mind when I recall the long trip sitting in the back of what seemed to be a half-truck from the solitary prison of Gadera in Israel to the prison camp at Ansar in the south of Lebanon.[8] Under the blindfold, seconds, minutes, and hours seemed much longer than they really were.

I don't know how much time had passed when I began to hear a loud humming sound, as though we were approaching a huge beehive. As the truck drove nearer, the humming was more like the sound of human beings.

---

8. The U.S. State Department, *Country Reports on Human Rights Practices for 1982*, Israel and the Occupied Territories, p. 1163, states: "Large numbers of the prisoners captured in June [1982] were transferred to Israel, according to the Israeli government, due to the lack of facilities for them in Lebanon. By July most of the prisoners had been concentrated in a newly-built prison camp near Ansar in southern Lebanon."

When we stopped, I could distinguish individual human voices, with the loud humming still droning in the background.

I got out of the truck. The soldier ordered me to walk faster from the truck to the place they were leading me. I couldn't walk faster because the shackles were too narrow to allow wider strides. I just walked.

When the blindfold was taken off, I was in the middle of a large tent. I found myself surrounded by a few soldiers and one officer. I gazed at the officer with a sense of astonishment: he would have passed as the twin brother of one of my cousins — dark complexion, with a mustache and a little goatee, and the same medium, well-built stature. The familiarity that I felt while gazing at the officer evaporated when he exchanged a few words in Hebrew with one the soldiers, and then resumed talking to me in English, pointing at the duffel bag where my belongings were.

They gave me some brown clothes which did not fit. They were too small. So I had to remain in my camouflage uniform which they provided me when I was in solitary.

The officer told me what was not allowed. Everything was not allowed. Then I asked him, "OK, you told me what was not allowed. Tell me, what are my rights?" He was shocked! "Your rights?" I told him, "Yes, my rights." "We'll tell you about them later." Then they led me into Ansar.

When I first saw Ansar, it was as if the whole universe were engulfed by barbed wire. It was in the late afternoon and one could even think that the barbed wire was marring the face of the sun itself. Everything was brownish: people, earth, tents.

Each section had a double gate. They opened the first gate, then the second gate, and I could recognize immediately the guy who was standing behind the second gate. His name was Khalid Arif. I knew him from the south of Lebanon. He lived in Ein El Hilweh refugee camp.

The second thing I saw, maybe three or four yards beyond the gate, was a sort of monument built with stone pebbles. It had a slanted surface that faced the entrance, so that you could see it as you went in. Engraved on the slanted surface were the words, "Peace, Shalom, Salaam." In the center of the monument there sat a model mosque with a Star of David painted on the minaret. I photographed it in my memory and put it in the back of my mind.

Everybody was welcoming me. I was in a sort of haze. Just having other people around me gave me the sense of tremendous strength. I felt I could conquer the whole world. I thought Ansar was like Paradise, just because there were human beings to communicate with.

My first night there was in September. They insisted that I should sleep in the kitchen tent because it was warmer and, for special treatment, my colleagues and friends offered me a sheet of corrugated paper from the boxes of bread and vegetables to put under me, and a blanket. They offered me tea.

The solitary cell seemed so far away, as if it had never existed; yet it was deeply entrenched within me. The taboos in solitary had turned into mental habits, resurfacing at moments when I wanted to go out of the tent for a walk in the yard or to go to the bathroom or even when I wanted to talk to somebody in the neighboring tent. My colleagues had to remind me that I was no longer in solitary whenever they felt my hesitation. They would approach me and tell me, "Yes, you can go out," "Yes, you can go to the bathroom," as though they were reading my mind.

I was still dizzy with happiness that I was with other people. The feeling of security generated by the thousands of people around me made it easier for me to doze off that first night.

The Count

At about six in the morning, there was a bustle of activity. Most of the prisoners were shuttling to and from bathrooms and tents. Then all of a sudden everybody disappeared into their tents.

I asked Khalid Arif, "What's wrong?" He said, "It is the daily count." "OK, so what are we supposed to do?" I asked him. "Sit down and put your hands on your head until the counting is finished and the officer, guards, and soldiers are out of the section." "I'm going to sit, but I'm not going to put my hands on my head," I told him. "Please, brother Salah, don't start problems. Just do what others do. It will not last for more than five minutes," he said in a begging tone.

When he realized that I was adamant and steadfast in my refusal, he went away and came back with some of my colleagues. One of them was Jamal Saleem, an old colleague and friend of mine. "Brother Salah," Jamal said in his gentle and calm voice, "Do you think you are the only person for whom it is difficult to sit in such a position to be counted like an object? We too resent that. We have no power to change it, and we would hate to see the Israelis break your bones to make you do it."

I was more stubborn than ever, until he said, "Please do it, if not for your sake, for our sake." I conceded, but I told him, "It will be the first and last time that I do it."

Two Israeli armored vehicles, mounted with machine guns, took their position at the corners of the section. A third controlled the gate to the section, with its machine gun pointed and a soldier's finger ready on the trigger. One or two officers and no less than five soldiers came in without arms other than what seemed to be cannisters of tear gas, wearing their bullet proof jackets, carrying their clubs. The moukhtar (the prisoner assigned by the Israelis to be in charge of the section) stood at the gate, keeping a distance from the soldiers as they requested.

They proceeded to count the prisoners in every tent. Each prisoner would be sitting on his blanket with his hands on top of his head. The officer would stand at the entrance, with a soldier holding him by the belt to yank him back in case the prisoners in the tent attempted to pull the officer in, whether to harm him or take him as a hostage.

I could feel the officer's eyes resting on me for a fraction of a second. I was restless, and I was scratching my head rather than holding my hands passively on top of it. The officer chose to ignore it, and moved to the neighboring tent. The counting of my section lasted over five minutes.

After the counting was over, I remember very vividly, a prisoner from the neighboring section was standing against the fence and he waved to me. He was an old colleague of mine from Cairo. We never got along together when we were students. We always clashed. We hated each other. Allah, to be in prison is bad enough! To have that guy in prison with you would make it hell! And I was surprised. From the first second, he was so friendly, supportive, and in fact he turned out to be one of the nicest colleagues.

The Owl

When the count was over, the prisoners rushed to the kitchen tent to take their ration for breakfast. They looked like street beggars, with their long shabby beards and hair, their ragged clothes. They carried in their hands a mosaic of things that served as eating utensils — empty cans for cups, some of the cans larger than cooking pots. Three or four prisoners would share one plate. Spoons were scarce. Knives and forks were nonexistent. And almost nonexistent was the food to use them on. One piece of cheese, a piece of bread and a half tin of tea was breakfast. Rations were kept in the kitchen tent and distributed by the moukhtar at each meal. Many devoured the triangular piece of cheese in one mouthful and gulped their tea. I asked some of the prisoners to slow down. They muttered, "The boomah (the owl) may come before we finish our breakfast. We may be taken out without breakfast."

"What owl?" I was bewildered.

"That car," one of them said, pointing at a van running along the dirt road surrounding the compound. It had no windows except the one by the side of the driver. It stopped in front of the section. Then an officer or a soldier came out. The head of the section, the moukhtar, rushed to the gate and he started reading numbers. Those prisoners would just come and they would be handcuffed, blindfolded and pushed into that car.

After a while I asked the moukhtar, "Where are they taking those prisoners?" He said, "Well, they are taking them to interrogation. This happens every day, except for the Sabbath sometimes." "When are they coming back?" I asked. "We don't know." "Do you take their names?" "No." "Do you ask the Red Cross about them?" "No." The boomah disappeared, leaving a cloud of dust behind it.

How false were the feelings of security I derived from the multitude of people around me. The multitude didn't provide any protection. Any one of us could be taken out. Anybody could be tortured, beaten, or even killed. To feel the contentment of sharing the same fate of others is one thing; to be protected by the multitude is another thing. We were so vulnerable!

My happiness at being among people was increasingly coupled with feelings of frustration, resentment, and anger that could not find a proper meaningful outlet.

Breaking the rules — standing by the barbed wire to talk to other prisoners — was not enough. The Israeli guards chose to ignore my violation of that part of their rules. The high tower controlling my section was manned by two guards instead of one. One of them followed my movements with a pair of binoculars. Many prisoners told me they never saw binoculars used by the guards before. In fact, they were all expecting trouble but as time passed by without any of the guards approaching me to order me away from the barbed wire the prisoners were encouraged to come closer to the barbed wire fence and talk to me.

The Monument

I spent the day absorbing what was going on. There were thousands of people. Many of them were smarter than me, more educated, but they were shattered. They were terror-stricken. They didn't know where their strength lay. They were reduced to items and they behaved accordingly.

Towards afternoon I realized that nothing was more of an embodiment of the situation, be it the humiliation in which the prisoners lived or the arrogant brutal dominance of Israelis over the lives of those prisoners, than the monument that I had seen when I first entered Ansar. It was the symbol of both the arrogance of the occupier and the involuntary submission of the occupied. All my deep frustration and anger were directed toward that monument.

I asked the moukhtar, "Who built that monument?" He said, "We, at the bayonets of the Israelis."

I stood right in front of it, reading the words, "Peace, Shalom, Salaam," in English, Hebrew, and Arabic. The sight of the Star of David, painted on the minaret, was like a slap in the face.

I had pulled one pebble out of the monument when Naji, a distant relative of mine who lived in Sidon and ended up in Ansar, pulled me gently but firmly by the arm, as if he knew what my intention was.

"What are you doing?" he asked. "I want to pull it down," I said. "For heaven's sake, don't do it. Don't bring a disaster on yourself and on us." He was unable to hide his panic. I yanked my arm from his hand. I said, "I'm the only one who will be hurt. If you don't want to help me, you can go back to your tent." I was more determined than ever to demolish that monument.

I resumed pulling one pebble after the other out of the monument when Yahya, one of the young people from Ein El Hilweh Refugee Camp, approached me.

I said, "Yahya, would you please come and help me make a little pavement with pebbles between the tent and the toilet because it will be muddy if it rains?" "Oh, certainly, absolutely," he answered immediately.

So we started collecting pebbles from the ground and making paths from tent to tent. Then we were short of pebbles. "I think there are some pebbles in that monument," I commented. He said, "Do you want me to take some from there?" I said, "I'll take them from the monument." "I'll do it with you," he said. One pebble, then another, then another, passed from the monument.

Then I told him casually, "Get me one of the long poles of the tent, the one in the corner that has a tip of steel where it goes into the tent." He looked concerned: "What if the tent falls down." I told him, "Taking just one will not make it fall down. It may lean to one side but it will not fall."

I got a piece of rope. With the rope, and the pole of the tent, I made a plow. I said to Yahya, "I will pull. You just hold the pole like a plow." And I pulled my plow over the monument for many minutes. When I had finished, the monument was gone. Nothing but flat earth lay where it had been.

Then I said, "Don't you think it looks better now?" "Absolutely," he said.

I stood and looked around. Not another prisoner was in the yard. They had all disappeared into their tents in fear. But no disaster took place. No guards, neither officers nor soldiers, came near our section. Except for the binoculars pointed at our section, there was nothing unusual.

The Second Night

That night, I stayed awake after everybody else in my tent was fast asleep. Why was it all happening? How could such a place exist in the middle of a civilized world? Where *is* the world? Is it true that nobody knows about Ansar? Impossible.

I didn't know the exact number of prisoners, but I knew they were in the thousands. I would have understood and comprehended a prison camp for PLO members, but there were not ten thousand members in the PLO. In fact, most of the detainees had nothing to do with the PLO. A large percentage of them were not even Palestinians, or even Arabs.

There were thousands of people in Ansar and they didn't know their strength. The enemy knew that he was dealing with a quantity. The Red Cross knew also that they were dealing with quantity. How could we send the message to both the Israelis and the Red Cross that the prisoners were *not* a quantity?

We had to know how many prisoners were in Ansar and we had to know, in detail and precisely, who those prisoners were.

Our Own Count

I asked my friends, colleagues, and the moukhtar of my section, "How many prisoners are there?" Some people said five thousand, others said ten thousand. None of them could give me an exact figure as to how many prisoners there were in Ansar. We had to find out ourselves.

But first we needed to know our rights. I turned to the prisoners around me. I asked them, "Do you have a copy of the Geneva Convention." "No. What is the Geneva Convention?"[9] They had never heard of it. "You don't

---

9. The Geneva Convention Relative to the Protection of Civilian Persons in Time of War, 12 August 1949, also referred to as the Fourth Geneva Convention, "reaffirms and ensures, by a series of detailed provisions, the general acceptance of the principle of respect for the human person in the very midst of war. . . ." (The Geneva Conventions of 12 August 1949, Commentary, published under the general editorship of Jean S. Pictet, *IV Geneva Convention Relative To The Protection Of Civilian Persons In Time Of War* [Geneva, Switzerland: International Committee of the Red Cross, 1958], p. 9). Article 4 states that the Fourth Geneva Convention applies to persons "who, at a given moment and in any manner whatsoever, find themselves, in case of a conflict or occupation, in the hands of a Party to the conflict or Occupying Power of which they are not nationals."

have books with the Geneva Convention in them?" The prisoners said, "No."

It was a Sunday and the delegation from the Red Cross was not there. So there was no way to get a copy of the Geneva Convention.

I told them, "OK, we will start by learning the number of prisoners." "How?" "You send letters to prisoners in other sections. You write on a piece of paper, wrap it around a stone, and throw the stone over the wire. You send the letter to your friend or your brother or your cousin. This time, I will send a letter to each moukhtar, the head of each section, asking for the exact number of prisoners in his section. He is the one who will know because he is in charge of distributing the food."

I wrote a communique. It was the first time in that prison camp that a communique was written and sent. It asked the moukhtar in every section how many prisoners there were in his section. When the responses to the communique came back, we had the answer: there were over ten thousand prisoners in Ansar.

Ten thousand people! It seemed impossible that amongst them no one knew that the Red Cross was obliged to get them a copy of the Geneva Convention.

"War in a Different Form"

I remembered that during the war, on the radio in Arabic, the Israelis used to address us in the singular. That was a technique to divide people. "Ayyo ha al musallah?" "Are you an armed person?" "Musallah" means "armed person." "Musallahin" is the plural of "musallah." They did not say, "Ayyo ha al musallahin?" which means, "Are you armed persons?" They talked to you as an individual. On hearing that, I would feel I wanted to stick to my colleagues. "We are together. Don't listen to them. It's not 'musallah.' It's all of us together."

They coupled their messages on the radio with the continuous bombing and bombardment that would make people yield and concede. It was like twisting someone's arm while convincing that person to accept something. Most often, he would be convinced as long as the alternative was to break his arm.

In their psychological war, they wanted to make the individual hollow. How did they make the individual hollow? The first step was to divide, to isolate the individual. The second step was to make him feel hollow from within.

They started with Israel's presumed military supremacy. The Arab human being, seeing Israel's actual military supremacy in 1948, 1956, 1967, and 1973, took it for granted that in any conflict, the Israelis would win. So the Israelis didn't need to prove their military supremacy. It was there.

From military superiority they expanded: "We are not super only in the military. At present, we are super economically, culturally, politically, and socially." Then they expanded in time: "We are not only super in the present time but we have always been super, all through history, the people of the

Book. Everything that was good and great in the world was Jewish." That would lead to an inexorable conclusion: there is an inevitable superiority in the future.

Talking about Israeli superiority was always coupled by undermining us. By us, I mean, Palestinians, Lebanese, Arabs, Muslims, Shi'ite Muslims, Sunni Muslims, Christians, Maronites. It didn't matter who you were. I heard it: if you were Christian, Christ was a bastard; if you were a Shi'ite Muslim, Ali was a hypocrite; if you were a Sunni, Muhammad was a big bluff, a womanizer who got married to so-and-so. The culture? We didn't have a culture.

Under such an atmosphere and with the physical pressure under which they put us, people became hollow. They were reduced to just responding to whatever the Israelis asked them to do. After the ceasefire, the only way to expose people to physical pressure and hardships was in a concentration camp like Ansar. That explained Ansar. Ansar was the continuation of the war in a different form.

I wrote a communique to the other prisoners. First I defined what the Israelis' objective was in Ansar and then I defined *our* objective. We had to redefine imprisonment: imprisonment was not a status in which the human being was neutralized and incapacitated; imprisonment was simply a new arena in which the human being had to continue his struggle. The rules of the game might be different, but it was still an arena for struggle. The victorious one would be the one who had the better organization, the stronger will, and the better defined objectives. Our objective was to turn Ansar into a burden on the Israelis themselves, to carve it into a thorn in their flesh.

The Prisoners' Demands

I said to the moukhtar of my section, "Let's send another letter to every other section and ask them what they need."

"And who is going to supply their needs?" he asked. "Just send that letter," I said, "and the answer will come."

The demands were very humble. We need meat. We need books. We need blankets. We need family visits.

I told him, "Write down our needs. Number one: A copy of the Geneva Convention. Number two: Seeds. Number three: Books. Clothes, hot water, family visits, blah, blah, blah, blah."

And I told him, "Each section should have the same demands." Then the moment the Red Cross representative read them, he would know that there was a central leadership among the prisoners and that would make him respect the prisoners and take things seriously. "Send it back to the sections and tomorrow the heads of the sections will give their demands to their ICRC representative." And that's what happened.

The head of the Red Cross delegation came to my section and he asked for me. He asked me, "Do you know of these demands?" "Yes. I know of these demands." He said, "Are you aware of number two?" "Absolutely, number two is the seeds," I said. "How could you put the seeds as a priority when you guys don't have enough food or enough blankets?"

When I asked for the seeds, it was based on how I found the prisoners. They had no purpose. "You'd better have seeds as a priority because I want them," I answered. He said, "I don't think I am going to bring seeds." "If you don't bring the seeds, you are not coming into the section again," I retorted angrily.

And I went on. "Why did you not supply the prisoners with their copy of the Geneva Convention?" He said, "Simply because they never asked for it." "Isn't it your role to bring it, to supply it?" "No, I cannot. I know they need it but they should have asked for it. If they had asked, I would have responded to them."[10]

It was shocking. At the beginning I even thought of the ICRC [International-al Committee of the Red Cross] as cold-minded. At a later stage I came to respect them and admire what they did. It took me a long time to realize that they were victims, sometimes as much as we were, and that the alternative was not to have them around.

So I said, "Now you know. Now we ask. Now you are obliged to give us answers." He said, "I'll discuss these demands with the Israelis."

The Owl Comes for Me

Within a week things started changing. More prisoners dared to come and stand at the barbed wire separating my section from theirs to ask me what I thought of this and that or simply to chat. More letters poured into my section from other sections, not only from the sections neighboring mine. Most of the letters came from old colleagues or friends who responded to my letters and communiques to the prisoners.

Many of the prisoners in my section were involved in one activity or another. Some were busy copying and handwriting letters to be sent out to prisoners. Others were busy wrapping those letters around stones to throw them over the wire to the neighboring sections, where other prisoners would pick them up and throw them over to other sections, and so forth. A web of mail routes was created.

Every day, when we woke up in the morning, one prisoner would ask another, "Whose turn is next?" for the interrogation. I knew I would be taken out of Ansar. One afternoon a senior Israeli officer with a sort of cowboy hat drove his GMC pick-up to my section and stopped outside. He stayed there for a few minutes examining the section as if the prisoners were a herd of sheep from which he wanted to choose one for slaughter. I could feel his eyes resting on me most of the time. Deep in my heart I knew I was the one.

That night was a restless one. I was eaten up by worries over what might happen if they took me back to solitary again. I worried over both the prisoners in Ansar and myself. But I consoled myself with the fact that in

---

10. Article 99 of the Fourth Geneva Convention, regarding administration of an internment camp, states in part: "The text of the present Convention . . . shall be posted inside the place of internment, in a language which the internees understand. . . ."

spite of the short time I had spent in the prison camp, less than two weeks, the prisoners' eyes were opened to many things. I was sure things would not go back to where they were before I came to Ansar.

I woke up at dawn, a couple of hours before the rest of the prisoners woke up. I scribbled a letter to some leading figures in the various sections. I told them about my fear of being removed from the prison camp. "In case I'm taken out," I wrote, "keep informing the prisoners" and "stick to your demands."

As the rays from the rising sun penetrated the barbed wire, into the tents and the yards in every section, the owl approached my section. It was accompanied as usual by a couple of armored vehicles which positioned themselves at two corners of the section, controlling the section as well as the gate where the owl stopped.

An officer stepped out of the owl and shouted out a few numbers. After each number he shouted, a prisoner headed toward the gate. Some would ask their colleagues to look after their letters in case the Red Cross brought any from their families. Most of them had anxious faces, etched with fear.

When the last number was called, no one responded. No prisoner came forward. The officer repeated the number several times, his voice rising a pitch higher each time he uttered the number. There was no response from the prisoners.

The moukhtar, who was standing at attention right at the inner gate and who often repeated the numbers after the officer, approached me and whispered, "Brother Salah, they're calling for you." "No, they are not," I answered him. "I didn't hear my name being mentioned." "Yes, they did," he responded. "They're shouting your number. Your name is your number." I told him, "I have a name, not a number."

He insisted, begging me to accompany him to the gate. I refused. I insisted I would only respond when they called me by name. He went back to the officer and exchanged a few words with him.

The officer pointed his finger at me from afar, and called, "Salah, it's you who I'm calling." I walked to the gate and went through the same rituals as other prisoners taken for interrogation: I was handcuffed, blindfolded, put into the back of the owl.

The owl made several stops in front of the sections, picking up more prisoners. Then it headed towards the outskirts of the camp to unload its cargo in "the hole," the prisoners' code name for the interrogation section. "The hole" consisted of a few tents surrounded by high walls of earth which made the place like a large hole in the ground.

I was led out of the van. When they took the blindfold off, I was in the middle of a tiny wooden hut. Three more prisoners were already there. They knew me and I recognized one of them. They were from the Liberation Army. The three of them looked in bad shape. They made a space on the floor for me and invited me to sit. We chatted for some time, exchanging news.

I remember, I started singing. The three guys were terrified. "Don't be terrified. Just sit. What could they do to us?"

I spent the night there and in the morning they took me out.

Back to Solitary

They took me through the muddy yard of the section to an adjacent yard where many soldiers were waiting. One of them fixed a black blindfold tightly on my eyes. And then he, or another soldier, held my hands behind my back and applied metal handcuffs, clamped too tightly around my wrists. I was dumped in the back of a car and I sat on the floor, leaning my back against one side of it.

The car drove for hours. It seemed endless because of the pain I felt in my wrists and my back. Apart from the physical discomfort of sitting on the floor of the car, each time the car bumped, I felt acute pain in my spine. There was no way to protect myself against the bumps. I tried to press my hands against the floor to absorb the shock, but because I could not see the road, nor was I warned before the car went into a bump on the rough road, my reflexes were too late. The pain in my wrists and in my back was agony. It was one of the most hideous experiences of my life.[11]

I remained silent. I was hungry and thirsty, and I could feel foam coming out of my mouth. The car stopped for a few times on the road. The cracking of the shells of sunflower seeds and the munching of the soldiers indicated that they stopped to eat and drink. At some point, a soldier asked me if I wanted to drink. I said "No." I was boiling with anger and too furious to accept water.

I had no idea where we were going or what their intention was. Behind the blindfold in the back of a closed car, I couldn't tell where we were or the direction we were taking. Then, at some point, the car left the highway. The mildly rough road and the curves that the car took brought memories to my mind. "They must be taking me back to Gadera," I thought. I was sure I was there when I heard the barking of the dogs.

They led me out of the car. When the blindfold was taken from my eyes, I realized that I was in the same cell where I had spent three and a half months. The handcuffs were taken off my wrists, and I was terrified at the size of my hands. They were swollen to at least two times their normal size. I kept rubbing my wrists to relieve the pain.

"Junkie" — that was the code-name of the guard, the one friend that I had there — was standing at the door. He had a club in his hand, and kept at a distance from me — something he never did before. He was on his alert, and he didn't seem friendly. He did not stay for more than a few seconds before he closed the heavy door of the cell behind him.

I looked at myself in the tiny broken mirror glued to the wall. I was as horrified at how my face looked as I was at how my hands looked. My eyes were red and swollen. My lips were dry and framed by dried foam. My beard, shaggy and long after weeks of not shaving, was painted white with the foam

11. Article 127 of the Fourth Geneva Convention, regarding transfers of internees, states in part: "The transfer of internees shall always be effected humanely . . . and under conditions at least equal to those obtaining for the forces of the Detaining Power in their changes of station." Article 128 states in part: "In the event of transfer, internees shall be advised of their departure and of their new postal address. . . ."

that had come out of my mouth during that long, horrid trip. I simply looked inhuman.

After less than an hour, "Junkie" came back again. He opened the door of the cell. He looked at me and in a few seconds he regained his usual smile and friendly attitude. But the club was still in his hand. He asked me how I was. I pointed at the club in his hand. He understood what I meant.

"You didn't see yourself when you first arrived an hour ago. You were terrifying. You looked like a beast boiling with anger. Nobody could predict how you would react once your arms were free. I insisted that I should take off your handcuffs because I thought you would react less violently with me than with others. If they took them off and you acted violently, they would have broken your bones. I thought I would take the risk and do that mission myself."

He hesitated before he spoke again. "It was so cruel to bring you here this way. Why didn't they loosen your handcuffs when they saw your hands were so swollen? That was cruel, too cruel."

I enjoyed the first night back in solitary because I was very tired. In the prison camp, sometimes a prisoner would wake me up in the middle of the night and tell me, "I dreamt that my wife had deserted the house." So I had to sit for hours with him, trying to calm him down. Or the Red Cross would come to me and tell me, "This prisoner is writing letters to God and he expects an answer."[12] I enjoyed uninterrupted sleep and at least it was warm.

I could have lived ten years in Ansar and to me it would have been a picnic, simply because solitary was hell. The mere fact that I had colleagues, human beings to talk to, gave me so much confidence at Ansar. In Ansar, if you had a nightmare, when you woke up you had friends to talk to. In the cell, you woke from one nightmare into another which was more real.

They kept me for about ten days. Then the director of Gadera came to see me in my cell. "You know, we don't know what to do with you. You spent more time here than we can keep you." At Ansar, when I met with the Red Cross, they had told me about people who contacted them about me, from Indira Gandhi to the Pope. So the Israelis couldn't keep me in Gadera for more than three months and a half. "They don't want you in Ansar. And they don't want you here," the director said.

They sent me back to Ansar, blindfolded and handcuffed. But at least I was handcuffed with my hands in front of me and not behind my back.

The Commander of Ansar

When I arrived at Ansar again, I thought they would put me back in my section. Instead, they took me back to the interrogation section and put me into solitary in Ansar. It seemed to be larger than it was ten days earlier. They had added to it what seemed to be prefabricated rooms, so small they looked

12. The U.S. State Department, *Country Reports on Human Rights Practices for 1983*, Lebanon, p. 1328, states regarding Ansar: "Psychologically disturbed prisoners reportedly remained unsupervised among the other detainees."

like boxes of concrete, with one door and one transom. These rooms were used as cells. I was kept in one of them.

I knew I was in Ansar because the humming of thousands of people reached my ears. It made this solitary more agitating than the one in Gadera. In Gadera, I was all by myself. I could hear the sounds or screaming of agonized prisoners, which was bad enough. But here, in solitary in Ansar, I could hear the hum of life. It gave me the feeling of someone who was dying of thirst while water was within reach, but one couldn't reach it because a glass wall stood between one and the water.

The next morning, the door of the cell opened. Standing in the door was the man in the cowboy hat who had been looking searchingly at my section the day before I was taken away to Gadera. I had a closer look at him while sitting in the corner of the cell: medium height, in his early sixties or late fifties, red face, red hair, piercing, narrow blue eyes. The wrinkles on the sides of his eyes gave the impression that all of his facial expressions started there, laughter as well as anger. It was a nice face.

Without introduction, he began. "I was relieved when they took you away. I didn't know what to do when they brought you back. Some have suggested that we keep you here, in this section, in this cell. I think that's unfair. What would you do if I sent you back to your section?" "I would like to change it," I answered. "No, no, what would you do?" I said, "I told you, I would like to change it if you send me back to my section." "Would Ansar be quiet? Or would you resume creating problems?" I told him, "I know the surest way to have it be quiet." He said, "What?" "Send everybody home. You remain with the barbed wire, and Ansar will be peaceful and quiet."

I could see the shadow of a smile at the corners of his eyes. It soon disappeared. "OK. Get up," he said. He took me in his car, back to my section. He himself opened the two gates and led me in. He closed the gates, and left wordlessly.

Who Were We?

In my absence it rained and, as I expected, it was muddy. The only section that was not a mess was my section, because of the stone pebble paths that had been made from the monument. This gave more credibility to my suggestions.

Living conditions were still unacceptable by any standard.[13] Winter was approaching. It was already cold during the day, and even colder at night. The three blankets allocated to each prisoner, to serve as both mattress and cover, were far less than what were needed to keep us warm. Lucky were those who managed to collect corrugated cardboard to sleep on.

Lack of shoes resulted in a large number of prisoners walking around

13. The U.S. State Department, *Country Reports on Human Rights Practices for 1982*, Lebanon, p. 1197, states: "Conditions at the Israeli prison camp in Ansar (south Lebanon) were reportedly quite bad with severe overcrowding, inadequate shelter, unhealthy sanitation, and lack of effective medical care. Living conditions at Ansar improved as 1982 went on, but remain unsatisfactory. . . ."

barefoot or wrapping their feet with whatever ragged cloths they managed to find. Most of the prisoners wore worn-out clothes, whether it was the outfits given to them by the Israelis or their own in which they were arrested, which they kept because the Israelis did not have enough prison uniforms. Food was far from adequate.

At the emotional and mental level, the situation was devastating. Family visits were not allowed.[14] The only link between a prisoner and his family was the Red Cross whose understaffed delegation could not cover the requests of thousands of prisoners, some of whom had families living outside Lebanon.

There was not a single soul who lived in the south of Lebanon who was not detained for a few hours or a few days or a few weeks or a few months, and I don't exclude anybody — children, women, infants, people in wheelchairs — everybody. They would declare a zone or sector of the city a sealed-off area. Everybody should go to the church or to the mosque or the main yard. The main yard turned into the detention center for a few hours. The beach of Sidon was the detention place where thousands of people were detained — men, women, ill; it didn't matter. Everybody was screened.

In Ansar, one of the things that we needed to know was who we were. We wanted to know how many doctors we had, how many teachers we had, how many students we had, how many members of the same family were there, what ailments did we have? We documented everything.

There were students, teachers, headmasters of schools, mayors, ex-police officers, Lebanese government employees, U.N. and UNRWA employees, poets, lawyers, artists, everybody was there. There were Muslims, Sunni, Shi'a, Christians, Druze, even Maronites. There were Egyptian workers, Pakistani, Bangladeshi, Yemenis, Koreans who had been working on construction sites, old and young, rich and poor, all rounded up and put in Ansar. The eldest prisoner was 83 years old. The youngest was 12. There were people who were handicapped and people with serious ailments.[15]

Our survey led to one conclusion. The Israelis were aiming at dismantling not just the PLO but the Palestinian social structure in Lebanon. They were

14. The U.S. State Department, *Country Reports on Human Rights Practices for 1982*, Israel and the Occupied Territories, p. 1164, states: "As of the end of 1982, the Israeli government had not made public a full or partial list of names of the detainees, had not permitted relatives access to the detainees, and, while granting the Red Cross access to most of the prisoners, apparently maintained some of them incommunicado and unaccounted for. . . ." The U.S. State Department, *Country Reports on Human Rights Practices for 1982*, Lebanon, p. 1197, states: "As of the end of 1982, the Red Cross still did not have access to all Israeli-held prisoners. . . . Communication between prisoners and families was generally not permitted. . . ." The U.S. State Department, *Country Reports on Human Rights Practices for 1984*, Israel and the Occupied Territories, p. 1262, states: "[Israel] has stated that under the Fourth Geneva Convention it has the right to intern persons who constitute a danger to the security of the detaining power or its armed forces. The Israeli Supreme Court has confirmed the applicability of the standards of the Fourth Convention, while holding that, for security reasons, Israel is permitted to deny the detainees access to family members and legal counsel. Israel has permitted ICRC representatives to visit the detainees."

15. The U.S. State Department, *Country Reports on Human Rights Practices for 1982*, Lebanon, p. 1198, states: "From 9,000 to 15,000 persons, primarily Palestinian but also including thousands of Lebanese and hundreds of other nationalities, were detained without charge by the Israelis. Various accounts, including at least one in the Israeli press, contend that many of the prisoners were not suspected of any direct involvement in military or terrorist activities. Persons who were old, crippled, or blind allegedly were included among these prisoners."

trying to push the Palestinian population out of the south of Lebanon — something like half a million people — by breaking up the nucleus of the Palestinian society, by sending all the males above age 12 to the prison camp[16] while the rest of the family — infants and females — were left vulnerable, facing all kinds of insecurities, physical, financial, and social. The Israelis aimed at forcing the broken Palestinian families to leave the south of Lebanon for some other place, be it the north or the neighboring countries, like Syria. And all those Lebanese who opposed Israeli policy in Lebanon would be forced to leave with them.

There was a basic difference between the prisoners in Ansar and prisoners in the Occupied Territories. A prisoner in the Occupied Territories had usually done something — maybe been in a demonstration, maybe thrown a stone, maybe protested. They were activists and they were politically aware. Prisoners in the Occupied Territories didn't have a problem in forming a committee to deal with their jailers.

But Ansar was the microcosm of our society. We had to deal with people who had never belonged to anything. What strategy would suit all of them? What was something that all of them would adopt? How could we maintain unity?

The image of the owl, the van that came day after day to take prisoners away for interrogation, was always in the back of my mind. I knew I had to stop interrogation. It was illegal. It was against the Geneva Convention.[17] And I knew that the objective of interrogation was not to obtain information from the prisoners, but to break their spirits. The prisoners would come back to their sections in bad shape. They would be demoralized, despairing.

At that early stage, it was impossible to tell a prisoner, "Don't go out for interrogation." He would not obey. The Red Cross couldn't do anything to stop it. So we had to stop it step by step. I crystallized the attack in my mind. I wrote it down and I talked with those who were close to me. What helped me was the greatness of so many who were in Ansar from all organizations.

How could we demoralize the Israelis? By performance. Ansar was a place of performance and waiting to perform.

The "We" Instead of the Individual

As I said, the prisoners at Ansar were hollow. They had no purpose. They had no faith, either in themselves or in what they belonged to. To start building them up, they should feel they were important as human beings. But how could they feel important if their days were aimless. There was no schedule, no program. How could we make our will dominant?

We started with getting up. It was the Israelis' will for us to get up at

16. Article 42 of the Fourth Geneva Convention states in part: "The internment or placing in assigned residence of protected persons may be ordered only if the security of the Detaining Power makes it absolutely necessary."
17. Article 31 of the Fourth Geneva Convention states: "No physical or moral coercion shall be exercised against protected persons, in particular to obtain information from them or from third parties."

six-thirty. OK, we can get up at six. That will be *our* will. So, we got up at six. Exercise. Everybody! Why should the 10–15 minutes inspection in each section every day be a demoralizing experience for the prisoners and not for the Israelis? Keep the tent tidy. It was easy to demoralize the Israeli soldiers. We were no longer shabby, desperate, helpless objects. We were human beings and we were full of life.

And, of course, we stopped putting our hands on our heads during the count. For this I give credit to the commander, because I told him, "Tomorrow, no one is putting his hands on his head. So if you want to oppose them, you better open fire." After the first section refused, he told them to forget it.

We started the slogan, "Ansar is the family reunion in the Israeli fashion." At one point, a father and six sons were in Ansar. The problem was that they were not in the same section.[18] So we got members of a family moved into one section. Some families had not met in ten years except in the prison camp. Of course, every achievement created its own problems. Some sons refused to join their fathers because they learned smoking. The headmaster of a school kept pressuring me to move his son to his section. I was afraid to tell him that his son didn't want to go to the same section with his father. The son told me, "Prison is enough. I don't want a papa in prison."

Once we wanted to go on strike. It was suggested that we sit in the yard for one hour. I told them my opinion: "Sitting in the yard in the sun — we have six people who can't do it. And there are cowards who would not do it. If we sit in the tents, then we are going to have 100 per cent participation. The sick are inside. The cowards are inside. And no one is allowed to move, even to the toilet."

Nothing portrayed the effect like the reaction of the chief of the Red Cross delegation until he realized there was a strike in the tents. He said, "I came to Ansar. I saw nobody and I panicked. What did the Israelis do? Then I thought, it's impossible. They couldn't have gotten rid of ten thousand people."

Even from our tents, we could see, we could feel, we could hear, the hectic engines of the vehicles and the nervousness of the soldiers: "What are those people doing inside?"

We performed through singing. Imagine, in the middle of the night, seven, eight, nine, ten thousand men — the moon is full — we would sing one sad song. And there was so much sadness! That would just shatter the Israelis. Just one song. "That's it. Go back to the tents."

This oneness, the "we" instead of the individual, was something new. Instead of ten prisoners creating problems and becoming burdens for the Israelis, the performance by everybody was dominant and it was the more powerful because it was everybody.

---

18. Article 82 of the Fourth Geneva Convention states in part: "Throughout the duration of their internment, members of the same family, and in particular parents and children, shall be lodged together in the same place of internment, except when separation of a temporary nature is necessitated. . . .''

A Concession: We Were Detainees

Our status in Ansar was ambiguous. We were not dealt with as prisoners of war and we were not dealt with as detainees.[19] In fact, the Israelis used a new term for us — "brought-ins" — a term that was never defined.

The way the Israelis dealt with the prisoners was to select one person in each section to take care of the rations, etc. These were the moukhtars. Being appointed a moukhtar didn't mean that person was bad. Some of them were bad. But others were pushed to accept this position by their colleagues.

Because our status was ill-defined, it was impossible for the prisoners to coalesce under any kind of leadership. It was easy for the Israelis to play individual prisoners and groups of prisoners against each other and maintain control.

The Red Cross told the Israelis that, according to the Geneva Convention, we were detainees. And the Red Cross told them, "If you want to talk to those prisoners, let them choose their committee."[20] If we had been prisoners of war, then the hierarchy of the military would have governed the situation.[21]

The commander of the camp was the first officer to dare to take the key from the attending officer, open the gates, and come right into the section. He said to the moukhtar, "I want to talk to Salah." He called me from my tent and I went out. I said, "Yes, commander, what do you want?" I kept the moukhtar standing with me.

"Instead of us dealing with all those moukhtars, let's deal with one person. Would you accept? You are the highest ranking officer here." I told him, "I thought we were not prisoners of war. Do you want to deal with us as prisoners of war?" He said, "No, no, no, no, no." "OK, then. We are detainees and, according to the Geneva Convention, we have the right to elect

19. The commentary to Article 4 of the Fourth Geneva Convention concludes, p. 51: "Every person in enemy hands must have some status under international law: he is either a prisoner of war and, as such, covered by the Third Convention, a civilian covered by the Fourth Convention, or again, a member of the medical personnel of the armed forces who is covered by the First Convention. *There is no* intermediate status; nobody in enemy hands can be outside the law." (Emphasis in original.)

20. Article 102 of the Fourth Geneva Convention states: "In every place of internment, the internees shall freely elect by secret ballot every six months, the members of a Committee empowered to represent them before the Detaining and the Protecting Powers, the International Committee of the Red Cross and any other organization which may assist them. . . ."

21. The U.S. State Department, *Country Reports on Human Rights Practices for* 1982, Israel and the Occupied Territories, p. 1163, states: "During Israel's invasion and subsequent occupation of southern Lebanon and Beirut in 1982, large numbers of prisoners, including members of armed Palestinian and Lebanese groups and non-combatants, were detained by Israeli forces. . . . Approximately 300 of the prisoners were Syrian military personnel who, after a delay of up to two months in most cases, were accorded treatment due to prisoners of war in accordance with the Third Geneva Convention, including access to them by representatives of the International Committee of the Red Cross. The Israeli government did not accord POW status to any of the other prisoners and did not acknowledge the applicability to them of the Fourth Geneva Convention, relating to civilians in military-occupied areas. Nevertheless, in mid-July the Government agreed to treat the prisoners in accordance with the humanitarian provisions of the Fourth Convention and to allow the International Committee of the Red Cross access to all of them."

our committee. In fact, we have the right to run our business while in camp."[22]

He wanted to tempt me into becoming the representative of the prisoners. It was a bait and I wouldn't bite. I could have raised hell in the prison camp without being a representative of anybody. I told him, "I'm sorry, I will not accept that. Whether you like it or not, we are going to elect our committee." The commander left without answering.

I was not the highest ranking officer and many in the military would have rejected prisoner-of-war status. But if we maintained the status of detainees, then everybody would go for it.

I had the support of the Red Cross, despite clashes between me and Philip who was the head of the delegation. We became very close and I learned a lot from him. He was in utter support of a committee to be elected under the sponsorship of the Red Cross.

The next day the Red Cross sent a delegate to tell me, "I think they will concede." And I said, "They *will* concede. They cannot handle this situation. There is something new that is going on in Ansar and they know things will get worse." To make a long story short, they conceded and the head of the Red Cross delegation told me the good news that at last we could form a committee elected by the prisoners.

A Committee of Prisoners

Forming a committee was a huge step forward. The Israelis had conceded! Most of the prisoners gave their support, but some were hesitant. A committee of prisoners to deal with the Israelis? That would be collaboration; the committee would be in the pocket of the Israelis.

Many wanted to be on the committee but they were afraid to take responsibility. Opportunism was there at its ugliest when it came to certain individuals. They wanted a comrade to be the trial balloon — let that person be doomed, not me. If the committee failed, the members of the committee would get burned, and if it succeeded, they could take over the committee.

Some still thought in terms of organizations and representation. But you could not apply the rules of the external world in a prison camp. You could not say, like parrots, "Our enemies are Zionism, imperialism, and the reactionaries."

Once you stepped inside a prison camp, it was a totally different situation. You were dealing with the enemy every day. You dealt with the officer for food. You dealt with the Israeli doctor for medical care. My enemy was not the fundamentalist nor the Marxist who was next to me in prison, nor the many reactionaries who were with us in prison. My enemy was the barbed wire and the bayonet of the soldier.

22. Article 103 of the Fourth Geneva Convention states: "The Internee Committees shall further the physical, spiritual and intellectual well-being of the internees. . . . In case the internees decide, in particular, to organize a system of mutual assistance amongst themselves, this organization would be within the competence of the Committees in addition to the special duties entrusted to them under other provisions of the present Convention."

Each organization had its infrastructure, and each major organization picked somebody to be on the committee. Four of us were nominated. The names were transmitted to the Red Cross. The Israelis never knew each one's affiliation. They knew me — I was a well-known figure — but not the rest. I was from Fatah. Ahmed Abu Leila was an officer from the Democratic Front. Dr. Nabil, a radiologist, was from the Popular Front. And Nami Jumaa, a Lebanese, was a Shi'a from the Arab Front. He was a lawyer. That was the committee.

They were courageous people and we came to trust each other. It took some time to gain each other's trust. They respected me. They trusted me. I loved them. I trusted them.

Having the right to be accompanied by the head of the Red Cross delegation into other sections made it possible for us to communicate in a better way.[23] We sat with people and talked about our strategy. It didn't take more than a few days to establish the importance of the committee and the attachment of the prisoners to the committee.

Justice was of utter importance. People should be equal in clothing, in blankets, in food, in cigarettes, except because of old age or illness. No one should be given special treatment, no matter whether they were leaders or officers. Unity could never be achieved without justice. Without unity and justice, you could not talk about morale.

To be absolutely honest and authentic, in our meetings with the commander we refused to take more than what we had back in the camp to eat. I told my colleagues, "Don't ever bite on the bait," because corruption starts innocently.

Once we were offered halveh. "I am sorry. We don't have it in the camp."

We were offered a battery lamp. We said, "Sorry, we don't need it as a priority." They said, "But you work late at night." I said, "No. It is needed in the clinic but not for the committee."

They brought us a special tent. We turned it into a library or a meeting place.

The Israelis couldn't play one of us off against another. When any one of us would talk, there was no contradicting each other. We were defending humanity and we did it in a spirited way. When we defeated the commander in conversation, I could see in his eyes that he was very happy, and I thought it was strange.

Ansar was plagued with rumors. And if you listened to the rumors, you would think every other person was a spy or an informer, which was illogical. It could not be true. So we passed a law: if anybody has a complaint about somebody, he should go to a certain committee, bring his proofs, and everybody should have the right to defend himself. Once the case was filed, then the person who filed that case should not go on talking against that person, and he should accept the verdict passed by the committee.

23. Article 104 of the Fourth Geneva Convention states in part: "Members of Internee Committees may appoint from amongst the internees such assistants as they may require. All material facilities shall be granted to them, particularly a certain freedom of movement necessary for the accomplishment of their duties. . . ."

When we did have an informer, we passed another law: "if two-thirds of the prisoner is with the Israelis, let's pull him back by the third that is left." Because the alternative would be to push him, fully, into the Israelis' hands. All those who made mistakes were given the chance to defend themselves and, we promised them, they would be pardoned. Many came to us and talked, and they were pardoned by the leadership.

We also explained to the prisoners the difference between an informer and someone who was pressured to confess. Such a person cannot be dealt with as an informer. Some people had been pressured in front of their sisters or wives. If a woman were repeatedly raped, it was not surprising that her brother confessed or her husband confessed. These were not collaborators and it was a crime to deal with them as collaborators. If we dealt with them as collaborators, we'd make them collaborators.

Mohammed Al Khalili

How could we talk about unity or morale or justice when they took prisoners for interrogation every day? Interrogation was the main factor that kept those values hollow. Number one, we had to stop torture or bad treatment during interrogation. Number two, we had to stop them from taking the prisoners to the hole for interrogation. Number three, we had to stop interrogation.

So we informed the Red Cross that there was to be no bad treatment in interrogation. At our meeting, we and the Red Cross informed the Israelis. But that was not sufficient.

One day they took somebody by the name of Mohammed Al Khalili, an admirable gentleman, for interrogation. Instinctively, I said to one of my assistants, "Get me some cardboard, and charcoal, burnt wood." And I wrote on the cardboard: "Our brother, Abu Mohammed, number so-and-so, was taken out. His meal is waiting for him. So are we." And I pushed it against the gate. And I told the moukhtar, "Put his breakfast there and make sure that his breakfast is larger than ours."

In the past, prisoners thought, "Well, ten were taken out for interrogation, we have ten extra meals." No way! Call the Red Cross. Let them come. Inform them that this person was taken out for interrogation and we want him back.

We decided that when any prisoner was taken out for interrogation, the head of every section and every sub-committee in the sections would take the name of the prisoner, the date, and the hour in which he was taken for interrogation; and when he came back they should sit with him and take a report from him about how he was treated.

Mohammed didn't come back that day. I thought, something else should be done. I asked the prisoners in the sections that were closer to the hole to stand by the wire and start singing so that the prisoner would hear the singing.

At noon his lunch was added. At dinner, his dinner was added. The next day, his breakfast was added. Then lunch was added.

He came back the next day. He looked at the bowl and the food we had put in. He looked at the cardboard and said, "That is my name." We said, "Yes, that is your name." "Those are my meals?" We said, "Yes. Who would eat your meals if you were in solitary?" He said, "You know, yesterday, during the interrogation, I heard you singing. I felt you were singing for me." I said, "Yes, we were singing for you." He said, "I thought so! I became different! The moment I heard the singing, I felt different." "We meant to support you."

The Flag and the Commander

The commander was always testing me and the committee. An incident that made me gain the confidence of the prisoners, as well as the Israelis' respect, was a confrontation between me and the commander.

One day I was sitting in the section. The Red Cross head of delegation was there. Then all of a sudden the moukhtar told me, "The commander wants to talk to you."

I went out of the tent and the commander was outside the gate, surrounded by two or three armored vehicles with the machine guns pointed at us. He told me, "Pull down that flag!"

I looked behind me. A prisoner had raised a Palestinian flag in the section. I said, "No, I will not. I did not raise the flag. Why should I pull it down?" His face turned red and he started being menacing. "Too bad," I told him. "You can open fire but I'm not going to pull it down."

I was not aware that hundreds of prisoners were standing against the barbed wire in every section and watching what was going on. I thought it was only the few who were in the section where I was visiting. I turned around and told them, "It will be a traitor who pulls down that flag."

I turned back to the commander and said, "Go ahead. Open fire. Now!" All of a sudden his face relaxed. He turned back and looked at the Red Cross man. I think at this point the commander realized that when we said something we delivered it. This was a turning point with the commander. We became friends.

One time as we went out for a meeting with the commander, I was surprised that we were led to the stone building that was the commander's quarters instead of to the hut where we usually met. They took us in. It was swarming with officers. We went up high into his quarters and there was the commander lying on a bed, quivering with fever. He was not completely covered. The blankets were on the floor. None of his aides, none of those people in the room, troubled to cover him.

Instinctively, without even thinking of it, I covered him. I told him, "Colonel, I think our problems can wait until you recover. We spent a few months so far and we can take a few days more until you recover." And I said to the soldier in command, "Come on. Let's go."

It was Ahmed who said to me, "Do you realize what you just did?" "What?" He said, "You covered the man. Good for you."

Another time we were walking, the five of us. The commander was walking with us back to the section. He started walking in the opposite direction. It was dark. We could easily have killed him there. In fact, he stumbled and one of the committee supported him so that he would not fall down.

One time he asked me, "Salah, should I renew my period at Ansar or not? I know you are plotting something. Should I renew?" I told him, "Why should I tell you or not?" Then I thought, that man was honest with us. He was an enemy. He belonged to the enemy. But so far he was courageous. He was decent. And he was in trouble because of us. His colleagues had told him he was defeated by prisoners. "No. Don't renew," I told him. He said, "Thank you." And he did not. A week later, Ansar was burned down.

The End of Interrogation

I wanted an incident in which a prisoner was badly treated before we moved to the second phase, to stop taking prisoners to the hole. I waited until a boy was taken out for interrogation and, when he was brought back after a few days, he just dropped.

The sub-committee in the section immediately reported that to us through the wires by urgent messages. I told them, "Call the Israeli doctor. Let him examine him." He came and his report was, "This guy was forced to stand up for three days."[24]

The commander was not in the camp. It was the weekend, the Sabbath. When he came back, they sent a report to him. He came to calm us down, but I knew what I wanted. It was not calming down. I wanted to reach the ultimate objective: stop interrogation.

"That will be the last case [of bad treatment]," he said. I told him, "No. No one is going to the hole for interrogation and that is our decision."

The commander was caught between us — the prisoners — and the intelligence. His role was to keep control because he was with the military police. The bad guys were the intelligence. I did not want a clash between him and the intelligence. I told him, "It's up to you. But next time no one is going out."

In fact, I was hesitant because the prisoners were not yet tested in moving as one person. I was preparing them gradually. I wanted to postpone confrontation until the prisoners were more solid. I didn't want a setback.

One day I was in the hospital tent having a glucose transfusion when Nabil, a member of the committee, was shouting at me from outside the wire. I jumped out of the tent carrying the bag with me and asked him, "What's wrong?" He said, "They are taking twelve of us to the Occupied Territories. I jumped out of the bus saying that I forgot my jacket. I just came to tell you."[25]

24. Article 100 of the Fourth Geneva Convention regarding discipline states in part: "The disciplinary regime in places of internment shall be consistent with humanitarian principles, and shall in no circumstances include regulations imposing on internees any physical exertion dangerous to their health or involving physical or moral victimization. . . . In particular, prolonged standing . . . [is] prohibited."

25. Article 49 of the Fourth Geneva Convention states in part: "Individual or mass forcible transfers . . . of protected persons from occupied territory to the territory of the Occupying Power or to that of any other country, occupied or not, are prohibited, regardless of their motive."

I looked. The bus was still standing there. The officers took Nabil back to the bus. In such a case, I couldn't convene the committee for a meeting and I had only a few seconds to respond. So I started a song, "Unadeekum," ("I call upon you").

Every prisoner knew that when I sang that certain song there was something urgent and they should move without questioning why. Soon the whole of Ansar was singing "Unadeekum" and everybody was on alert. They knew something was wrong.

The commander came all of a sudden and he was shouting at me, begging me, to calm down. He promised to bring them back the next day, because the bus had moved already. I told him, "No way!"

For the first time ever, I gave orders to burn a tent. The prisoners would not do it. They hesitated so I burned it myself. It was a moment of truth — whether we could deliver. Unless I could make good on my word, there would be no possibility of unity or high morale. That was the moment. I was agitated and I burned the tent.

And I told him, "If they don't come back . . . ." and I just dropped. I was so tired and with the smoke — I'm asthmatic — and the transfusion, I dropped. I remember waking up in the back of the hospital tent with the doctor there.

Then the commander came in and the Red Cross head of delegation was there. "Listen," the commander said, "I give you my word of honor. Tomorrow they will be back. And there will be no sending people out for interrogation. This I promise." I told him, "You promised before. It happened." He said, "Give me that chance." I was afraid that solitary would kill one of the twelve who had problems in both kidneys. The commander said, "I promise." "OK. Let them come tomorrow." The next day they brought them back.

A few days after that, they wanted to take a group for interrogation but this time we knew of it. We had a meeting with the commander. He told me, "Listen. Let this be absolutely the last time. As I promised, no harm will happen to them." I told him, "I don't think that will work. Let me think about it."

We went back and examined things. Then I told what our decision was: I would go to solitary with them. That was the one time when I went to solitary in solidarity with the rest of them. "Why should you?" the commander asked. "Why shouldn't I? You said there will be no harm. I want to make sure there will be no harm. I want to be one of them." I went with them. We spent a week in solitary and we were brought back.

A colleague of mine on the committee told me later that one of the guys who went to solitary that time was a big shot in his faction, and this guy was provided with over fifty sleeping tablets. So he could sleep the time off while I was agonized for the whole week.

After that, messages were passed to every prisoner in every section, "No prisoner should go out for interrogation. If a prisoner refuses to go out for interrogation, the section is *obliged* to protect him. And the neighboring sections are obliged to protect that section, and the whole compound is obliged to protect those sections. In brief, confronting one prisoner should bring about a confrontation with every one in Ansar. It's as simple as that. If the Israelis say that this person will be released — don't go for that. The Red Cross should take the prisoner out, *not* the Israelis." That was the end of interrogation.

Our Objective

Our Objective Number One is to survive as a people, united, maintaining our identity. The objective set by the enemy is to end our identity.

Independence is in the back of my mind — it is not an immediate objective. It is a mistake to respond to the question, "Do you recognize Israel's right to exist?" The right to exist is a human right. No establishment can determine a human right. If you answer the question, "No," you are regarded as anti-Semitic. If you answer the question, "Yes," you are losing your rights. I want democracy all over Palestine and I want to co-exist with Jews.

We speak of unity as if it were only political unity — unity amongst factions. There is a more essential unity, a unity that is more relevant to our being. Unity is spontaneous among our people who are on their land. We need to maintain that unity between our people in exile or diaspora and the people back home. Awareness of unity starts with education, discovering our collective memory, and creating memories that become part of the collective memory.

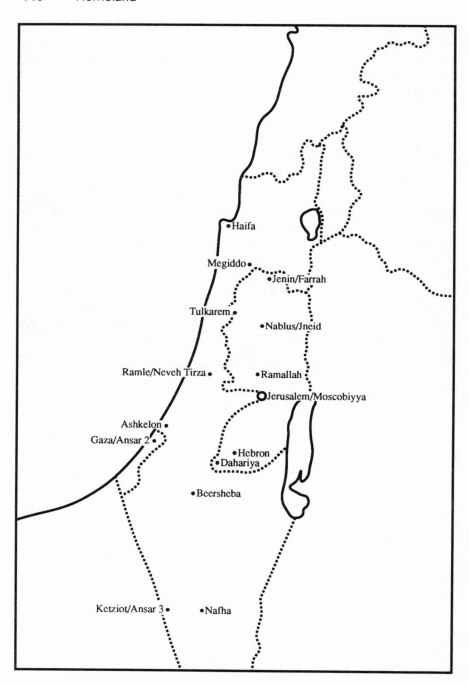

6

Prisoners

Within the Occupied Territories, Palestinians suspected of security offenses are normally tried in Israeli military courts with a military judge presiding. Israeli settlers in the Occupied Territories accused of security offenses are tried in Israeli district courts presided over by civilian judges under Israeli law rather than military occupation law.[1] "Israeli settlers involved in security violations have been treated far more leniently than Palestinians guilty of similar offenses."[2]

> In October 1987, a special judicial commission, headed by former Supreme Court President Moshe Landau, issued a report which found that since 1971 the General Security Service (the Israeli internal security agency or Shin Bet) had routinely used physical and psychological mistreatment to obtain confessions, which were often the only evidence against persons accused of security offenses. . . . The Landau Commission report stated that by 1974 it had become "well-rooted practice and the accepted norm" for Shin Bet interrogators to lie to the courts about their interrogation methods and that by the early 1980's Shin Bet interrogators "had been given written instructions" on how to lie to the courts when accused persons tried to retract their forced confessions. As a result of Shin Bet assurances, which the Landau Commission found to be systematic perjury over the last 17 years, the courts had refused to accept these retractions. . . . [T]hey routinely perjured themselves by denying in court that such mistreatment had occurred.[3]

The Landau Commission approved the use of "moderate physical and psychological pressure" to secure confessions and to obtain information concerning terrorism.

★   ★   ★

1. U.S. State Department, *Country Reports on Human Rights Practices for 1991*, pp. 1444–45.
2. Ibid., p. 1452.
3. U.S. State Department, *Country Reports on Human Rights Practices for 1987*, pp. 1181–82, 1191.

Lawahez Burgal

"From that suffering, I promised myself that I am going to continue."

In 1975, when I was fifteen and a half years old, I entered prison. One day, about thirty-five Israeli soldiers came to our house. They surrounded the house. They asked, "Is Lawahez here?" My mother was shocked! She accepted the fact that they might come for a man but not for her daughter.

They entered the house. They started kicking the children. They started searching every single thing in a way that suggested something big was going to happen and to say to my mother, "Your daughter, she is criminal, she is dangerous." Also, to show the neighbors: take care, look what we are doing to this woman and these neighbors; if you want to do something, look what we are doing to this house. They wanted the people to hear what was going on. So they came shouting, breaking, and with guns.

It was winter, December, and very cold here in Jerusalem. I asked my mother, "Where are my socks, Mama?" She couldn't speak. She was sitting on the bed and looking at me and the soldiers. "Where are my socks?" She didn't say anything. I knew that my mother was in shock. She didn't want her daughter to go to prison because of what she thought was going to happen inside the prison.

They took my father with me. One reason was because I was young. And, the second thing, they gave my father an order not to work any more in any Israeli hotel. Also they confiscated some land from us. They gave my father these orders before I admitted anything, before trial!

Interrogation

After that, I went for interrogation to the Moscobiyya Central Prison. All the security people that interrogated me were men. They are supposed to have a woman in the room at all times. But if they want to beat you or to torture you, then the woman will go out and the men will continue interrogating you. If they just want to ask a question, the woman will remain and she will sit and listen.

It wasn't easy in prison at that time. We didn't have an organization among the prisoners with an educational program that told prisoners what to expect in prison and how to handle it. They didn't tell us that you do not have to confess. They didn't tell us about how the security men are going to deal with you.

For example, it was a shock for me to hear the security men talking in Arabic better than I could myself! They knew about the arts. They knew Islamic history, poetry, exams, everything! They knew every detail about Arab society. You were sitting in the room with eight security men surrounding you and you felt as if you were in an Arabic university or mosque. You could not believe that these men were Jewish, and that they were interrogating you.

So I knew that I was in a place where they knew everything about the

Arabs. And that meant they knew everything about me as a person, as an Arab, as a Palestinian, and the ball was in their hands. I could understand this from their speech. We had to share our language now.

When I entered, they called me by my secret name, my political name. They knew my secret name. That didn't mean that they knew everything, but they wanted you to think it meant that they knew everything.

During the first half hour, I started to hear someone shouting. He was crying in Arabic, "Please! Help me! I'm going to die." One of the security men entered the room and said, in Arabic, "They are torturing her father. He is bleeding. She's not going to admit anything. We are going to kill him." Another security man said, "Don't speak in Arabic. She understands."

I was thinking to myself, "Is that my father who is shouting?" I had never heard my father shout. It was now maybe two o'clock at night, and eight men were surrounding me. I started to think, "If my father is going to die, who's going to feed my family?" We are a big family. My father had thirteen children at that time. "Will society say about me that my father died because of me?"

But something inside me told me, "He is not your father. Don't believe it!" This is not a normal feeling. You can't say that I was educated to think in this way, yet something let me feel that he was not my father. And, of course, he wasn't my father. But I want to tell you that I was very glad — two weeks later — to look into his eyes.

To this day I am still suffering from the interrogation and torturing process in 1975. I was seven days without sleep, four days without food. I was tied for periods of time with my hands behind my back and my weight on my hands. I was beaten on the head, and in my stomach. They held my head by my hair and swung it in a circle as if stirring a bowl for a quarter of an hour, a half an hour. They kicked me in my stomach and my back, and they were men, huge men sometimes.

The thing that really disgusted me was that the security men who interrogated Palestinian women threatened to rape them. And they didn't just threaten. Two Palestinian girls who were raped during interrogation in Moscobiyya Central are in Jordan now. To tell a Palestinian woman, "We are going to rape you," means the end of her life, because we are educated that the honor of a woman is her virginity. This is the honor of the family. This is the honor of the brothers, the father, the husband also. The security men know this about our society. They think that if they threaten a Palestinian woman with rape, she's going to admit something.

Three times they brought black men to me. Imagine, not white men but black men. It was a racist thing to say to me, "It's not a white man who is going to rape you. A black man is going to rape you." They told me about this black man, who was standing right there, "He is not going to touch you with his body because you are a cockroach. He's going to rape you with a stick." This is something scary. But at the same time I saw somehow, maybe in their eyes, that it was not going to happen.

Each of the security men who did interrogation had a secret Arabic name. This was so that if, in the trial, you told the judge, "There was a security man and he tortured me," or he did this or that to me, the judge would say, "What is the name of this security man? Can you tell us?" You would tell him, "Abu Abed." Then they would tell you, "We don't have anyone by this name." We don't know the real names of the security men.

Abu Hanni was an elderly white-haired man with blue eyes. It was raining and icy outside and he wore an open shirt and you could see the hair on his chest. He was sitting on a table. He was maybe sixty-five years old and I thought perhaps he was going to play a grandfather role. But he said to me, "Stand up, beside the table." I stood up. He said, "I want everything in five minutes!" He didn't look into my face. He was looking at the table. "I want everything in details. My name is Abu Hanni. I killed Im Hawaja" — this was one of the persons killed when he was a prisoner under interrogation — "and I did" this and that, in Ashkelon, in Hebron, in Ramallah, in Jenin. He wanted to show me that he was very dangerous. "I want you to speak. And I have no time for small talk."

So I said, "Please, Abu Hanni, really I am very tired, and I don't have anything to tell you." I didn't have time to finish my sentence. He told me, "Take your clothes off." I thought that maybe he was going to rape me. I took off my shirt in a way intended to show that I was not scared. And I started to take my trousers off. He said, "No, stop." He wasn't looking at me, only looking at the table, but he could see what I was doing.

I began to think, "What is he going to do to me if he is not going to rape me? Why undress just the top and not further down?"

I knew nothing about sexual life. Maybe he was going to rape me in some way. I didn't know. At that time I thought that if a man kissed a woman she was going to be pregnant. That was our education. At fifteen years old, we knew nothing. One didn't ask what went on between men and women.

Abu Hanni said, "OK, put your hands under your leg," and I did. Suddenly he took a stick from the table. I can't describe how long it was. I don't know. It was over in seconds. He took this stick with a nail in the end of it and he struck me on my breast. I lost consciousness.

I opened my eyes. I saw a doctor. He was making some stitches. And he was treating me as if I were a criminal. He wanted to show me, "You are disgusting." When I started to see the blood, it was shocking to me. I became hysterical. It was painful. It was a sensitive area. There were three open gashes.

Then they had someone who interrogated me and told me, "If you don't want to speak, we are going to do the same thing on the other side." I was bandaged and he was pressing his hand on the bandage, making it bleed again.

They want to show you that you are alone, and that you are in the hands of the security men to kill you or to save you. No one is going to save you from outside. No lawyer. No Red Cross is going to enter. There is no visit from your family. You are in that place and you don't have contact with the part of your life which is outside. You don't know day from night. You don't know the time. You know nothing when you are in isolation. You don't have good food. You aren't allowed to sleep, because interrogation continues day and night. You are tired. You want to sleep. You want to think. And, of course, they are beating you. And now I had a wound in my breast.

They put me in a small room and made me sit on a chair for hours, while they tapped on my head with a pencil. After that, they put my head under a lamp. It felt as if something was going "bang, bang, bang," pulsing in my head. I started to think I was crazy. This was hurting more than the wound in my breast. It was maybe two days I was in this situation. I couldn't hear anyone talking. I didn't want to move my leg because if I moved I felt it in my head. I can't explain.

They wanted you to hear the other prisoners crying and shouting. One time they brought a man and they began torturing him. I didn't know him and he didn't know me. But they brought him and they said, "Look what we are doing for the Arabs." And they started beating him in his face. He was bleeding. It is difficult to see someone who is being tortured and you are looking, just looking. This affects something inside you, psychologically. At that moment I was ready to do anything! I prepared within myself for them to torture me and not to torture that man.

If one of the security men was huge, solid, and had an ugly face, he would beat you. After that they would bring you a nice handsome man, young, with blue eyes. He would come, and salute as he should, then say, "Oh, my God. What happened to you! What did they do to you? I don't believe it. This is happening here? Who is on your case? Please, don't cry. Give me the name. I'm going to make a report. It's forbidden to torture you. It's forbidden to beat you. Don't let them come again to you because they are criminals." He was trying to get you to tell him about everything. If you said, "No," the other man would enter and the man that was talking in a nice way, suddenly would change and be an animal. "OK, you don't want to speak? Let them beat you! Let them kill you!" This is a psychological technique that they used.

They used another method that wasn't easy for me. They would say, "OK, we'll bring a prostitute for you." They would bring a Jewish woman into interrogation who would say ugly words, dirty words — you are like this, and you are like that. To sit with this girl also meant that you were dirty.

Mother

All this happened in maybe ten days. I didn't see my mother for eighteen days. After eighteen days, they have to take you to court to get you another fifteen or eighteen days. There is a street between Moscobiyya Central and the court.

The soldiers surrounded me. I was bleeding from my breast. I heard the voice of a woman. I started saying to myself, "I know this voice. From where does this voice come?" I was looking and suddenly I saw my mother. She was running. I'm not going to forget this all my life. She was coming and she said, "Is she my daughter? I don't believe it. I know Lawahez." I looked into her eyes. I told her with my eyes, "I'm Lawahez!" She was expecting me to be beautiful but instead I was ugly, dirty, smelling bad, and also bleeding. She looked at me and she said, "What did they do to you?"

"Please," she said to them. "Please. Let me touch her." A soldier came up and pushed her, "Go! Don't touch her." She started kissing the ground. She said, "Please, God, help her." She was always praying to God. And she said, "I'm not going to pray to you any more, God, if you leave her in this situation." It was ninety degrees and she was kissing the ground and looking at me. She was saying, "Just let me touch her, to feel that she is my daughter." I'm not going to forget this thing, because it affected my mother to see her daughter suffer.

After that, I admitted in interrogation that I was a member of a certain political organization, and they took me to prison to wait for my trial.

Prison

The prison was called Neveh Tirza Prison for Women. It is in Ramle.

The trial was in a military trial court. At the trial, I showed the judge my breast. After he saw me, the lawyer said, "We want an Arabic doctor to check what is going on with her." So the judge gave an order to the doctor inside the prison to check me. Of course, the prison doctor was working for the security men. The doctor came and he said, "No, the torture was done outside prison." There was no proof at the trial to show that there was torturing. Even this experience was difficult for me. They sentenced me to four years.

Inside Neveh Tirza Prison there are two buildings, one for the Jewish Israelis, and one for the Palestinians. They treated us as criminals and not as political prisoners. At that time, delegations would come to see Neveh Tirza Prison because the authorities wanted to show the world that it was a nice building and there were beds in the rooms. But the treatment inside the prison was the same as in any other prison.

Every room had six beds. The room was small, like the room of my two children. Six persons lived in that room.

If the prisoner wants to go outside the prison under the sun, she has to work in the fields, digging and picking stones, and after that, she has to bring stones to the same place. You don't feel that you are making something. It is just to keep you busy and to make you feel that you are going to die from doing this job, because it is very hot there in Ramle. It's to break your psychology.

The food was not enough. I was even taking bread from other prisoners who shared their breakfast, because there was not enough bread to eat in the morning.

The only treatment for disease was akomod. It's like aspirin. If you had ulcer, cancer, or headache, anything, the only treatment for you was akomod.

The aim of the Israelis is to break prisoners. They try to force you to forget *anything* about the society and about the reason that you are inside there. But I started to learn about myself in prison. I came to know more about the world when I was in prison.

The first four months, maybe, I was thinking about what had happened to me under interrogation. If I suddenly saw something red, there went through my mind about the blood when I was bleeding from my mouth, from my stomach, and from my breast.

I was psychologically and spiritually weak. I would see something red, and I would start shouting, "I want Hitler now. Hitler must come and kill you! I'm going to kill you."

My comrades in the cell started saying, "You must not say that. Hitler was a criminal. Hitler killed Jews, Arabs, and others who were innocent." One said, "Don't say 'the Jewish.' Say 'soldiers.' The Jewish are people and there are good and bad Jews."

This was the first time in my life that I started thinking like that. Look, the comrades that told me these things were sentenced to life sentences, and they had been tortured more than me. R. was raped and she was teaching me what it meant to be a human being. After that I was ashamed.

The Jewish women were in Building A and we lived in Building B, but it was close. We could see each other in the break, for example, in the work, in the kitchen. I was working in the kitchen and the kitchen was in the Jewish building. Day by day, in the afternoons, I started to sit with Jewish prisoners. I would speak with one about her life. Soon I started to hear why she was there, why she stole. It was because she was in a bad situation, because she was poor, or because of discrimination between the Jewish from the West and from the East or from Arab countries.

The kitchen work was always given to Arabs. We were cooking just for prisoners, not for the policewomen or officers. We were punished many times for this because they wanted us also to cook for the policewomen. But we refused. We were Arabic cooks just for the prisoners.

I finished my high school proficiency test inside prison. Believe me, we were all the time educating ourselves. Any book we had was brought in as a present. But if we made a strike or anything, they would take the books. And we had to wait another six months or one year to ask for books again.

Also in prison, I learned Hebrew, French, and English. For a time we had a girl from Holland. She was helping us to learn Dutch. She was charged as a spy for the PLO. French girls taught us French. One from within the Green Line, from the University, knew Hebrew and she taught us Hebrew.

We were always thinking. Some girls were writing. Sometimes we would discuss an article. They always were feeding our minds. They educated me about the Palestinian problem, and about poor countries that are helpless and under occupation.

I started to feel like a human being. Inside prison I started also to feel the real relationship between one human being and another. You can't find this relationship outside, just in prison. Inside prison, you do not think about yourself as a separate person. We are not fighting for ourselves. This is about Palestinian women and about Palestinian men.

Inside prison, they didn't break us. After a while, I started to get used to seeing red colors. I forgot that this interrogation was going to leave me with hatred against Jews. I was ready to sit with Jews. I was ready to like them. I was ready to love them. I started to know the wisdom place in my personality and then I could give.

From that suffering, I promised myself that I am going to continue. This is the real life. Even if you are not in prison and you are not a member of an organization, you are living under occupation, so you can't live as a free person. You have to do something to make changes. This is the only thing to do, to think like this. That is what I learned from prison, from the suffering.

When I was released after four years, I had asthma. I had an ulcer. I had rheumatism. I had a weak hand. This was not from the interrogation. This happened in the prison itself. I remember the invasion of Lebanon. They wanted to show that what was going on was between Muslims and Christians. So they said they had to separate the Christians from the Muslims and the Arab Jews. At that time, a Dutch girl was living in the room with me and we refused to be separated. We were political and we were happy that she's Christian and I am Muslim. They brought soldiers and they started beating us. One soldier beat me on my hand and something happened to this [right] hand. Sometimes I can't hold my son in this hand because he is heavy and I feel that he is going to fall.

Changes in the Family

So, now came the big experience, to leave prison and to see what's going on. Four years is a long time. You don't know anything and you have new thinking now, a new feeling also. I had been fifteen. Now I was twenty.

The first thing, really, that forced me to continue in my life was our society, the people that came to my house, people I knew and people I didn't know and had never met in my life: men, women, students from school, coming to see the stupid you, or bringing gifts to be sure you know that you are something.

Also, during my life inside the prison, I started to see changes in the personalities of my mother, my brothers, my father. As I said, during my first two months in Moscobiyya, my mother was scared and praying to God! After that she began to go to demonstrations. She went to the Red Cross. "Should we make a strike?" "I was in the mosque. I heard a woman come and shout." "Outside of the prison, I was shouting with the policewoman." All families were saying that they had someone inside prison. So she was thinking now about prisoners. I started to see that my mother was also living in a new life. Everything changed in my house.

For example, I started smoking cigarettes in prison. When my father came to visit me, I never smoked, because you have to respect the father. But when my mother came I smoked. One day, my father came to see me in prison and he handed me a pack of cigarettes. "Here," he said, "Take all you want to smoke." He was a simple man, a very nice man, this father. I said, "You know?" He said, "I know that you are smoking." It was not easy for him. He never smoked in his life and he never let one of my brothers smoke. So to tell me to take cigarettes from his hand, this was something! A big change! After that, I started to decide everything. I shared with my father, taking a position.

The hope of my mother was that, when I was released from prison, they would get me married. She would tell the society that her daughter can marry, they didn't touch her inside the prison. She wanted to show this to the whole world and especially to our big family, the Jaberi family. And she wanted me to marry a doctor or an engineer or something like that. This was her thinking. But later, she confessed, she realized that Lawahez was going to marry the one that she was going to choose. And she knew that I was going to marry one that was in prison. Why? Because he was going to think the way that I was thinking.

Arrest as a Mother

I was arrested again when I had two children. This was a new experience for me because it was inside the Green Line. Now I was being arrested as a mother. I was feeding my son, Ahmed, from my breast at that time. My daughter, Yara, saw the soldiers coming. She knew that the soldiers were going to take her mother or her father or her uncle or someone. So she started crying and shouting, "Mama, they are going to take you. They are going to kill you." I told her, "No, I am going to bring you a gift. Don't cry." The soldiers were surrounding us. She cried, "I know they are going to torture you."

When she was crying, my son woke up. He needed feeding from my breast. So I asked two men, "Can I feed him?" One said, "No." So I told him, "This is the last thing that I have to give to my son. This is a human being. He's a baby. Let me feed him." You know the noise a baby makes, uhhhhhh, he was making noise like that. He wanted my breast. He was not taking the bottle.

So they took me. I was ready to kill that soldier! "This is a human being! How can you stop me from feeding this kid?" From that morning until I finished interrogation, I didn't forget that picture. I was just hearing my son's voice and he wanted me.

The interrogation was in Haifa. The first seven days it was without food, without sleeping. You can't keep yourself awake all the time. They were asking me questions and I was nodding. The policeman there used to bring water and to throw it in my face to make me wake up again.

There was milk in my breast and it became very hard, like stone, and I had fever also from that. I needed water to make a compress. Sometimes the guard would come up and snip with his finger on my breast, pop, pop.

They told me that they were going to bring Yara into the jail. I heard a girl shouting, "Mama, mama." It was a real human being, but I didn't know whether it was a recording, and they wanted to tell me that this was Yara. So I told them, "If it was Yara, she cries. Because this is the end. If you want to kill me, kill me. I am not going to say one thing, because I am not going to forget what you did to my son."

They were talking to me for hours, trying to get me to forget this thing. They knew that I was ready to die and I was not going to speak or spell my name.

After seven days they brought my husband, Mohammed, to see me. He couldn't believe that I was his wife. I couldn't walk and I could hardly speak. My whole system was changing.

I went to court in Haifa. My mother expected to see me walking from the police car. But when she saw them holding me in their hands, she was shocked. She was shouting, "You are killing her." And she started telling me, "Your son is talking. He's eating." I was crying because I couldn't ask her about my son.

Back to Moscobiyya

After ten days in Haifa, they brought me back to Moscobiyya in Jerusalem again, and I met the old security men who had interrogated me in 1975. They brought me before this captain called Abu Nihad. He's very famous. He started saying, "Please forgive me for what I did to you in 1975. Don't forget that I am a human being. I have daughters your age." Imagine! I saw tears in his eyes. He wanted to convince me that he was feeling guilty and he was always dreaming about what he was doing during interrogation. So I looked at his face as if to say, "So, if you are feeling guilty, why you are here?" He told me, "Please, Lawahez, let me help you. Because I tortured you in 1975, I won't let them put you in the chair." It was like he was telling me, "I'm your uncle." I thought, "No uncle of mine."

I said, "Ask me, what is my name?" He was shocked. I said, "No, I mean, just ask me, what is my name?" So he said, "What is your name?" I told him, "I don't know. I know that you are vain, and you are not going to trick me with these tears."

He started to shout and make a big noise: "You . . ., you are dirty!"

I was bound in many positions. This is what we call "shabeh." First of all they put a sack on your face which is dirty with shit from the toilet. You can't breathe from that, and you can't see anything. Shabeh has many positions. In one of the positions, you sit in a chair with one arm over the back of the chair tied behind your back, the other arm tied under the chair, and your feet tied behind another leg of the chair. Your hands are tied to one leg of the chair and your feet are tied diagonally across to the opposite leg of the chair, so that you are off balance. Hours! That means all your muscles here are affected. You get to the point where you want to die. Try it for ten minutes and imagine it for hours and days, this position.

In another position, there is a pipe on the wall. They will tie your hands to the wall in a way that you are not standing and not sitting, but squatting with your knees bent, your back thrown forward, and your hands high up behind, also for hours and days.

There is another position that was used on me also. They brought two towels and water. They put you squatting down and with your hands tied to the chair. If you are tired, and you fall to one side, you fall in the water. But your hands stay in the same place; they stretch but you fall. And if you want to lean back, there is a pipe that would strike your back.

You are sitting like that and suddenly a policeman comes and goes [wham] on your head or on your back. If you were a woman the guard would call you a bitch or something like that.

I was not conscious all the time, so they made little cuts in the sack to let me breathe.

They put me in an isolation cell in Moscobiyya. It was like a grave. It was a small room without windows, without light.[4] I sat beside the door. I was scared to enter inside. Maybe there was a big hole or a big pond that I might fall into. And I heard something walking, like mice, inside the cell.

For the first time I felt I knew the meaning of death. I felt that everything was going to stop. I couldn't breathe. I couldn't talk. I couldn't do anything. Even if I wanted to admit something, I couldn't tell them any information. I couldn't write. I was a dead person.

They brought my husband, Mohammed, to me. He was also under arrest at that time. Mohammed just looked into my eyes as if he was saying, "They are going to release us. You are going to see your children, so tell me that you are going to close your mouth."

One night I tried to shout to the surrounding prisoners, "I have two kids, Yara and Ahmed. They are killing me. If they say that I committed suicide, it is not true." Mohammed believed at that moment that I was dying, and the other prisoners were shouting, "What's going on? What are they doing to you?" It took a long time because I had difficulty speaking. At the end I said, "Say hello to Yara and Ahmed, my kids."

They brought a nurse to take my blood pressure. It was so low that they started to worry that I was going to die. Then a military doctor took my pressure and they brought me medicine. The doctor said to take me to the hospital but they didn't. I couldn't give them any information, and they saw that there was no point in keeping me, so they released me.

When I came home to my family, Yara didn't come to kiss or hug me. She came running and she lifted my shirt and started looking to see whether there were signs of torture on my back. Because, after my mother saw me in Haifa she said, "This is the end of her life." And Yara was listening.

For one week, my son didn't call me "Mama." I had left him alone and stopped feeding him and I went away. He didn't want to come to me because of that. He would say, "Mama" to his grandmother, my mother. This hurt me a lot, because I wanted to show him, "I'm your Mama." But after that, he started to understand. Now, he is very close to me. He doesn't like me to go anywhere without him. He is afraid, maybe, I will go and I will not come back.

[Continued below, Section 10, p. 296.]

---

4. Article 118 of the Fourth Geneva Convention states in part: "Imprisonment in premises without daylight and, in general, all forms of cruelty without exception are forbidden."

Hunger Strikers
I. Walid

"Our slogan was,
'Yes to hunger [strike], no to concessions'."

I was arrested in 1975. After six months, I was sentenced by a military court to seven years. The charge against me was being a member of a political organization.

I was taken at midnight to the central command post in Nablus. Eight of us were arrested at the same time.

At the post, we were faced with various types of interrogation. The first stage was physical harm: blows of the hand and with billy clubs, lit cigarettes burning the flesh where it does most harm. I was forced to sit on a piece of leather with nails sticking up.

We were put in dark cells with pools of water on the floor for one month. Then I was taken to a place near Haifa, and put into a room that is supposed to affect a person psychologically. After that I was taken back to the Nablus command post and from there to the Nablus prison.

In prison, the mattress was a piece of material about two centimeters thick. We spent twenty-two out of twenty-four hours inside the cell. We had one hour in the morning, and one hour in the afternoon, in the yard.

Conditions were better than at the beginning of the occupation. Nevertheless, cells made for five to ten prisoners held thirty to forty, waiting for transportation to Ashkelon by truck. The jailmaster's first question was, "What is your name?" If you answered, for example, "Mahmoud," you would be beaten with electric cords until you said "sir" or "master" before each sentence.

We were given five blankets (I used two under me, two over me, and one as a pillow), one shirt, one pair of pants, one plate, one glass, and a spoon. The day started with the count at 6:00 a.m. For inspection, we had to place the cup on the plate and the spoon in the cup; your shirt had to be buttoned to the top, your socks pulled up, and your blankets folded. You sat on your mattress.

From 6:00 a.m. until 6:00 p.m. we were not allowed to speak to any other prisoner except at lunch for an hour. During our breaks in the yard, we had to walk single file in a military manner, keeping our hands behind our backs, and remaining silent without turning our heads.

Any officer could take any prisoner at any time, strip him naked in front of other prisoners and whip him. Any cell could be emptied for collective punishment at any time. They used American-made fiberglass night clubs. One at a time, prisoners were made to go naked between two rows of jailers. The punishment was the same for not folding your blanket properly or for spitting at the jail master.

The food was terrible, lacking much of what the body requires. I asked for lentils but was told that this kind of bean causes kidney stones. For breakfast, we had one raw egg for two people, two olives per person, one half teaspoon of jelly, ten grams of butter, and one round loaf of bread for four prisoners. We had soup like mop water for lunch, with freshly-killed fish, not cleaned, but put through a grinder with water and then cooked, and fifty grams of raw rice. For dinner, we had one half teaspoon of yogurt, one half egg, and one half dish of bean soup made from beans that had been returned as not saleable.

There had been a strike at Ashkelon in the early 1970s. A prisoner was martyred. He was injured in a military confrontation before he arrived at Ashkelon. The prisoners excused him from the strike. He chose to participate and he died as a result. Collective gains were won through this struggle.

In the mid-1970s there was a long hunger strike at Ashkelon. The prisoners struck, took several days off, and then struck again. They accepted only water and salt.

They forced milk into strugglers through the nose. It caused many illnesses, one being ulcers. Tubes were inserted from the mouth into the stomach and were moved up and down, cutting the walls of the stomach.

As a result of the Ashkelon struggle, my two centimeter mattress was replaced with a five centimeter sponge mattress. This was in my eighth month in prison.

Then I was moved to Sabea jail. There our chief demands were better food and more healthy conditions. There were many cases of hemorrhoids not addressed by the prison administration. The soup was "improved" by adding an ingredient used to feed cows.

In Sabea, the policy was that prisoners must work. Moshe Dayan said that for each Israeli killed, a prisoner would make toys for the rest of society. After Dayan said that, the prisoners at Sabea refused to work. I was one of the first. Prisoners in Nablus and Ashkelon also refused to work. By 1980 the prisoners in all jails took the same position.

The authorities created a committee of five, headed by a general, to study how to control prisoners. They believed a very small minority were organizing behind the scenes and the authorities tried to find out who they were.

Nafha jail in the Negev was opened for "hotheads" from all jails. Ninety such "hotheads" were taken to Nafha from Sabea. There was not enough space in Nafha for all the "hotheads," so some were put in a jail in another city.

The authorities at Sabea responded to prisoners' activity with a policy of no visits, no use of the bathroom, no use of the yard. This lasted for seven months.

The prisoners organized for their rights. Our slogan was, "Yes to hunger [strike], no to concessions."

At Nafha there was a thirty-day hunger strike. After two weeks, several "hotheads" were taken from Nafha to Ramle and force-fed. All but three submitted. Three refused. They were badly beaten. The prisoners added three days to the strike because of this.

The three who refused had milk forced into their bodies. The tubes were mistakenly put into their lungs rather than their stomachs. Two died instantaneously.[5] The lawyer, Felicia Langer, saw the third man while he was still alive. She insisted that the authorities open his back and drain the milk from his lungs. He lived for two more months in jail, then died.

The strike ended when the authorities agreed to meet the most basic need of all prisoners: a bed. Israeli civilian prisoners received all the same things and more without asking for them.

One accomplishment of our strikes was to end the count. The practice of counting began in the late 1960s. As a result of the strikes you no longer had to be counted.

In 1982, the last portion of the Sabea jail was added. I remained there. Sabea jail rooms held eighty to ninety people. After the "hotheads" were removed, the remaining prisoners including myself were put in two-person cells the size of a bathroom.

When we sang, we were told to stop. As punishment they would take us to the yard and squirt gas in our faces. The gas was made for outdoor use but it was also used for punishment inside the cells.

In 1984, a former Jordanian hospital in Nablus was converted into the Jneid prison. The Israeli press described it as a "five-star hotel." The highest level of oppression of prisoners took place there. I was there during my second imprisonment.

I lost my teeth at Jneid. I was due to be released and the other strugglers asked me to swallow a message contained in a capsule, which I would pass with my stool once I was free. Six guards entered the cell before I had time to put the capsule in my mouth. I put it in my mouth anyway. They knocked out my top front teeth.

I was in prison for a total of thirteen years.

Hunger Strikers
II. Badran Bader Jaber

"Why do you confiscate any book speaking about the strugglers for freedom all around the world? This is our spiritual food."

I am Badran Jaber from Hebron. I completed my studies in 1970 at the University of Jordan. Since then, when I was not in prison, I have worked as a teacher and a journalist.

---

5. The U.S. State Department, *Country Reports on Human Rights Practices* [1980], p. 1003, states: "Overcrowded prison conditions continue to be a problem. At the Nafha prison, a newly opened maximum security facility for West Bank detainees, two Arab prisoners who took part in a mass hunger strike protesting the conditions of incarceration died in July. The Israeli Ministry of Interior appointed a special committee to investigate the circumstances surrounding the deaths of the two prisoners. The committee stated that one prisoner, Muhammed Hulwa, died from 'aspiration pneumonia,' due to aspiration of acid and food from the stomach to the lungs. It found a reasonable possibility that this was due to his objection to being force-fed and to the misinsertion of the tube used for force-feeding. The committee recommended some changes in prison conditions and certain improvements in prison regulations concerning hunger strikes and their definition. Israeli authorities allowed newsmen and photographers to visit the prison during the hunger strike, which ended in late August."

I have been arrested many times beginning in 1971. Altogether I have spent about ten years in prison.

In 1985, I was accused of working as a member of a political organization and I spent about two years in prison. They said someone told them that I had a leaflet by a political organization and that I gave it to a man in 1980. And they arrested me in 1985![6]

All the detainees, all the prisoners, used the hunger strike as a last resort when they reached a breaking point. Hunger strikes were to defend yourself, to defend your rights as a human being.[7] If anyone asked me now to go on hunger strike even for one day, I would feel afraid of the pain, even in the free atmosphere outside prison.

I was involved in more than twenty hunger strikes in the jails. One of them was the hunger strike in the Jneid jail of March and April 1987.

Jneid

Jneid jail was opened in 1984. They transferred to Jneid prisoners from Beersheba jail, from Ashkelon jail, from Nablus 1 jail, from Hebron jail.

At Jneid, the Israelis tried to treat the detainees or the prisoners as they had treated them in the first days of occupation after 1967. But many of the detainees had the experience and the determination and the personal power to organize themselves.

There was an initial hunger strike in September 1984.[8] The prisoners negotiated with the director of prisons and the minister of police not only about the Jneid jail but about all the jails and about the Israeli policy toward prisoners. When one of them asked who could speak for the prisoners, they told him, "You must meet with our whole committee." So he was forced to ask for the representatives and at that time seven persons appeared and said, "We are the representatives of Palestinian detainees in the Occupied Territories." He promised to solve many of the problems they presented.

In May 1985, there came the big exchange of prisoners between the Israelis

---

6. The U.S. State Department, *Country Reports on Human Rights Practices for 1982*, p. 1159, states: "Membership in, contact with, or expressed support for the aims of proscribed organizations (e.g., the Palestine Liberation Organization or its constituent elements) is grounds for arrest." And, pp. 1158–59: "Educational materials, periodicals, and books originating outside Israel are censored for alleged anti-Jewish or anti-Israeli content and for perceived encouragement of Palestinian nationalism. The occupation authorities maintain a list of forbidden publications. . . . Possession of such publications, many of which are legal in Israel and East Jerusalem, by a West Bank or Gaza Arab is a criminal offense, frequently resulting in fine or imprisonment; however, according to Israeli press reports, the list of forbidden publications is not made available to the public."

7. The U.S. State Department, *Country Reports on Human Rights Practices for 1985*, p. 1269, states: "Palestinian prisoners at a number of West Bank and Israeli prisons conducted hunger strikes through the year protesting conditions. The head of occupied territories prisons said inmates at Jenin prison spend 23 hours a day in 30 square-meter cells holding 14 people each."

8. The U.S. State Department, *Country Reports on Human Rights Practices for 1984*, p. 1273, states: "Palestinian prisoners at the newly opened Jnaid Prison near Nablus conducted a hunger strike during September in protest of alleged overcrowding, poor food, lack of exercise, and the prison's extensive television monitoring system. After an inquiry, the Police Minister granted some of the prisoners' requests and the strike ended peacefully."

and the PLO.[9] Jneid lost many of its leaders and the authorities felt that it was the time to reconquer. They put into effect a new policy of isolating certain prisoners. They said that they were isolating the "dangerous" prisoners.

They also stopped the policy of permitting visits between prisoners in different sections of the jail, and between rooms in the same section. They refused to give us rooms for educational purposes, and they confiscated many books, including all the handwritten copy books made by detainees. We said, "Why? These books were brought to the jail by the Red Cross and by lawyers. Now you confiscate them. What do we have the right to read?" They said, "You can ask for the Holy Bible." And we replied, "We are strugglers for freedom. We want to know what is happening in Peru, Lebanon, Argentina and in Brazil, in Costa Rica, in Managua, in Panama. We have the right to know about Israel and about Israelis and about ourselves and about the Islamic world and the Third World. So why do you confiscate any book speaking about the Palestinians, the Arabs, and the strugglers for freedom all around the world? This is our spiritual food."

When I heard about an Irish hunger strike in Great Britain, I felt as though I was one of their comrades and I spent two days in solidarity with the Irish strugglers, because they live in jail and I live under the same conditions! So, we asked the Israelis, why do you confiscate the newspapers that are speaking about that hunger strike?

I did not leave Jneid jail in 1985. Of about 800 persons who were in the jail, about sixty of us remained after May 1985. The majority of the detainees in 1986 were new detainees.

We began to educate our colleagues about the hows, the whats, even the alphabet of a hunger strike: what the person will feel when he begins the hunger strike, the movement of the stomach, the smell of the mouth, the taste, how we must go to the bathroom, how we must take water, how we must take salt. We told them how to maintain the strike if they were placed in isolation or transferred to other jails. We said that even if they were released they must continue the strike with their colleagues who were still imprisoned.

Before we started the strike, we made sure that everyone knew what to do if the administrator of the jail came to them and said, "Please, I want to speak to you about the hunger strike, about how to solve this problem." Everyone knew that the answer was to be, "Sorry. There is a representative committee of the detainees and I am not one of them."

We spent sixteen days without anyone asking us, "Why you are on hunger strike?" After sixteen days, the director of the jail came to my cell and asked, "Badran, what do you want?" I told him, "We are detainees. It's not a question of what Badran wants. You must ask, 'What do the detainees want?'" He left, angry.

Then they sent one of the other prisoners to my cell, a man nobody

9. The U.S. State Department, *Country Reports on Human Rights Practices for 1985*, p. 1259, states: "On May 21, 1985, under the auspices of the ICRC, Israel released 1,150 prisoners, including 879 who had been convicted of security offenses . . . in exchange for 3 Israeli military personnel who had been captured in Lebanon."

trusted. This man went to the other detainees and told them that Badran wanted the detainees to die, that *he* was the best leader of detainees in the Israeli jails, and that discussions should begin without Badran. But my colleagues disagreed. They said to him, "Badran is the spokesperson of the detainees; you must speak to him."

Finally, the minister of police and the director of prison services came to Jneid jail and we held a conference about the requests of the detainees. We regained *all our rights* in 1987, even our copy books.

But they refused to give us the chance to transfer anything to the outside. Even poems, short stories, messages for the strugglers for freedom in Nicaragua, a message from the detainees to a Palestinian delegate to the United Nations, they refused. We showed them the Geneva Convention and the rules of the International Red Cross and asked for this right. They said it was refused for security reasons.

I made a copy book out of a dictionary of English to French and I made it into an Arabic-French dictionary. I spent about twelve months working on it eighteen hours daily. They confiscated it. More than once I have dreamed that I had it and I took it to my colleagues at the school where I teach and to my comrades and said, "This is what I did in jail."

Ali Mohammed Jiddah

"Sometimes you are obliged to be a candle, which burns itself to give light for the others."

My name is Ali Mohammed Jiddah. I was born in 1950 in the Old City of Jerusalem. My father is African. He came from Chad with a group of Africans, mainly from Chad, Nigeria, Senegal and Sudan. They had been to Mecca, the holy place in Saudi Arabia. Some of them managed to go back home but some of them could not, merely for financial reasons. They stayed in Palestine and began to associate with Palestinians.

My mother is a mixture. My grandfather, her father, was from Nigeria. My grandmother, the mother of my mother, is a Palestinian Christian from a village very close to Tulkarem. So my mother is second generation African, but she was born and grew up in Palestine.

I grew up in a neighborhood which is called the African Quarter which is close to the Aqsa Mosque. There you will find people who came originally from Africa.

I was educated in the Friends School and I can say that I was a clever student. I had my own ambitions, thinking about becoming a lawyer or something like that.

I was seventeen years old in 1967 when the Six Day War broke out. The Six Day War made a crucial change in my life. As a young Palestinian, all my ambitions and aspirations were totally undermined by the occupation.

First, I couldn't go on with my studies because my father could not afford to pay for my education. My father used to be a guard at the electric company, which meant that the salary was not very large. We were a family of eleven, and he was the only supporter of the family. So I said to my father, "I suggest that I leave school for one year, work and earn money, then go on with my studies." I quit school and began to look for work.

At the same time, I began to feel the negative impact of the occupation on me as a young Palestinian. I couldn't stand to be stopped in the middle of the street by border guard soldiers or by the police to show my identification card, to be harassed and humiliated.

The occupation gave me a shock on the issue of color. I felt my color, which was a new experience for me. I had been living among Palestinians for seventeen years. I felt and feel as one of the Palestinians and very welcome among Palestinians. Most of our friends are white Palestinians. We can marry them. White girls can marry us. I began feeling that because of my color I was doubly oppressed. I was oppressed because I am a Palestinian, and secondly, I was oppressed because I am a *black* Palestinian, which was hell for me.

I felt I had lost my dignity on the personal level and on the national level. That pushed me to look for various means to change the situation, so I began talking with friends of mine who had the same experience. From that moment I became politically active.

Violence between Palestinians and the Israelis reached a summit between 1967 and the early 1970s. Israelis bombarded various places in Jordan and Palestinians reacted. Sometimes Palestinians attacked Israelis and the Israelis reacted.

So one day I took part in this circle of violence. I went with a group of comrades. We placed several bombs in the west side of Jerusalem. They exploded at the same time in the evening and it was called "the night of the bombs" in Jerusalem. In my case, seven Israelis were wounded.

The day before, Israeli planes bombarded a Jordanian city called El Salt. Many civilians were killed and we had seen that on the TV. We wanted to deliver a message to the Israeli civilians: "All the time you don't do anything against the inhuman activities of your government, you'll pay the price at the end of the day."

Months later, when I was just eighteen years old, I was arrested. I was sentenced to twenty years of which I passed seventeen years in Israeli jails. At the beginning I was sent to Ramle where I passed twelve years. Then I was taken to Beersheba where I spent another four years. The last year, I spent six months in the desert in a jail called Nafha, and the last six months were in Ashkelon.

In 1985, I was released in a big exchange of prisoners between Palestinians and Israelis. Three Israeli soldiers (who had been captives in the hands of Palestinians since the invasion of Lebanon) came back home, and in exchange 1,150 Palestinians were released. I was among those Palestinians.

To pass seventeen years in Israeli jails is not a joke. It is not a picnic. The most horrible experience you can have as a human being is the day you are obliged to see your best comrades dying in front of your eyes and you can't do *anything* to save them. That experience played a very crucial role in developing my personality.

It was Israeli policy that jails were to be collective cemeteries for the political prisoners. They wanted to make of you a number: just a number. When you came out of prison, you would be worthless, of no more use. On the contrary, you would be a problem for yourself and for your people.

When we became aware of this policy, we said, "Can we stand it here? We can stand it!" That meant we had to organize ourselves in order to confront this policy. We began organizing our internal apparatus, beginning in Ramle, and contacting other prisons to carry out this same process. When we found that our internal apparatus was strong, we could then begin confronting the administrative services of the prisons. We began launching struggles: the open hunger strikes that lasted up to forty days in which we had our own martyrs.

We reached the point where we had the ability to transform collective cemeteries into the most academic revolutionary schools. Our people who graduated from Israeli jails were well-educated, politically and ideologically.

We achieved a lot of rights. Now they are attacking those rights: no representation for political prisoners, more crowded cells, humiliation during family visits. They think that by this they can crush the political movement. This is stupid.

I tell the Israelis, "You are doing a favor for us as Palestinians. You pick up a boy thirteen years old when he throws a stone. You send him to jail for nine months. He doesn't know how to read or write. When he comes out of jail, he is a real reader, in the struggle."

At the beginning of my imprisonment, I was an extremist. I couldn't stand the suggestion that I learn Hebrew. I spoke French, English, and Arabic. I had such an ability to learn languages that my comrades used to say to me, "Ali, you should learn Hebrew." I used to say, "I'll be the last among the political prisoners to study the Hebrew language. I don't want it." But I realized that I was an idiot. So I began learning the Hebrew language which I now speak and write fluently.

It is not a hobby for us to throw stones or Molotov cocktails. We are normal people. But all the time you exercise oppression on me, it accumulates, and it comes to such a point that it will express itself. From 1967 to 1987, there was a lot of accumulation of oppression and it had to express itself by what we call the Intifada.

Psychologically, I still suffer from my experience in Israeli jails. I may be just sitting with you and I want to talk and to have a good time. Suddenly, I pass from a good mood to a very sad mood and I want to be alone with my own thoughts. I still feel that the prison experience is dragging me. It is so very strong that I cannot escape from it at home. The one who is really affected by my psychology is my wife. At home, I can't sit for five minutes. This is the negative side of that experience.

But on the positive side, it sharpened my political opinions and the way I regarded all conflict. I came out of prison with a strong belief that I had been fighting for justice.

In my struggle, I am not dealing only with the Palestinian issue any more. I have many issues. The more you read, the more you find out that a lot of Jews who are oppressing us nowadays are in the same boat with us. It is a Palestinian issue and a Jewish issue. Maybe I am doubly oppressed, but at the same time they are oppressed. A really just peace would guarantee that the Israeli and Palestinian communities would live together in the same area, in equality, and as good neighbors.

So when I came out of prison, I believed I should practice on the ground. I said, "I am going to work with Israelis." And I began working at the Alternative Information Center, a joint center run by Palestinians and Israelis. The main intention behind such joint work was that both Palestinians and Israelis should be the bridge over which coming generations would come and meet each other, the Palestinians from one side and the Israelis from the other.

I worked there for four and a half years. For me it was a very rich experience to be a Palestinian among Israelis. I didn't feel alienated. They didn't feel strange or alienated while dealing with me. They forgot I'm Arab.

While working with those Israelis, I succeeded in creating a connection between a group of young Palestinians — fifteen, sixteen years old, girls and boys — and a group of Israelis of the same age. They had meetings together. It was during the Intifada. The first meeting was very, very difficult, psychologically, for both sides. But it became easier in the second meeting, third meeting, fourth meeting. They even reached a point when they began talking about social activities together, going to a movie together, playing chess together.

Because of the Intifada, I felt that it was very important for me to be on the Palestinian side. I moved back to the Palestinian side as a journalist.

I am married. My wife is from behind the Green Line, from Akulp. It began as a joke in prison. Whenever we had empty time, we used to just sit and talk. "Well, Ali, when you are outside the prison, from where are you going to marry?" I used to say, "I will be revolutionary. I will marry from behind the Green Line." I was emphasizing that we Palestinians are one people, whether behind the Green Line, in the Occupied Territories, or in the diaspora. So when I came out of jail, those comrades began saying to me, "Well, you said you wanted to marry from behind the Green Line."

I have two daughters. One of them is four years old; the other one is two and a half years. In the meantime my wife is pregnant. When we get the third one we'll have to stop because of the horrible economic situation.

We have a very beautiful saying in Arabic that says, "Sometimes you are obliged to be a candle, which burns itself to give light for the others." I look at my daughters sometimes. The most beautiful thing in this world that I can imagine is the innocent smile on the face of a child. Today it is very difficult to see it on the faces of most children. So I look at my daughters and I say, "Are you ready, Ali, for your daughters to have the same experience as you?" I answer, "Never! Never!" So if you are not interested that your daughters, your children, will have the same experience of sacrifice that you had, you have to create the conditions such that they can have a real human and normal childhood. The only way is to be involved in the struggle. You can't be neutral over here.

Maha Nassar

"The faces of my children were never away from me, but I thought of them in a way to make me stronger, not to make me weaker."

1988

I was arrested in 1988 when I had two children. The army came to the house after midnight. They arrested me and they warned me if I did not confess they would imprison me and the children would be left alone because of the absence of their father in Ansar 3. They thought that it was a critical time when they could take a confession from me because I would be under the pressure of having my children alone in the house. So they started threatening me and they wanted me to confess.

My children were three years and a half and four years and a half. The older one, the daughter, was strangely steadfast. She took my hand and we walked hand-in-hand all the way to the army vehicle. She said, "Bye, Mama." I told her, "Bye. I promise you I'll be back home very soon. I promise you."

Their grandmother lived nearby. She heard the trucks and she wanted to come out and come to our house. The army forbade her to do so until they had finished searching my home. They locked the door of her house and stationed two soldiers there. But two minutes after the army jeep had left, all the neighbors came to my house saying, "We will take care of the children. We will take care of them." I was sure that this was going to happen. That was why I was not willing to give one word to the Shin Bet.

I made no confession for the whole interrogation period. I was taken to the Russian Compound. They put a hood over my face so that I couldn't see who was around me. And they subjected me to the shabeh, which means that they handcuffed my hands behind my back and connected them to a pole that was higher than my body. You remain standing or sitting or extending your body in this position, with your hands above your body, hanging by your hands. The handcuffs are very tight.

And I was put in what they call "the grave." It's a specific cell with two doors. You enter the first door and it is very dark. Then you have another door. You enter it and they close both doors and you are kept in a very small cell where you cannot stretch your legs, you cannot sleep, you don't have water, you don't have food, you don't have light. It is totally black. It comes to a point where you feel as if you are suffocating.

They moved me from one cell to another, very dirty cells. Some cells have the bathroom in the ground just beside where the prisoner is. There is a mattress, very thin, and blankets full of water. You have a bucket with dirty water that you drink. And in some other cells you have a bathroom such that if you push, the water comes directly in the center of the cell so you are all wet and your mattress is wet. There are crusts of food around you and a lot of insects on them so that if you move a little bit, the insects fly up. You stay huddled quietly all the time so that the insects will not fly up from the remains of the food.

They brought cassettes into the "grave." On the cassettes were the words of children saying, "Oh Mama, come back home. We want you. We are hungry. We want you back home." They wanted me to believe that these were my children calling for me. And the Shin Bet the next day said, "We saw your children without shoes in the streets, hungry and very dirty." And I told them, "Never mind. One day they will have something to wear and to eat. I don't care. I have full confidence in my people and I know that my people are going to take care of these children. I am confident of this."

It was a struggle of wills. I was not willing to give anything to the Shin Bet. I wanted to see my children happy for me to come out and not ashamed because their mother was the one to talk about other people and put them in jail and maybe expose their children to the same experience as my own children. The faces of my children were never away from me, but I thought of them in a way to make me stronger, not to make me weaker. I was held for fifteen days.

1990

The last detention was in 1990. I spent fifteen days in interrogation, during thirteen of which I was on hunger strike. By that time I was very well known so that a lot of signatures came to the Russian Compound asking for my release. Even Women In Black, a group of Israeli women, made a big demonstration in front of the jail asking for my release. It had a very big impact on people because I was also on hunger strike. I was released because I had nothing to confess. Nobody had confessed so as to implicate me. There was no reason to keep me in jail since they didn't have any charges against me.

For the first four days, they didn't give me food, water, or sleep. I would fall asleep for a few seconds and then be required to wake up, a very tiring situation. I was under shabeh all the first four days. Sometimes shabeh was used at the same time that they put very cold air into the interrogation room. The fifth day I was taken to a cell. I didn't know night from day. I couldn't tell because there was a sack over my head. After they took me to the cell, I slept for about half an hour and then the soldiers returned and put the sack over my face and took me back to interrogation. And I told them, "I will not eat." They started worrying about this because my health started to deteriorate badly. I lost ten kilograms [about 22 pounds] during this period of time.

The first interrogation after the fifth day they started asking the same questions again: about my relation to the Popular Front, who was the leadership, and things like that. I noticed that their question was whether I was a member of the Popular Front. I answered, "No. I'm not a member but I have the political beliefs of the Popular Front. It is very well known that I have the political beliefs of the Popular Front. I'm well known. My husband is well known." They couldn't take me to court for my beliefs. If they took me to jail I would be out of the dirty cells. I told them, "You cannot charge me and take me to court for my political beliefs. Take me to jail if you want to."

They said, "When will you end your hunger strike?" I said, "When you take me to jail." At that time, I was sure that they were not going to let me out. I didn't know what was going on outside.

I saw my lawyer after eight days of detention. I was very weak at that point: not weak in the will, but weak in the body. After that they continued to take me to shabeh, to interrogate me, and to threaten me. They also sent collaborators to look at me through the window of the cell at night, so as to make me afraid. These were men. I was not adequately clothed.

I started shouting. I had already made friends with some of the male prisoners to whom I could talk through the wall. Some of them I knew by voice. I later met some of them a year after I was out of jail, and I would know that this person was so-and-so from his voice, even though we had never met, we had never seen each other.

The fourteenth day they told me, "You belong to the Union of Palestinian Women committees." I said, "Well, this is recorded in the files of the United Nations, so you can charge me for being at the center of that." So they said, "OK, who is your administrative committee? Tell us the names." I said, "We don't have an administrative committee." They said, "No. You have." I said, "OK, we have but I don't want to tell you. It's not my job to tell you. You pay somebody else to bring information for you." That was the first time that they slapped me several times on the face.

At the end of the fourteenth day they brought me to interrogation and tied my hands to a chair, took hold of my hair, and began knocking my head on the wall. The wall was cement, very rough, with holes in it, and they banged my head on the wall several times and said, "You belong to a political organization. You don't confess. You have the slogan that confession is a betrayal. But you have no choice except to confess." They were acting very frustrated because I wouldn't confess. They said, "Your organization is forcing you, it will punish you if you confess, and we know you have this slogan not to confess."

It came to the point where I didn't feel anything in my head and I went back to my cell. I slept a little. I was half dead, but I was at the same time very happy, because I knew that I had won the battle. The Shin Bet was defeated. They could only retreat.

Two days later they fetched me from the cell and told me, "We are a democratic state. You know nothing. We are human beings. We don't want your children to be alone so we have decided to release you." And they said, "You can call your husband." I was laughing. I thought this was a game. I said, "Believe me, I will call my husband." They said, "You go and call him." I took the telephone. I called my husband to come. It was late at night. Did they expect to release a woman at eight o'clock at night? Who would dare to come? Who knew what would happen? I didn't believe it myself until I was really out of the Russian Compound.

Mousa

"We were so tired and thirsty for our families."

First Arrest

Right when the Intifada began, in December 1987, I was arrested and held in
the Dahariya Prison in Hebron for eighteen days. It was not because I did
anything wrong. It was a time when they were arresting all men my age. The
charge would be the same: throwing rocks and building barricades. I was one
of many who were jailed at that time. They picked up twenty-five of my
friends on the same night they picked up me. The intention of the authorities
at that time, during the first two months of the Intifada, was to make massive
arrests and quell it as they did uprisings before that.

Second Arrest

I was arrested again in the fall of 1989. By chance, a car was stopped in El
Bireh and Molotov cocktails were found in the car. Two individuals who
were in the car were caught and arrested. These two individuals were leaders
of a popular resistance committee. They were in charge of the strike force in
town. When they were arrested they were interrogated and the authorities
found out the names of other members of this group. I was one of the
members of the strike force.

In El Bireh, the strike force is made up of cells of three individuals who
meet together. Out of those three, one would meet with other individuals
who were also in charge of a group of three. The person who meets with the
other cell leaders would bring directives back to the cell. One of the two men
who were caught in that car was one of those who distributed directives, not
one like myself who received directives. During interrogation, he could not
remain steadfast, and our arrest was the result of his interrogation.

The soldiers found their way to our house. They said to my father, "You
have two sons. Where are they?" He said, "They are sleeping." They said,
"OK." They left the house completely. I was sleeping. I did not know what
was happening. My family was thrilled that they left and they did not take
anyone this time.

About ten minutes after this, they came back and told my father to wake
up his son. They came into my bedroom. It was about 2:30 a.m. I was told to
rush — get my clothes and get out. I had on some kind of slip-on sandals.
They didn't even give me time to put on proper shoes. When they took me
out of the house, they did not have anything to wrap around my eyes. I was
wearing a homemade yarn sweater, so they brought the sweater up over the
back of my head and covered my face with it while I was still wearing the
sweater.

The soldiers who came for us were the Border Patrol. They came in what
we called the "porch." The porch is a vehicle like a jeep but longer, with a
bench on each side. There were four soldiers on one side and four soldiers on

the other side. Between the seat and the spare tire there was a space just as wide as I am and that's where I was placed.

We went from my house to the next house where they wanted to arrest someone else. We stayed a half hour while they went to get the other one. It seemed as if the soldier that was guarding us was bored: every once in a while we got beaten. I got my share of beatings that night. Then the brother of the person they wanted to arrest made a problem with the soldier and they were yelling at each other. So the soldier that was guarding me left me, and they beat the brother of the person being arrested. I got out of it but someone else got it, so either way someone is getting hit, kicked or punched.

After they arrested the second person, they arrested a third person. This guy was fat and his seat was on top of me! The soldiers would hit him and he would press on me. I started screaming. I was telling the guy on top of me to get up and get off me, but the guy was so scared, he thought if he would move he would get beat. The soldiers wanted to walk quietly to another house to surprise arrest a fourth person, and they had to have us quiet, so the soldier told me, "Shhhh!" I said, "Stop hitting him so he doesn't put pressure on me and I won't yell." They took the guy and put him on the soldiers' bench so I would stop yelling. They got the person they wanted to surprise arrest.

A homemade yarn sweater has little holes in it, so I was the only one who knew exactly where we were going on this trip. I could see everything. They did not find the next two persons they wanted to arrest, but they got another person. We stopped at the police station. Some soldiers got out, someone got in, and we kept going to the Ramallah jail.

It was a Friday when we were arrested. We were seven people. They took two of the individuals directly into the interrogation room and beating rooms. Five of us went to a tent. The jail master told us where each person should sit in this tent and he told the guard of my tent, "These individuals are to sit where they were told and not to move or talk."

There were more people in my tent than just the five of us. There was a total of maybe fifty people in the tent I was in and the tent next to us which had more people. I knew the other prisoners. They were from Ramallah.

The tents were surrounded by barbed wire, then maybe a two foot space, and more barbed wire. So it is a confined tent. You cannot go out.

The food they brought was stewed tomatoes with eggs, mixed together, but the egg shell was mixed with the food. It used to crunch. They brought us cold tea.

We stayed until Sunday in these tents. On Sunday afternoon they came and called my number and someone else's number. They told us we were leaving. I was pretty happy — I had not stayed long this time. They were walking us together until they took the other guy into a room. I thought, maybe this guy is going into interrogation. But I thought, for sure, I was going just a couple of meters further, out the door, and home. I asked the guard, "I'm going home?" The soldier just cracked up laughing.

Interrogation

They took me to a very large door. There was a small door in the larger door. They opened the smaller door and they put me in. It was the torture cells.

In the first room there was a computer. An interrogator began asking me social questions: "How old are you? Where do you work? How many brothers and sisters do you have?"

Then they put me in front of one of the cells and told me not to move. They went and got metal handcuffs and they handcuffed my hands behind my back. A soldier brought a canvas sack, like the material that the tent is made of, and they put it over my head down to about the bottom of my neck.

The soldier would come and ask your name. You would say your name in a very low voice. You were not allowed to raise your voice because in the solitary confinement or torture cells, they don't want anyone inside the cells knowing who is outside, or who is outside knowing who is inside. So your voice remains very low.

In the area we were in, there were five cells on the right and five cells to the left and in the middle was the standing area. This is where you stand, handcuffed, canvas over your head. You can't tell time. They purposefully make it very hot and you have a canvas hood over you and you are very tired. You have no conception of where you are.

In the standing area, our heads were always covered. I used to shake my head so I could see a little bit. At times I would raise the canvas hood as much as I could to see what was around me and if I heard a soldier coming I would bring it down fast.

They also made us wear the hood when they were walking us between the cell and the interrogation room. When the guard came to walk us, he grabbed us from the bottom of the canvas and pulled us along.

They entered me into one of the rooms and the canvas was removed from my head. However, the handcuffs stay on. Four interrogators came to me. One of the interrogators asked, "Do you have friends?" I said, "Yes, I have many friends." He said, "What do you do with them? Have you thrown rocks? Have you participated in these activities?" Up to this point I had no idea that someone had spoken of my activities. I still thought they were asking general questions. When I answered that I had no activity, I was thrown against one of the walls of the cell and given some punches in the stomach and some kicks. After some time, and I am not sure of the time period, I was taken back out to the standing area between the two sets of cells.

Then I was taken to another room in this section for interrogation by a third person. He also had a computer. This interrogator told me, "You worked in a plastics factory. You have three brothers. Their names are these." All of this was information that I already gave. But he had information that I had done: one, two and three. When he threw out this political stuff at the end, I said, "I have no knowledge of this. I am not active in what you are talking about." He struck me and I fell from the chair. The method that they use of striking is very scientific — it does not show if the Red Cross or other organizations investigate.

In this same section, they also have cells that are as big as one chair. You are entered into one of these cells and you sit on this chair. You don't see anyone. You hear no one. You are not allowed bathroom facilities. You are not given water. You don't know how long you stayed sitting there. Every once in a while they come and take you back to this interrogator again. It is a very, very stressful situation.

After several times in and out of the interrogation room, I was told specifically that this person (one of the guys that was arrested from the car) said that I had done one, two and three. I responded, "My relationship to this person was, 'Hello, how are you doing?' No more. No less." The questions that were coming now were all very detailed, very specific, on my activities.

Of course, during all of this I would get a punch here and a blow there. With my hands behind my back, I was knocked to the ground. They would put the handcuffs on the ground and jump on my hands. My hands were very much swollen and a piece of metal protruded from my skin. I remember the handcuffs had imprinted on them, "Made in England."

We called the smallest cell a "closet." It seemed like it used to be a shower. There was a shower spout but there were no handles. I was able to move my pants down and I moved my bowels in that room where I was sitting. Then I played with one of the teeth of the gear where the handle was supposed to be, until the water dripped a little bit and I was able to drink a little from the shower spout. The water had a terrible odor. I was hit in the inner leg when the soldier opened the cell, smelled the smell in there and saw what I had done!

They took me from this cell to an interrogation room where they brought me a sheet of paper written in Arabic. It was a confession, to be signed by me, and it had very detailed information as to who I was with and what I was doing. They asked me to sign and I refused. I told them, "I have no knowledge of this. I don't know what you are talking about."

I was taken back to the cell. This was all happening in this special section. I was put back in this room with no sleep. Every hour or hour and a half or couple of hours, the door opened and if I was dozing off the soldier would wake me up. I do not know how long a time it was but it was at least four or five days without sleep.

Then I was put into a solitary confinement cell with two blankets — one I used as a mattress, one I used as a cover.

After two weeks or two and a half weeks, I had my hearing for renewal of my detention without charge. I did not see a lawyer or anyone from my family — not one person.[10]

Before you go to the court you are required to take somewhat of a bath: they spill a bucket of water on you and they let you wipe off. And you have to

10. The U.S. State Department, *Country Reports on Human Rights Practices for 1989*, states, p. 1434: "An attorney is normally not allowed to see a client until after interrogation is completed and a confession, if obtained, has been made."

cut your nails in order for you to present yourself in court. This happens before court and every Saturday. Because the interrogators are off on Saturday, it is the duty of the guards that come on Saturday to make sure that we get our "hygiene."

The court was within the Ramallah jail facility. The military judge read the charges. If you pleaded not guilty, the judge gave you a thirty-day extension. The charges against me were the same as everyone else: throwing rocks, setting up barricades, writing on walls, distributing literature, and being a member of the Popular Committee. I pleaded not guilty.

From One Jail to Another

Two days after my court hearing I was put into a military police car and I was transported to Dahariya jail. It was Friday night and the soldier was hurrying so that he could take his day off. This was in November, 1989.

This time when I went to Dahariya, I was directly taken to the cells. I was so tired, I probably spent most of the first two days sleeping.

In this jail it was different from the other jails. In other jails there was an organizational structure among the prisoners. That was not present in this jail. Each person was on his own.

November 15, 1989 was going to be the first commemoration of the Palestinian declaration of independence. People in the jail were organizing, singing and clapping for the commemoration. We were told that if we did *not* do that we would be able to go from the cells to the tents. There was some activity on November 15, but not as planned. So we were able to move from the cells out to the tents.

I stayed two months in the tents. I was allowed family visits every two weeks in Dahariya. They brought me some clothes and I was able to get them.

A judge comes every Wednesday to Dahariya prison. They would have a hearing for anyone whose extension was going to end. I went in front of this judge in Dahariya. He would come into the room, tell you the same thing he told you before, and ask you, "Guilty or not guilty?" I said, "I am not guilty." "Extension." They call it an extension court to make it sound legal, but they just go through the motions of justice.

In my file, there were seven people. They knew that we were one group. Therefore, they charged us as one. It was like a group hearing. All seven of us would go to the court and the judge would ask each person in that file: "Plead guilty or not guilty?" He would go down the row in that file and extend.

The prisoners called the last court hearing in Dahariya the "blank check" hearing. That's when the judge would give the prisoner a 101-day extension. When you get this extension, you knew that you were going to be charged and have a prolonged jail sentence.

I stayed in Dahariya until one day in January, 1990, when they came and called out our numbers. They told us we were being transported. We did not know where. We thought we might be going to a jail that was newly being used for uprising individuals, outside of Jerusalem, called Anata. We thought this was pretty bad because that was an old storage place for Jordanian tanks, and they had it set up where you could not see anything around you.

We made a stop at Farrah, which is a jail that is well known for its torture techniques. The entrance to the Farrah jail is right next to the entrance to Farrah Refugee Camp. As soon as the residents of the camp saw us being unloaded from the truck, they started throwing rocks at the soldiers. One of the prisoners and one of the soldiers were wounded by the rocks, and glass was broken in the truck that we were in.

This stop at Farrah was to be a rest stop for the soldiers and then we were supposed to go on to Megiddo jail. But the bus driver got so upset about what happened with the rock-throwing, they decided to stay that day and we slept in Farrah that night.

They searched us inside and out. I don't know what they thought they were going to find. We were coming from one jail to the other.

When they were taking us to the cell inside Farrah, a soldier came and started speaking to me in Hebrew. I told him, "I don't know Hebrew." He told me to stand there. About fifteen minutes later, another soldier came. He slapped me and told me to go. I went to the group of people that came with me and I asked one of my fellow prisoners who knew Hebrew, "What did the soldier want from me?" He said, "He asked you in Hebrew to tell them who threw rocks at us outside of the jail." This was ridiculous. How would I know?

There were forty of us who came in the bus and they put us in a small room. We had to sleep on our sides.

The next day, we were taken from Farrah to Megiddo. The soldiers would tell us to raise our heads when we went through Arab villages so the community could see that there were prisoners in the truck and they would not throw stones at the truck. This was the only time that we were able to raise our heads.

When we got to Megiddo, we had to stay in the bus for about two hours while they took care of the administrative work. When you are transferred from jail to jail, your files are transferred with you.

We were given new numbers. We had to hold up our numbers and they took mug shots. This was the first time they took my picture while in jail.

Once again, we were searched. We were able to bring in with us clothes that our family had brought, but everything had to be solid blue. If it was not blue, or if it was blue and had a red stripe, it would not go into the jail.

They gave each prisoner five thin blankets, a cup, a dish, a spoon and a fork. A friend of mine was in the next cell. We used to talk to each other between the cells.

Within Megiddo there was a prisoners' organizational structure. We used to meet within the prison and talk about different things. We talked about the political atmosphere. We talked about other prisoners who had left this jail. We talked about some of the martyrs. We talked about the possible development of the Uprising, where it's going, and other things.

It used to be that prisoners were taken from Megiddo to Ramallah for hearings before the military court. But a few days before I arrived, something happened, a rock was thrown and a prisoner was wounded when he was being transported to Ramallah. So they stopped taking prisoners from Megiddo to Ramallah. That meant that I couldn't get out of jail for anything — not even travel time — and it is good to get out sometimes.

In Megiddo, we were allowed one visit per month for half an hour. There were about 1,500 prisoners in Megiddo, so they had different visiting days for different parts of the jail. Visiting took place like this. Thirty prisoners were taken one at a time and we were lined up in a straight row for about fifty yards. Three people from the family could visit each prisoner. They were on the other side of the fence. So there are thirty prisoners with ninety people in front of them. Try to understand your family talking to you from a distance with ninety people talking at once!

My main question to my family was whether they had heard anything about my court hearing. I had no idea where my hearing would be. I knew they had canceled hearings in Ramallah, and I had heard that they had started sentencing people in Jenin, which is the closest other court, and I wanted to find out whether they had heard anything from Jenin about when my court hearing would be.

My mother arranged for an attorney to come and visit me in June, 1990. That was the first time that I was able to see an attorney. He told me that the lawyers were going to go on strike for fifteen days to protest how the courts were held. The lawyer said, "I don't want to send you to the hearing without me there. I would rather extend it fifteen days and I'll go with you." I didn't have a choice. I said, "That's OK."

Two days later, they took me to the court anyway — without a lawyer. The same seven in our file were taken together. The judge always speaks Hebrew, even if he knows Arabic. If you don't understand Hebrew, the judge brings in an Arab translator. The translator told us our options: "They are not going to give you a fifteen-day extension in order for your lawyer to come. Either they are going to give you an automatic three-month extension before your next hearing, or they are going to give you a sentence today."[11]

We went into the courtroom. There was one "lawyer" — a collaborator who acts as a lawyer for them. We used to talk about him within the organizational structure of the prisoners. As soon as he opened the door and walked in we all knew about him because we had discussed him and how he treats people.

So the first person of the seven said he was not guilty. He was given two years. The second was twelve months. The third was mine: fourteen months with 1,500 shekels fine. Two others nine months, another one eighteen and another one two years. One of the guys had the same name as one of the leaders of the Palestinian movement. They ridiculed him throughout the whole hearing and he was one of the ones who got two years.

11. Article 71 of the Fourth Geneva Convention, regarding penal procedure, states in part: "No sentence shall be pronounced by the competent courts of the Occupying Power except after a regular trial. Accused persons who are prosecuted by the Occupying Power shall be promptly informed, in writing, in a language which they understand, of the particulars of the charges preferred against them. . . ."

Three of the seven prisoners had their families come. They were at least happy that they could see the family before being sentenced. I was sentenced Thursday. Monday was the day I was supposed to see my family again. Sunday, I was transported back to Farrah to sleep one night and then go on to "Ansar 3" where there were no family visits.[12] My family did not know this. They came on Monday. When I was not there they went on to Farrah in hopes that I was there.[13]

"Ansar 3"

We were lucky. We had older guards with us who didn't really give a damn and who weren't bothered by us. They were just transporting us. One of the prisoners in the back of the bus had a pin and he opened the handcuffs of a few of the prisoners. When they saw the guard coming they would relock them.

We left Farrah at 6:00 a.m. and we got to Ansar before noon. Once again the administration process began. Our files were transferred. We were given new numbers. (In every jail you are given a new number.)

About 4:00 p.m. the bus started taking the prisoners to the different sections. Ansar was huge. There were about 7,000 prisoners. There were five sections — Section A, B, C, D, and E — with six tents in each section. It was in a military security zone. There was a military base nearby and you could hear tanks and planes landing.

Again we were searched. They were looking for letters sent from jail to jail. We went into a room one by one. We removed all of our clothes, including underclothes. We had to walk around the room one at a time in front of the soldier, then put our clothes back on and leave.

Each person was given a slender pallet, like they use in a warehouse, made of two-by-fours. It was for sleeping. But it was not flat and it was not smooth. You were a king if you got a five centimeter mattress. If you got a one

12. The U.S. State Department, *Country Reports on Human Rights Practices for 1988*, states, p. 1380: "Since March [1988] the IDF [Israeli Defense Forces] moved over 2,000 administrative detainees at various times from the occupied territories to a detention camp in the Negev desert [Ansar 3] near Ketziot inside Israel. . . . Transferring prisoners from occupied territories, in the view of the United States, contravenes the Fourth Geneva Convention. However, the Israeli Supreme Court, in dismissing a petition brought by Ketziot detainees, held the Convention's provisions could not be enforced by an Israeli Court since they have not been incorporated into domestic Israeli law. . . . Conditions at Ketziot are rigorous and there is overcrowding. Prisoners are required to live in tents not designed for extended periods of confinement." The U.S. State Department, *Country Reports on Human Rights Practices for 1991*, states, p. 1444: "The authorities continued to transfer detainees and prisoners out of the occupied territories to detention facilities in Israel, especially to the Ketziot camp in the Negev Desert and Megiddo Prison near Afula. In the view of the United States, the transfer of prisoners from the occupied territories to Israel contravenes Article 76 of the Fourth Geneva Convention. . . . Family visits to Ketziot Prison began in November 1991."
13. The U.S. State Department, *Country Reports on Human Rights Practices for 1991*, p. 1444, states: "Israeli authorities claim that they attempt to post notification within 48 hours; Palestinians assert that families and lawyers are normally notified much later and often locate the detainee through their own efforts. The ICRC attempts to help by passing on to families (by telephone) the information it receives from Israeli prison officials. A military judge may delay notification of arrest to immediate family members, attorneys, and consular officials under the law for up to 12 days. . . ."

centimeter mattress, it fell through the cracks and it was just like sleeping on the wood. At one point we had a hunger strike for thirty days to get a little thicker mattress.

After I had been in Ansar for several weeks there was a demonstration. Let me tell you how we communicated. We would take the inside of the bread — that dough was flexible. We would insert a letter, wrap it with dough into a tight ball, put it in water, keep it for a day until it got hard and — if you know a shepherd, you know he can make the throw — use it as a stone to be thrown into the next section. It was a long distance between sections, but we had shepherds with us and shepherds are specialists at throwing rocks.

Every section in Ansar was built on asphalt except Section A. Section A still had gravel. So Section A would provide other sections with rocks. Section A would throw rocks to Section B. They would hide those rocks and then they would be used as tools of communication.

The technique was to throw a rock without a letter first and then throw the one with the letter. That was to alert the prisoners to prepare in case the letter fell outside the section. Around each section the dirt was piled up. There would be a patrol on top of the dirt. But the person throwing could not see to take aim. When the first rock fell, they would whistle or send some type of signal from the other section.

It is very important to understand that these messages were absolutely not allowed to be caught by the Israeli soldiers. Once the communication was sent, all efforts were made to get that communication, so communication was very, very dangerous.

Someone threw us a letter. It landed outside of the barbed wire. One of the prisoners threw himself through the barbed wire to get it. (The special police were in charge of internal affairs and the army was in charge outside of the jail.) The police told the soldier in the tower to shoot the individual. He shot him in his side and he died. Two people were injured.

The organization of the prisoners within Ansar put out a communique saying, "That soldier must be hit. He must pay for what he did."

The prisoners from Gaza were very steadfast, very dedicated. By chance it happened that the guard who gave the order to shoot walked too close to a metal door with bars. So one of the Gaza prisoners took the guard and hit his face against the bars.

This time the army came into the section to take the prisoner who did that. They took him out into the road area between the tents. The prisoners in the rest of the tents in that section started throwing all of their spoons and their dishes at these soldiers, trying to stop them.

The major in charge of my section was injured as well as two soldiers. This is something very, very big when the major of the section gets hit. They take it very, very seriously when that happens.

They surrounded the section and they started throwing gas. The whole section took to the ground because we knew that gas rises, but it was choking. It was overwhelming. For one half hour they would throw gas. Then they would let us go. Then in a half hour they would spray water. If someone left the tent to go outside of the tent in his own section, if he did not go back to his tent, he would be hit with gas. This took place for about four hours.

The prisoners in the tent next to us were mostly from Gaza. They went to that tent and they handcuffed the prisoners. They would throw them between the barbed wire while they were handcuffed. We watched. There was nothing we could do. We broke the pallets that we were given as beds and we were throwing them as part of the resistance.

At three o'clock in the morning, they announced that they wanted to do a count because there was so much chaos they were scared they were missing prisoners. After this count, all of the pallets were taken out of this section.

For eighteen days our section had increased punishments: no soap, less food,[14] no cigarettes. We used to take the tea, after we cooked it, and roll it and smoke it as cigarettes. We were no longer given a dish and spoon. You used the dish that was brought to you for a meal and then you gave it back five minutes after the meal.

After that they brought us soldiers that did not understand anything but hitting. That was their specialty.

I was one out of about twenty who got sick from the gas. I started getting a rash on my hands. The other people got better after a while but I did not. They sent me to the doctor in the section. He gave me something to spray on the bed so I would not itch but it did not help. I was itching the whole time. The rash became infected. My infection was contagious.

Each section had a person who spoke Hebrew who was appointed to talk to the prisoners and the guards. I was one of the two cases in my section that was always brought up in negotiation: "He has a medical condition. He cannot remain like this." The other prisoners wanted me released very badly because they were afraid I would infect other prisoners. I did not get the rash taken care of until after I was released and went to a doctor. It took three or four days with medicines and then I was OK.

Release and Back Home

One day in November, 1990, I was told my number was up to leave. After they took me to the door of the section, they told me, "Your number is wrong. You are not going."

A week later, I was told again to get ready to leave. At nine o'clock in the morning, they took me out to the bus. It took from about 9:00 to 12:00 going to the different sections, calling the persons' names that were leaving that day.

With my first imprisonment, at the beginning of the Intifada, they gave me my ID card on my way out. This imprisonment, they gave me a temporary ID card on my way out that was good for 24 hours only. Within 24 hours, I had to show up at the civil administration in my home town.

---

14. Article 100 of the Fourth Geneva Convention on discipline in places of internment states, in part, that "In particular, . . . the reduction of food rations [is] prohibited."

Because no cars were allowed in this military zone, when I was released we were taken in a bus outside the military zone, and they put us out on a street where they knew that cars would be coming and going.

In Dahariya, which is the Arab city closest to "Ansar 3," there is a volunteer committee that sends cars every day to this area where they know that prisoners are released. Volunteers would pick up the released prisoners. The volunteers told us, "Stay and sleep here tonight. We'll freshen you up and then you can go back home." But we were so tired and so thirsty for our families, we asked to be sent home that same day.

★   ★   ★

Note

In 1991 international, Israeli, and Palestinian human rights groups published detailed credible reports of torture, abuse and mistreatment of Palestinian detainees in prisons and detention centers. The practices reportedly included hooding; deprivation of food, sleep, and sanitary facilities; forced standing; confinement in a narrow, small space; slaps, blows and beatings; and threats against the detainee or his family. Most such abuse takes place immediately after arrest and during the first few days of detention and interrogation when detainees are denied access to family members, attorneys, and the International Committee of the Red Cross (ICRC). The ICRC cites this isolation period as an issue of great concern. . . . The ICRC is not allowed access to detainees until the 15th day after arrest. Human rights groups point to this prolonged incommunicado detention of security detainees as contributing to the problem of abuse.[15]

According to an Israeli human rights group, there were about 90,000 arrests in the Occupied Territories between December 1987 and October 1991.[16]

---

15. U.S. State Department, *Country Reports on Human Rights Practices for 1991*, p. 1442.
16. B'Tselem, *Violations of Human Rights in the Occupied Territories 1990/1991* (Jerusalem: 1991), p. 63.

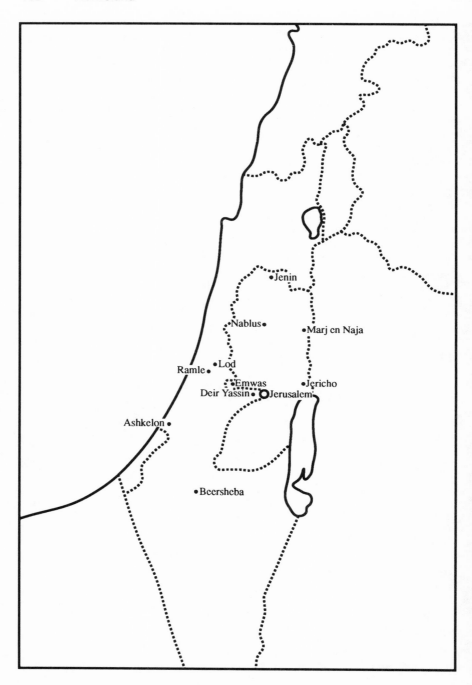

7

Workers and Farmers

Trade unions in the Occupied Territories are relatively small and generally confined to urban workers in skilled crafts. According to military order, the occupation authorities must approve all candidates for union office. In practice, trade unions conduct elections at the workplace level without seeking the approval of the occupation authorities, because they fear that the authorities would exclude candidates who have served in administrative detention. According to the United States State Department:

> Israeli authorities, citing security concerns, actively discourage many activities by unions in the West Bank and Gaza. The authorities assert that the West Bank umbrella federations and many individual unions are fronts for illegal political organizations rather than trade unions. Measures taken against trade unions include arrests, administrative detention, searches of trade union premises, and confiscation of union property, according to the 1991 report of the International Labor Organization (ILO) Director General.[1]

As of 1985, there were approximately 40 labor unions in the Occupied Territories. Only 15 new labor unions had been permitted to register in the West Bank since the beginning of the occupation in 1967, but over 100 applications had been turned down and a number of Arab unions had been disbanded by the occupation authorities for alleged security reasons.[2]

In 1991, there were 32 registered unions operating in the West Bank in addition to approximately 100 unregistered unions with a total membership of over 100,000. In Gaza, six unions that existed in 1967 operate out of one office.[3]

At the end of 1991, 84,000 Palestinians from the Occupied Territories worked in Israel. Palestinians who live in the Occupied Territories and who

---

1. U.S. State Department, *Country Reports on Human Rights Practices for 1991*, p. 1453.
2. U.S. State Department, *Country Reports on Human Rights Practices for 1985*, p. 1273.
3. U.S. State Department, *Country Reports on Human Rights Practices for 1991*, p. 1453.

work in Israel may be members of the Histadrut, the Israeli national labor organization, but they may not organize their own trade unions within Israel. Although deductions for employee benefits are taken from their wages, Palestinians do not receive most of the benefits granted to Israeli citizens including old-age, survivors, and disability pensions, unemployment compensation, insurance for long-term care or injury in nonoccupational accidents, children's allowances and other welfare programs.[4]

Many Palestinian farmers have been forced to become day laborers when their land was taken for Israeli settlements. Both Israel and Jordan frequently restrict export of agricultural products from the Occupied Territories. "Israeli agriculture and manufacturing are protected against Palestinian competition from the Occupied Territories, whereas all markets in the territories are open to Israelis, subject to extensive Palestinian boycotts."[5]

★　　★　　★

Salah Abu Kteish

"I refused to solve the problem for myself individually."

Emwas

We had a home in Emwas. It was one of the best built houses in the town. My parents had four daughters and one son when they left Emwas. I was not born yet.

My father was active with the resistance. During the 1940s, my father worked in a British camp. Also during the 1940s, he was arrested and imprisoned in Lod, in Ramle prison. (Later on, I was imprisoned in the same prison.)

My mother and father fled Emwas in 1949. Due to the disaster of 1948, two things struck our family: one was that there no longer was a British camp that my father could work in; and two, the land was taken. The majority of our land became part of the No Man's Land. We could not grow crops on it. We could not make a livelihood. That's when my father took the decision to move to Jerusalem.

Jerusalem

When my mother fled, she was pregnant with me. She lived one month in the Salaheiya School in the Old City of Jerusalem with other refugees. I was born in this school. Then my mother's family, who was living downstairs here, gave her one room because she had a newborn child. We had access to a kitchen and a half-bathroom. Since that time, I have been living in this same house in the Old City of Jerusalem.

4. Ibid., pp. 1436, 1438.
5. Ibid., p. 1452.

When my father came to Jerusalem, he worked with the municipality of Jerusalem as a construction worker. He made 35 kroosh per day (about one dollar at that time).

When I was going to school, the first job I had was by the Damascus Gate. I worked for someone who used to sell yogurt in glass jars. Every afternoon after school, I would go to all the places that bought the yogurt, collect the empty jars, and bring them back. I used to make 3 kroosh, which is insignificant when compared to the dollar.

In the summers I worked for a watermelon company. I stayed with the truck, helped to load it and unload it. I used to make 20–25 kroosh per day, which meant I had significant change during the summer.

Beginning when I was fourteen, I worked in a buffet for the Jerusalem cinema. I used to take ten per cent of sales, which was rather good. I worked on this job around four years, until the 1967 war.

1967

Before 1967, we used to go to Emwas. My father had rented out our house and he used to go to collect the rent. We went to the lands that were not in the No Man's Land and we used to collect fruits and wheat if there was any. We never broke our connection with Emwas during our time of being in Jerusalem.

Before the 1967 war, I was not a burden upon my family. I used to work so I paid for my schooling. My sisters were married. So the money my father brought into the family provided even more than a decent living. In 1964, my brother went to Kuwait, and he used to send us 10 to 15 Kuwaiti dinars from time to time. This was almost the income of a person here, so we found ourselves really having two incomes, my brother's as well as my father's.

After the war in 1967, my father's work stopped because he was working with the municipality. My work stopped because the cinema closed. Any income and support we got from Emwas was gone: we no longer got the rental money from the house; also, we were no longer able to go and find food there.

Options

I learned to smoke and I spent my free time in the coffee shops. I found myself without money to eat sometimes.

I was an average student in school. Because I had to work, I could not excel in school. But I did think about school. I wanted to finish.

One of the guys in town saw that I was wasting a lot of time in coffee shops and that I was spending a lot of money on cigarettes, just sitting there, not really doing anything. I was asked if I wanted to become part of a student movement. This was October of 1967. The General Union of Palestinian Students was just a seedling; it wasn't formed yet.

I had two options in front of me: one was to continue on the negative side of life, staying in the coffee shops and spending money on cigarettes; or to become organized in the student movement. We didn't know what we were getting into.

First Arrest

By March of 1968, I had started working in Deir Yassin with a company called Tedarah. (Deir Yassin had been rebuilt as an industrial Jewish area.) It was an Israeli refrigeration company. I was helping to move refrigerators. We were young guys. Everywhere we would go we would be harassed. We were hit several times.

One day we were coming home and we had no idea that there had been a military operation within the borders of Israel that day. We were in buses. They used to drop us off at the Mandelbaum Gate, the gate that separates East and West Jerusalem. There in front of us were police and soldiers. They forced us off the bus and began striking us. Remember, we didn't know what had happened this day. We were coming home from a normal day of work in Deir Yassin.

I was arrested at the gate that day. I was taken to the Moscobiyya prison which at that time was horse stalls in the field with manure and hay on the ground. It was a harsh experience. They used to hit us, then leave for a while, and come back and continue hitting us.

They put a curfew on the city of Jerusalem because the civilian population was in a rage. On my fourth day in prison, they let me out at 1:30 at night. There was still a curfew. I asked them to give me a ride to Damascus Gate because there was a curfew.

When I got out at the Damascus Gate, there in front of me was a patrol. The patrol began interrogating me in front of the Damascus Gate: "Who gave you the ride?" "Why are you out so late?" "Why are you out under curfew?" I told him, "I was in Moscobiyya. I just got released." They acted as if they were going to arrest me once again. I told them, "Go ask the people at the top of the street. The police are still at the top of the street. They will tell you." They walked me up to the top of the street and the policemen who were at the top of the street said, "Let him go. He just came out of Moscobiyya an hour ago."

Student Movement

I started working in the student movement in October 1967. But you have to separate working with them and actually becoming organized. They were not organizing people until at least six or seven months after getting to know the individual. I was not yet organized when I came out of jail.

I was still a high school student. But school was not a daily event like it was before. If there was a curfew there was no school. One day it would be open. One day not.

It is no secret that the student movement was begun by a specific political faction. I straight out told my colleagues that I was not willing to continue in that type of political movement if we were going to continue to be faced with sticks and arrests and beatings. I told them, "I'm not convinced that your work is going to make a difference. I want to become part of the military aspect of the struggle."

They continued to express the need for me to read and to educate myself, to become interested in the larger aspects. I was not convinced about any of this. I was considering dropping out of school. I stayed in school for about a month after this discussion, and then I took my decision that I wanted to drop out. And if they could not provide me with the type of struggle that I wanted, I was going to another party. Several others were emerging at this time and I was ready to move on to somebody else.

After they saw that I was very serious and had already dropped school, they gave me the opportunity to go to Jordan for training. I went there for nine days. This was in about June 1968. I did not get what I expected. I was expecting full military training. Rather, I received mostly educational lessons on the importance of being an educated struggler and methods to mobilize people as individuals.

When I came back, I was arrested for forty-eight hours. After I was released, I became a laborer, a construction worker. I used to work in the day and practice my political life at night.

Prison

On February 26, 1969, I was arrested once again. It was a big Muslim holiday. I was working at a butcher shop within the Old City of Jerusalem. I had weapons at home. They came into my home while I was at work and they found the weapons. They followed me and they caught me at my work.

I spent two months under interrogation. It was probably the most horrendous time for interrogation in the life of our struggle. This is the word of prisoners that have gone through all the different stages. The 1969 time was the beginning of the harshest. Most prisoners spent two months in interrogation before they were ever brought to trial.

After interrogation I stayed four months in Ashkelon. When we were in Ashkelon prison, there used to be cells in the shape of a circle. Soldiers would come and encircle us, and laugh at us and spit on us as if we were animals. After breakfast we would have a beating. After lunch we would have a beating. And after supper we would have a beating. This was after interrogation. This was normal prison life.

During this period my mother used to go to Moscobiyya and request to see me. They refused to tell her that I wasn't even in that prison.

I was moved, after four months, to Ramle prison where my father had been before me. I was put directly into a solitary cell. Just as an animal, they used to feed us through the door — they did not even open the door. It was about 140 or 150 centimeters long and a meter wide [approximately 3 × 5 feet]. If we were lucky, we would go out for one hour.

I stayed in the solitary cell for one month. Neither myself nor any of my comrades had any idea what prison was like, or the difference between prisons, or that there were different cells for different purposes. When I stayed in the solitary cell so long, I thought I was going to spend the rest of my time in prison in this cell.

When we were moved from these solitary cells into the general prison population, we found a different life. I found my comrades who were with me in town were with me now. Also, I got to be introduced to a lot of different types of people, people that were organized for a lot longer than I was, people that had different experiences. So we began to program our days in order not to waste time.

Trial

Then trial began. I was taken to several meetings with my lawyers. They said there were two charges against me: being organized, and having weapons in my possession. These were too concrete to defend; to bargain would be better for me. The lawyer guaranteed me that I could get four years if I would say "yes" to the charges that I was given.

Me, personally, I wanted to continue in the court, not to bargain. I wanted my voice to be heard. But my comrades said it would be better for me to accept the four years — which was a rather short sentence compared to some of the sentences they were giving to people who were going the whole way in court.

Once we agreed, we went into the courtroom. As I said, knowing that I was going to get four years, I went in. The charges were read to me. I pled guilty to the two charges. After the judge heard my confession, the prosecutor surprised me by telling me to ask the judge for mercy. A little debate came into play in front of the judge. I told him, "I'm here to plead against my charges, not to drop my dignity by asking for mercy." The prosecutor then said, "You have two choices. You either beg for mercy or I drop the plea bargaining agreement."

The judge then asked if I wanted to say anything myself. I told him, "I am here to plead guilty to the two charges against me and I refuse to beg for mercy because I feel that I am under occupation and it's my legitimate right to fight this occupation." I was sentenced for seven years.

They took me back to prison. I got a visit from the boss of the prosecutor. This chief prosecutor came and said, "You should not have taken seven years. If you appeal and ask for mercy, I guarantee you four years." I refused to appeal because I would not ask for mercy. I spent my seven years in prison.

Work and Refusal to Work in Prison

I began serving my term in Ramle prison where my father was before me.

We were given a job by the security officers to make camouflage nets for tanks. We refused. We were going to be punished for this so we announced an open strike, a hunger strike, refusing to work in any military aspect of the operations.

We spent twenty-three hours a day in cells because of our refusal to work on the nets. We were given one hour a day to leave the cell and that one hour would be split into three: we were given a half hour to walk in a circle with our heads down, hands behind the back; we were given a half hour to kneel against the outside yard wall, as if there was a chair there but in a kneeling position; and we would be given four cigarettes, but we had to finish those four cigarettes within that one hour.

In the cell, they would give us one sheet of prison stationery. We would write a letter on the front of that stationery sheet, give it to them, and they would send it out. Our families were required to respond on the back of that letter. It would have to be the same sheet of paper. I have one of them that my mother just kept and never returned.

Anything that was given to us for our use, for instance, razor blade, pen, pencil, paper, anything that was used during the day, had to be returned back to them. Ramle was split into two sections: civilian prisoners and political prisoners. Arab prisoners used to smuggle paper and pens from the civilian section into our section.

I was still a young boy at that time. I was very active and hardy. I worked in the kitchen. It was agreed upon that we would work in our section only, cleaning our section and feeding our section. We used to get up at 5:00, work in the kitchen until 5:00 or 6:00 in the afternoon. I learned cooking so well that you could classify me as a chef right now. I was given the responsibility to cook meals for sick prisoners in order to give them a special diet.

When I came back to my cell, I would activate myself in the education program. If there were things to write, things to read, letters to translate or whatever, I used to work with that. I consider myself one of the many who has been built by prisons. I learned Hebrew fluently in prison and I took three English courses.

My father died while I was in prison. I had not seen him for ten months. My family postponed the burial one day, even though that does not go with our religion. They postponed it in hopes that if they requested for me to come out just for one day that I could be at the burial. The authorities refused. I didn't know this was taking place, and I read about my father's death in the papers.

Supporting a Family

When I was released in February 1976, I was in a hurry to get caught up with my own life. I stayed away from the life of education. I wanted to get married. I wanted to straighten out my life. Life in prison had changed me politically and psychologically. I can say now, thank God, that it has had a positive effect on the way that I deal with my wife and my children, and on the way that I have built my household.

When I got out of prison in 1976, I was almost alienated from my home community because I was a political prisoner. There was a factor of fear there. Even part of my own family refused to come and greet me when I came back. The community was not yet very receptive to political prisoners.

Twenty days after my release, my brother in Kuwait sent a visa for me to go to Kuwait to work. I went. I was hired at a place where they were going to train me to do interior decorating. The pay was going to be about $400 per month in Kuwaiti currency. That was a big amount of money. I accepted and I went home. That night when I was sleeping, I had a discussion with myself: after my comrades spent so much time building me as a person, and after I sacrificed so much time myself, working hard to build myself, is my place to build an economic life outside of the land or to go back and be steadfast in the Old City of Jerusalem? I woke up in the morning and I quit.

When I came back from Kuwait I had three offers. I had a sister in the United States and her husband gave me an offer to go there and work; he needed help and he wanted somebody from the family. The second offer was for me to go to Jordan, which would mean to leave again. The third was that my relatives in Abu Ghosh were willing to buy my father's land in Emwas. I refused all three. But my younger brother wasn't dealing with responsibility yet, and I felt that I had to support the family.

I became a laborer again. I worked building settlements in Jerusalem, until the head of the security forces came and warned the builder of the settlements that I was a threat and I should not be working there. I was fired. They made sure that it was very public that I was fired, and that made it very difficult for me to work even with Arab contractors.

I was hired by the Jerusalem Electric Company. My job was to dig the holes for the utility poles of the electric company. I had in mind that I needed to finish school in order to get a better job, but it was very difficult financially. Then my younger brother was arrested and imprisoned for four years. I was the only breadwinner.

I knew I could not support my family if I remained a laborer. I just couldn't make ends meet. So while I was working I attended a training school on electricity, which was given through the Jerusalem Electric Company.

Labor/Management Relations

I became aware of labor/management relationships through this apprenticeship. I was supposed to work for six months during my training period and then I was supposed to become registered and get my certificate. This six months turned into a year and some months, and during that time I was always in conflict with the management.[6] I was doing the exact same work that I would have been doing if they had given me my certificate, but my salary was not the same.

There were about eighteen apprentice electricians in my section. All eighteen of us were delayed in getting our certificates. There was a union there, but they refused to permit us to strike, so we struck anyway.

We became a problem to our own union. First, the union did not believe that the delay was significant enough to make an issue with the management. Number two, the union did not want this to become an open discussion in its ranks. And number three, which blew the top off, was that the union leader

6. Management of the Jerusalem Electric Company was, at this level, Palestinian.

came to me personally and said, "Speak to me one-on-one. We'll take care of what you need to finish this problem," and I refused. He liked me. He knew me from prison. That was not the issue. The issue was, I refused to solve the problem for myself individually.

During this period, I also was learning how to drive and I got my commercial driver's license. I took a decision to confront this company. I wanted to stay with the company. I wanted to be a thorn in their side. I continued working as an electrician and, at the same time, I applied to be a driver for the Jerusalem electrical trucks. They continued to refuse. They would not allow me to become a driver because, they thought, applying for this new job I must not like my old job, therefore, sooner or later, I'll leave. I stayed longer than the boss! When the boss quit or was fired and the new one came, I became a driver.

In June 1978, I asked for a vacation so I could get married. I had earned the vacation, but my boss refused my vacation saying he wanted to leave town that day. I told him, "Anyway I'm getting married, and I'm not going to be working that week so deal with it." In the end they did give me the leave for one week.

When I got back I found I had a new job. It was the electrician job that I had before! I asked for the reason why I was transferred. The boss of that section told me that they just had internal changes. I said, "That's not good enough. I want you to bring my other boss and I want to talk to everyone at one time." The boss of the electrician section said, "OK, just come meet with me, tell me what's the problem. I'll get you transferred back to wherever you want to go." I said, "You bring me the other guy and the worker who was involved in this transfer. I'll talk to all of you at once. Then if you want to transfer me you can transfer me, but I won't transfer because I had a special meeting with you." There was no meeting.

I ended up staying four months in the electrician section but I wasn't quiet. I was a thorn in their sides. I was not yet a certified electrician. I had finished the course and I had nothing more to do but I wasn't certified.

Second Jobs

I worked from 6:30 to 3:00 with the electrical company. At 3:00 I would head straight to Deir Yassin where I worked in a printer's shop. I used to get home at 11:30 or 12:00, dead! The income from the Jerusalem Electric Company was not enough to support the marriage without the supplemental income from the print shop.

One good thing was that the owner of the print shop was religious. So we had a lot of days off, religious holidays, which gave me the opportunity to go and train for a bus chauffeur license. That's what I did. I went on days off from the print shop for six months to get my bus and taxi license.

I stopped working in the print shop in 1980. I worked with my chauffeur's license along with my Jerusalem Electric Company work up until May 20, 1990. This was Black Sunday when seven Gaza workers were killed. I was working at that time as a taxi driver in the afternoon. Political and professional people went on a hunger strike in solidarity with them. For fourteen days I was on a hunger strike here in Jerusalem.

After those fourteen days, most of us in the opposition were faced with tax people coming to our homes. From me they requested 5,000 shekels for every year I worked in the taxi. I couldn't afford it so I quit. I never made 5,000 shekels in one year.

Elected

I became crystallized in the labor movement as someone who would not be bought by the management. I was more interested in being principled and standing by my brother in work, and I came to be well-known for my confrontations, both during strikes and in my debates with management and union leaders.

We had a strike at the Jerusalem Electric Company in 1979 over a cost-of-living increase, working conditions in the field, and a contract that defined the workers' rights. I was one of the ones that gave a lot of input on how that strike should take place and how our requests should be proposed.

After this strike it was decided that we would have union elections. I was elected for the first time in 1979 and from that day until now I have been in the leadership of the union in different positions. I am still a worker and the union is an extra responsibility. We have no paid staff.

I was also elected to be the representative of my union in the General Federation of Trade Unions. In 1980, the Federation was split. I was one member of a committee that tried to rejuvenate, to rebuild, this Federation. This committee was not totally successful. So we and others decided to create committees to work in the meantime.

The rules of the Federation require that representatives come from the union membership. However, we also have people who are paid staff members of political organizations. This has deteriorated the condition of the Federation because then you're no longer talking only about union workers. As our rules for the Federation state, I am still a worker. I was elected by my Jerusalem Electric Union. The other unions have not held elections but yet they send representatives.

I was a founding member of the Popular Workers' Committee. We have been very successful in our work. We have been responsible for creating several unions. We have carried on the work even though the Federation is not there. In 1985, we took a conscious political decision to work within our committee until a unified Federation can come back.

When we saw that a mass union movement was surrounding us, I felt that I needed to spend most of my time in the organizing field. It has not been easy because I have been personally harassed for my exposure in this activity. I was arrested four times, sometimes for a couple of days, and interrogated. I am not allowed to travel outside of the country.

On August 3, 1988, they came here and I was arrested for six months for administrative detention. There was no charge against me. In my interrogation it was brought up several times against me that I am a leader in the

Popular Workers' Committee. I went back to my father's prison in Ramle and put in my six months.

I have now four children. The oldest is thirteen. The smallest is four years old. He is named for Naji Al Ali.

Yacoub

"It was the head-hunter's job to bring ten workers."

I was introduced to a "head-hunter" from Jerusalem who took Palestinian workers from the West Bank to Haifa in Israel to work in a bakery.

It was the head-hunter's job to bring ten workers to this bakery. It didn't matter where the ten workers were from or who they were. The head-hunter was the person responsible to the bakery owner for these workers. If the worker did anything wrong, the management would come to the head-hunter and the head-hunter would solve the problem. And vice versa, if we had a problem, we would go to the head-hunter.[7]

So I went to work in a bakery working at night, going and coming every day. They came for me at 8:00 p.m. and took me to work. We would get there about 11:00 p.m. and we would work until about ten o'clock the following morning. I used to go home and sleep, eat, and go back to work.

A Palestinian can have a permit to travel back and forth only to work. You are not allowed to sleep overnight in Israel but you can work all through the night for an Israeli factory or business.

It was a mixed group of workers. There were about 30 of us from Jenin, Nablus, Ramallah, Jerusalem, and Gaza. There were also Israelis working with us. They were in charge of us.

Sometimes my work in this bakery would consist of going with an Israeli driver and delivering our product to the bakeries within the city. There were different kinds of truck drivers. Some would make sure that it was known that you were Arab, which would cause you to be harassed in the city. Others were nice. They would not mention that you were Arab. You could stop at many bakeries, leave them their stuff and not talk to them and no one would really know.

I would be paid by the head-hunter, not by the owner of the factory. For ten hours of work, we were paid twenty-five shekels [about $10–12].

I worked for about a month. Then we could not work any longer. To get to work we had to pass through Arab villages and we started getting stoned. The first day we got stoned, we tried to explain to them who we were and what we were doing. When there was not one piece of glass left in the van, we took a decision that we did not want to work in Israel.

7. According to the U.S. State Department, *Country Reports on Human Rights Practices for 1988*, p. 1374: "About half the West Bankers and Gazans who work in Israel come illegally, with labor contractors or individually, evading taxes and social contributions (which their employers also evade), but losing social benefits. In unorganized enterprises, their wages and working conditions are often below Israeli legal standards, particularly in seasonal agriculture and small restaurants, garages, and construction sites."

Mohammed

"The rebuilding of the union movement was adding to the fire of the Intifada."

My family came to Jenin camp from a village outside Haifa in 1948. My father was a farmer. He had land before '48 and he used to work on his land.

The goals of the Zionist movement, from the beginning, were to take land to build the country, which meant to kick the inhabitants off that land, but at the same time to keep the working hand on the land because he was the person who had experience on that piece of land. My father is a prime example. We were working with the land. Then, when it was taken from us, my father became a worker on the same land. This made my father an indispensable resource to Israel. He was an educated hand who was working at a very cheap labor rate, because he had no alternative.

I grew up in the Jenin camp. I studied Business Administration in Najah University and I graduated in 1987, just as the Intifada was coming about and mass arrests started taking place.

I was arrested several times, first in 1988 at the beginning of this barrage of arrests. I spent sixteen days in interrogation and was released. But right after that, I was arrested a second time and I was sentenced for ten months.

Arrests were for activism in general. At the beginning of the Intifada, there was no organized union activity. The union bodies were defunct. The majority of labor leaders had left, were exiled or in prison. There was a lack of leadership and a lack of interest in organizing factory workers or the agricultural sector, even though in Jenin these were the two main types of work that we had. I saw this lack of interest both within Jenin and from the PLO as a whole.

In 1988, there were many prisoners with us who were union workers and who were the seeds of the rebuilding of the union movement. Administrative detention was used to arrest these people without actually charging them with unionism, because the Israelis felt that union activism was political. The rebuilding of the union movement was adding to the fire of the Intifada.

When I left prison I wanted to begin working with unions. I was released from prison in December 1988. I joined a union in Jenin. That was my first step. In February 1989, the preparatory committee to try to rebuild the General Federation of Trade Unions was formed and I was nominated to that committee.

I worked inside the '48 area in a plastic factory. We produced whatever the mold was for that day, anything from dishes to stands for fans. The factory had about 400 workers. Between 35 and 40 per cent of the workers were Palestinian, the majority of which were from Jenin. Besides us there were a lot of Arabs from the Nazareth area that worked there, as well as some Jews.

It was not long before I was arrested again. When I was released in December 1989, I was given a green ID card which cut off my employment activity within the State of Israel.[8] When I was first arrested they didn't have

8. A person with a green ID card is forbidden to enter Israel or Jerusalem. The U.S. State Department, *Country Reports on Human Rights Practices for 1990*, p. 1490, states: "Approximately 15,000

this idea of two different color cards. This came out in 1989. Since I have not been permitted to go into Israel to work, I have spent my energy in Jenin solely on building the movement here.

Mamdouh

"We will never leave."

This area is a part of the Jordan Valley called Marj en Naja. The population of the area as a whole is about 1,500. This village is about 200 — twenty families, on average ten per family.

The individuals who established this village were refugees. There are two neighborhoods in the village. One neighborhood is from villages in the far northern part of Palestine. They came here in 1948 when they were exiled. The others were Bedouins from southern Palestine near Beersheba. The U.N. provided motorized wells and basic housing.

I came here in 1960. We came from north of Beersheba. I have my grandfather's deed for 13,000 dunums [4,250 acres] of agricultural land that we had in Palestine before my grandfather was exiled in 1948. When we left, we were looking for some place that would be a safe haven until we would be able to return home. This was one of the places that would take us.

When we arrived, this was Jordanian government land. We rented the land from the Jordanian government for seven years. Under Jordanian law, after seven years we were supposed to own the land. We were self-sufficient during those first seven years. We were able to dig wells and to apply motors to them.

After the 1967 war, the Israelis took two-thirds of the land in the Jordan Valley, and they created a buffer zone with barbed wire. They left one-third of the land to be cultivated by the residents. The Israelis also formed a village of their own in this area. There was no recognition of the legal arrangements between the Palestinians living here and the Jordanian government.

The land has been confiscated. This village has twenty farmers who have been turned from partners in land ownership and development into hands working for someone else who is the landowner. Many individuals in this area work as wage laborers. The kibbutz with date trees is on confiscated land. That kibbutz hires Palestinian labor to work the land.

I now rent 64 dunums [16 acres] from people who are Israelis. That is a very small parcel of land for a family. There is no ownership in this renting contract. We rent from year to year.

Palestinians are affected by the Government's issuance of distinctive identity cards which prohibit the bearer from entering or transiting Israel or East Jerusalem. These cards have been issued for several years to Palestinians considered to be security risks. In November the Government began to issue several thousand more such cards to any Palestinian ever detained or incarcerated. Some of those who received such cards at that time claim to have been administratively detained for their political views. Others, including lawyers, human rights organization employees, and journalists, say they had never been arrested or administratively detained. Such identity cards not only prevent Palestinians from working in Israel or East Jerusalem, but also from visiting the many key Palestinian institutions located there, such as hospitals, schools, and religious institutions."

We try to be as self-sufficient as possible. We grow eggplant and tomatoes. We also grow some chickens and livestock. We have some sheep. We buy what we do not have from the marketplace in Jericho. We do not yearn for luxuries. We have the basic diet that we need here.

The water resources have been drained by the Israelis and the water that is left here for the Palestinian farmer has become salty. Therefore, we are only able to produce eggplant and tomatoes and very minor crops.[9] Settlers have solved their problem of salt in the water by making a linkage between all of the settlements[10] and installing water purifiers. We are not allowed to install water purifiers. They have enough quality water for agricultural use, but we are prohibited from having this water.

When a well is drained, it is illegal for us to drill a new well. Thousands of dunums of bananas have been lost down the road, twenty kilometers from here, because the water resources were depleted and they were not allowed to link to any other water resources or to drill new wells. When your well is finished, your livelihood is finished.

We have one six-month growing season. We produce for six months straight and we sit for a long period of time without doing anything. October first is when we start to harvest the new crop. Now [in July] we are in the preparatory stages.

The Israelis have a year-round growing season because they have technology. When they don't grow crops, they grow flowers. Five hundred meters from here there is a kibbutz where they grow grapes and flowers. The kibbutzes here are funded by American institutions or American individuals. They work under the umbrella of the government. They have the money, the tractors, the resources and the permits to put up greenhouses.

Because of the technology and because of this money and resources, there is an Israeli I know up in the hills who took one dunum and planted grapes, and those grapes produce as much as three hundred of ours. We cannot be expected to produce this much. We do not have the water purifiers. We cannot have the essentials for farming.

There is also a problem with transportation of goods. At this time we are not allowed to take anything outside of this area to the Jordanian market, and we are not allowed to take anything into the Israeli market. The Palestinian market — the West Bank and the Gaza Strip — is continually under curfews and strikes and this presents difficulties in transportation and marketing. Our market is mainly Nablus and Jenin.

In the days that we were able to export to Jordan, we would take our product in trucks. Before going over to the Jordanian side, the Israelis

9. This is corroborated by Al Haq, West Bank Affiliate of the International Commission of Jurists: "Excessive use of water results in salination of water supplies, restricting the crops that can be grown to low-value tomatoes, eggplants, and the like. . . ." (*A Nation Under Siege: Al-Haq Annual Report on Human Rights in the Occupied Palestinian Territories, 1989*, p. 432, n. 20).
10. According to Al Haq: "In 1977–1978, 17 settlement wells in the Jordan valley pumped 14.1 million cubic meters (mcm) of water while the 106 Palestinian wells in the same region were permitted to pump only 12.1 mcm. Many Palestinian villages in the Jordan valley are consequently short of water. Meanwhile, military orders were passed connecting the water grid to the Israeli grid and Jewish settlements to the Israeli electricity grid, further entrenching Israeli control and *de facto* annexation" (*A Nation Under Siege*, p. 410).

searched the trucks. Every piece of product on that truck had to come off the truck and go back on the truck. By the time that produce reached the market it was bad and could no longer be sold.

As for exportation of products to Israel proper, there is a special military contingent on the border that looks for fresh fruits or vegetables coming from the West Bank. Nothing is allowed to go through. It is a completely closed market. Even with their lack of technology, Palestinian farmers were able to compete with Israeli products. But in order to control the price of Israeli products, a decision was made to cut off the transportation of Palestinian agricultural products. This way Israeli products would be sold because theirs would be the only products on the market. In the market in Israel, they sell one kilogram of eggplant for a dollar; here, we sell thirteen kilograms for half a dollar.

The European Economic Community [EEC] has given us some opportunities to transport produce outside the West Bank. Last year we were able to get some eggplant out but the eggplant was damaged by the amount of time it had to stay in the coolers because of paperwork problems. More essential is that any market that was opened up to us in the European Community was saturated before our product got there. In one year's time, no one would buy from us any longer.

It has become harder during the Intifada because of curfews and strikes. There are days when the entire West Bank is closed. There are strikes, and a strike means that the worker does not go to work, which means that the consumer no longer has money to purchase the product.

But the Intifada is also attempting to help us in the agricultural sector, for instance, by the boycott of Israeli products and fruits. This is not just a political slogan. It is a practical thing. They are trying to promote our products. This is good.

During the Gulf War, there was a twenty-four hour curfew in this area as well as in other areas. Because we are used to this type of life, we store essentials that we need, like flour, and we go back to primitive methods. We are not dependent on gas. If the gas is cut off, we go back to charcoal.

In the beginning of the war, we were not allowed to go from village to village or city to city. During the climax of the war, for forty days, we were not allowed out of the house itself. Every couple of days they used to give us two hours to do anything we had to do outside of the house. First we would give our livestock water and then we would go get some food for the children.

We as farmers had an extra burden on us in the Gulf War. The worker stayed home and didn't work but the factory was still there when he went back. When we went back we found that no water got to our land, the crop died, and we lost what we started with. We lost the whole season.

The war caused very complex problems, one being our not being able to work properly. Another is that Jordan used to produce exports for the Gulf States. With the closure of the Gulf area, the Jordanians had a surplus so their surplus was going to their population. They didn't need a Palestinian product.

The Israelis patrol the Jordanian border. Under normal circumstances, every once in a while a jeep comes here, turns around and then goes back. When there is a problem or a tense situation, they will remain present and put at least twenty families under continuous curfew.

Collective punishment is the harshest punishment that the Israelis practice against us. Something could have happened twenty kilometers from here and the whole area is put under curfew when we don't even know what's happened. Down the road from here where the troops have been hit by rocks, one of the punishments would be to uproot the trees. Here there are no trees to uproot.

As an individual farmer, I am in debt 15,000 dinars [$30,000], partially because of the Iraqi war and partially because we do not have a market open to us for the small quantity we are allowed to export. The war explains most of my debt. But it was one blow in a series of blows. Now the war is over, we still cannot export nor cultivate in the proper way.

I have a personal problem trying to finance my own harvest. But it is not only my problem. Many are not going to be able to harvest this year.

The smallest cost to produce on one dunum is 1,000 shekels [$500]. This is just to prepare the land — plowing, seeding, covering the land with plastic, mulching — not the labor. The person who funds the harvest takes a commission on whatever I make. But I must pay before he will give me anything else.

The person who loaned me the money had $100,000. He loaned that money out. He gave the first person $5,000, the next person $10,000. Now it is gone. He's stuck now because he has no income for himself. He is very lax in asking for the money because he knows the person on the other end also has a problem. True, there is a class difference. But there is a collectiveness in the Palestinian community that allows us to be calm and not to press, "Give me my money now." I know this individual cannot continue giving.

In a few cases, an individual will give a small piece of his land to a person who takes on his debt for him. They let us get into debt to where we cannot harvest. Finally, there is a wealthy Palestinian who will buy the land and pay off the debt. But he will never sell the land to the Israelis.

The last resort this year will be to plant only half of the land and sell part of the livestock, but this is very dangerous because your livestock is your only backup if your crop does not produce as you expect.

After that stage, the next stage is to sell my labor. Then I will grant Gorbachev and Bush and others the ultimate thanks for sending us the kibbutz people [immigrants], Israeli settlers that are able to give us work. Have we come to this, that we have to sell our labor to work on *our* land?

It is not so analytical as I have explained to you — three stages for me to lose my land and become a working hand on a kibbutz — but there are the emotions and characteristics of the person. To sell his labor to work on his land gives the person a sense of explosion. It is not intellectual debate. It is the feelings of persons, of individuals, family structure, that is being sacrificed. If the person becomes a desperado, anything could happen at that point.

Every year we go back to our land in Beersheba. The discussion is always the same. They ask us, "What are you doing here? This is private land." I say, "This was originally my land." The hardest thing in my life is to see our land being used by another person. They grow the same crops as my parents used to grow, but it is grown in higher quantity and quality because of the access to technology, the irrigation, the continuous water resources. You see the fields organized in an orderly fashion.

Does the world expect me to get up and leave? We left our land once and look what has happened to us. There is a Palestinian saying, "does one leave the sprinkle of a rainfall to stand under a waterfall?" We will never leave.

The Israelis understand that moneys from the PLO could help so this is banned. That channel is closed as an alternative funding source. They want us to leave or die.

Don't ever think that there is any national liberation movement that is rich. But it is not the money that is going to provide victory or not. It's the people and the will of the people.

The Intifada has brought hardship but it is also helping. We are 100 per cent with it because we know that it is trying to address our problems. When a family comes into economic hardship and needs support, there is a relief effort through the Intifada. Food is provided for that family. But our problems are basically economic problems which are the hardest to solve.

There are rumors continuously that the European Market, United States, other economic markets, are going to give us relief here. But the relief comes in the form of giving us a factory that makes cookies — which is not for us essential. We want essential help. We don't want chocolate factories and cookie factories. We want the basic pillars of agriculture.

I do not need the 120 pounds of flour that comes in the relief bags from the European Community. Nor do I need the bags that come from different parts of the world that say: "Not for sale. For relief efforts." Relief organizations could help a specific family in need of something, or might offer moral support.

We are struggling for land. We need to have freedom to develop our land. Land is the basic resource of agriculture. If land is confiscated we no longer have the basis for building any kind of agriculture in this country.

I am addressing all the people in America that want to work on this issue. You are able to come here and see. Go. Do your own live study. Find a project or an institution that you think is trustworthy, and support it directly. See the results of your work. From abroad and from the West Bank, there are volunteer groups and individuals that come here with their expertise and technology and they help us to develop what we have.

Let's learn a little bit from our enemy. Israel is a self-sufficient state agriculturally. It does not need any outside support in agriculture. But they are convincing people from around the world to come to work as volunteers to set up new projects, coming to work for nothing in order to build the land. They are collecting dates and flowers. They are not putting any of their own production money into this. It is collective work, it is volunteer work, and they are making millions off of it.

Let's not wait until we have a state. We should always have the sense of collectiveness and everyone who wants to work could build the land.

I am appealing to the conscience of mankind, even though I am not convinced eternally that mankind as a whole has a conscience. Look at what happened in Kuwait. This small country that had a problem for a few months got the attention of the world, whereas millions of people here have been economically deprived and socially deprived and politically deprived, and no one can raise a finger. Where is the humanitarianism? Where is the democracy that everyone speaks about? Where are the human rights?

The future looks bleak if the situation does not change quickly. The current peace efforts are morphine, to keep us quiet for a little bit longer. Today, thousands upon thousands of foreigners are coming into this country and taking the land from under our feet, and at the same time the political entity is talking about settling these lands. It doesn't make sense. I have lost hope in all aspects of trying to make the situation better except, when American and European delegations come, I have hope that that my voice and the voice of my people will reach these foreign lands.

I need freedom. I am willing to sleep hungry as long as I can behold freedom and independence. Freedom is essential before any of this relief effort comes to me. I also need political solidarity with my work. My hope is that one day we will be able to be together because one person has technology, another has oil, another has fruit — each of us need each other if we are going to survive as a human race.

You base your foreign policy on the basis of what you call terrorism or extremism in this society. If terrorism and extremism is here it is because of the policies that have been implemented against us. If terrorism means confrontation with the authorities, then I am willing to become a terrorist.

The Palestinian people are the most steadfast people in history. As a whole, the Palestinian people have put their hands out for peace. We are a people who want to live. We are a simple, practical people. All we are asking for from this large house is one small room, but give us freedom and peace. If the Palestinian people achieve this peace, they will be the best friend of the person on the other side of the table. We will reach out. We will not even think of war but we will think of building the society together.

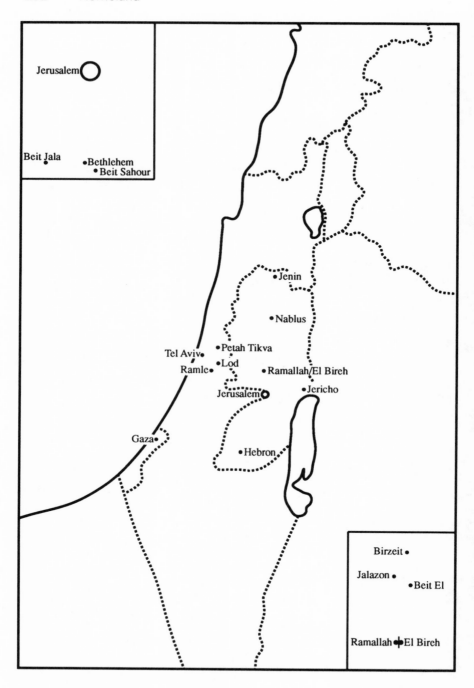

8

Families

Palestinian families face many problems in maintaining their solidarity. These include a maze of obstacles in connection with foreign travel. Individuals like Abu Sam and Husam Rafeedie, who obtained foreign citizenship after emigration but who were born in the West Bank and own property there, are permitted to return to the Occupied Territories only as tourists for a three-month period. Um Elias' daughter is now permanently restricted to non-resident status because, while residing in Lebanon for study, she lost her travel papers. When we interviewed Um Sa'alem in the summer of 1992 we were unable to speak to her husband. After a brief visit to Jordan, he had been waiting for weeks for permission to return.

The restricted status of Palestinians contrasts sharply with the status conferred on Jews by Israeli legislation. "The Law of Return of 1950, which abolished all restrictions on Jewish immigration, and the Citizenship Law of 1952, which granted every Jew the right to citizenship upon arrival in Israel, confer an advantage on Jews in matters of immigration and citizenship."[1]

*   *   *

Leeka Bahour

"We are always looking out for everyone else."

Making a Living from the Land

I am more than sixty years old. I was born in the house right behind here. It was my grandfather's house. Thirteen individuals lived in that one-room building. I had four brothers and three sisters. I was the fourth child in my family.

When I was young, I used to work in the fields around the house. I used to spend my time with the sheep and the roosters. We had a cow. I would milk

---

1. U.S. State Department, *Country Reports on Human Rights Practices for 1985*, p. 1261.

the cow or sheep. My mother would make the cheese and yogurt, everything fresh.

In my mother's time you ground your flour at home. We used to rotate two rocks to crush the grains. In my time, we would get the wheat from the field, put it on the roof of the house to dry, and then take it to the flour mill. Grinding was the only part of the process that was automated. In our house there was a stove; my mother would pat the dough with her hands and put it in the oven.

My grandmother did the same work my mother did, just one generation back. And when my generation came, I did the same thing. I learned embroidery from my mother.

My grandfather was crippled so he did not work, and my parents were old, so my brothers and sisters and I did the major work of planting and harvesting.

We produced from our land. I used to pick olives during the olive season, grapes during the grape season, and figs during the fig season. We had lentil beans, and we used to pick them.

We had a lot of land. The whole family had between 120 and 140 dunums. It was spread out in separate parcels. We used to walk back and forth, about five or six kilometers each way. We carried loads of fruit in straw baskets on our heads. Sometimes we went barefoot.

We had an ox to help with the plowing. The person who didn't have an ox would give us something nominal and we would plow their land. If we needed them to help us pick the crop, we would hire them to do that. So each family helped the others with the different resources that it had.

Whatever was needed for the family would go to the family. Anything left over would be sold at a cheap price to those who did not have land. They would come to the house. There were no scales so we would sell by the bag. We would fill a bag and say, "This is about five rutal." [One rutal is about six pounds.]

I started working in the fields when I was eleven years old. We would begin at six in the morning, sometimes even before dawn, and we would stay until seven in the evening. Even in hot weather, there was no going home to take a nap. We worked the whole day. If there were sharp thorns in the plowing and you got scratched, that was part of the work. You didn't go home. You just finished the day's work.

Most of the boys went to school up to the fourth or fifth grade. When they were old enough to work, they would go to work. As soon as they were old enough to chase the donkey, they would chase the donkey. Studying was only to the sixth grade anyway so it was not a deprivation of education to go through fourth or fifth grade. That was the norm at that time.

In my time, the daughter's priority was traditional work. The daughter should go and work in the fields; the son should study. It would be a disgrace for the daughter to read. After my time, both men and women got education.

When I was forty-seven years old, I went to an adult education class at the Friends Girls School. In thirteen months I reached the sixth grade level. It wasn't anything political. I used to get letters from my brothers. I couldn't read them so I had to take them to someone to read them to me. By the time I found out what was in the letter, the whole town also knew what was in the letter.

I went to one of the schoolteachers I knew and I said, "I want to learn how to read. Don't say I am old and I won't be able to. If I can't do it, hit me and make me learn." I learned arithmetic on the streets from buying and selling — and I don't need a calculator!

When I was young, they used to throw movie advertisements on the field around the house. I thought they were throwing papers that meant we had to pay taxes for the land, so I would go and hide them. But after I got my sixth grade education, I went back to the house and I found a whole trove of papers. At that point I knew what they were and I threw them away.

There was no running water in the houses. We used to get water from a well. There was a well next to the mosque that was down the street from where we lived. There were three separate faucets from the well for all of this side of town. In the summertime, the spring that fed the well would become low, so the water would trickle down from the faucet. It could take from two o'clock in the afternoon until eight, just to get one full vase of water to take back, because there were so many people waiting in line. If you wanted to get two vases which would hold you for a day, it would take a whole day's work to get that. Sometimes, if our well was busy, I would walk to a little village on the way to Birzeit where there was another water well. We carried the water in a vase (called a jarra) on our heads.

Only the people who were really needed to go for water would go because it took so much time. My parents were old. They couldn't carry the water. The kids carried it, both the girls and the boys. When my older brother became mature, he bought a mule and we used to go with the mule and get all the water at one time which made it easier.

The well was like the marketplace at that time, very busy. Communication and gossip would happen because we spent so much time there.

In 1976, the Israelis confiscated about 50 dunums of our land. When they took it they offered me a small sum. For twelve years I refused to take that sum until I felt that if the land were not going to come back to me I might as well take what I could get for it.

They are not using the confiscated land except for one parcel where they store ammunition and rifles. The rest cannot be used and cannot be bought or sold. Our income came from the land. If we were still able to grow crops on that land, we could make a lot more money.

Marriage

I was seventeen years old when I got married. My husband had a little grocery store across the street from our house. He was the only grocer in this part of town. He used to pass by my parents' house. He saw me carrying all I could carry, and I didn't have much fat on me. He talked to his family and they came and asked for me. I knew he was a man in town, but there was no relationship there. Then it was dishonorable if you built a relationship before you got married.

My family did not pressure me to marry. They encouraged us to marry but we weren't forced to accept someone we didn't want to marry.

A long time ago, to show prestige and honor, the lady would go on a horse when she got married. They put me on a horse, and we went from my father's house less than half a block to the house of the father of my husband and that is where I stayed.

My husband's parents were very elderly too so my work didn't change. My husband's mother had ten children and she was on her deathbed when I got married. I basically took her role.

During the 1948 disaster, my husband became very sick. We went on the mule, he and I, a couple of kilometers away to a big fig tree on the high mountain across from where we lived. It was on a parcel of land that was ours. We stayed under the fig tree for seven days, I and my sick husband.

We left because we were scared. Planes came two or three times and they made a big commotion here in town. They would swoop down. It was like a warning that they were coming. We were scared for our lives, so we took off. When we came back to our house, everything was the same.

My husband died six months after we got married. He was twenty-two years old when he died. It was a sudden natural death. After that I wore only black for thirteen years. Only my eyes showed. Nobody came and asked for me again. Probably they were scared of me because I dressed that way. Remarriage was acceptable but I didn't want to remarry. There wasn't anyone of the same quality as my husband.

I stayed with my in-laws for seven years after his death. After seven years, my brother, the oldest son of my father, sent a letter to my in-laws and said, "In the same way we gave you our daughter, after seven years we would like to ask to have her back into our family." They agreed and I came back here.

I was about twenty-five years old with no children. I took care of my mother and father. And I did a lot of sewing. I sewed for myself first and then I became a seamstress. Customers would bring all of the material and all of the thread, and I would measure and sew at home. I do the same thing now.

I worked by hand until I had enough money to buy a sewing machine. I made so much money from my machine that I paid for it many times over. Thirty-six years I have had my machine. It was a treadle machine when I bought it but it was converted to electric. I built myself up with my machine. I put 8,000 dinars into remodeling the old house. I have stocks now in Palestinian companies. I put forth 4,000 dinars to help my brother marry. And I donate a lot to the mosque, to people in the refugee camps, and to anyone that I think needs a donation.

Becoming Aware

I began to become aware of what was going on around me in 1948 after my husband died. I had no political speculation before that time. We were solely concerned about harvesting from the land. That was our priority. If a lady spoke of politics, it was unacceptable.

In 1948, we used to go to the health facility up the road from here. They would bring the refugees in trucks — the mother who had lost her son; the child whose father had not shown up anywhere. Truckloads of injured came. My mother almost lost it at that point. She was not really involved in taking care of people, but my mother made bread for them. Some refugees stayed in the field where this house is right now.

Thirteen people came from Lod. We opened our house to them. They stayed for six years in one of the rooms. We had three rooms and they stayed in one of them. My uncle opened up a store in their name and they worked together. Also we bought them cattle, groves of trees, beehives, and they made honey.

After a couple of years, my uncle pulled out of the partnership and gave his share to the refugee family. Now they have built a home, but if you go and ask them, they will tell you that it was the Bahour family who put them on their feet. You have to remember that we were a rather wealthy family compared to people in the refugee camps.

My uncle gave the Jordanians thirteen dunums when they were building a hospital here before 1967. The hospital is now part of the Beit El military establishment.

When I was young I lived under British rule. I got married under British rule. Then came Jordanian rule. The British weren't as repressive. They at least had pity on the population, unlike Jordan.

For example, the Jordanians arrested my sister's son, Jimah. The Jordanian jail master put his foot on Jimah's neck and pressed on it saying, "Until you tell me the king is great, I will not take my foot off." When Jimah said he didn't like the king, he took twenty-two years in prison. He was charged with being a member of the Communist Party but they didn't prove anything. This is an example of the petty things that took a man's life in jail.

At the hearing when Jimah was sentenced, there was a young man who was sentenced to four years. Jimah was so troubled by that, he said to the judge: "Can you just let him go and put his four years on top of my twenty-two? He is yet young. Let him live his life. I am willing to take his four years."

I got first aid training about six months before the Six Day War. Every town and village in the West Bank was to train ten people in first aid. They wanted to pick people who were well known in town, would be accepted in all the homes, and were strong. The mayor, who was one of our relatives, came and asked me to join the first aid crew. There were two trained doctors with us. I used to go around with the ambulance.

The first notion I got that something wasn't going right was when they brought us two wounded soldiers who were Palestinians. I asked about the Israeli forces, "How far did they get?" One said, "To a village a couple of miles from here." I asked, "Is there resistance?" He said, "There are about seven guards, lightly armed."

Then I saw the Jordanian army retreating along the road here. Their guns were pointed down. They were not in a fighting stance. I ran home to tell my father. My whole family was hiding in part of the house. My father had fought in the days of the Turkish so he knew military style. When I told him that the Jordanian army was retreating with their guns down, not in a fighting stance, he said, "If that's the way they are and they are heading back this way, we have lost."

We turned on the radio and we could hear the Israeli army saying, "Pick up the white flags and you won't be hurt." When we heard that we looked outside to see what was going on.

The first tank we saw had pictures of Arab leaders on it. We thought it was an Arab tank. I took a white bedsheet, I split it in half, I put it on a stick and I put it out. I used it as a flag, because I could hear on the radio, "Put out your white flag and you won't be hurt." I thought maybe we really did win if the tanks got this far. We thought everything was OK. We thought we were safe. What a surprise that was!

We expected something was going to happen but we were expecting a war, not an occupation, not a takeover with no resistance.

Israeli Occupation

In the beginning the Israelis didn't bother us. They would even pass out cookies to the kids. They wanted to infiltrate the community. They wanted to become part of what was going on. They would come to our marketplace to be involved with buying and selling. They took over strategic places, like the radio tower, that had been controlled by the Jordanian army.

The population refused to deal with the Israelis. We wouldn't talk to them. After six or eight years, it reached a boiling point. The population had to deal with the Israelis to get a building license or a car license. Basic day-to-day things that you had to have to continue life came through the Israeli authorities. It took about eight years before they knew, "This individual is a Ba'ath" or "This individual is a Communist."

The Intifada should have been at that time. It would have been overwhelming because the Israelis were not as strong as they are now. We waited until they built settlements and they built an economy around us, and then we had the Intifada. That was mistiming.

The Israelis took over the municipalities and that was when I started openly to resist. The Israeli soldiers used to sit on the roof of the municipal building with their legs over the side, and they would use profanity, night and day. I would be very blunt with them.

As a widow I was able to move about when other people were stuck with the burden of raising children. I was free, so if there were a demonstration or a strike in Jerusalem or a sit-in at the Red Cross, they would come and get me because I would not be scared. I was the one who carried the flag. Until today, if I see the Israelis catch a child outside, I'll go and pretend that I am his mother and take him away from the soldiers. I lost my fear a long time ago. But understand, when they first came to this country, they wouldn't hit a woman.

An Act of Solidarity

A few years after 1967, a house was demolished because a seventeen-year-old girl was said to be a commando, a military person. They came and arrested the girl and they demolished the house of her entire family on the same day. Because this was the first time a house had been demolished in our town, it created a commotion. The entire town was there. News reporters came and took pictures. But the Israelis are slick. That night the Israelis brought bulldozers and when we got up in the morning, we found an empty parcel of land. They had taken all the rubble away. There was not one trace of the house that had been demolished. Until now, it is a vacant piece of land.

My nephew, Sami Bahour [see below, this page], was there when they blew up the house. His eyes opened up in astonishment. It was hard not only on Sami. It was hard on the whole town. But he expressed it in front of everyone. He said, "We're going to build you a better home than that. Our eyes are your eyes and you can have anything we have." I kept telling him, "Shhh. Be calm. Something's going to happen to you if you keep this up. You're going to hurt yourself."

While they were doing the demolishing, the Israelis did not allow anyone to come within 200 meters. They blew up the house and left. So Sami's act was not an act of defiance face-to-face with the occupation forces, but it was a show of solidarity with the family. All of us do that. I finish my work day only after the children are in their homes, because we are always looking out for everyone else.

The biggest tragedy that our people face is that people leave town and don't come back. Every time someone takes resources out of this country, whether they sell land here or don't open a business here but do that in America, every one of those moves makes us weaker here. One should live in his town. One should live in his country. The alternative is to give it to Israel. If we are going to give it to Israel, why all the struggle and sacrifice? The Israelis are trying to reduce our lot. Shall we fall into the trap of reducing our own lot? If I could convey one message it would be: get an education, work for a few years, and come back and use that knowledge here.

Abu Sam

"I can close my eyes and see those people in the fields, the kids crying."

"I Was One of the Poor"

I am from a city in Palestine, El Bireh, about six miles north of Jerusalem.

My father was in the United States in 1935. He served in the U.S. Air Force. In 1939, he returned to Palestine and married my mother. My father was forced to marry my mother. He had seven sisters and they wanted him to marry an Arab girl, so they chose my mother, who was his first cousin.

My father stayed twenty-five days and then went back to the States. I was born on May 16, 1940. My mother took care of me. She used to sew and embroider dresses for a living. At that time most women wore hand-made dresses.

I can recall events that happened around me since I was eight years old. Two things I remember very clearly. One thing I still remember was how my mother used to put me under the table for protection when the Israeli planes were bombing our city in 1948.

The second thing I remember is also from 1948. We used to live outside the city limit. We had a lot of fruit trees — apples and plums and all kinds of things. And I remember a lot of people came and lived in the field next to our home. These were the Palestinian refugees of 1948. I didn't know at that time where these people were coming from. Somebody was chasing somebody. They said the Jewish people were chasing these Palestinian Arabs.

I remember taking food to these people. My grandmother gave me bread and my mother gave me different things. I took the food to the people in the field and just gave it to them. I can close my eyes and see those people in the field, the kids crying. I was eight or nine years old.

At that time we weren't expecting the visitors to become long-term refugees. We expected that in days, at the most weeks, they would be able to return to their homes.

Every one told you their story. I remember one lady who lived under one of the trees on our property. She was listening to the radio and heard that they had found her five-year-old son near Jerusalem, about thirteen kilometers. Nobody would take her. She was taking dirt and throwing it on her head out of frustration.

From 1940 to 1951 I lived under my mother's care. There was no father so I could do anything I wanted, most of the time. This made me a "hard head."

In 1951 my father came back from the States. My father had remarried in the States. He never sent us money. He never took care of me or my mother. When my father came back he divorced my mother.

The family decided to provide my mother and myself with a place to stay. They gave us a room in a commercial district of El Bireh. The kitchen, bedroom, and everything was in one room. I started to go to the Hashemite school near where we lived.

There was not much money. My mother was a seamstress. People from the villages would come to the market and bring my mother either material or money to buy material. She would buy the threads. A dress would take her maybe a month to embroider, all the designs, stitch by stitch. Later, she would give the yard goods to other women to sew, so that my mother would make some money and the other woman would make some also.

That money wasn't enough to buy the necessary things. A family needed a can of olive oil, a hundred-pound sack of flour, fifty pounds of sugar, twenty-five pounds of tea — if you had that you could survive. My grandfather on my mother's side used to furnish most of these items for us. What my mother earned from her sewing would buy us a can of corned beef or meat. My shoes always had holes. The socks were only from the shoe up: the rest of the sock wasn't there.

I began to hate the life I was living. I looked at my cousins who had fathers and mothers and money in their pockets. It seemed that I was the odd person.

We lived in that one room until 1953. I was then almost fourteen years old. It was decided that my mother should go to her parents and I should live in my father's house with my grandmother. My mother and I were separated, and I began to live with my 80-year-old grandmother.

I started to feel hatred toward the society in general. I wasn't doing very well in school. Everything that I could see was dark. For instance, I wanted to be a Boy Scout. It took fifty cents for a hat. I could not get fifty cents. My grandmother was too old. If you asked her for a hat for the Boy Scouts, she would tell me to get something to eat instead. The rest of my family could afford the luxuries in life. They could wear hats.

I decided I had to look for something to change the whole society. Even if I was fourteen, I felt that I needed to join with others that were like me. So I started looking around.

In 1955 there used to be all kinds of parties, from the religious parties to the political parties, including the Communist Party. I started listening to them. If somebody was running for office, or he wanted to spread his political view, he went to a coffee shop. So every time I heard there was going to be a lecture, I used to sneak in and listen.

I decided I wanted to join the Islamic political party called Hizb al Tahrir ("Islamic Party of Liberation"). It was a party that wanted to overthrow all the regimes in the area. I went for it. They talked about justice in an Islamic society, that Islam could do this for you and do that for you. I was really listening. I wanted something to change.

So I joined when I was fifteen. Joining the movement meant you had to go to weekly lectures about Islam. They didn't just read from the Qu'ran. They explained it. They showed you how Islam is not just a religion between you and God. They put it in three ways: religion is your connection between you and God, the connection between you and yourself, and the connection between you and the people, which means dealing with the government and society. We had discussions and we used to ask questions for more explanation. Then we would go to the masses and we would try to convince them that the Islamic Law is the best law to govern with.

I was very, very loyal to it. As young as I was, I used to go to different villages, sleep in the mosques, and talk about Islam and how we should overthrow the government. I used to go collect people from the farms. I would tell them, "Tonight I will be in the mosque at seven o'clock. After the prayer, be there. We'll have a lecture." It was all men. The women stayed home. So here I was, fifteen years old, lecturing about Islam to maybe about 25 or 30 men. I went to refugee camps and to the poor ghetto communities to spread the word of this movement.

Now I ask myself, "What was I telling them when I was fifteen years old?" When I started being active in this movement, we were under the Jordanian government. But we were not looking just at the Jordanian government. We were looking to overthrow all the regimes in the area and to make one Islamic government. Most of the Arab governments were dictatorial, one-man rule or family rule. We talked about justice in Islam. So I believed, when I joined this movement, if we govern with Islam and enforce this justice it will get rid of one-man rule, family rule, dictatorship, and the people will love it.

What encouraged me to join was that under Islamic rules there would be no poor people. There would be free enterprise but the distribution of wealth would be handled fairly. They would share the wealth of the country.

Later I came to feel that free enterprise would not help the poor to share the wealth. Because if you are rich and strong you are going to stay rich and strong and the poor are not going to have a chance to pick up and be rich. I say about free enterprise that it is free to be cut-throat: as long as you can cut the throat of your neighbor to satisfy yourself and get away with it, you will do it. That is the way I look at free enterprise. Since Islam does believe in free enterprise, I felt it would not help me — especially me — because I was one of the poor. I wanted to better myself and the masses but every human being looks for his interests first. I felt, "I am poor. All these rich around me have these businesses. How am I going to get a start?" Since there is free enterprise in Islam too, it will stay the same thing. I asked myself, "Is this the law I want?" And I decided not.

If it hadn't been the Islamic movement, I would probably have grabbed whatever movement came along because of the way I was oppressed. In a well-to-do family I was the only poor one. I was distressed with my father and mother being divorced. I looked at the society and it seemed like all the animals wanted to eat me. So I wanted an exit. When I think of it now, it was not so much Islam. If anybody else had come and talked about justice when I was fourteen or fifteen years old, I would have grabbed it.

I started thinking about what I was doing during the last four or five or six months before I came to the United States. The more you go into religion, I thought, the more you want to work for all the people. Much as I wanted to do for myself, I refused to be isolated from all the human beings around me. "You want to work for all the human beings around you, and not be prejudiced against certain sectors of society," I said to myself, "but if that is what you are looking for, you have got to change." I felt like: "I have to change. I cannot keep going with this Islamic movement."

The economy in the area was deteriorating. There were many refugees from 1948. They took most of the business. Educationally, they were better than us. They had lost their homes and working was their only hope to survive. I would say they entered into 80 per cent of the business in the area.

I heard of people going to different countries, looking for a better living. So I decided to call my father and get him to prepare travel documents for me. I wanted to go to the United States. That's where the money was. My idea was to go to the States, stay a couple of years, get a lot of money, and come back here and try farming. I would buy some tractors. I could do a lot of good for the people, especially for the people like me — the poor people.

I sent my father a letter and told him I would like to come to the States. He didn't answer right away. So I asked different uncles and aunts to beg him to help me come to the States. He sent me the papers.

I had an aunt living in Youngstown, Ohio. My father lived in Belzoni,

Mississippi. I decided I didn't want to go see my father. I had never had a father. Since I had come to the land of opportunity, I didn't need a father. I would make it on my own. I came to Youngstown, Ohio. . . .

"Justice for All the People"

When we came from overseas, we didn't come to work in a steel mill or to go to school. We ran from our country because of the economy and we were looking to make a fast dollar. We had in our minds, especially I am talking about myself, before my home town was occupied by the Israelis, we wanted to make that fast, fast dollar and go back home and work.

So coming to Youngstown, working in a bakery where I made $35 a week, I looked at some of my people who were peddlars. They went from house to house and, I heard, they made very big money. So I wanted that very big money.

Somebody explained to me, "There's two ways to make money. Stay in the north, Ohio or New York, and it is rough because people are a little bit smart. Another way is to go down south where you have a lot of black people and they are dumb." This is exactly the way it was put to me. At that time, I did not take into consideration dumb or not dumb, or oppressing people or not oppressing people. I ended up in a country that I did not enjoy, I could not speak the language, and I wanted to get rich fast. I was almost going crazy because I wanted to go back home. So I took a decision to go south.

My father was in Belzoni, Mississippi. I decided to forget about his divorce from my mother. I would go to the heart of the south which was Mississippi. I thought I could make that big dollar. So I took the bus to Mississippi.

I arrived in Mississippi and I found two or three peddlars selling goods. They went to plantations. They avoided any good-looking house. They avoided any middle-class people. And they went to the poor, poor, poor people, especially on plantations.

They explained to me how to work. "These people are black. They cannot refuse to open the door for you. Kick their door so they have to open it for you." This is *my* people explaining to me! "Don't worry about what time you go — night, morning, any time." So I did what they told me.

I started going to plantations and started selling watches, bed covers — we could sell anything we could buy. On the plantations, they got paid once a year, around Christmas. My father used to have a dry goods store. He used to tell me, "There is a payday in X plantation, so go there." Different people knew there was a payday and we all wanted to get there before the others. So one time I was knocking at the doors at four o'clock in the morning to sell goods before the people went to shop.

We would go to these poor, black people and tell them a story about ourselves. We felt that these were good-hearted people. Since they were oppressed, if you told them something about yourself, how oppressed you were, they would help you. For instance, I would tell them, "I just came from overseas and I left my mother behind and I don't have a father. I want to bring my mother here so I can go to school, so she could help me. I have a watch I want to sell you." We used to buy the watch for $2.50 to $3.00. It says on it $79.95. So we used to offer it to them for $40 or $50 or $30. If they bought it, fine. If they didn't, we would ask them, "How much would you give me for it?" They really didn't want to buy it, so they would say, "Ten dollars," to discourage me. For ten dollars, you were making seven dollars on that watch. So we sold it. At the same time, you are oppressing them!

It started bothering me right away. This was not the way I was raised. I didn't like cheating people. They gave me $20 for a watch and it worked for two hours and stopped. I remembered the political body I had been involved in and the justice I was talking about. I wanted justice for all the people, not just for the people of Palestine.

Beside what we were doing, I started seeing how the white people in Mississippi were treating the black people. I saw a black guy waiting in line in the post office, when a white man grabbed him from behind and threw him back and stood in his place.

So I felt very, very upset. I was making money but my conscience was bothering me too much. I couldn't do it. I felt, "They are no different than my people. Let me try to work with them." Since then I have been interested in listening to any black movement in the United States. . . .

Taking Care of the Family

I decided to go back to Youngstown, Ohio. I liked this girl I had met. I wanted to be around her. I would stay away from cheating people if I could find a job in a steel mill. I could not find a job then, and I went back to the same bakery.

In 1964 I brought my mother to the United States. She decided to come because of the poor economy and the hard life over there. She took a big chance to come. She was coming to see a son who had married a girl in America. There was the possibility that she would not be respected, since marrying in the West was not commonplace. Palestinians have the feeling that they take care of their families better than Americans take care of theirs.

When my mother came, I didn't have much money. We were just surviving, struggling. One time I would sell merchandise. Another time I would work at GM, or Chrysler, or in a bakery.

My mother lived with us for a year and a half. Before I married my wife, I said, "If you accept me for a husband, there are conditions. If we have only one loaf of bread, we're going to put it in front of my mother. We're going to say that we're full, go ahead and eat, Mom. After she finishes, if we have anything left we're going to eat. Otherwise we're going to sleep hungry. If we have five dollars we're going to buy her a dress and patch yours." She agreed.

My mother was so close to my wife, you could see it. If you asked my mother what was the best time of her life, she would say: "Well, my age is a year and a half. The only time I lived was when I lived with Sarah and Sami, and especially with Sarah."

The Six Day War

In 1967 I was going to work at General Motors, and I turned on the radio one morning and there it was: the Israeli army was attacking. I loved my people. For ten years I had not been home. The picture of the refugee camps was constantly in my mind. That was my direct family that was being attacked.

I went to work but I just couldn't concentrate. I asked my foreman if I could go to the nurse. I said I had a headache. I needed a couple of aspirin. He said, "Yeah." I went to the nurse at GM. She looked at me and said, "What are you?" I said, "What do you mean?" She said, "What nationality are you?" I said, "Arabian." She said, "From where?" I said, "From Palestine." She said, "Do you have a headache because war has broken out there?" I said, "Maybe." She said, "Would you like me to give you a paper to go home?" I said, "Please." She gave me an excuse to go home.

So I went home and I started listening to the news. It affected me. All the things to which I had been looking forward — to make money, to go back, to farm, to have my land, my house, and give my mother a better life — disappeared. I would turn on the TV, listen to the radio, open the newspaper. "They're talking nonsense, they're talking lies, this can't happen," I said.

They were saying that because Nasser had closed the Suez Canal, Israel had to take this land for their own security. And they were continually repeating that this land really belonged to Israel anyhow. They said it was the promised land.

I said, "What do you mean, 'it belongs to them'?" My name is Sami Salem Saleh Ibrahim Sulemein Bahour — without going any further, that's five generations. I mean, you just make us disappear? You just wipe us off the land?

I have seen my grandfather's birth certificate. It is in Arabic, in English, and in Hebrew. I have money from before 1948 and there is Hebrew on it as well as Arabic. We all lived in one country. We used to live as one.

The Six Day War consumed all of my thinking. It froze all of my social activity. I started thinking, "They can't take my country just like that! We have to help our people." I was watching the news. The Israelis were entering my home town. They came from Jerusalem on the road to Jericho. I saw pictures in the news of my cousin on the street: the army was holding him at a checkpoint. I said, "This stranger people can't do that to us!" So I got more involved in the Palestinian issue.

The PLO had formed in 1964 to ask for the liberation of Palestine, the area in which the State of Israel had been created. They called for a secular state in which Muslims, Christians, and Jews could live together as they had lived before 1948. We got hit. Instead of things going as the PLO desired, the Israelis took the rest of the country.

Going Home as a Visitor

In 1969 I decided I wanted to go back home. I went with $300 in my pocket. If people had known I had only $300 after twelve years away, they would

have made a fool out of me. To go away from your home town and come back
with only $300? You could have earned that back home!

At that time the PLO was starting military operations against the Israeli
occupation. The Gaza Strip was especially hot. I wanted to see the PLO
coming up and struggling.

When the plane began circling Ben Gurion airport, I became very nervous.
I had so much hatred for the Israeli soldiers and the Israeli government that if
they could have gone inside my heart and seen how much I hated them, they
would have put me in jail for the rest of my life. I hoped something would
happen to the plane so it would have to return to Cyprus or to London. I
didn't want to go back home any more.

As we got close, the religious Jewish people in the plane started praying,
according to their custom. I felt like a stranger.

When we landed, the Palestinians were asked to enter an army truck that
was waiting for us. They asked us all kinds of questions and stripped us
almost naked. After they finished I went to El Bireh and stayed with my
aunts.

El Bireh had changed almost 100 per cent. The streets had changed. I
almost didn't know how to get to my house. There were soldiers with guns in
the streets. There were jeeps and tanks. There were more people. They
seemed more involved in the struggle than when I left them. There were
more lectures. There was more activity in the schools. About 75 per cent of
the people were talking about how they wanted to kick out the occupation.

I took a trip to the Gaza Strip. There it was very tense. There were
demonstrations. There were checkpoints and a lot of harassment.

The Israelis gave me a visa for three months. I stayed for twenty-one days.

In 1974, I took my wife and family. Again we were stripped. My wife
didn't care for that kind of search. She was not used to it. In Jerusalem, they
searched my wife no less than three times within about two blocks. I can take
it, but Americans get more upset.

We stayed with my aunt. Her husband was a successful businessman in the
United States and he left her a lot of money. She went out of her way to take
care of my family and myself. We ate so much we could hardly breathe. After
dinner my wife said, "Let's go sit on the porch." We had coffee. Next door
there was a refugee family. They lived in a shack made of bricks and
aluminum siding (and they still live there). There were five kids, the mother,
and the father. We looked down and this refugee family was about to eat their
supper. It was watermelon. They cut the watermelon and sat around it on the
ground. They started eating. You never saw such fast eating. My wife asked,
"Why are they eating so fast?" I said, "Because each one wants to eat before
the other one in case there is nothing left."

That is the life of the refugees. This makes me remember when I was
hungry. This is where we have some class struggle beside the struggle against
occupation.

I have another aunt, my mother's sister, Aunt Leeka [see above, this
Section], who isn't scared of anything. Her house is on the public square.
From her house the Israeli military government officials can be seen when-

ever they come to town. There was a time when they deported the Palestinian mayors and took on the functions of running the municipality. To get a permit to build a house or to get a permit to leave the country, you had to go to the Israelis at the city hall.

The population boycotted the military administration. But a few people, especially the businesspeople, wanted to go there. So Aunt Leeka would open the window of her house and cuss those men out in front of everybody.

When we were visiting in 1974, the people of our city wanted to take flowers to the martyrs' cemetery where people who had been killed by Israeli soldiers were buried. The Israelis ordered a curfew. We were not allowed to go to the cemetery. Aunt Leeka told the people to go to the cemetery starting from her house. She would have a taxicab come to the door of her house, she would put the flowers in the taxicab, and she would meet us there with the flowers. I took a picture of it. I took the film to West Jerusalem to be developed and when the pictures were returned, they gave me all the negatives except the negative for this picture.

In any demonstration she is in the front. The Israelis don't put her in jail because she is almost sixty years old and has a medical problem. My uncle left her some apartments from which she collects rent. She spends much of her income on the needy. Once there was a curfew on the refugee camps. I witnessed her take food and sneak it to the refugees. She takes part in many activities. At her age, you don't see that too much.

One time when I was in El Bireh, a house was blown up right in front of me. The girl who lived in the house was accused by the Israelis of poisoning collaborators.[2] They gave her half an hour to take what belongings she could. The Israelis brought engineers and they planted bombs all over the house. When they exploded the bombs, the house fell like dominoes. This was a two-story house.

Everybody stood around crying. But the sister of the girl who lived there jumped on top of one of the stones. She said she didn't want to see anyone crying. She started saying slogans: "We will perish in blood to protect the martyrs!" I jumped up with her. I couldn't help it. I said: "These stones, we will build them back!"

Thinking of it here now, I'm scared. But at that moment, 75 per cent of the scaredness in me went away. The girl was standing there in tears. I couldn't help expressing the slogan in solidarity with her.

---

2. The U.S. State Department, *Country Reports on Human Rights Practices for 1982*, p. 1171, states: "Houses of the families of individuals believed to have been involved in security incidents or located in the vicinity of terrorist incidents have been demolished or sealed and the families displaced. . . . As a result, families were rendered homeless because a member was suspected of a security offense. . . . There is no judicial process prior to a decision to seal or demolish a dwelling in security cases." The U.S. State Department, *Country Reports on Human Rights Practices for 1991*, p. 1446, states: "Security forces assert the right to confiscate and then to demolish or seal all or part of the house of a suspect, whether he is the owner or only a tenant, and to do so before a suspect is brought to trial. . . . The United States believes that the demolition or sealing of a home as punishment of families contravenes the Fourth Geneva Convention. This type of house demolition or sealing is enforced only against Arab residents in the occupied territories."

Zahwa Rafeedie

"My dream was to be a doctor."

Childhood Memories

I was born in Ramallah in 1924. I stayed forty days in Ramallah. Then we moved to El Bireh. I had three brothers and four sisters. I was the baby of the house.

My father was a construction worker. On a normal day, he would leave at seven in the morning, take his lunch with him, and not return home until four or five o'clock in the afternoon. He built houses. The man who wanted a house built would buy the materials. My father would bring his own workers with him and they would put it together. He would pay wages to the men he hired. All of the work was in town.

My mother was a housewife. That was the norm. My mother would take care of us and my big sister would help her.

Our home had four rooms. There was no electricity. There was no running water. There was only a well. We had a kerosene lamp. We burned wood to keep warm in winter. About every two weeks we would go to Jerusalem and purchase food in bulk. Because there was no refrigeration, we did not buy for more than fifteen days because it would spoil.

We had apricot trees and almond trees. One of my tasks was to pick from the trees. We planted everything from zucchinis to eggplant, peas and everything else. I worked in the garden. We had a hand sickle and we used that sickle on a donkey as a plowing tool.

The members of the family had different jobs. One was making bread. We made lots of bread. We washed clothes outside behind the house. Four or five times a day, we would take a small amount of laundry, do it by hand, and dry it outside. When it was dry we would fold it, take the next batch, and wash those things. Carrying the water from the well was mostly boys' work. Girls didn't carry water. Girls made the dough.

I went to school until the seventh grade (which at that time was excellent). I went to the Friends Girls School in Ramallah. The school day was from 8:00 until 4:00. We would have lunch at home and go back to school. Just like other kids, we did our homework, and played a little bit. And we repeated the next day.

We studied Arabic, English, math, embroidery and handwork. I was one of the best in gym class. The history of Palestine was taught but it was geography, treaties, textbook material. There was no political or revolutionary material.

They taught religion in school but they did not connect religion to political reality or to our life. I was brought up with an orthodox emphasis which was very different from the religious teachings in school. We studied the Old Testament in this Quaker school, whereas in the Orthodox atmosphere outside of school it was more of a life situation kind of teaching: "Where did Christ come from?" "Where did he go?" "What did he say?" "What did the prophet say?", and so forth. It was not teaching from books.

There were many Jews around. My brother used to work with a Jewish carpenter named Zacky. They were both hired at the same place. They got to know each other and after a while they became partners. After the occupation in 1967, Zacky and his wife came to our house and visited us. Zacky gave us the address where they lived and directions if we wanted to go to visit them, but we would not take a chance.

There was a six-month general strike in 1936. A cousin of our family used to be the attendant for a gas station in the center of town. A car came with people who were working with the strike — revolutionaries, nationalists — and they asked for gas for their car. He refused to give them gas because there was surveillance going on and he was scared he would be seen giving gas to the Thuwar, the revolutionaries. That evening, he was beaten severely.

It was a tense time. The Thuwar, the Palestinian fighters, had control of the area. The uprising made us scared because we thought things were changing.

Abdul Dayim, who was a neighbor of ours, was one of the leaders in the struggle. He went to a graveyard and brought back the head of a Jewish soldier. He walked through town with it and took it specifically to a family whose son had been killed. And the mother cut the ear off the head as a kind of revenge. It might not sound good but this is what I remember.

The whole population was scared to go anywhere. It was like a curfew. We were out of meat. We were out of oil. There was nothing coming from outside.

We played a role. When food or fruit was needed from our house, we would give it to the revolutionaries. They would come to sleep.

I do not exactly remember what my parents used to tell us but in general they would say, "Be patient. Our day is coming. This is just a beginning. It is nothing to be scared of. Justice will be done."

Marriage

I got married on October 15, 1939. I was fifteen years old. My dream was to be a doctor. My brother said, "Don't get married. I am going to support you. You go and get an education." But I left school in the middle of the seventh year to get married and that was the end of school.

My parents were very much in agreement that I should get married. The decision was taken and I followed the decision. I was told, "This is an excellent man. There are not many like him. He is the only son in his family. You shouldn't pass him up. He's a solid man." I was told by my father, "Think about it. Because once your mother and father are gone, if you don't have a family you're basically lost. So you need to start now."

The whole plan was all worked out. I was playing in the marketplace when my father came and said, "Come to the house. We're going to get dressed." And that dress was my wedding dress!

I didn't know what was going on. The engagement is when the religious ceremony takes place. It was a fifteen-day engagement. They made it a real wedding. From my father's house to the house where I live now, there were people the whole way. But I wasn't ready for it.

We lived in my husband's home. It was built on the main thoroughfare, right across the street from the mill. It is an old, old home with a rounded roof. That was the first type of house that was built there. It was three rooms. The entire family of my husband lived there. I moved in with them.

I didn't have a hard time adjusting to the lifestyle of my husband's family. Their lifestyle was very similar to our lifestyle. My sisters and father and mother would come and visit. There was no separation. It was a very tight-knit family.

My mother-in-law taught me the ropes of married life: cooking, washing. When I first got to the house I wanted to become self-sufficient. I said to my mother-in-law, "Give me some flour. I want to bake. I want to learn how to make the dough." So I started mixing the dough. My sister came and said, "What are you doing? You are making a mess of it." And my mother-in-law said, "Do me a favor. Let her do it. I want her to make a mistake and learn on her own. It's OK if the dough doesn't come out to be bread this time. Just let her have the experience of working with it."

The living part of it was not hard. But it was the change in status that was hard. I swear to God, that was the hardest time in my life. My dream was not to be married at fifteen but rather to become a doctor with the support of my brother.

I used to be home all by myself. My cousin was small at that time. I used to dress him up — put powder and stuff on him — because I had nothing to do. I used to play with him as if he were my doll.

Then my in-laws said I shouldn't stay home by myself all day doing nothing. I should learn sewing. So they sent me to Ramallah to a trade school to learn embroidery and sewing. I studied how to sew for almost two years until I had my first daughter.

My husband drove a bus from Ramallah/El Bireh to Jerusalem and on his days off he drove trucks. Then he took over the flour mill from the old folks.

1948

I remember that a few weeks after the '48 war I was pregnant with my third child, Issam. I recall people fleeing, carrying things. They had sticks on which hung bags with their stuff. The refugees that came had kids sleeping outside under the trees. And the next day after I had my son, I said, "I'm no better than they. I'm going to get up, and I'm going outside to help." I got a fever and ended up very sick.

Behind the flour mill we set up a tent. People used to sleep under it. We used to feed them. We gave them blankets. We used to make daily meals. Hundreds of times refugees slept in the mill. Many of them stayed for weeks until they found someone to take them in. There is one family that stayed about one year in our back yard and on the porch. A lot of them were from villages known to have been destroyed in 1948.

It never crossed our minds to leave. Abu Tayser was a neighbor and a very good friend. He would always come over to the house. I would tell him, "Don't ever think I would just get up and leave to go to no-man's-land, and not know where I was going." And Abu Tayser would tell me, "Don't worry. If you have to go, I'll help." I remember being very steadfast and saying, "You don't have to help me because I'm not going anywhere." Until now, if they destroy my house, even if they demolish my house while I'm inside, I'm not going anywhere.

1967

When the Six Day War happened, we were in the process of preparing an engagement for my son Mousa. Everything was bought. Everything was set up and arranged. The meat was cooked. The almonds were in little favor trays. They cut the electricity, so we ended up eating the meat that was all prepared for that party. We ate meat for the longest time!

Because there was no electricity, people were bumping into each other and falling over things. We had to use the restroom outside. Another family brought their kid to our house because they were scared that something would happen.

The mountain called "Jabal Al-Moukaber" or the large mountain in Jerusalem is where the first battle took place. All the news media were saying the Arabs were victorious. We were encouraged. We thought, "This is the day. Things are going back to our side." The news would say, "Put out your white flags," and "Everything is good, we're winning."

Then trucks started coming with no identification marks. Everybody went out. Issa, one of my sons, was giving them cigarettes until one person in the neighborhood said, "You dummies, you stupids. Don't you know? These are the enemy. These are the Jews. Everybody go back into your homes."

When we saw them passing our house I thought, "Oh-oh. Now, in less than a mile, they'll reach the Jordanian base that was there. All hell will break loose!"

Everyone was so scared. We were petrified. We remained in our homes, thinking there was going to be a battle. Twenty-five individuals lived in one room for a period of time, waiting for that battle to happen, because we thought there was going to be a bloodbath.

The Israelis reached the Jordanian base and there was nobody there. There was no battle. Not one bullet was fired. There was occupation.

My father said, "Since there was no battle, and now that they have occupied this area, the population transfer is coming. They are going to make us move." So my father said, "Give each one of the kids so much money and put it tight in their pockets. In case we become split up, everybody will at least be able to live on their own."

People in the neighborhood were saying, "Let's leave until the atmosphere calms down. Then we'll come back." My husband was one of the ones that said, "I'll stay. I'm not leaving of my own will."

My son, Issam, was in Jordan. We received messages saying, "We hope you're OK. What we hear on the radio and from the people coming is that the people's homes are being demolished, and they are cutting the breasts off the females to scare them. Some people are saying that you are on your way. Is this true or is this not true?"

My husband worked hard. He watered the crops around the house. He was not leaving. It was his. He said, "What am I going to do with mama? Look at her." She was old. "If they're going to kill us, let them kill us right here. We're not moving."

After time passed, the soldiers went from house to house, collecting weapons, collecting anything they felt was bad. I asked one of them, "The people outside, are they allowed to come back?" And the soldier told me, "No, no. Those who are here are here. Those who are outside are outside." The borders were not open.

When the war took place in 1967, Issam was cut off from us. He had gone to Jordan to study political science. Before the occupation, every fifteen days Issam would come home. And he would take money so he could live because he wasn't working in Jordan. When the occupation came, he got stuck. There was no more income from the family.

He had two alternatives: leave school and go to work, or go to the United States to continue his education.

My oldest daughter, his sister, was already in the United States. So Issam contacted his sister. She sent him enough money so that he could get his paperwork taken care of and go to the States. He was drawn to the only relative that he could reach at that time.

My son Issa was studying at Birzeit University. When Issam got enough money to come to the States from Jordan, he sent a message to us saying, "All the paperwork is done. We are leaving the twelfth. If there is any way possible, make sure Issa comes across the Jordan River and meets me at so-and-so place. If he is late one day, all of our paperwork that it took so long to do, will be gone."

Issa smuggled himself out. He went with some guy who now lives in Cleveland. They left and crossed the Jordan River. That was the first leg of their trip. A sickness that I now have started on the day they left.

[Continued below, this Section, p. 226.]

Husam and Salwa Rafeedie

"And God said, 'Not in my time!'"

Marriage and Travel

Husam Rafeedie: I came to the United States in October of 1968. I went back in 1974 and met this young lady, Salwa! She was going to the same school that I had gone to.

My mom and I went into her town, Birzeit, about eight miles from our town. One of the Rafeedies was married in that town and she told my mom that she knew a few of the girls if we wanted to go meet them. We went into a couple or maybe three houses, and I saw two or three of them. And I got frustrated. I felt, "What the hell am I going in there for? This is not the way to get married." I told my mom, "Let's go. That's it. I'm not going to see any more. I don't want to visit any more."

On our way to find a taxi, the lady who was with us said, "I just have one more house for you to see." She said, "You know, I've never seen that girl (which was Salwa, now my wife). But I have been told she is a nice-looking girl and she has a nice family. Why don't you see just this family and then you can leave?"

So we went into the house. Her father had just come from work. He was sitting on the carpet and he was smoking a water pipe. As soon as I saw him, I remembered my dad, who was always smoking a water pipe!

"Hello, how are you?" And the lady told them who we were. We were just coming in to say hello. "Well why not? Come on in." Of course, I guess they got the message right then and there that this guy was coming to take a look at one of their daughters. So Salwa went out and they threw a dress on her. I remember, she put her new dress on and she brought the coffee. And she sat and I started talking to her. "What school do you go to?" "Well, it's the same school that I went to." "Who's the teacher?" I started naming some of the teachers to her. She knew my brother, Fouad. And we got to talking and, "Thank you very much. We'll see you." And we left.

We got in a cab to go home. And do you know who was the cab driver? It was her uncle. We didn't know that. We sat in the back seat, my mom and I, talking. I said, "That girl didn't look too bad. The whole family seems to be very poor, and that's the kind of family we should look at. They are very poor and very nice and I don't see anything wrong with that family. Maybe we'll go back one more time and talk to them," or stuff like that. And the driver, he was driving. When we finally got to the house, I offered to pay him for the ride of course. "No, no," he said, "that's on me." I said, "Why?" This was late at night. He said, "Well, I was supposed to take you over to that house. But I didn't." I said, "What do you mean?" He said, "Well, the lady sent her kid to tell me that you were coming to see my niece. But I do not talk to her father and I refused. So I am not going to charge you for it." I threw the money at him anyhow.

Two days later, I took my dad and my mom. My dad knew just about everybody in the area. He said anything at any time, he didn't care who he was talking to. It was over fifty steps up to Salwa's house. Going up the steps I kept telling my dad, "Don't make me look bad. You don't know those people. Please, don't say anything." My dad was an old fellow. He was huffing up the steps. He was tired. He got to the top of the steps and he looked at Salwa's dad and he said, "I know you. You so-and-so." I said, "Daddy, please!"

Her dad would bring her mom into our shop. She would bring wheat, and my dad would make flour. Then Salwa's dad would come and take her mom home. My dad noticed Salwa's mom because she was the only Christian woman that came to our mill. She had a cross and he always gave her a seat somewhere so she wouldn't be covered by a lot of dust. And he wouldn't let her carry anything. He or the workers would carry the stuff for her and help her, make sure everything is fine with her. Salwa used to bring her mom's dough into our bakery.

We saw them the second day. And then we went the third day. Finally we sent them the message that we were interested and we would like to have an engagement party. We got engaged for two weeks. I rented a Volkswagen and took her around. I told her who I am and what I'm looking for and what I had. I had a house already bought for her, furnished. I had a store. I had a business. I had a few handy dollars and I was ready to have the responsibility. I don't think she had a choice. She liked me. We got married two weeks after the engagement. We got married on November 17, 1974.

Salwa Rafeedie: My father was the type that didn't like girls to go out and talk politics. So we just kept busy in the house helping Mom, going to school in the morning and coming back in the afternoon. In school, we had to choose between history and geography or math and science. I chose history and geography. We were never involved in any demonstration. Just housework and homework and that was it.

I was about twelve years old when the 1967 war broke out. My mom has eight kids. I am the oldest. We used to live in Ramallah. That Sunday my dad knew that something was going to happen. We bought some meat and extra bread just in case. My mom was pregnant with the seventh kid and she was ready to have it at any time. So my dad put us in the car and took us to Birzeit so we would be with relatives in case anything happened. We stayed ten days. The only thing I remember is that my dad walked from Birzeit to Ramallah to get us a permit so he could drive us back to the house we used to live in.

After the war, everybody went back to working. We never were involved in any politics.

Now my sisters are working and feeding the family. One of them is a teacher. One of them is a beautician, and one works in a factory that makes medicines in Birzeit. She had a three year course on a computer. The pharmaceutical company is owned by a Palestinian from Jerusalem.

Husam: My wife and I and our two daughters went back to the West Bank in 1979. I was thinking about going back and staying there. I had a place to stay. It was my house. I knew I could manage back home with no problem.

We had heard many times about people going through interrogation. And she was worried. "What am I going to do if they do this? What am I going to do if they do that?" I said, "Hey, they can't do nothing. We have American passports. We have two kids with us. We're not carrying anything. We have done nothing wrong. They can't do too much. Don't worry."

As soon as the plane landed, the pilot jumped up and said, "Everybody remain seated until security check. We have a group of security coming on to the plane." They came right to the tail end of the plane. I had picked a few seats for the kids at the tail of the plane so they would be close to the bathroom. He came and he called us by name, "Mr. and Mrs. Rafeedie." "Yes." "Please come with me." So we went.

A special van was waiting for us. Julie was only four at the time. Samia was two. It was one day before her birthday. They took us to a room, specially designed, I suppose, for all the Palestinians. "Where are your suitcases? You come with me. Let's go get your suitcases." We had about five suitcases with us at the time — our clothes and a few gifts. We got them and went back to the room.

They took me by myself. They wanted to know all the names and details: where did I come from, where did I go, what do I do. And my question to them was, why all these questions? What is it that you want? I'm a guy coming to visit my dad and we're going back home. At one point, I think, the answer was, "Just shut up and answer."

Before he finished with me, all of my clothes were taken off. As a matter of fact, after I took off my clothes, he told me to bend — to see if I had something stuck up my butt.

In the meantime, they opened every piece of material that we had. I mean, Wrigley's spearmint gum, they broke it loose; toothpaste, they broke it to see what was inside of it. They searched. Then they took the empty suitcase somewhere to test it or check it, and brought it back.

The kids were crying and my wife was sitting there. Then they took her and searched her. She had one of those shoes that's got a big heel in the back. The guy looked at her and he said, "I have to go and test this one." I said, "What are you going to do with it?" He said, "I'm going to drill a hole to see if there's anything in it." He walked about two or three steps, and then I looked at him and I said, "Hey, wait a minute! Here's the other one. Take it and give it to your wife. After you drill a hole in it, what in the hell do we want it for?" And I started screaming in English, right in the middle of the airport. They frisked the babies too.

After about three and a half to four hours, when we got done, we went out. As soon as I saw my family outside, I started crying. I was so mad! If I hadn't cried, I'd have probably exploded. I started using some filthy language.

I was still in front of the airport. My mom grabbed me, saying, "Shut your mouth. You're not out of here yet." I said, "I don't give a goddamn. I didn't do anything. What the hell are they trying to do?" Finally they got me in the car and we left.

I had the documentation with me to prove that I had been a resident of the West Bank, but, at the time, I was single. Once you become a married person then you are allowed to bring in your wife and your kids on your documentation. I tried to change it through the authorities. They refused. The question was put to me, "You lived that much in the United States and you became an American citizen. You ought to go back to where you came from." I said, "This is my house. I have the title for it, and I want to live here." They said, "It's not yours. Get out!" I was chased away.

So we tried with the wife. She had the same documents. She went to the authorities and she told them, "I have married an American citizen, and we would like very much to live here." They asked her, "Where's your husband at?" She said that I was in the United States. He took the documentation from her and tore it up and threw it away, saying, "You go back to your husband."[3]

3. The U.S. State Department, *Country Reports on Human Rights Practices for 1987*, p. 1451, states: "[West Bank residents] who have acquired foreign citizenship are ordinarily not allowed to resume

Coming back out, believe it or not, we went through the same routine. We had already been searched outside, about two blocks before you get to the airport. They open your suitcase and everything else. And then inside the airport, you go through the same doggone thing over and over again. If your plane leaves at nine o'clock in the morning, you have to be at the airport at three o'clock in the morning.

I would like very much to go back, there's no doubt about it, if things would get a little bit better than what they are now. I'd love to take the kids, especially now when they are old enough to realize where their father and mother come from, and see the house that we have and the property that we own. I have thought about it many times, but the way things are now, it's like a jail.

I'll tell you a little joke about how long it is going to take or when is it going to happen. A Lebanese woman told me this joke. In 1981, we took a trip to Lebanon, and we were talking to some of the Lebanese villagers, down in the south. I guess at that time Gorbachev was the leader of the Soviet Union, and Reagan was the leader of the United States. So this very nice lady says that Gorbachev and Reagan and Yasir Arafat, all three of them got together, and they went to see God. And they asked God, "When will we have peace in the world?" Well, Reagan jumped up right away and he said, "The minute I destroy the communists in the whole world and take over Eastern Europe, everybody will be happy and peace will be upon all the earth." So God looked at him and he said, "Reagan, I don't think that's going to be in your time."

Gorbachev said, "Well if we take over Western Europe, and we destroy the United States and the whole world becomes communist, then everybody will have everything that they want, and that's when peace will come to the earth." Well, God looked at him and said, "I don't think that's going to happen in your time."

Yasir Arafat, what was he going to say? He asked him, "God, can you tell us, or give us a hint at least, when the Palestinian problem will end and peace be in the Middle East?" God hesitated, and all of a sudden he cried, and the tears streamed down his face and God said, "Not in my time!"

Zahwa Rafeedie

"When Wissam gets out of prison, I will have one more marriage to take care of."

Wissam's Youth

My son Wissam was born in 1959. He was eight years old at the time of the 1967 war.

Every single penny he got, he would use to buy comic books. He would

residence in the West Bank. Persons subject to these restrictions are permitted to return to the West Bank as tourists only, and are sometimes refused entry entirely. Entry or residency permission is frequently denied to spouses, relatives, and children, following the emigration of the head of their household."

put them together and bind them. He had two volumes of comic books. Later he was a coin collector.

He was fifteen years old when he became involved in political activity. I think he became involved because he was very tall and very skinny and he looked more mature than he was. His birth certificate was all crinkled because he had to keep showing it to soldiers as proof that he was not sixteen: "I don't have an ID card because I'm not sixteen yet. Here's my birth certificate." I knew something was wrong because his birth certificate was in the worst shape of all of my children.

He took part in demonstrations. Of course, he would not tell us. He used to come home and his tennis shoes would be full of mud. I would say, "Where were you?" He would say very casually, "Oh, I cut through the back yard and it's all muddy back there." He would come and go on his own.

We weren't completely dumb. Someone would see him and tell us he was in a demonstration. We knew what he was up to. Once in a while we would make a scene and try to cool him down and tell him to stay out of trouble. But do you think it worked? It didn't work with Wissam.

He used to be very popular. He would go to the classrooms and tell the teachers there would be a demonstration on this day at this time. And the kids would listen to him. This was a government school. The principal, Hamdi Kade, became very disturbed by what Wissam was doing. He would call the authorities to tell them. So Wissam became involved directly with the principal: "Yes, we're going on the demonstration." "No, you're not going on the demonstration."

The first time Wissam was beaten it was because of a problem with the principal. The principal sent a notice home to me saying, "Be sure Wissam goes to the military police station at this particular time, because there is a problem." It didn't say what the problem was.

Wissam was in Beit Sahour that day. He was intrigued by coins from different countries, and he would go to Beit Sahour where they would encase them in wood and glass for his collection.

When he came back from Beit Sahour to Jerusalem, and from Jerusalem to El Bireh, I told him, "I'm glad you're back home because you got a notice to go to the police station." Wissam asked, "For what?" I said, "How do I know what you're up to now? Anyway, eat before you go." He said, "I don't want to eat. They'll give me a beating and if I eat my stomach will hurt. We'll see what happens." He went without food.

They asked him to go to the police station because the principal's car was hit by a stone that day. Wissam was taken and blamed for this whole incident. The principal said it had to be Wissam that did it. So they blamed Wissam without seeing Wissam. He said, "I tried to say, I was not here. I was in Beit Sahour. Come see the coin boxes that I bought for my coins."

They beat his feet with a stick and a whip. When he came home, his heels and his entire feet were swollen. That was his first beating.

The second time, he was one of four people who were asked to go to the police station in Ramallah. When he left, I did not know for how long — for an hour, for a day or whatever. He stayed for twelve days in Ramallah prison.

I did not know what was happening. How was I going to know? During the first eighteen days you are not allowed to ask where he is, or how long he's going to be there, or what condition he is in. I got off the couch only to go to sleep, those whole twelve days.

In Ramallah prison they were held next to the outdoor sewer system. What they did to all four of them was they dipped sacks into the sewerage and covered their heads with the sacks.

When they got out, all four came to my house first because it was the closest to Ramallah prison. Their heads were as if you took sand and dirt and mud, and rolled them in it. So I told the other ones, "Go home. Go and get cleaned up." And I took Wissam and said, "Go into the bathroom to get clean. You're in bad condition."

Those two incidents were before he was sixteen. The first major arrest was after he was sixteen years old.

They came to the house looking for him. It was twelve o'clock midnight. They looked in the window and they saw me.

Wissam ran to get dressed right away because he knew they were coming to arrest him. They came into the house. I said, "You can't beat my son." One of them told me, "I'll shoot him right here." I said, "You will not shoot him in my house. If you want to shoot him, take him into the street."

That arrest was for five months. The charges were burning the principal's car; people throwing rocks at the principal; and participating in demonstrations.

It was less than a month before the big final test that they take at the end of high school. He had set up a little makeshift tent on the roof of the house where he and his friends were going to study so no one would bother them. This was all set up when he was arrested, and it remained set up.

The next time he was arrested, he came home in the evening. He wanted some hummus with meat on it. I told him, "Go and get washed up and when you come out you'll find it ready." He ate and went to sleep.

When he got up in the morning, I told him, "You better have breakfast before you go out. You are studying and you are going to have a long day." This was the second time he was studying for the high school graduation exams. The first time he failed, because he had just got out of prison.

He told me, "I am on my way to Jifna," which is on the way to Birzeit. "I'll stop and get breakfast at my aunt's house when I get there."

When he was on the Ramallah-Nablus road, he came to a jeep with three or four soldiers, and a car that was burnt. He had to see exactly what was going on. He knew the soldiers. One of the soldiers said to him, "Hi, Wissam." He responded, "Good morning," and he kept walking.

As soon as he passed them, the soldier that was in charge told the other soldiers, "Chase him. Follow him. Catch him." They followed and caught him and put him in the Ramallah jail.[4]

I had no idea what was going on. I was still at home. One of his friends saw

---

4. "Any soldier may arrest without warrant a Palestinian who has committed, or is suspected of having committed, a criminal or security offense." U.S. State Department, *Country Reports on Human Rights Practices for 1991*, p. 1444.

him enter the jail. He called me on the telephone and told me, "Wissam was just arrested." He told me to go to Ramallah and see what was happening.

Who was I going to send? I was not going to go by myself to the jail. They would not let me in. I called an uncle to go. When he came to the house, I said, "Here, I prepared a sandwich to take to Wissam because he did not have breakfast before he left and I'm sure he's hungry."

So my uncle went. They would not let him in. They would not let him talk to Wissam or give him anything. They said, "This is a closed case. You stay away."

He was sentenced to two years in prison. For three months he stayed in Ramallah while they were bringing the charges. Then he was moved to Nablus.

While he was in Nablus, I went to visit him. He said, "I did something and I'm not sure I should have done it." I asked, "What are you talking about?" He said, "They brought me a paper in Hebrew and I made a mistake. I didn't have anyone around who could read it to me to see exactly what it said, but I signed it. They told me, now I have one year less."[5]

I started yelling, "How can you sign something and you don't know what it is? No way, from God's open sky, would they give you a year off!"

What happened was that one of the lawyers in El Bireh had gone to Wissam when he was in the Ramallah jail and told him, "Listen, just say that you were the one that burned the car, like they want you to say. I'm a lawyer and I'll take care of it." And Wissam told him, "I didn't burn anything. I don't know what the soldiers were talking about. I was on my way to Birzeit. I refuse to confess to something I didn't do."

Until now, we do not know what he signed. Most likely, he signed something that said, "Yes, I burned the car."

Into Hiding

Wissam was missing from our life for nine long years.

Early one morning, a white car came to the corner where we live and the men in the car asked some of the kids that were playing, "Whose house is this? Whose house is that?"

As soon as they left, my grandson told my son, Mousa, "A white car came and there were four men in it, and they were asking about who lives in every house on the street." Mousa said, "Something must be coming up. Tonight, I bet you, they're going to try to arrest people."

---

5. "Most confessions are still written in Hebrew, a language which most accused do not understand" (The Report of a Mission by Jordan J. Paust, Gerhard von Glahn, and Gunter Woratsch, *Inquiry into the Israeli Military Court System in the Occupied West Bank and Gaza* [Geneva, Switzerland: International Commission of Jurists, 1989], p. 33). And, "we recommend . . . that *all* signed confessions be written in a language which the accused readily understands or be ruled inadmissible" (Ibid.). The U.S. Department of State in its *Country Reports on Human Rights Practices for 1991*, p. 1445, indicates that the writing of confessions in Hebrew continues: "Most convictions in military courts are based on confessions. Physical and psychological pressures and reduced sentences for those who confess contribute to the likelihood that security detainees will sign confessions. Confessions are usually recorded in Hebrew, which many defendants cannot read. . . ."

People were being asked too many questions in the neighborhood. We felt that something was going to go wrong. Wissam said, "I'm leaving for Birzeit. I don't want to sleep here because it seems like something is going to happen."

I was worried. I said, "Where are you going to sleep?" He said, "I have a lot of people I can sleep with. Don't worry about it. I'll see you in the morning." So Wissam left.

My husband had just died and my son, Issa, was there with me for forty days. About 12:00 or 12:15 that same night, I heard knocking on the kitchen window. I went to look. It was Wissam. "Wissam, what do you want? Where were you? Did you eat?" "Yes, I ate." "Come on in."

We sat down and started having tea. We were sitting in Wissam's room on the road side of the house where you could see when the army came and went. We were sitting, just talking, when I saw and heard the Israeli walking patrols on both sides of the road. They were not in a jeep this time.

I said, "They're coming for you! They're coming straight to the house. What are you going to do?" He told me, "Take my cup and put it in the sink so they do not see that there were three people sitting here." He opened the back door and he left.

He went to the top of one of the houses in our back yard, watching what was going to happen to the house. We put everything together as if we were sleeping, and we left just two cups out.

There was a knock at the door. It was the army. (Now I talk calmly but then I pulled myself up to make myself stronger than I really was.) They knocked several times and I yelled at them. I wanted to tell them that I was sleeping. I told them, "Wait a minute. You guys are in a hurry. I've got to get dressed."

They asked, "Whose house is this?" I said, very fast, "You mean you come knocking at a house at twelve o'clock at night and you don't know whose house you are coming to?" "No, we know everything."

The second question they asked was, "Who's living here?" I said, "Nobody. My son is here from America for the father's funeral." "Who else?" I said, "I have a son named Wissam. He's not here." "Where is he?" "He's in Birzeit." "What's he doing in Birzeit?" "He's studying. His father just passed away and he got behind in his studies, so he went to Birzeit to study." "When is he going to come back home?" I said, "If there are taxis or buses, he'll come. If not, he'll sleep there." "Where is he going to sleep there?" "I don't know."

They got a little smart, trying to ask me, "Have you seen buses or taxis that travel at twelve o'clock at night?" I told them, "Yeah. It happens. You can get a taxi if there is an emergency."

Then they asked, "What time does he usually come home during the day." I said, "About 4:00 or 4:30." "Well, here's this notice. Make sure he comes at 4:30. We want to talk to him. We want to find out if anybody threw rocks at your house or anybody's bothering you." They changed the subject: now they were coming to protect us.

I knew they were looking for Wissam specifically. And I knew he was not going to give himself up. Until now, we do not know why they were coming for him.

He left the back door open when he left. He didn't even close the door behind him. We were very lucky that they came in the front door and they didn't try to come in the back door or he would have been caught at that time.

Wissam was gone. We didn't know where he was. The following day at 4:30, Maurice (who was the civil administrator) called and threatened me saying, "Either Wissam shows up here or we'll hunt him down and kill him." I said, "Wait a minute. The bell is ringing now. Maybe that's him." I went to the door. It was Issa. I went back to the phone. Maurice said, "God willing, it's he who came." I said, "No, it's Issa."

Maurice said on the phone, "You are his mother. How can you not know where he is at? You can go to the school and get him." I said, "You're the one that wants him. The same way I can go to the school and get him, you can go to the school and pick him up if you want to. I won't go get him for you."

Then Maurice talked to Issa and told him the same thing, "You're the older brother that's in the home. You are now responsible for making sure Wissam shows up at the police station."

For two to two and a half months, they drove us crazy. They would come in the middle of the night, put the searchlights on the house, and come and ransack the house.

One time they came and they found a big picture of Wissam that we had and they took it off the wall. I asked them, "What do you want with that picture?" The captain who was in charge said, "We are taking this picture and we are going to make copies and pass them to the army officials at all of the checkpoints and all of the airports and the bridge." This was a scare tactic to try to open me up.

Nine years passed. From time to time they would come back and ask about Wissam. Every so often they would tell me, "We have news that he died," and they would leave the house — leaving me a wreck — and they would watch the house to see whether I would leave and go to see my dead son. That affected me even more emotionally than physically. I didn't know where he was.

Wissam Arrested

They caught Wissam after nine years. People started coming to the house and saying, "Did you hear about the news? They caught a cell." I said, "That's news? Every day that happens!" But this was different because more than one person came.

I started asking, "What is this all about?" Some of the people said that the people who were caught were people that had been underground for some time. They said, "It looks like there are wanted people involved."

I thought this was just like any other incident until Munir, a good friend of mine, came and asked me, "Did you hear about this cell?" When Munir came I knew something was up. I said, "Listen. I'm not a dummy. If you guys know something, tell me now. If you know Wissam's got caught, tell me. I want to know." He said, "We'll find out. To be honest, we don't know."

That night I didn't sleep. In the morning I sent Mousa to the Red Cross and I went to see Lea Tsemel, the Israeli lawyer. I said to her, "Everybody's talking about it. Something must be up. Can you find out for me?" This was the first time I ever met Lea.

The Red Cross said it was less than twenty-four hours since the men had been caught and they had no names. Lea Tsemel picked up the phone and called the Ramallah jail and asked specifically, "Is Wissam Rafeedie one of the four that got caught?" I was sitting in Lea's office and Lea was the one that broke the news to me.

I didn't break down. I'm glad that he got caught because I know where he is now. My dream was to see him. I got to see him.

The lawyer, Lea, tried day after day to get me in to see Wissam. They refused. Lea said, "The only way you can see him is to set up a bond hearing. They will have to bring him to the bond hearing. You will be there and you will at least be able to see him." So we did that.

When they brought him in, there were three or four soldiers around him. He came, handcuffed, limping. He had stitches on his chin. He did not have a change of clothes and he looked like he was in very bad condition.

I had with me some aspirin I wanted to give him. I asked the person in charge, "Can I kiss him?" He said, "No, no, later you can do that. Now we have a court hearing."

We went into the court and they brought up the request for bond. It failed and he went back. The only thing I got out of the whole thing was just to see my son.

On the way out, when we were getting ready to leave, I pushed through the soldiers and I went and hugged him. I asked him one question, "How are you?" "I'm OK, don't worry about me." They told me not to talk to him, not one single word, but I did.

Three times I saw him: the fourteenth day, the twenty-fifth day, and the forty-fifth day. Then Mousa saw him once after that.

Wissam was in and out of interrogation for five full months. They added 101 days of administrative detention, after the first eighteen days, just to figure out what the charge was going to be. This was part of interrogation, not part of being sentenced.

They accused him of being a member of the Popular Front. He said, "I'm a member of the Popular Front, period. That's all I'm saying. I'm proud of that. Ask me no more." He gave them that and his name and that's all he gave.

I was able to see Wissam when he went to the hospital. That's where I found out something about how he was treated in interrogation: hands tied behind the back; feet tied; head with a sack on it, between the legs; not allowed to sleep for three days straight. Any time he would doze off he would be punched and poked to wake up.

He had a weak stomach anyway. He was also hurt from the beating. He started yelling at the top of his lungs. No one would respond until other prisoners from the entire prison floor began yelling as loud as Wissam was yelling to draw attention to him. And that's how a doctor was brought in who put him in the hospital.

They took him to the hospital at seven o'clock at night. He stayed that night and the following night. The third day, Lea called me and said, "Do you want to come see Wissam?" Lea was always laughing when dealing with such serious situations. I laughed with her, "What do you think? Do you think I'd like to see Wissam or not?" Lea told me, "He's not feeling well. He's in the hospital." I had a cup of coffee in my hand. I threw it out and said, "I'm on my way."

I went with Lea. This was a day and a half after a serious operation. They would not let us into the hospital building itself. Lea tried all of the entrances to Hadassah Hospital until she found an entrance where there were Arabs who must have been workers there. Lea asked the Arabs, "Did you see any prisoners brought in a day or a day and a half ago?" One of them said, "Yes, he's in room whatever. We saw him brought in."

We went straight to the room without asking anyone. Once we got to the room, a soldier told us there was no way anyone could visit Wissam. Lea took a very strong stand and told them, "No way except this mother is going to come and see her son." Lea went and got a chair, put the chair in front of the bed and said to me, "Come, sit here." I went and sat there.

We found Wissam with a soldier — in full gear with a rifle — sleeping on one of the beds, and a soldier with a pistol sitting in front of him in the closed room. Wissam had gauze in his mouth. He was recovering from an operation.

Lea and one of the soldiers took care of the paperwork: "What are you coming here to do? Who is this?" The other soldier stood by the door. Every time the soldier would turn his face I would talk to Wissam. Wissam couldn't move. I told him, "I'm scared to get up and help you because if they see me touching you, they're going to kick me out." He said, "Don't even worry about it. I'm OK. It's no big deal."

After we left, Lea told me he couldn't move because he was tied to the bed. This was one of the complaints that Lea was raising with the soldier who was outside. Wissam was covered. He wouldn't even tell me, his mother, that he was tied.

He was there for six days. On the seventh day they took him to Moscobiyya prison in Jerusalem. He ate tomatoes with dried fava beans. He got sick from this food, especially after the operation. He threw up and became very, very sick. He requested Lea and he got to see Lea. Lea came and reported to the family that he was in worse physical condition than he had been in before the operation. Lea took him a peach. He could hardly eat the peach, that's how sick he was.

I tried many times to visit Wissam. Several times we stayed all day and were not able to see him. They told us to come at eleven o'clock. We stayed from 11:00 a.m. until 5:00 p.m. and they would not let us in. So we had to return home.

One day when we were halfway back they stopped us at a checkpoint. They said, "There is a curfew now." When we left there was no curfew.

"Now there is a curfew. You can't go back." I said, "It's our home. We've got to go back. Then we will stay home." We had to go home by a different road.

Wissam was in prison in Israeli territory for interrogation. The army called me to come and be interrogated at the prison in Tel Aviv. They asked me, "Did you know where he was? Did you ever see him during this period?"

I got to speak to three interrogators. They kept saying, "You must have seen him within those nine years." I told them, "Listen. On the graves of all the prophets," and I named ten prophets, "I didn't see him. Because if I knew my son was in Ramallah, I would have done anything to visit my son after nine years." The response of the soldier was, "I don't know any of these prophets you are talking about." I said, "If you haven't been introduced to the prophets, that's your problem, not mine." He told me, "Are you coming to interrogate us or are we interrogating you? Shut up and answer the questions!" I said, "OK, ask me and I'll answer." He said, "What answers!"

After that interrogation, I told the interrogator, "You brought me here. I stayed all day. I've been answering your questions. I'm not leaving now until I see him because he's in jail here." He said, "Whatever you want." So they brought Wissam and the head interrogator.

The head interrogator sat and talked with me and Wissam. I said to the interrogator, "I want to get to know you better. What is your name?" The guy responded with the Arabic name he must use in jail, Abu Sharif. Sharif means trustworthy, honorable. Wissam, in front of the interrogator, said to me, "Do you believe he is the father of Honorable? God knows what his name is, but we know it is not Honorable."

I asked this Abu Sharif, "What do you want? You have just interrogated him. Why are you keeping him here? It is enough that you exploded his insides to the point where he had to have an operation." The interrogator responded to Wissam, "Did I do that to you, Wissam? Did we do that to you here?" Wissam said, "No, you didn't bust my intestines. But you put me in a room, twenty-four hours a day, where I count how many ants there are. And I yelled for two hours to go to the bathroom and no one would take me out to the bathroom." After two hours, when they finally took him to the bathroom, they kept him in this bathroom for an hour and a half, refusing to take him out, after he was knocking on the door, "I'm done." He was knocking and no one would come. When they finally came, they pushed him inside the bathroom. He pushed the soldiers back. Now that is one of the charges against him, that he attacked a soldier in prison.

He was forty days in solitary in this prison in Israel. He had food but they would not give him tea. God only knows why they didn't give him tea.

When we were sitting with the interrogator, one of the things he asked Wissam was, "Are you bored in solitary confinement?" Wissam said, "Sometimes it's good. Sometimes it's bad. But life sometimes is good, sometimes is bad, so I'm not too worried about it."

Abu Sharif said, "Would you like us to bring somebody for you?" "If you brought somebody, that would be good. And if you didn't, that would also be good." This happened in front of me. Abu Sharif said, "How would you like

Sami," which was someone Wissam knew who was in jail. "If you want to bring him, good."

Wissam wanted to show, "Whatever you do, it's up to you. You play the shots. I'm not going to like it or dislike it."

They asked, "Shall we bring him now? Would you like to sit together with him?" I said, "Yes, bring him. Because I am going to go and be the messenger and tell his family that I saw him. It's as if you are bringing him to his mother."

When Wissam gets out of prison, I will have one more marriage to take care of. Then my role will be finished.

Wissam Rafeedie

"The best of days are those which we have not yet lived."

January 4, 1992[6]

To my family, my brothers and sisters, my loved ones, I send my warmest greetings. From within the walls of the central prison in Hebron, I have started a new page of my political life after living underground for many years.

First I would like to apologize very greatly to each and every one of you for not writing to you during the past ten years. The reasons are known to all of you. However, I was always convinced that the brotherhood and sisterhood between us and the family connections we have would remain alive and well. I felt that your solidarity was an active part of my struggle.

I am writing to you only days after my interrogation period. I spent four and a half months of my life as a prisoner being moved from cell to cell, and from interrogation rooms in Ramallah to torture cells in Moscobiyya and to solitary confinement rooms in Petah Tikva (which is Hebrew for another one of their miserable prisons). I have exited these prisons as the same Wissam Rafeedie that entered them, the same brother of yours that you knew and heard about.

My health is stable and the intestinal condition that I suffered from while under interrogation is getting better after the operation. As I understood from the prison doctor in Ramallah, they cut the veins from the pancreas which was reacting abnormally during the high periods of stress that I faced together with extreme cold and days on end of being deprived of sleep. My stomach has become smaller which causes it not to be able to digest some foods. My stomach is exactly like what they say about the Mercedes car: when it tries to climb a steep hill it feels like it wants to roll backward.

My left foot is unpredictable and has a mind of its own. It is in need of an operation to remove some internal buildup. To date I have not been permitted to have surgery done. When the Gulf War broke out, I was forced to stay in one place for over one month which gave my foot a much needed rest.

---

6. This is the first letter to his family from Wissam after more than nine years of living underground.

There does not seem to be any risk of bone problems occurring, so I don't think it will be critical if the surgery is postponed. I'm going to check with the Red Cross if there is any chance of getting an Arab doctor to perform the surgery. If not, I will probably be taken to the hospital in Ramle.

I lost over twelve kilograms during the interrogation period. But I'm not worried because I know, once I am released, Mother will make sure I get all of my favorite meals.

I must let you know that I felt great when I heard news about all of you. I was undergoing interrogation and working through the process of administrative detention hearings and bail hearings and meetings with representatives of the Red Cross. Your solidarity as well as the solidarity of all of the friends that worked so hard was deeply felt at a much needed time.

Every prisoner needs the support that you demonstrated for me. When you send a letter to me, it is as if you have sent a letter to every prisoner. I have become aware of all of the activity that was initiated on my behalf. I will not, however, give personal thanks to all those who acted on my behalf since there is no thanks to be given. Your solidarity is a human and brotherly responsibility bestowed upon each and every one of us. I will say that I firmly embrace your hand in solidarity — person by person.

I am confident that, regardless of the terrible days that have passed, the future is yet bright. My conviction of a better, brighter future is overwhelming. For me this conviction of a better future is like the conviction of a young child knowing that his mother will feed him when he becomes hungry. The ultimate future that history holds for our people is bright and flourishing. No matter how long it takes, the suffering of our people will be abolished.

On the personal side, I am going to attempt to address the questions that I can anticipate your asking: marriage, family life, and my studies.

Let me be very clear and up front with you from the beginning, that the road I have chosen is a road of deep conviction. It is a road that I do not plan to diverge from until I am in my grave. The routines of life, such as having a wife, kids and getting a degree, do not mean much to me. If I am able to fulfill these, all the better, as long as it is not at the cost of my convictions. If I am not able to achieve these, I will *never* regret one day of my life or look behind into my past! Long live the life which has as its titles: change, adventure, and struggle. As for my field of study, Arabic literature, I challenge any master's student to match my skills.

The only thing that saddened me throughout the years is that I was not able to be beside my mother whom I know has passed through some very difficult times. I felt saddened during our separation that I was not able to call, write, or meet any of you. It is true that during exile, life was very difficult. But life being difficult is one thing, and being able to withstand and deal with it is another. I did and will withstand.

I am writing now in the morning hours. We have just finished the morning count and breakfast. I had fava beans, olives, and tea for breakfast in the company of some of the finest comrades I have known. At 10:00 is our break for one hour and a half. In the afternoon we get an hour. Life here is routine but I will be OK.

The only time I really become disturbed is during a few hours when prisoners are allowed to talk to each other. During these breaks, tens of prisoners speak at the same time and a television and radio are going full blast. My head feels like it is going to burst sometimes. I'm not used to all of the noise. For many years I lived alone, in complete silence, so it may take some time for me to get used to the new environment.

I am embarrassed to say, but it is the truth, that I forgot all of the youngsters' names. I know many are no longer youngsters. There are so many and I hope the future brings even more. I believe that limiting the number of children a family has is treason in the Palestinian family. Say "Hi" to all of them, especially the ones that I met before 1982, Nelle, Jeanne, Brenda, Nader, Samia. Is it Sonia who is Samia's sister or Rania who wouldn't let anyone carry her but me? I know I have left out some of the names of people I met before the many years of separation but please understand that my memory has worsened during the months of interrogation. Not being able to remember everyone's name bothers me.

Special greetings to my oldest sister, Nigmeh, who holds all of the precious memories of my oldest brother, Abu Mousa. I wish that I could meet her and I hope that she will come back with Mom when she returns from her trip to America.

Send pictures as much as you can. The Red Cross showed me some pictures when I was undergoing interrogation in Moscobiyya. When I saw some of the kids' pictures, I was delighted. I really got a barrel of laughs from the picture of little Wissam swimming in the pool. I'm going to ask Mom to put all of the pictures everyone sends into an album. Of course, little Wissam, my prophet on the ground, will have the first page.

While I was in Moscobiyya I was able to read the Bible. I could only wonder what Jesus would have done if he underwent the torture that I did. I must admit that when I read that it is easier to put a camel through the eye of a needle than for a rich man to enter heaven, I thought that it was a progressive idea and an idea against the wealthy. But following that, I read that I should love my enemies and wish them well. How am I to love my enemy while I am within these prison walls?

Eighteen years after finding the road of a Marxist party, I do not believe that the road of Jesus is for me. He has his religion and I have mine. To put it simply, I sense my Arab being and not my Christian being. That is why I hate the traditional Christian names such as Meta, Scander, Boulus. I have named myself, and the other prisoners call me by the name, Abu Yazed.

Sami, Randa's friend, is in the same section I am in. Tell Randa and her family that Sami is fine. Every time I smoke he starts to lecture me on the hazards of smoking. But when it comes to discussing smoking I somehow lose my ability to hear. Like the Syrian saying goes, the three good things in life are a cigarette, a wife, and a glass of whisky. For the whisky, I tried it when the Intifada first broke out. Since then, I only drink occasionally. As for the wife, I tried once and she was cowardly.[7] If possible I would like to

7. Wissam was engaged to a woman in 1982 who decided to get married to someone else when she learned that Wissam was underground.

meet a woman that has a strong, independent personality, and who is organized. I despise those women that only nod in agreement to everything their husbands say. This I will leave for history to determine.

I have returned to writing after lunch. We had dried beans, a small bowl of soup and a piece of meat. I must complete this letter before our afternoon break.

My stay in Hebron is possibly temporary because as soon as they want to put me into the court process they will most likely transport me to Ramallah. There is also a possibility that I can request that I be moved to Ramallah, because it is difficult for Mom to connect with the Red Cross from El Bireh to Hebron.

No court hearing has been set yet. As for the charges, they have phrased them in an exaggerated way. I don't waste much time thinking about the sentence I may receive. Three or four years is most likely. Whatever it may be, I am up to the responsibility and challenge. It's like the saying, he who wants to get drunk does not count the number of drinks. I, likewise, was not raised to count the years.

Thinking of my family and everyone else, too many to name, especially of our people who reside in America — I don't know their names, and if I did it would require a letter of its own — during this holiday season I send you my greetings.

Wissam – Abu Yazed

January 21, 1992[8]

To my loving mother,

Good morning if it's morning, and good evening if it happens to be evening. I send my deepest and warmest greetings.

This is the third letter that I have written to you. I write again because I feel like gossiping with you from Ramallah this time, not from Hebron.

The other comrades are looking out of the window at the falling snow which has been ongoing for three days now. This means we now live in a prison within a prison, because at break time we are not allowed in the field. Rather, we spend the two and a half hours visiting other cells and discussing politics with the other comrades while smoking and drinking tea.

I will probably be in Ramallah for a week or two during my court appearances. Today is Friday, the day set aside for those who worship Muhammad. This is the third hearing and I am yet to be sentenced. The trip to Ramallah, however, was not a waste of time. There have been many good things that came with my being transported here. Just like the old Arabic proverb says, "In travel there is much good." I have met some new comrades and we have become good friends.

Here in Ramallah, one finds prisoners from all of the prisons waiting for their court hearings. I have met Nasser who is here from the Jenin prison. I currently am in the upper bunk writing to you and Nasser is resting on the

---

8. Wissam sent this Mother's Day letter to his mother while imprisoned by the Israeli authorities.

lower bunk watching the Friday Arabic movie called, "We Wish You Well and Hope to Meet You."

I think Nasser's wife is going to visit me soon and I hope she brings their son, Omar. I really got to like Omar whom I got to see during exile. I enjoyed playing with him. I even changed his pampers one day. In front of me is a beautiful picture of little Omar. It is a wonder how this youngster has grown into a handsome child.

Visiting day in Ramallah will be two days after tomorrow. I heard that you went to visit me in Hebron the same day that I left for Ramallah. I guess that was just bad luck. As you know, I had no means of letting you know I was leaving because the mail day for the prisons is the day we are allowed visitors. Ramallah is easier for you, anyway. On Monday I will be permitted to visit. It will be an hour visit, in other words a halfway decent visit.

More important than all of this is that my being sent to Ramallah has given me the opportunity to see the flour mill and the house. Nothing has changed. If my memory serves me correctly, the only thing that looks different after ten years is the hanging plants on the front porch of the house.

How is Um Mousa? I hope you are fine. Please always take care of yourself and your health. Rest and do not worry about me. My health is good and the food here in Ramallah is better than that of Hebron. Please keep me informed about your health and how you're managing.

Do you know what the difference is between the love of one's mother compared to the love of one's brother or wife? Let me tell you what I think the difference is. The mother loves for free without asking for anything in return. The mother always loves her son — whether the son respects his mother or not, whether he loves her or not, whether he helps her through the difficult points in life or not. Can a son wish for more than this non-stop love from his mother?

Even believing this, it causes me distress because my life has dictated that I be away from my mother for so many years, and the life that I have drawn for myself may not be what you had wished. Even with this anxiety, I yet feel a great love for you. I feel that I hold upon my shoulders a tremendous amount of responsibility to figure out how I am to express this love for you when I am so close to you but yet so far out of your reach and sight.

Whatever I am able to do to express my love, I will. Be assured that however I am able to express my love to you, I will express the same love to all mothers. This is the deep-rooted conviction that I have chosen, to lead us all to a free, progressive, bright life. Do you accept this conviction?

My gift to you today from behind these prison walls is tens of kisses on your rosy cheeks. After the kisses are some hugs and ruffling of your hair as I used to do when I was a youngster. Is there anyone in America that can give you this present? I think not. This is my role and I will not permit anyone to fill my shoes.

I hope your health is good because you yet have ahead of you years and years that we will live together, side by side. Like the revolutionary Turkish poet, Nazim Hikmet, once said, "The best of days are those which we have not yet lived."

Um Sa'alem and Family

"If someone from the army came to your house, how would you deal with this?"

Um Sa'alem: Let me begin with the most difficult family problem. That is having a son in prison. What does that really mean to a family, especially to *our* family?

It's true that when my son was arrested, I cried. I cried at the moment. And then I quit crying, because the reason my son was arrested was not a wrong reason. I want my sons to be strugglers, to be morally taking the high ground, and when they are arrested, that is part of the struggle. I am convinced that they are not criminals. They are arrested for taking a correct road in their life, which is to struggle for their homeland.

Me, within myself, I cry twenty-four hours a day. When I take a piece of bread, sometimes I can't swallow it, so I drop it back on the table. I will never let my kids or my husband or anyone notice that it affects me twenty-four hours a day, because I need to be strong for this family to continue.

In 1968, my mom had to face the same thing. They came and took my brother when he was sixteen years old. I remember when they took him from the house. I was breast-feeding my son, the one who is in prison now. My mother said she told the soldier, "His life does not mean to me as much as our resistance to you. So go ahead. Do what you want with him." She yelled an Islamic saying: "At the end, justice and life are one." What we live for, we die for.

Our family, historically, has been a family that loves their land. My father was arrested during the British time for his resistance activities. So my strength was not acquired after one arrest, but rather I was brought up with this moral high ground.

In 1967, the relationship between myself and my husband[9] flared up, because in '67 he proposed that we leave and go to Jordan. I told him, "I will never leave this land. If you want to leave, my kids will stay with me and you are more than welcome to go. I was born in this land. I am going to live my life in this land. I am going to die in this land."

I think that there are good and bad people everywhere. I am a Muslim. My family in Ramallah are in Fatah. My brother in Amman is Hamas. My kids are Popular Front. I think there is good in all of them, and I don't have a problem with any of these people. As long as they stay clean and their spirits are clean, I don't care who they are, I like them. But if my brother was a collaborator who turned against the people, I would hate my brother.

My third son, Samer, was arrested in 1986. He's been in prison six years now for killing a Jewish settler. Samer was arrested for eighteen days pre-

9. Abu Sa'alem, husband of Um Sa'alem, was not present during the family interview in 1992. The following is from notes on a conversation with him in 1991: "Previously, all three religions lived together. Now, live shooting is a daily event in the marketplace. With every home having someone martyred or in prison, it's a human problem not just a political problem. How can I convince my sons that co-existence is possible? They face more harshness in what they see and experience."

vious to that time, when he was taking his high school proficiency test. Faris, my second son was also previously arrested, so I had had an introduction to how an arrest can affect the family.

Sa'alem: When my brother Samer was arrested, I felt I needed to be the moral backbone in this time of crisis. When they surrounded the house and closed the area off as a military zone, I, myself, and the authorities were clashing at the doors of the house. But then my father was even more aggressive than I was. When I saw how my father was reacting, I realized that he didn't need me to be supportive. Rather, we were working in orchestra, not as individuals, trying to help each other out.

My main interest at that time was to insure Samer's safety, to make sure that he would not be physically harmed in prison to the point where he might pass away.

Um Sa'alem: When they came to arrest her brother, Hala was crying at the top of her voice. But at the same time she was yelling to them, "Take whoever you want, because we have so many more, we are not worried."

Ahmad was very young at the time. He was astonished. He didn't know what was going on. He started crying. I went to the soldier and said, "No, he's not crying." And I started whistling (like the sound we make at weddings) and singing.

The moukhtar of the town came and said to me, "You shouldn't be doing that. Your son is going to jail and he may be gone for a long time." "I am singing because he took one of the settlers," I replied. "He [the settler] took my land a long time ago."

For four days, people coming out of the prison would tell me about how Samer was bleeding in the face. They were hitting him when he was blindfolded.

One time when they came to the house, they took all of my sons except Ahmad. At the door of the house, I told them, "Why don't you just go ahead and take Ahmad, because six is not enough kids to bring to Palestine. I'll just start working on six more." He said, "Go ahead and start."

Ahmad: Everybody's waiting their turn to go to prison. I'm not scared of prison. My brother's like everybody else.

Um Sa'alem: There is not one mother who lives in this country that does not want to see her son get out of prison. However, if the release of my son means that we aren't going to be able to achieve freedom for everyone in this country, I want my son to be in prison. I'd want him to have three lifetimes in prison if that meant the ultimate goal would be achieved. Because we can no longer live like this and my son is just one paying the price for many.[10]

Don't think that when we go to the marketplace and find the soldiers that we are not scared. We would be lying if we told you we were not scared inside. Also, don't think that when they come to arrest our sons that deep inside we are not worried about our sons.

We have two alternatives when they come to arrest someone or when they hit someone. It's either, we're going to shut up and accept it, or we're going

10. Similarly, Abu Sa'alem said in 1991 that he did not want Samer to be deported. "Even if he's in prison, he's still in Palestine."

to save our dignity and make our voices heard. This family, our people, our dignity becomes higher than anything, so we will speak up to save our dignity.

Sa'alem: You may be surprised at how this steadfastness comes about. We were raised on an Arabic proverb that says, "That person who is drowning doesn't care if somebody squirts him with a little bit of water."

Um Sa'alem: My son sends me a lot of letters. He never once told me that he was in bad condition. He is asking about me only. I know some of his comrades in prison and they talk about wishing they could have this kind of food or wishing they could go and see that place. Never, never does Samer talk about his own condition.

When I last wrote to my son I told him, don't ever think I forget you because you are in prison for life. When I walk in the marketplace and I see the young men walking in the street, I see you walking with them. When I come home and make food and we sit to eat, I see you eating with us. When I go to sleep and dream, I see you in my dreams.

Do you think I'm worried about only *my* son in prison? I wish I could show you the letters I have from other prisoners. All of his friends send me letters. I get to know them when I go to visit my son. I talk to them. We become friends. Friends have to write. We write. Some I used to see but never really knew. Some brought me messages from Samer when they got out of prison, and when they got imprisoned again, I knew them because they had been to my house. If I don't respond to each and every one of them, I have a problem when I go visit!

When I come to visit, my son says to me, "There are four or five people who want to hear your voice. First, yell for what's-his-name up on the second floor so he can hear you." So I will yell a greeting to that person. Then I will yell a greeting to another person. And that's how I keep connections with the other prisoners that are in the prison.

Sa'alem[11]: Two-thirds of the prisoner's life is trying to build social relationships within prison, with other prisoners and with other prisoners' families. Those who are in and out of prison can make a connection between the families. When a mother comes to see her son and she sees that her son now has new friends in prison, she relaxes.

We make sure that the family relationship among the prisoners is very strong. A lot of problems occur in the families of prisoners or with the prisoners themselves that the families can't take care of. But with the relationship that evolves out of being together, we can address some of these problems. Sometimes we even write to the families about specific family problems that we try to help them solve from within the prison.

Um Sa'alem: Let me give you a specific example. There is a boy who came from Jalazon Camp. He had no one to send him letters. So once he sent a letter to his father in the grave and he addressed it to "My Father" at the cemetery in El Bireh. My son in prison found out about it. So the next time I visited my son, he asked me to write a letter to this boy. I wrote to him in the

---

11. According to notes taken in 1991, Sa'alem spent three and a half years in prison.

name of his father. When I saw him, he said: "I really believe that you are my real mother" (even though there was no family relationship there). Ever since that time, we have been writing back and forth.

When we go to visit, they make us feel like nothing. When I went one time, I was wearing my headdress. There was a new girl there checking us. She said, "Take off your headdress." I told her, "What do you mean, take off my headdress? I never took off my headdress any time I came to visit." I started yelling and the person in charge came and asked, "What's wrong?" I told him, "I never took off my headdress. Who is this girl? She told me to take off my headdress." He said, "You mean, the other person never told you to take off your headdress?" I said, "Yes." The person in charge said, "Then this one's the smart one." I said, "OK. I'll take it off this time. Next time, I'm going to come with a hattah [man's headdress], two headdresses, and another hattah. I'm going to make you tired as you take off my headdresses."

Fatmeh: I am very proud to be engaged to Sa'alem, because he was in prison so I know he has been tested by this society and he won, and he is still a struggler even after he came out of prison which is even more important to me.

Marriage should not be an obstacle to the struggle. To be married does not mean that you continue your activity as it was before. You have an added responsibility that needs to be worked into the overall framework of the struggle.

Sa'alem: Marriage is not a goal but marriage provides several things for a struggler. It provides a companion to help in building the future society, or the atmosphere of future struggle. In a normal life, marriage should bring stability. But under occupation, whether you are married or not, stability is not there. So the essence of marriage you will never see. We have to become very creative in the ways that we remain supportive of each other, supportive of the family, and supportive of the general work as a whole.

Um Sa'alem: When they came to arrest Faris, waking all of us to arrest him, he asked for one thing. He asked for a drink of water from his mom before he left because he was thirsty. The soldiers started picking him up and taking him out and said, "That's OK. He'll drink where we are." I chased them out the door with a cup of water. At the end, I gave up. I threw the water. I said, "That's OK. He doesn't have to drink." After that we heard that they put water in front of him for two days and they didn't let him drink. If they took your son and he wanted a glass of water and they wouldn't let him drink for days, what would you think?

You didn't answer me. If someone from the army came to your house, how would you deal with this? What would you tell them?

Um Elias

"I felt they were _our_ kids, Palestinian children."

My first name is Emily. Everybody knows me as Um Elias. It means mother of Elias. Here in the area, everybody is called as the father or the mother of the oldest son.

I am from Bethlehem. We are a Christian family. My uncle was the mayor of Bethlehem. I was born on the third of June, 1930.

I went to school in Jerusalem. It was a German school. There was no difference then between Palestinian people or Jewish people or any other kind of person. I remember a small story. It still remains in my heart. One of our friends — her name was Mahoba — was a Jewish friend. She was so close to my older sister, Mary, that each pricked the finger of the other, and each took the finger of the other in her mouth to take some of the other's blood, to be sisters in blood and to trust each other always. It made me so happy to think that we could spend all of our lives together.

We had a lot of Jewish friends but that was before 1948, the year in which I married. I was going to marry and go to the Gaza Strip, because my husband and his family lived in Gaza. When the problems started between the Zionists and the Palestinians, I said to my mother, "Look, Mother, we have got a lot of Jewish friends. So if any problem happens, please, Mother, protect them and keep them in your house until everything is over." This was the thing that I asked my mother for, to protect the Jewish people whom we knew and who were so close to us.

My mother said, "I can protect them until everything is OK. Perhaps the Red Cross will come, we don't know who will come, and then you can tell the people, they are in our house." We did not expect that we would lose and they would win!

1948-67

At that time, when people were married, it wasn't for us to choose. The grandfather and the father and the mother came to see the girl, they asked the neighbors (who said what a good girl she was). So they came to our house.

My father-in-law was a priest. He was from Beit Sahour and that is where his father's house was. But my father-in-law lived in Gaza. He didn't want his son to marry a girl from Gaza because he felt that if his son were to take one from Gaza, his son would stay in Gaza, and he wanted him to come back to the area of Bethlehem, Beit Sahour, and Beit Jala.

So they tried to find him a girl to marry from this area. They asked for a girl, first of all, who had studied and could speak well. In my time, before 1948, there were very few girls who had studied.

My family did not want to push us to do something which we would not like. So when I saw my husband and they asked me to marry him, my mother asked me, "Would you like to marry this man?" I told her, "I don't know him. We would have to sit together."

We sat together maybe two or three times and then, one day, when he left he kissed me and I never forgot that kiss! At that time, it was very difficult for a girl to let anybody kiss her.

After that, there was some problem between my family and his family and my family said the engagement was over. I said, "No, I want him." My mother was worried. She said, "What's happened?" I told her, "Nothing happened." "No, what's happening? I want to know why you want this man." I told her, "Yes, he kissed me. So I will not let anybody say, 'Another man has kissed her'."

When I was still newly engaged, my husband used to go to the doctor in Jerusalem. One day he came from Gaza to Jerusalem. That day, when I listened to the news, I heard about the Stern and the Irgun gangs, and I heard that a bomb had been thrown at people who were coming from Gaza, and a lot of people had been killed. I couldn't see anything. I was just weeping and weeping and waiting.

My husband did not see the doctor in Jerusalem and managed to get back to Gaza. But he told us, "Oh, I couldn't tell you what I saw there. A lot of blood — a lot of people have been killed. I don't believe that anybody could do this to animals." It was very terrible. From here, we began to have some hate in our hearts.

I lost my husband on April 15, 1967. He died from a heart attack but he left me eight children, six sons and two daughters, and all of them needed me to protect them. My youngest son was only two years and three months old when his father died. Before that I lost a son who was seventeen years old, not by war but by sickness. Elias was in the first year of university when his father died. At the end of the forty days of mourning for my husband, the Six Day War began.

I remember at that time, my father-in-law was standing beside me on the balcony and said, "Look. I know that you are very sad and that you have lost your husband. We don't know whether the Israelis will enter into this area or what they will do with us. But I want to ask you a question: would you like to stay here or would you like to take your children and go away, I don't know where." I called him "Father" because my father had also died. My mother had gone to America and there was nobody here from my family. I told him, "Father. Where my husband has died, I would like to die with my children. I will not be a refugee. I saw what happened to other people and I will not let my children grow up in a camp." So we stayed.

My father and my brother were living in Honduras and they helped me much so that I could stand on my feet and begin to build myself here. I began to build my family, to do everything for my family, and, in front of God, I feel that I have won.

My Daughter Can Only Visit

I will tell you a small story about my daughter. In 1971, she was working as a social worker in Bethlehem. She got permission to go to Lebanon to study for her examination in the Arabic University. While she was there she lost her visitor's paper. I called the government and said, "Please. My daughter is in Lebanon. I want to bring her back. Please help me." The officer in the police station in Bethlehem was a good man. When he saw me he asked, "What is the matter, Mrs. Rishmawi?" I told him, "I have a problem here." He said, "I'll try to help you." Another one also asked, "What is the matter?", because we are peaceful people. We never do anything hard to the other side. "OK," he said, "we will try to help you." I felt that I was dealing with human beings. They gave me messages to the office of identity cards and told me, "Maybe they will help you."

When I went to the identity card office, I went to Captain David. I told him, "I have two messages for you," from the captain in Bethlehem and from the person in charge of the entire area here, "and they ask you to help me." He read the papers and he said, "Where is your daughter now?" I told him, "She is in Lebanon because she went to study for her examination and she has not come back." He said, "Tell her to come back." I asked, "How can I tell my daughter to come back?" He said, "Make her a visitor's paper."

I thought when he spoke with me softly and gently that the man would help me. I did not know what would happen. So I wrote to my daughter, "Come back quickly. Everything will be OK." I prepared the visitor's paper. When she came back I went with my daughter and the visitor's paper to the identity card office and I told the man, "Here is my daughter." He said, "How did she enter?" I told him, "You told me to make her a visitor's paper." He said, "Did you make a visitor's paper?" I said, "Yes, as you told me." He said, "Where is it? Go and make some photocopies of it."

I believed until then that the man would help me and that everything would be all right. I went and made the photocopies. Then he told me to give him the photocopies. He brought the identity card of my daughter and all of the papers for her and he said, "Is this your daughter's identity card?" I said, "Yes! Give it to me." He said, "Go away. She will never get it. Do you see what is written here? If she is coming with a visitor's paper, she will never enter this area."

Put yourself in my place. What had happened to us? I started to shout. My daughter started to cry. But what could we do? Nothing.

She went back to Lebanon. She married there and she has her own house and her own children. Until now, she can enter only with visitor's papers. That is one of our problems and why we started to feel that we had to change.

This year, she was in the south of Israel, and she tried to enter the West Bank to visit us. She waited there seven days. She called me and said, "They will not let me enter." I asked her, "Why?" She said, "Because my birth was in the Gaza Strip." Would you believe that? She could not enter to visit her family.

Good and Bad Soldiers

We deal with the Israeli people. There is no problem when they are not officers. A lot of them say when they come to our house, "Mrs. Rishmawi, we feel that you are like our mother." One of them said, "I tell my mother that I have another mother in Beit Sahour. Her name is Um Elias." I feel the same about another one: when I speak with him I feel that I am speaking with my son.

But when you need anything from the officers, you feel the difference between us and them. You never feel that they are dealing with human beings. They always make us feel as if we are not more than slaves. They can enter into any house, to arrest anyone. They do not care. It is not as if you are dealing with a people like ourselves. You are dealing with another people.

When they killed a boy here in Beit Sahour named Yihad Abu Sa'ada, I tried to speak with the soldiers gently. I asked one of them, "Haven't you got children? Why do you use guns to kill our children? These are not animals. They are not birds. These are human. Do you know what it means for a woman to lose her son? It is very difficult." Maybe I feel more with the mothers who lose their sons because I lost one of my own children. I always remember my son and I know that I lost him. "Can you tell me, how do you feel when you see that one of our children is dying from a shot by a little pistol like this?" And they ask why the Intifada started!

I am telling you, the soldiers are not all bad. I asked these soldiers, "Can you tell me you haven't got children, you haven't got a brother? Feel with us!" One of the good soldiers said, "Look, Madam. I can't speak with you. I know. But we have an order, 'Don't speak to the people'." They tell the soldiers not to speak with the people, but to deal with them in a hard way. They do not want the soldiers to know about our problems.

One time a group of women was visiting a family who lost a son. The soldiers caught a boy and they were going to take him. We said, "No, we will not go away until you let this boy go." We stood there until they let him go.

A little while before, my children had come to me and said, "Mother, the soldiers entered our house and they are up on the roof." I would not let my children go to see the soldiers because I was afraid they would beat us or kill us. I went to the roof to speak with the soldiers. A boy who was here with my son said, "I will not let you go alone." "Please. Don't come with me," I said. He said, "No. I will come with you."

One of the soldiers started to speak bad words. My son told him, "Don't use those words. We don't like to hear those words in our house." The soldier said, "Oh, why? I hear that in another family, when the small boys repeated these words about us, his mother kissed him." My son said, "You can go to that house, but not in our house. We do not speak and we do not hear these words."

I saw the same soldier outside the house of the boy who was killed. I told him, "I remember your face. You were there." He said, "Look. We don't like to come to you, but it is the order." I said, "I believe that it is the order. But can I come to your house and go on the roof? Can I go to your house and do anything I like?" He said, "We know that you couldn't. It is the order."

If we would start to speak, there are a lot of stories. One day my son, my daughter-in-law, four of us in all, were sitting here taking our lunch and, I remember, it was cucumbers, potatoes, and chicken. The door opened — we did not lock the door, we just shut it — and a soldier entered with his gun saying, "Who threw stones at me?" We said, "Oh, nobody is outside. We haven't any children here. We are all of us as you see — old, nobody small." And, as he was taking our lunch, he said, "Somebody was throwing at me." I carried the dish to him and I told him, "You can taste it. You can try some of our lunch. Just try it." Then he was ashamed of himself. At the end he said, "Somebody threw stones at me but not you."

Another time we had a visitor, a German girl. We were sitting at the table.

A group of soldiers — maybe eight or ten — came quickly into the house, and ran into this room, and some of them entered into other rooms. I said, "What is the matter?" My children would not speak. I said, "What is the matter, people?" They said, "Somebody threw stones at us." I answered, "Nobody threw stones from here. You can see."

A lot of soldiers climbed the steps and one tried to open the door to the roof. He couldn't open it because it was old-fashioned. I told him, "Just a minute. I will open it for you." I opened the door and said, "Come. You can see if there is anybody on the roof. There is nobody."

On the way back he entered into my son's room. My son had just been paid at his job. He had put the money on the cupboard and he was sitting downstairs with us. When I came by with the soldier from the roof, the soldier said: "Go away." I said, "But I want to see what you want to do." He said, "No. Go away." As long as they left my children alone I didn't care about anything else. I said, "Let them do what they want. I know that there is *nothing* in my house."

After they went away, my son remembered his money. He went upstairs. Then he said, "Oh, Mother. They stole my money." He had worked for a whole month only to have his money stolen.

We are not worried about money or anything but our children. One day, they said that children had thrown stones and that it was beside the school. They came to a place far from the school, where vegetables are sold. They caught three children. I was passing. The children were so young, maybe ten or twelve years old, not more. But because they were carrying their bags, they caught them. I looked at the children and said, "What is happening?" The soldiers said, "Go away, woman." (Those are the best words we hear.) "Go away, woman. Go away, woman." "Yes, but these are kids. Why are you taking them?" They said, "Go away." But I couldn't go away because I was feeling, "These are *my* kids." It didn't matter whether they were my kids or my neighbor's kids. I felt they were *our* kids, Palestinian children.

So I waited. These small children had no identity cards. They had nothing on them. We come again to the good people and the bad people. The leader of this group of soldiers was very bad. He caught the first one of the children and he tried to beat him on the neck. "But he is a *kid*! What are you doing?" He beat two of the boys very, very hard. Another soldier let one boy run away.

When the children were gone, I went to the captain and I said, "I want to ask you just a small question." He snapped, "What do you want?" I told him, "Look. I will ask you this question. Can you tell me, these kids who you beat, how they will grow? In which heart will they grow?"

One day I was standing outside and two children, maybe eight years or seven years, were carrying stones. I said, "What are you doing here, children?" These children are so small, and these are a danger to the State of Israel? I don't believe that.

I will never forget when I saw the Israeli soldiers with ten young men standing at the wall and they were kicking them with their feet! I stood in the street and shouted, "What are you doing?" The soldier told me, "Go away, woman." I said, "Not me, go away! You go away! It is my land. You have to go away." I was beside the church here. Maybe because I am an old woman he did not kill me, he just said, "Go away." I told him, "I will not go away. This is my land and I will stay here. These are human beings. These are *our* children. Why do you kick them with your feet? Can you tell me?"

He didn't know what to say except, "Go away." Because I feel that it is my land, it was my father's land, it was my grandfather's land, how can I go away?

Military Law

If they arrest anyone, no one can give you an explanation. My daughter, May, studied in Bethlehem University. They had a university magazine and she wrote in it. Under the university rules, those who write for the magazine must get approval from their leader, not from the government. But what happened is that the soldiers entered the university and arrested a group of eight and sent them to court. One of them was my daughter.

They had put out a magazine under the university rules. They had permission from their leader. They were told, "No. You have to get permission from the government and they have to check whether it is good that you wrote it or no." But it was under the university. They should not have to have any permission from outside.

My daughter was secretary of the group, of the magazine. They translated what my daughter wrote. The judge said, "When I read it it is nice, it is good." It was about a green garden and the birds flying and the sun shining — I don't remember what was written. "It is wonderful writing," the judge said, "and we have to translate it into Hebrew. But, the law is the law, and so you have to go to jail for six months or you have to pay money." Can you believe that?

We are dealing with a lot of laws: Turkish law, Jordanian law, Israeli law, and, if there is no good law to judge us, there is the military government law. So, whatever they do, we can't say anything. How can we continue? If you were in our place, could you continue in this life?

Grandchildren

Now we have the youngest, my grandchildren, and this is who we want to protect. We want to return the smiles to their faces.

I have twelve grandchildren but none of them have been to church at the Church of the Nativity in Bethlehem. They don't know how we pray, because all the area is a "closed area." There are more soldiers there than other people. For twenty-five years we have not been permitted to go to pray in the Church of the Nativity on Christmas! We live here and this is our church. But if we want to go to church, we have to get permission. What is this? Why?

Would you believe that there are boys of ten or twelve years who do not know what the word "sea" means because they never have seen the sea? It is very difficult to send them to see the sea.

I have a very small story of what happened with my grandson when he was maybe seven years old. The children were in the grade school in Bethlehem when the soldiers started to say, "Curfew in Beit Sahour." The driver proceeded to bring the children back. When they reached the father's house and the car stopped, a soldier started to shoot at the car so the children could not get out. They were so worried, the driver brought them to me and said, "Here is your grandson. I don't know what to do with him. You can send him to his father." Now this child, he would not come down from the car. He said, "No. They will kill me. They will shoot me. I will stay at your house." But it was curfew and I did not know how long it would be in force, so I had to take him to his father's house. I took the child's hand and I said, "I will take you to your father." A lot of soldiers were calling, "Where are you going? Go back. There is a curfew." I told them, "Yes, I know there is a curfew but I have to bring the child home to his family." This boy, how can I tell him that he is safe? He will never forget something like this. Never!

After my son lost everything, it was not enough that they confiscated everything from the pharmacy, but they went to his house and confiscated everything in his house, even the children's toys. [**See below, Section 9, p. 276**] My grandson had a computer that he bought with his pocket money and the soldiers or the tax people came and took his small computer. Can you tell me how he will feel? They took the desk from the children's room where they study. It was my children's desk, it was not my grandson's desk. I had my husband get it for my son when he was just a kid. How do you believe I felt when I saw them take the desk with them? It hurt me especially because it was from my husband. I had protected it a lot of years to let my grandchildren feel that it was from their grandfather to their father and now it was for them. I felt that it was something nice, but they took it.

During curfew, I saw my ten-year-old grandson standing beside the window and hanging a piece of nylon with a thread. I said, "What are you doing, boy?" "Grandma, Grandma, look! I made a flag and it will go!" I was worried for him.[12] When they enter any house and see a flag, or a flag is hanging outside, they get it and make the boy cut it or burn it. "If the soldier would see you, you would be in trouble, boy. Go away from the window." "No, Grandma, they will not see me. I am standing beside the window. See? I am standing here where nobody will see me."

We have our flag and our children feel that they have their own flag. They feel that they have their own nationality. They will never forget it.

Peace and Freedom

We are a normal family. We are not a problem family. No one of our children has ever thrown stones or done something like that. We are still a simple family living in peace. But, if the Israeli soldier comes and enters my house carrying his gun, of course, I will hate him. The soldier who stole the money

---

12. The U.S. State Department, *Country Reports on Human Rights Practices for 1987*, p. 1194, states with respect to the Occupied Territories: "Proscribed acts include displaying the Palestinian flag, its colors, or Palestinian nationalist slogans, and publicly expressing support for the PLO."

of my son after he was working all month to get his money and the soldier put it in his pocket and went away, how do you want me to feel toward him?

When we see that they demolish a house, when they kill a boy, when they do something hard, it hurts us all. We are going to feel with these people, their tears. We feel with any boy, whether he is Christian or Muslim; these are *our* children. He is a Palestinian boy and he is our child. There is no difference between Christian and Muslim here.

But a lot of the Christian people are leaving. They don't want any problem. There are very few still remaining in Bethlehem. For example, I have four brothers and two sisters and all of them have left the country. Some of them are in Honduras. Some of them are in El Salvador.

With all these problems, something starts to happen in our hearts. We lived with Jewish girls as friends and we tried to feel that we were sisters. We feel sad that we cannot continue like that. One day I was in Jerusalem and I saw Mahoba, the friend of my sister. I said, "Oh, Mahoba. How do you do?" This was maybe twenty years later. She had a friend with her. I spoke to her with enthusiasm, but she looked at me and said, "I am sorry I have an appointment with my friend." And she went away with her friend. I was just standing there. I lost something at that moment.

We hope that one day peace will come. We always think about peace. We are peace people. We are not hard people. We try to do everything in peace because we have very close friends among the Israeli people who are always feeling with us. I shall never forget an Israeli peace group that was with us after they arrested Elias. They came and said, "Um Elias, what happened with the government?" "They confiscated everything and that is not enough. Now they arrest him." They stood beside me. When we were sitting in church, they came and sat with us.

So, I feel that we can do something by peace. We do not always have to use hard things. We can do it by peace. But after what we have seen, it is very difficult.

I think that trust will never be built by hardness. Trust should be built by good things, exactly as we started to build trust between ourselves and the Israeli peace group. At the beginning, when they said they wanted to speak to us, we didn't believe that they could. They were very few. We tried and they tried. I hoped that their group would grow. When our children were with their children, in this peace group, from both sides we could deal with each other. A lot of Israeli people came and visited us.

We want to end the occupation. This is the problem. I think, without the occupation being over, peace will never come. They have to deal with our problems as equals. If we have our own state we want a freedom state, not *any* state, not *any* peace.

At the beginning, it was all Palestine. There was no Israel. Great Britain sold our land, land that was not theirs. They sold our land with the Balfour promise. When Great Britain left Palestine, they gave everything to Israel, all the power, all the guns, everything. I was a kid but I remember, my brother carried a small pistol and they were going to protect the area with this small pistol. We didn't know.

How can you protect the people with guns and soldiers? If peace does not come from the heart, how will it come? If we want to trust each other, we have to build love, to build peace. After we build this, then peace will come.

What we want from the Intifada: we want our nationality; we want our own land; we want our children to grow in a good situation, to return the smile to the face of our children; to let them feel that they are free, that they are not under occupation, because if they will remain in the same situation, they will never feel that they are free, always they will have suffering in their hearts. We are proud of our children when we see them. They are small but they are feeling the same as the old people. We feel that we are strong.

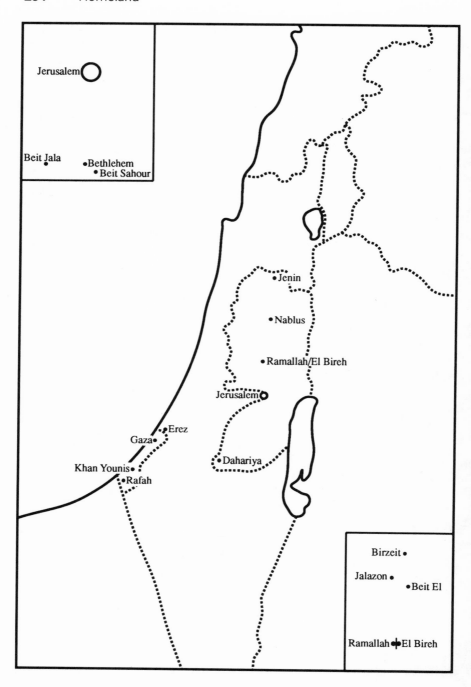

Jerusalem ◯

Beit Jala ·   ·Bethlehem
                ·Beit Sahour

·Jenin

·Nablus

·Ramallah/El Bireh

Jerusalem ◯

·Erez
Gaza·
Khan Younis·
·Rafah

·Dahariya

Birzeit ·

Jalazon·
       ·Beit El

Ramallah ✚ El Bireh

9

Resistance in the Occupied Territories

The West Bank and Gaza are ruled by a military government established after Israel's victory in the 1967 war. No formal political parties or overtly political organizations are permitted. Municipal elections were last held in the Gaza Strip in 1946. In the West Bank, municipal elections were held in 1972 and 1976, and according to the United States State Department "were widely regarded as fair." Most of the Palestinian officials elected at that time, such as Bassam Shaka'a, were later removed or deported by the Israelis and no further elections have been held.[1]

Within a few weeks after the Intifada began in December 1987, and before its magnitude could have been recognized, the State Department summarized the causes of the Uprising:

> The complex human rights situation in the occupied territories arises from the absence of a peace settlement; the territories remain under military administration, and communal conflict continues between occupation authorities, Israeli settlers, and the Palestinian population. Among the signs of friction are active resistance to the occupation, including episodes of violence, sometimes encouraged by outside groups. Friction also arises from security measures taken by Israel to counter terrorism or other perceived threats to security. Other concerns include Israel's denial of residency rights to spouses and relatives of some residents and to those who try to return to the occupied territories following prolonged absences. Discontent is also caused by civilian Israeli settlers who are governed by different rules from those imposed on Palestinians, and who sometimes engage in violent activities against Palestinians.[2]

In response to the Intifada, the Israeli authorities increased repression. Between December 1987 and the end of October 1991, in the words of an

1. U.S. State Department, *Country Reports on Human Rights Practices for 1984*, pp. 1279–80.
2. U.S. State Department, *Country Reports on Human Rights Practices for 1987*, p. 1189.

Israeli human rights group, "1,413 people lost their lives, most of them Palestinians killed by security forces, . . . [m]any thousands were wounded, tens of thousands were arrested and imprisoned, hundreds of homes were demolished or sealed, dozens of people were deported, the inhabitants of the territories were placed under curfew for protracted periods, and pupils were kept from their studies for weeks and months."[3] In 1992, 158 Palestinians were killed by Israeli security forces, 45 of them by undercover units disguised as Palestinians.[4] Also in 1992, five Palestinians died in custody either during the period of interrogation or shortly thereafter. "In three of these cases, autopsies showed that an aggravation of preexisting conditions (such as asthma or heart trouble) brought on by mistreatment during interrogation caused death."[5] On December 17, 1992, Israel deported 415 Palestinians alleged to be associated with Muslim fundamentalist organizations to Lebanon.[6]

Israel continues to discriminate against Palestinians in administering the Occupied Territories. The State Department reports:

> Israel has extended Israeli law to govern most activities of Israeli settlers who live in the occupied territories; Palestinians live under military law. Under the dual system of governance applied to Palestinians and Israelis, Palestinians are treated less favorably than Israeli settlers on a broad range of issues, including applicability of the right to due process; residency rights; freedom of movement; sale of crops and goods; water use; land tenure, ownership, and seizure issues; and access to health and social services. Offenses against Israelis are investigated and prosecuted more vigorously than offenses against Palestinians.[7]

★   ★   ★

Bassam Shaka'a

"I am the last elected mayor of Nablus."

I am the last elected mayor of Nablus. I was elected in 1976.

There were free elections in 1972 and 1976. All the councils in the Occupied Territories that were elected in 1972 resigned in protest. The Israelis tried to establish settlements near Nablus. The council of Nablus resigned and all the other councils resigned. The Israelis held another election in 1976.

The Israelis wanted councils as our legal representative, instead of the PLO. They were determined to get new leadership instead of the PLO and to

3. B'Tselem, the Israeli Information Center for Human Rights in the Occupied Territories, *Violations of Human Rights in the Occupied Territories 1990/1991* (Jerusalem: 1991), p. 11.
4. U.S. State Department, *Country Reports on Human Rights Practices for 1992*, Occupied Territories, Section 1a.
5. Ibid., Section 1c.
6. Ibid.
7. Ibid., Section 5.

cut the relationship between Palestinians inside and outside the Occupied Territories. They also wanted to destroy our unity inside the Occupied Territories.

Our people elected the national list in all the cities in the Occupied Territories. The Israelis fought these elected councils from the beginning. They wanted the councils to accept the occupation and to accept the military's orders. They wanted the military to make illegal laws. They wanted to change the occupation into a legal authority over our people.

The Israelis directed daily life. They tried to give the council responsibility for security. The council refused and the clash began to grow day by day until they tried to deport me in 1979. They deported two mayors in the beginning of 1980.[8]

After that they tried to kill three mayors when they bombed our cars. I lost both of my legs. The mayor of Ramallah lost his foot and the muscles of the other leg.[9] The mayor of El Bireh was lucky. He heard about the incidents in Nablus and Ramallah and he didn't use his car.

The Israelis did not make an investigation. No one has met with me or with either of the other mayors to ask for any information about the bombings. Some settlers were arrested. In prison, they lived in the guest house of the Israeli authorities. The Israelis let one of them go to America to visit his mother and then return to prison. When they were released, one of the settlers said that he believed the government knew about their activities against the mayors. And that man, who put the bomb in my car, said that he did not regret doing what he did.

In 1982, the Israelis dismissed most of the councils and began to administer the area by force. They removed the elected mayors of municipalities and appointed some Arab administrators. Three years later, Israeli mayors were appointed.

The Israelis refused to hold elections. They fought against any democratic solutions for our people[10] and they tried to oblige our people, by force, by the iron hand, to accept the civilian administration[11] until the Intifada exploded.

---

8. According to the U.S. State Department, *Country Reports on Human Rights Practices for 1991*, p. 1452: "Municipal elections were last held in 1976 in the West Bank, and most mayors elected then were later dismissed or, in some cases, deported on security grounds." Ibid, p. 1443: "The United States considers deportations to contravene Article 49 of the Fourth Geneva Convention."

9. The U.S. State Department, *Country Reports on Human Rights Practices for 1980*, p. 1106, states: "On June 2 the Mayors of Nablus and Ramallah were maimed by bombs allegedly set for them by Jewish extremists." Not until 1984 did the State Department report the arrest of Israeli citizens for the 1980 car bombings which maimed two Arab mayors, *Country Reports on Human Rights Practices for 1984*, p. 1272.

10. The U.S. State Department, *Country Reports on Human Rights Practices for 1991*, states, p. 1451: "The West Bank and Gaza are ruled under occupation by Israel's Ministry of Defense through a military government and civil administration. Israel does not permit Palestinians to participate in policy decisions concerning land and resource use and planning, taxation, trade, industry, and many other governmental functions."

11. The U.S. State Department, *Country Reports on Human Rights Practices for 1982*, states, pp. 1165–66: "Israel has made a concerted effort to reshape the politics of the occupied territories through the West Bank and Gaza Civil Administrations. The Civil Administrations were created in late 1981 and are under the control of the Ministry of Defense. They are staffed by military as well as civilian personnel. In 1982, they played a dominant role in such practices as the dismissal of elected and appointed officials, the deportation of university faculty, the imposition of house or town arrest and other collective punishments, the banning of newspapers, and the implementation

The Intifada, of course, is the answer of our people to the occupation. The Intifada is the peaceful revolution of our people. All of our people can act through the Intifada. The young, all the organizations, villages, refugees, the cities, all of our people express their determination through the big struggle which they have sustained for three years and a half and still continue. We believe that the Intifada will continue until we arrive at our aims and our rights. The public determination is very deep, very strong. No Palestinian has any hope that we can live for our future through the occupation.

The occupiers believe that this land belongs to them. They now use more than 65 per cent of our land. They use our water. They limit the water which we can use. They limit the electricity which we can use. They make these problems to oblige our people to leave the land and to emigrate, while they help Jews to immigrate to Israel.

When I was mayor of Nablus, we spent two years in struggle for a license to develop our electric station. After I said to them, with the council, that we would resign if we could not develop our own projects, they gave us a license to develop our water and electric projects.

When we had the generators and the station, they stopped us from giving electricity to some villages with which we had agreements. They forbade us from giving electricity to factories inside Nablus. And when we tried to defend our rights to give electricity to villages and factories, they arrested the engineers and the workers. We tried to defend our rights through the law. We found that there was a military order which gave the Israeli officer of electricity the right to control any activity involving electricity. He could stop our development without any reason. I asked a lawyer who said to me that this military order gave the officer the right to stop my wife from using electric machines in our house. If he wanted to stop it, he could stop it.

So they stopped our program to get electricity for the area. When they dismissed us, they cut off electricity to the villages outside Nablus. Then they connected Nablus itself to the Israeli electric system, without reason. Our station had started very well and could have answered all of our electric needs inside Nablus and in the area which we served before. Now, our electricity is from Israel. The Israelis always made problems for any simple services which we had.

We also had a project to make the water clean and to use it for agriculture. We collected the money to establish it. They made problems for us.[12] They

of broad restrictions on speech and assembly. The Civil Administrations also made major efforts to transfer patronage and authority from elected and established Palestinian nationalist leaders whom Israel objects to as being supporters of the Palestine Liberation Organization. As a key part of this effort, the West Bank Civil Administration actively promoted the spread of rural-based, quasi-political organizations known as 'Village Leagues.' These organizations were provided with arms and financial assistance by occupation authorities. . . ."

12. The U.S. State Department, *Country Reports on Human Rights Practices for 1982*, states, p. 1175: "Throughout 1982, there was a continual effort to create a role for the Village Leagues in the political process. There were constant efforts by the West Bank Civil Administration to interpose the Leagues as an intermediary between the inhabitants and the occupation authorities by refusal to accept requests for such services as the registration of births or marriages, building permits, bridge crossing permits, and family reunion applications without the participation of the local league. Village League members often exacted extra fees for their services. Many West Bankers complained that the Leagues' expanding activities undermine the elected Arab political structure."

did not help us to get the land which we needed. And they made propaganda that encouraged some villagers to believe that the sewers of Nablus were very dirty, that the project would be very difficult, etc. I went to the villagers and I said to them, we shall make a lake together and you choose exactly the land which we need. Then the Israeli officer asked the villagers, why are you silent now? And the Israelis dismissed us. Now our sewers go openly through the fields and it's very bad for our health situation.

Twice they stopped us from building schools. We built them after a very big struggle.

Even before the Intifada, the universities and the schools were closed for "security reasons."[13] During the Intifada our students have not been educated. We have spent about four years without education.

In the beginning of this dangerous situation for education, our people opened our houses for the students, and there were volunteers to teach the students. It was a very good action. The students came and accepted the education and I can say that our policy of education was better than the officer's policy.

The Israelis arrested teachers. They arrested students. They closed associations which started alternative education. There are military orders which give the occupation authorities rights to work inside the schools, even the elementary schools, to control education and to control teachers. They deported many teachers. They dismissed many teachers, objective teachers with great ability to teach, who respected themselves.

Now the universities, the secondary schools, the elementary schools need a new license every year. Every year they can be closed. The Israelis ask the universities and schools to give them documents about every student. Of course, our teachers refuse.

The Israelis encourage our students to graduate from secondary school without adequate education. They let our students cheat, without control. This year we tried to deal with the cheating. We willingly opened the schools for the students to get their education, freely, without money, to prepare themselves for the final secondary examination. We planned a public meeting with the parents, with the students, to educate them about the cheating and about the danger which some would face in the future. The Israelis stopped the meeting. That morning they forbade anybody to enter the hall. They prohibited the meeting by force. When the examination happened, the cheating went on.

More than six to seven hundred military orders control and direct our daily life. All of our schools and universities struggle against military orders.

13. The U.S. State Department, *Country Reports on Human Rights Practices for 1980*, p. 1008, states: "Following student demonstrations in the spring of 1980, the military government closed many schools, including Bir Zeit University, for a period of several months. Since then, the authorities have closed the high school in Bir Zeit (which had been the site of a number of confrontations), dispersing its students among a number of less well-equipped schools in nearby villages. In July 1980, the military governor amended Jordanian law regarding educational institutions to give himself the power to dismiss university students, bar professors and revoke university charters." The following year, the State Department states, *Country Reports on Human Rights Practices for 1981*, p. 1010: "Many activist teachers and school administrators were demoted and/or transferred to sparsely populated districts at the beginning of the fall term."

Everything connected with education has become very hard because there is a continuous clash with the authorities.

Those who have education learn by themselves. I have a daughter. She is struggling. Her educational program is in our hands. She is in the final year of secondary school and she wants to take the London examination and the official local examination. Many of our students learn by themselves in their houses. I have three sons who are volunteer teachers.

When I served as mayor, the Israelis controlled my daily life. When I returned from treatment and God gave me a chance to live again, they tried to destroy my socialization. A military group controlled my house 24 hours a day. No one could visit me without investigation. No one! No visitors came to my house without blood on their faces. They beat them very hard and let them enter my house, to harass me.

When I went out in the street, they followed me, shoulder by shoulder. They forbade some citizens from shaking hands with me. They beat citizens who said hello to me. They investigated and threatened some merchants when I bought some things from them. They continued this action more than five years until my children stopped having fellowship with any visitors or friends. I had a son in America. One year he came home for a holiday. He always used to stay in our house. I said, "Come on." He said, "I don't want harassment against my friends." Believe me. This is our daily life.

The Israelis do not accept democratic solutions. They do not recognize our human mission and determination. Until now, they fight against our unity. When any organization plans a meeting, the Israelis forbid it. Many of the mayors of village councils have always been connected with me and are my friends. Before they dismissed me, they dismissed other mayors because they had a relation with Bassam Shaka'a.

It's not against Bassam Shaka'a only. They are against any mayor. When they tried to kill me, they tried to kill three of us. When they wanted to deport me, they deported two other mayors also. All the mayors in Nablus, or in Ramallah, or in Birzeit, were dismissed or deported, or have resigned. Both mayors before me in Nablus resigned. Me, they dismissed after they tried to deport me and to kill me. They appointed Israeli mayors because our people refused to accept some Israeli-appointed mayor or some other council instead of us. It was no different in the other cities.[14] It happened to all of us, whether or not we were aggressive or we were radical. The Israelis did not recognize the facts, our facts. This is our situation.

---

14. The U.S. State Department, *Country Reports on Human Rights Practices for 1983*, states, p. 1301: "Twenty-three Arab mayors and municipal councils were elected in the 1976 elections. By the end of 1983, 14 of the mayors had been dismissed, as well as at least four of the town councils. The major towns of Hebron, Nablus, Ramallah, and El Bireh were ruled by Israeli officials; Halhoul and Jericho were led by mayors appointed from their town councils. Bethlehem was the only major town still governed by its elected mayor."

Nidal

*"If your heart is from a rock, no matter what they do to it, it remains in shape.
It remains a rock."*

Education

I was born in the Rafah Refugee Camp in 1973. My father was responsible for the extended family including my uncles and some aunts. I had six sisters and three brothers. Two of my sisters died.

My father was a worker in Israel: every day, he did whatever labor they would ask for. My uncles were old and could not work and there was no work for my aunts. So my father was the breadwinner for the extended family.

While my father went to work, there was a role for my mother to play at home. It was a community type of thing where the whole extended family worked together. Even after my sister married, we were still very close.

I became aware of hating the Israelis from the way I was brought up. The Israelis are an occupier, occupying our land and trying to remove our people from the land, so therefore I must hate or I must resist these Israelis. If someone tells you to leave your land, tells you not to live where you currently live, and hurts your family, you will hate that person. We were brought up to resist and to hate this enemy.

When I was small, we were never allowed to go out at night because our families were scared that something would happen to us. Now it is different.

When I was six years old, I started school. This was the only thing my family pressured me to do. They thought that having an education was the only asset I would have, so when I got to school I took it very seriously.

In first grade they taught us the Arabic alphabet. Also in first grade, once a week there were classes on the situation around us, on what has happened to our people. That was when we first were systematically introduced to our history and our culture. Because of this, hatred towards the Israelis is seen when the children are very small. Therefore, when they see the Israelis and they react by throwing stones or cursing the army, it is a reflection of what they learned in school.

When I was young I saw small kids being held by the Israelis and knocked on the ground, bones being broken, people being beaten, and I began to hate these Israelis even more. Every time I saw this type of scene my hatred became more intense and I became more dedicated to serving the struggle.

When people were going to school and there were lots of students together, sometimes the army patrol would come and try to talk to the students — especially the female students — or ridicule them or swear at them. And the female students, of course, would not talk to the army. So the soldier would come down from the truck and hit or slap or do something to someone. When the other students saw this they would throw rocks. Then you would have mass confusion.

As I became older, I also became more mature. It began to crystallize in my mind what the Israeli army was doing to my parents and to my brothers and to my sisters and to my community. I came to the point where I was looking for some institution or some sector of the community where I could work to fight this occupation. There were two concentrations in my life at that time: first education, then the army.

When we were in eighth and ninth grade, we would meet with other students and discuss as a group what to do. If a martyr had died during the past week, we would decide to go and visit the martyr's house and give our sympathy to the parents.

Even before the Intifada, the different factions, different institutions and mass organizations, coordinated with us the days that we would strike, the days that we would start burning tires, the days that we would have a demonstration, the days that we stoned jeeps, and the days that we wouldn't stone jeeps. On the days when the high school proficiency tests were going on in school, we would not throw stones because it might result in the closing of the schools for a couple of months, and those were critical times for education.

When the Intifada came, I was in my ninth school year. Before that we used to read about different experiences of Palestinians outside of Palestine, in Black September, in Beirut, Lebanon, and Tripoli. When the Intifada came, we became more aware of the struggles of our people inside Palestine.

The Intifada Begins

When the Intifada first started, we would fight and resist the Israeli soldiers when they came to our camps. Keep in mind: they have guns; we have rocks. So we could not stop them from coming in. But we did resist as much as possible.

When they brought in the half-tanks[15] and the army patrols, we would end up having to retreat. But when we did retreat it was because we were faced with gas. Gas was the army's first response to us so that we would be unable to breathe and to continue the resistance.

After the Intifada, my father stopped going to Israel. We went to the UNRWA refugee center and told the personnel there, "Our father is not going to work in Israel because of the Intifada. Therefore, we would like some relief." They gave us flour, bread, and so forth. Because my father did not work, we could not eat much. We had to minimize our consumption. My brother is a person who helps with different problems in the neighborhood and some people give him fruits or other food as gifts, and that comes back to help support the family.

In the second year of the Intifada, we engaged in national civil disobedience. The men would not go to Israel to work. Stores would strike at certain times.

The Israeli response to this was coming to the homes at night, banging on the doors, taking people out, and either beating them or humiliating them in

---

15. A "half-tank" is like a jeep and a tank. It has artillery on it. The back wheels look like a tank but the front wheels look like a car. It maneuvers very well in the sand.

front of the rest of the community. Many people resisted, but you cannot ask much from a person that has no weapons and no means equal to what the soldiers have. People would always resist to a certain extent.

I was pinpointed by the Israelis. Several times I was part of demonstrations in which soldiers were wounded or the glass of the soldiers' trucks was broken. When that happens, the soldiers become full of frustration. They don't know who did it, but if they can identify one person they will point him out. I was pointed out.

In all of the neighborhoods around us, they would always ask for me. At the end of the second year of the Intifada, I was told by other Palestinians that they were asking for me by name in a neighborhood near where I lived. They told me to be careful because it was possible that I could be shot on sight. I began to disguise my appearance when I went into the street so that I could not be readily identified.

Arrest

A couple of weeks after I learned that the army was searching for me, the army came and surrounded my house.

They knocked on the door around two in the morning. I looked outside and I saw that they were surrounding our house. Our extended family's home is all open and together except for a wall we built between our house and my uncle's house. When I saw the commotion around our house I jumped over this wall to my uncle's house, hoping that I could get out from there. But I saw from there that they had surrounded not only our own house but the entire extended family's home.

We are refugees and the door of our house had some holes in it. The army saw me when I jumped over the wall, so they knew that I was there and they knew that I had tried to get away.

When they asked my mother, "Where is Nidal?", my mom said, "We have no one here by the name of Nidal." The soldier asked once again, "There's no one here by the name of Nidal?" My mother told them there was no one there by that name.

They had seen me go next door, so they went next door to my uncle's house and they broke down the door. They didn't knock.

I knew I was going to be caught so I got in one of the beds in my uncle's house. When they came in I pretended my uncle was my father, because I did not want them to go back to my mother and say, "You lied."

My uncle told the soldiers, "Leave him alone. He's a young kid. He didn't do anything. You shouldn't do anything to him."

The soldiers began roughing me up and asking me, "Is this your house? Are you sure this is your house?" I said, "Yeah, do you think I came from America to sleep here? This is my house." They said, "Are you sure, tonight, you were sleeping in this home?" I said, "Yes, you saw, I was sleeping when you came in. I just went to bed." If I had known that they saw me when I jumped over the wall, I wouldn't have told them that story. But they had seen me so they knew I was lying.

When we were brought up, we were taught through books and through talking to people that we never give information or confessions to the army, no matter what. When you are asked a question, you make sure to avoid the answer. They ask you, "Where is your ID card?" You say, "I don't have it." You don't say, "It's at home." If they have your refugee papers and they ask you your father's name, you tell them your father's name is on your paperwork, or you tell them, "You have it," because you know that it is right in front of them. Other than that, you always give a general answer. From the beginning you make your answers very short and to the point, to make sure that they know you are in no mood to give anything more than they are asking for, and that you are not willing to discuss things with them. You don't offer anything for free.

They took me and my uncle out to the asphalt street and they hit us. They continued to ask my uncle, "Are you sure he was sleeping at your house?" And they kept asking me, "Are you sure this is your house where you were sleeping?" I said, "Yes." They told me, "You are going to go with us." I said in a very pitiful way, "Where are you going to take me? I didn't do anything." They said, "You are going to jail tonight."

While they were beating us and hitting us they were saying profanities to my uncle in Hebrew. (My uncle and I understand a little bit of Hebrew, so we knew they were swearing at him.) They beat my uncle pretty badly. In the morning, my uncle's family took him to the hospital.

They took me off to the side and kept interrogating me on the street. They wanted me to tell them where specific persons' homes were. I would say, "I don't know." They would say, "This is your neighborhood. You should know everybody in your own neighborhood. We know this kid is from your neighborhood." One of the names they gave me was our neighbor wall-to-wall. I told them I didn't know who he was and I didn't know where he was. I said I was young and I never went out of the house.

They put my hands on the asphalt and they beat my hands very badly. They would ask me a question, "Where is so-and-so's house?" I would say, "I don't know." Then they would hit me on my hands with the butts of their guns.

There were about fifty to sixty soldiers involved in this incident around our house. They came in four large jeeps. After they beat me and told me they were going to take me to jail, they said it was so I could prove to them whether I was lying or not lying.

They put me into a jeep. They tied my hands behind my back and to my legs. I asked them, "Why are you tying me up?" They said, "So you don't run away."

They took me to the military administration building in Rafah. The person who was in charge of my arrest, head of that military patrol, said, "Here is Pepper." They already had a nickname for me. The soldiers beat me because they thought that I was involved in some of the things that were being done in town.

There were no new jails yet so they took me to tents that were outside of the military administration building. Anything I would ask for, if I wanted to go to the bathroom or if I wanted to eat, they would say, "Schikit!", which is the Hebrew word for "Shut up!" I stayed ten hours in the tent. Then they came and said, "You are going to Ansar 2 in Gaza."

I was moved from Rafah to Khan Younis and from Khan Younis to Gaza. On the trip from Rafah to Khan Younis, they laid me in one of those jeeps that has a bench on both sides. I was lying on the floor with their feet and some of their equipment on top of me. They would hit me every once in a while. If I would say that my hand was hurting, they would say, "Schikit!"

When I got to Khan Younis, they put me into a tent. I recognized some of the people there. They were my friends because they were active with me. When I first came into the tent, they said, "Don't worry. Don't be mad. We are just like you. The same thing that happened to you has happened to us. Don't worry about it." The soldier who put me in the tent told the shawish (the head master of the tent), "This individual is not to be untied. He is to remain tied, both hands and feet."

As soon as I got into the tent and the soldier left, the other prisoners untied me. I told them I was hungry because I had not eaten for a couple of days. This tent had food — water, bread, very basic stuff — and my friends fed me. When they saw the soldier coming, they would tie me up to make sure that they did not catch me untied.

I stayed about four days in Khan Younis. Then I was told to get ready to go to Ansar 2 in Gaza. I and about twenty other prisoners were to get into a bus to go. I was the only one that was tied at the feet. The shawish, head master of the tent, asked the soldier who was taking us, "How is he supposed to walk? Undo his legs so he can get to the bus." The soldier replied: "Let him walk step-by-step." So everyone else got into the bus while I was walking step-by-step and the head master of the tent was with me, holding me so I would not fall down.

We sat in the middle aisle of the bus. The soldiers sat in the seats and every once in a while we would get a foot in the face. We could not see who did what because we were blindfolded the whole time.

Ansar

When we got to Ansar 2, I was the only one for whom they brought a straw bag which they put over my face, so that when I went into the jail, no other prisoners would recognize me. Everyone else, except one other person who was from a strike force in Gaza, went to a cell. I and that one other person went directly to change clothes into prison uniforms and then into interrogation. We were so tired and hungry and thirsty, but we didn't get one minute to rest.

Interrogation was approximately sixteen hours a day. You didn't know day from night for sixteen hours straight. The only time you would have to rest was when the person interrogating you wanted to rest: they would put you into a holding cell until they ate or whatever and then they would come back and interrogate more. Five days I remained in interrogation — no food, no nothing. I stayed very, very basic just to live.

They would start by, "Do you throw stones? Yes or no." I would say, "No." They went all the way down to, "Tell us where the people who do throw stones run when they finish throwing stones. Where are their hiding places?" I did not confess to one thing. I knew that if they took even the smallest confession it would become a gradual process whereby they would know that you were willing to give information, and you would give more information.

I was prepared for the interrogation because of the education process that takes place through our committees. Three times a week we used to meet to become educated on different issues: what to expect during interrogation, what are the methods they use to interrogate, what to say, what not to say. It was usually older activists, twenty-five or thirty-year olds, who had experience who would come and teach us. Also, they issued books where people who had actually gone through the process gave us their experience of how it is. One of the richest experiences we got was this education. People always find when they go to a cell a collaborator who will open a discussion and say, "I threw stones. I killed a soldier. What did you do?" Without the knowledge that this would happen, you would have no idea what to do.

I remained in a cell another four or five days until my court hearing came up. When the soldier came and told me I was going to court, I asked, "Why am I going to court? You don't have anything on me. You didn't prove anything." They came up with a paper with my name on it that said I threw a Molotov cocktail, that I threw rocks, that I threw wire rods, a whole list of things. When I told the soldier, "I didn't do any of this," he said, "Well, you're going to court now. They'll find out."

About twenty of us, the same twenty that were moved from Khan Younis to Ansar 2 together, had the court hearing the same day. When the military judge read me the list of charges, I said, "I didn't do anything. Take the list you just read and compare it to my age. Could I do all that and I am only fifteen years old?"

The judge delayed the court hearing until they could gather evidence on me. So the people who were in charge of putting me in jail returned to Rafah to the head of the military in my neighborhood, and used his statements as evidence against me: yes, I was the person who did so-and-so-and-so.

When I left the court and went back to the cell, I discussed with my comrades what had happened in the court, what their charges were, the delay, and so forth. We enter jail knowing a lot about what to expect, but time in prison deepens your whole awareness about jail, about the Intifada, about different things.

The next time I went to court, they asked for a seventeen-month sentence. In the meantime, my parents were able to get a lawyer for me. My lawyer came to visit me while I was in the courtroom holding cell at Ansar and he told me, "The best I can do is to get you five months." For me, that was excellent because I had been participating in activities. So I told my parents, "OK." I got five months.

During the time I was in jail, one specific incident sticks out in my mind. There was a prisoner from Rafah who had a metal plate that he made into a knife. He attacked three soldiers, killing two and wounding one of them. The soldiers opened fire on the prisoners, killing Abdullah Abu Mahruka who made the knife, and wounding three.

When I finished my five months, the prisoners stayed up until about 4:00 a.m. while they were bidding farewell to me. Every prisoner was saying, "Tell my parents so-and-so. Tell my wife so-and-so. Give my regards to so-and-so." I got maybe an hour or two sleep. Then they called and I got out.

Back to Rafah

When I got out of Ansar 2 there was a strike going on in Rafah so they dropped me off in Gaza City. I went to a mosque where there was a telephone and I called an ambulance to take me from Gaza City back to Rafah. Even the ambulance could not go into Rafah, so I walked the last part of the way. One of my friends saw me coming and called my parents' neighbors and told the neighbors, "Go and tell Nidal's family that Nidal got out of prison and he is walking home."

All of my friends, all of my family, came to see me at that time, even if there was a strike! When I turned into the street to go to my block, it took me three hours to get home. Everyone was saying, "Hi," and kissing me and shaking my hand. It was hours before I could get to my sisters and greet them. That is one thing that I have found, when you are wounded, or a person in your family was martyred, or you were in jail, you find the people to be there and you find the community to be supportive of it.

I was very tired when I came out of jail. I spent about a week at home recuperating. Then I went back to school. I even found the instructors at the school to be supportive, telling me, "It's not a problem that you missed school. You'll catch up."

After a while I became re-involved in the same activities I had been in before I went to jail, which were rock-throwing, writing on walls, and so forth.

Also, I became introduced to a new set of soldiers in the area and I was once again pinpointed. My family was harassed. They would come and ask my parents, "Where is Nidal? Are you sure he is not involved in anything?"

I lived for three months outside of the house. I did not sleep at home. I used to sleep at the houses of relatives or friends. I visited home maybe once every three to four weeks, only to get fresh clothes or whatever. They would come and ask my mother for me specifically. The family was scared for me to come home because the house might be staked out or they might have a sniper waiting for me, so I would not go home.

Writing Slogans

I participated in one of the popular committees. It is very important when people with the committees go out to write slogans that not one part of their bodies is showing. You have to have a thin sock over the shoes so you are not identified by your shoes. Your hands are covered with gloves so no one can see the complexion of your skin. Your face is wrapped.

One day after school I went to the mosque and prayed the afternoon prayer. There was an activity that had to be done that night, so I went home and took all of the clothes that I needed for that activity. I left the house and met my friends at a specific place where we would all change our clothes.

Before we could go out to write slogans, another group of men would go out ahead of us to check where the positions of the army were that night. If there were any army in the vicinity where we planned to write slogans, we would not go out at all because we were masked and there was an order, "Shoot to kill any masked Palestinian." We would take no chances whatsoever.

The men who went out before us reported that there were no army in the area. But that day there was an Israeli patrol on the rooftop of one of the houses where they could not be seen.

We went out to write slogans. I was writing on one wall and my friends were at another part of the street writing. I was the only one writing on the wall near the patrol. We finished writing the slogans. It seems the army had been viewing me while I was writing. The others who were with me were where they could get away, but the soldiers had me trapped.

I heard a signal that a patrol was approaching and I began to run in the opposite direction. I wanted to get back to my group so that I could see what was going on. I heard a shot. Then I heard another shot and my foot became numb. I realized that it was not random shooting. They were shooting at me. They were sniper shots. The next bullet was an exploding one and I felt it. I tried to run faster to get away. But for every three steps I took, the sniper put another bullet in my leg. I continued running until I had nine shots in my leg and my leg felt like a snake on the ground.[16]

The place where I stopped running was far away from the army. I found out afterwards that the other members of the group I was with knew that a committee member had been shot and they knew it was me because I did not come back to the meeting point. So they began agitating the entire community, all of the neighborhoods around, to go out into the streets in order to delay the time it would take for more army to come. The entire community came out into the streets, people came out with knives facing the army, just as a delaying tactic, trying to give me time to get away.

When I could run no more I went behind a tree. A lady came out of her house with a tub of water. I asked her to give me a cup of water from the tub because I was thirsty. She wanted to know what was wrong with me. I raised my voice and said, "Just give me water. That's all." She brought me water. Then I told the lady, "Leave! Go. Leave me alone." I did not want the lady to get caught with me.

16. The U.S. State Department, *Country Reports on Human Rights Practices for 1991*, states, p. 1447: "IDF [Israeli Defense Forces] regulations permit the use of standard ammunition only when (1) soldiers' lives are in imminent mortal danger, or (2) when a soldier is detaining a person suspected of a dangerous crime and the suspect attempts to escape after having been duly cautioned in various ways. Only a specific attacker may be fired on, except when facing immediate danger; fire is to be directed at the legs only; and fire may be directed at a fleeing suspect only if a serious felony is suspected, and as a last resort. Soldiers may fire at any fleeing masked person but may fire standard ammunition only after exhausting other methods such as tear gas, rubber bullets, and warning shots."

By that time the army had gotten to the point where I had fallen. The army took the water from me. I was very, very thirsty. I continued to ask for water. They refused. After I asked three times to no avail, I said, "To hell, I will never drink from you." I was in very bad shape. I foresaw my death that day.

One soldier cocked his gun while I was on the ground. The captain told the soldier, "You see, he is not going to run anywhere. Where is he going to go?"

Then they began to interrogate me. They continued to ask me, "Who were you with? Who told you to leave? Where is your ID card?" I told them, "I am by myself." They knew I was not by myself, but they could not get to the other people to shoot them. I said to myself that I would not answer one word because the worst they could do was to kill me and I already thought I was going to die right there.

The army saw that I was in no condition to answer any questions, and at that time the UNRWA ambulance came. The doctor in the ambulance said he wanted to take the wounded. The captain said, "He doesn't leave here until he tells us who he is with." They continued asking questions and the only thing I would say was, "No." I was in no condition to answer questions.

The doctor negotiated for me to go into the ambulance. They laid me in the ambulance. The doctor kept telling me, "You're going to be OK. You're all right." I knew I was in bad shape and I wasn't going to be all right.

Losing a Leg

The doctor took me to Khan Younis in the ambulance. At Khan Younis they gave me two pints of blood. That hospital was not equipped very well. They couldn't do more than that so they transferred me to Shifa Hospital in Gaza City.

At Shifa they saw that I was a severe trauma case. They X-rayed my leg and they saw what damage was done, but they could not do anything for me so they returned me to Khan Younis. At the same time, they said they would call Makassed Hospital in Jerusalem and see whether they could prepare a unit to deal with my case. I was bleeding very badly.

Gaza was very, very tense and the army had set up several checkpoints along the way from Khan Younis to Jerusalem. At every checkpoint we would stop and it would delay us at least ten minutes while they asked me why I was hit, where I was shot, and so forth.

When I got to the Erez checkpoint, they refused to let me pass because I did not have the paperwork. So the chief ambulance person called the UNRWA office in Gaza. A foreigner who was the head of UNRWA in Gaza came to the Erez checkpoint and negotiated with the soldier to let me pass. That's how I got through.

When I got to Makassed Hospital in Jerusalem, a bone specialist, Dr. Rustom Nammari, came to the emergency room to see me. He found that the most immediate problems were not with the bones but with the veins that were cut. Dr. Nammari said that the vein problems had to be solved before the bones could even be looked at and that Makassed Hospital was not the best equipped to handle the vein problem.

So they took me from Jerusalem to the Ramallah Hospital, where there was a specialist for veins. They took veins out of my left leg and fixed the thigh part of my right leg, and they took me back to Makassed.

At Makassed the bone specialist, Dr. Nammari, checked out my leg and braced it for a couple of days to see what was going on with it and how it could be fixed. At that point, gangrene had set in in my leg and there was no solution for gangrene.

The doctor told me, "There is no hope but to amputate your leg. What do you want to do?" I said, "What you see best for my leg, do." The doctor told me, "It would be best to cut it below the knee because if we wait any longer, since gangrene spreads, we might have to take your thigh too." So I told him, "Do it."

The shooting occurred at about two or three o'clock in the afternoon. I went from Rafah to Khan Younis, from Khan Younis to Shifa in Gaza, from Shifa back to Khan Younis, from Khan Younis to Makassed, from Makassed to Ramallah in one day. My aunt and my mother came in the ambulance with me and my mother stayed with me the whole time. My mother fed me everything. I did not even have the energy to eat.

I had three bullets in the thigh of my leg and that part was corrected through six operations after the amputation took place. But until now, my leg cannot flex all the way back because this part of the leg was also injured. I stayed in the hospital for six months before I returned home.[17]

This is my story. Many have been hurt worse than I but this is our duty.

The people, in the end, know what is in their own interest. For Palestinians, it is in our interest to be like one hand, united, as one fist. The fingers are held together. If you hit it, it remains a fist. In Gaza, we were united before the Intifada came about.

Hamas uses Islam as the basis of their work. Fine. Members of all of the factions pray just as they pray. We need to look at it in a more progressive way: you do not have to be part of Hamas to be part of the liberation of Palestine. They say they want to liberate Palestine, the same as we do. Their tactics are the same as our tactics. Because there is an army in front of us, we have to remain as one.

The Intifada is the voice of our people defining its strength while living the horrendous daily realities of occupation. The negative face that some put on the Intifada is only an attempt to cover up the heroic struggle of our people in the face of the Israeli occupation which arrests our men and women, demolishes our houses, confiscates our land to build new settlements, deprives us of our schools, throws us in prisons, and beats our clergy and those praying. The rank and file of the Intifada are armed with hope, power, and commitment. They face the enemy with sacred stones and a deep sense of hope in their hearts. The Intifada is an avowal of our willingness to make practical steps toward victory, through greater sacrifice, persistence, deter-

17. In July 1992, Nidal reported that with the assistance of Steve Sosbee, an aid worker from the United States, he was able to travel to the United States for treatment and fitting with a new prosthesis.

mination and conscious resistance. We are ready to continue against all odds to survive because we refuse to choose death willingly.

The last four years of our life has been like a rock. A rock is everything to us. In a human, if your heart is from a rock, no matter what they do to it, it remains in shape. It remains a rock.

Elias Rishmawi

"In the course of the struggle, the tax protest changed."

In February 1988 the Unified Leadership distributed a leaflet asking people to stop submitting tax reports and to stop paying taxes. This request by the Unified Leadership was not something imposed on the Palestinians. It was originally demanded by the Palestinian consensus and conveyed through internal mechanisms to the Unified Leadership. Taxes were a very heavy burden on Palestinians in the Occupied Territories. When the Unified Leadership asked people to stop paying taxes, it represented what the people wanted at that time. Almost everybody stopped paying. Personally, I stopped submitting my tax reports in February 1988.

In November 1988, along with most of the people in this area, I received a notice from the Value Added Tax Office in Bethlehem requesting submission of tax reports as well as payment of taxes. In this notice, they said unless I fulfill their request within thirty days, I would be fined and receive penalties, etc.

A few days later, I was taken by force from my pharmacy together with three other pharmacists who had been taken by force from their pharmacies. Three of us were Beit Sahourians; the fourth is a woman pharmacist from Beit Jala. We were taken to the military headquarters in Bethlehem; then we were transferred to the military court in Ramallah.

In front of the military judge, we were denied access to a lawyer. First, I requested that the lawyer should represent us and that we were not going to proceed without a lawyer but we were denied that. Second, I submitted to the judge the notice that we received from the tax office giving us thirty days. I tried to explain to him what it meant but he didn't pay any attention to it. The military judge decided that we must pay a fine of 5,000 shekels or we must be imprisoned for ten days.

We refused to pay. If the fine had been one agora [penny] we would not have agreed, for it was a matter of principle.

Jail

We were imprisoned for ten days. I, with another colleague, was taken to Beit Shemish police detention facility inside Israel. This is against international law which says that detainees from the Occupied Territories can only be detained inside the same territory, not within the occupying state.[18]

---

18. Article 76 of the Fourth Geneva Convention states, in part, that "persons accused of offences shall be detained in the occupied country, and if convicted they shall serve their sentences therein."

We were imprisoned with Israeli heroin and cocaine addicts, for ten days, twenty-four hours a day. It was my first experience in jail. The first night, we were kept in two opposite cells. We could look through the door holes and communicate. One of the addicts recognized that we were Palestinians. He pulled a small knife out of his mouth and started waving it in front of our faces, and he said: "Oh, you are Palestinians. Oh, PLO! Tomorrow I will bring you your comrade's head in a nylon bag." That night I could not sleep. I was near the door, watching the other cell in case my friend started to scream or call for help.

The second day I was transferred to the same cell so the two of us were with the same people there. We were obliged to play a sneaky trick to save ourselves from being hassled by the addicts. It was against our morals and ethics, yet it looked like the only available way. A doctor visited the prison every night at 8:00 p.m. The rules allowed each of the addicts to get five Valium pills of ten milligrams each, which meant fifty milligrams. (A normal person, with two milligrams would sleep twenty-four hours.) They asked us to take the tablets and pass the tablets to them. We used the pills to keep them calm: "If you are not going to be cool, we are not going to take the pills for you." It was most unfortunate that this was the only way to save ourselves.

The Court Case

After ten days we were brought back to the same court, the same judge. This time we had lawyers. The military judge admitted that our imprisonment was only to impose pressure on us to pay the taxes.

We refused to plead guilty. It was out of the question that we would accept being fined, not even one agora. The judge could easily guess that. He said, "I will free you if you will pay a *bail* of 1,500 shekels." (It was $1,000 each at that time.) "All that is requested from you is to accept interrogation by the Value Added Tax people."

After we were freed, we were subjected to a long, oppressive interrogation by the Value Added Tax Office for two or three months. We were kept two or three days a week from eight o'clock in the morning until two o'clock in the afternoon in their office. All the while they were interrogating us we didn't give them any kind of information. We simply said, "You don't have the right to interrogate us. You have no right to harass us." For them this was shocking. It was the first time that people were talking in such a spirit and attitude. We refused to sign any paper.

Being fed up with us they said, "Why don't you see the deputy in Beit El?" [the civil administration headquarters]. He was the director of the Value Added Tax for the whole West Bank. We thought that this might be an opportunity to gain time and we planned to tell them: "You cannot force us to pay, because no one is paying during the Intifada." This was the initial strategy.

We met the deputy who said, "In Bethlehem and Beit Sahour, more than

80 per cent of the people have paid" (which was not the fact at all). "Why are you trying to be stubborn? We can play together some tricks by which you can keep your image in your community from one side and start again paying taxes from the other side. We can then issue for you one thousand invitations to the military headquarters in Bethlehem. You just show them to the people of Beit Sahour and later throw them away. We are ready to play the game and show the people of Beit Sahour that you are nationalist and honest people through any kind of arrangement, or cover, whatever you like. You just mention the way you would like it to be and we will just do it."

I said, "Where are you living?" He said, "In Tel Aviv." I said, "Are you ready to be dishonest and cheat your people, your family and your friends in Tel Aviv? If you are ready, I am not. I can't be dishonest to my people. I can cheat no one." His face was blushed red and that was the end of the conversation.

Confiscation of Pharmacies

A few weeks later, we were told that they were going to attach our properties. We appealed to the High Court of Justice in Israel and we got an injunction on June 22, 1989, which said that any tax authority has no right to confiscate our property unless they notify us or our attorney ten days in advance.

Only four days later, on June 26, 1989, a large vehicle carrying a big container stood opposite my pharmacy with ten tax personnel. Fifty to sixty soldiers occupied the whole area including the roofs of the buildings: "This area is a closed military zone." Then the tax personnel started taking everything from my pharmacy and warehouse.

I had the Supreme Court injunction in the drawer. I took it and showed it to the officer in charge, Major Yaron. He laughed in a very sarcastic way — "Ah, ha, ha" — while throwing it into my face in a very disrespectful manner. He said in the same sarcastic way, "Well, go back to court, man." I said, "Listen, if you don't respect your own supreme court, don't ask me to go back to court." Until that moment, I did not believe that an Israeli, much less an officer, would not respect *his* own supreme court.

From everywhere, they were taking everything. They confiscated medicines, baby food, cosmetics, chemicals, medical supplies, etc. Goods worth $120,000 were attached. It was the first time during the Israeli occupation, since 1967, that pharmaceuticals were attached, a matter which was surprising. Later on we were informed that the orders of confiscation were given at the highest level of the civil administration.

After finishing their work, they took me with them to the place where they intended to keep the attached goods. I told them, "You put these things under direct sunlight and they are very sensitive to heat and humidity." They replied, "That's none of your business." I then protested, "These things will be spoiled in a few weeks." It was June and already summer. They didn't care. In the next few days, they raided the other three pharmacies in the same way.

A few weeks later, they submitted charge sheets against me and the other three pharmacists. The case is called *Elias Rishmawi et al.* We have to be judged by the military court in Ramallah.[19]

A Challenge to the Military Occupation

In the summer of 1988, the tax personnel of the Bethlehem office started a campaign against Beit Sahour. First, they took the boys' secondary school and made it into a military camp and tax offices. Having the lists for those who had stopped paying taxes, they went through the town's streets, stopping people, checking their names. Those who had their names on the list were sent to the above-mentioned building. While they were receiving fines and penalties, they had their cars confiscated.

Something had to be done. One morning, there was a whisper all over the town calling Beit Sahourians to gather at the municipality to discuss the possible means of retaliation. The Deputy Major was in charge and people started discussing.

Nobody knows or remembers how it started, but a process of delivering the identity cards to the Deputy Major started. He was supposed to send them back to the military governor. The Deputy Major, Mr. Khalil Kheer, was to represent the whole town in this operation and he was enthusiastic to do so in a very courageous way.

Giving back our IDs was the best answer for what the military occupation had initiated in the town. It was a reaction just fitting perfectly with the idea of *civil disobedience* that was prevailing during that period of struggle. The IDs were the symbol of oppression as it was the first thing requested by the military, and they were used for harassment, for anyone who would be caught without it would be subject to beating, humiliation and possible detention. So let us throw it away, let us get rid of this symbol of our oppression.

By afternoon, around two to three thousand IDs were delivered to the municipality. People who had gone to work that morning started coming back. The whole town was there. The crowd was about five or six thousand people, gathered in and around the municipality.

While the process of delivering back the IDs continued, the military arrived. It was about 4:00 p.m. They surrounded the area with special units (we hadn't seen before). The officer in charge of the operation was the same Major Yaron who attached my pharmacy. (He was the military governor's assistant for Arabian affairs.) He stood there in a very arrogant provocative way. He started speaking into his loudspeaker asking everybody to leave.

19. The U.S. State Department, *Country Reports on Human Rights Practices for 1990*, states, p. 1488: "Authorities assert that they face widespread opposition to tax payment, which necessitates extraordinary collection methods. Palestinians claim that these measures are excessive and that such tactics are not used in Israel. Palestinian residents of the occupied territories do not have recourse to the Israeli judicial system which serves as the arbiter of tax disputes within Israel; rather, appeals must be made to a special review board appointed by the military commander. Palestinians may petition the High Court for redress of any administrative action."

The people responded by sitting down so as not to give the military an excuse for provocation, and a whisper spread among the sitting crowds, "Do not shout and do not throw anything towards the army."

The military did not know what to do and for a moment they were stuck and hesitant. For Major Yaron himself, this was more provocative than anything else and more than he could tolerate, to see perfectly disciplined Palestinians. It was unusual. Major Yaron was not prepared for that. Minutes later he gave the only orders he knows: the army started shooting tear gas and rubber bullets while beating the first sitting rows with clubs. People started to run away and disperse.

All the scene was documented. Television reporters and journalists were invited in the morning. Some young men were instructed to wait for them in the nearby town of Bethlehem, and all necessary measures were taken to ensure their way to the town from back roads.

Beit Sahour had to live under curfew for two weeks afterwards. Some people were detained and later on got administrative detention.

The civil disobedience of Beit Sahour was a kind of a threat and challenge to the military occupation. At the same time it created a new image about the Beit Sahourians which helped very much to keep the tax gangs away for almost a year.

Beit Sahour Under Seige

During 1989 the military and tax officers started exploring the possibilities for raiding Beit Sahour. The first waves started during June. They arrested groups of old people, six, seven or ten at a time, keeping them at detention centers, trying to figure out what the reaction of Beit Sahour would be, and also trying to make a penetration through these groups.

On the other side, a perfect system of support was created in Beit Sahour, by which masses were visiting and comforting and showing solidarity to families of all those who were detained. At the same time, all those who were released were also visited and supported. Popular and neighborhood committees were in charge of all these arrangements. It was twenty-four-hour continuous work under severe conditions imposed by the military, for anyone who was identified as being active was risking administrative detention or even imprisonment up to ten years (as Yitzhak Rabin declared).

Both sides, Beit Sahourians and the military, were preparing for the battle which was coming. Mistakes could not be tolerated. When a famous merchant did not remain steadfast under the military pressures during detention, he started an argument calling for surrender. That very night on all the walls of Beit Sahour, graffiti were written: "Mr. . . . (Judas Iscariot), why do you want to hand over our Jesus Christ (The Intifada) for a few shekels?" This man could not carry on and had to come back to join the public movement.

The military failed to do the penetration and decided to move further. Rabin, who was the defense minister, declared that he was going to teach Beit Sahour a lesson. On September 19, 1989, the town was totally seized. All entrances were blocked. Thousands of soldiers supporting tax officers started the biggest taxation raid in recent history.[20]

Some Beit Sahourians were detained on suspicion that they might be the community leaders. Most of them got administrative detention.

The town was denied any access to medical or food supply. Anyone who was caught at the border coming from Bethlehem with any supplies had them confiscated. The soldiers, together with tax officers, took a building and made it their headquarters. They started to wake people at night, taking them from their houses to the military detention center in Bethlehem. The next morning they confiscated the contents of their houses or their businesses. Most of the people had both confiscated, one for the Value Added Tax, the other for the Income Tax.

On the night of September 21–22, 1989, the military started one of the longest curfews on Beit Sahour (it lasted forty-five days). After midnight, I was taken by force from my house, along with other Beit Sahourians. I spent eighteen days detained between the military headquarters in Bethlehem and the detention camp of Dahariya, after which I was released. But I still had to face daily arrest for another ten days, being summoned to the military governor's office in Bethlehem from 8:00 a.m. to 8:00 p.m.

Confiscation from Houses

During this raid the income tax officers attached the contents of my house. Before leaving, an officer said, "Listen, we will bring everything back if you will pay 100 shekels." I said, "Go to hell!" And then he said, "OK, one shekel, and that's final. For one shekel, I'll bring everything back." And I replied, "Don't even dream about that. Get lost."

This was not my attitude only. This was the attitude of all Beit Sahourians. Everyone was offered the same thing, to get everything back with one shekel, and they could not find in Beit Sahour one person who would give them one shekel.

After three weeks of the tax raid, some people who were waiting their turn started to be nervous: "Why is my turn not coming? Something is wrong." So they waited for officers in an armed car to come along. They stopped the car and a man said to the officers, "Listen, my name is —. I am on your list. I have been waiting for you. Tell me, when are you coming?" I saw this happen in front of my eyes. The officers were so furious that they started beating him.

At one house when they started driving away after they finished the dirty work, they heard a voice calling them, "Wait, wait!" A smile appeared on

20. The U.S. State Department, *Country Reports on Human Rights Practices for 1989*, states, p. 1439: "Israel, in response to a tax boycott, imposed a siege on the West Bank town of Beit Sahour. All access to the town was blocked for over 40 days, during which Israeli authorities seized merchandise and vehicles to pay outstanding tax bills. Israel claims these actions were justified by the tax boycott. Palestinians claim that certain Israeli tax practices are inconsistent with international law, including the imposition of a value added tax (VAT) and other taxes which did not exist before 1967, the summary seizure of private property, and Israel's failure to address whether the tax revenues were being utilized for the benefit of the population of the occupied territories."

their faces: "Finally someone will pay!" The lady who was shouting was carrying something in her hand. Without hesitation and with full confidence and courage, she threw the remote control of the TV while crying, "You forgot this."

A six-year-old boy was watching cartoons when his house was raided. The officer started using human emotions by saying to the father, "Your kid can keep the TV if you will pay 100 NIS [new Israeli shekels]." The answer was, "No." "OK, 10 NIS." Adham, the six-year-old, answered. He jumped up and switched off the TV, shouting "No! Father, let them take it. Don't pay anything." The officer muttered in a low voice, "Damn you."

Hundreds of stories carry the one clear message of Beit Sahour: "We are people with honor and dignity. We are very much proud of what we are doing and we believe in it."

The furniture that was taken from Beit Sahourians was sold at auction and no one in Beit Sahour knew when or where. When later on I was summoned to the Income Tax office in January 1992, I was informed that my furniture had been sold at an auction inside Israel for 1,500 shekels (not much more than $1,000). This furniture cost me almost $12,000.

Children's toys were not saved from confiscation. My children watched while soldiers carried away their toys and their studying desks.

Our children lost their childhood. They are not living as children. They are faced with experiences that are appalling to me after 43 years of life, and they have to face them while they are only ten years or seven years old.

Despite everything, it was not just a tax raid. Beit Sahourians could easily detect what it was. Beit Sahour is the last Christian town of what used to be called the Christian Triangle (Bethlehem, Beit Jala and Beit Sahour). Palestinian Christians are playing a major role in linking the Muslim Arab world and the Christian West. This could neither be accepted nor tolerated by the Israeli occupation, for the existence of Christian Palestinians would be a deterrent to what they have in mind. We all in Beit Sahour believed that we were the real target, not taxes.

The Occupier's Obligations

Before the Intifada we were totally ignorant of the tax system and the occupier's obligations to the people. We learned during the struggle that there are certain restrictions imposed on the occupier who wants to raise taxes. Failure to comply with these conditions deprives the occupier of the legal right to collect taxes.

The military occupation authority has failed to comply with the restrictions listed in Articles 43 and 48 of the Hague Regulations which form the legal basis for tax collection in the Occupied Territories. The main restrictions prescribed in Articles 43 and 48 of the Hague Regulations are that all revenue collected should come back to the Occupied Territories for its administration, and respect for local laws in force (Jordanian law of 1964).[21] The fiscal

---

21. The Regulations annexed to the Hague Convention IV of 1907 are referred to as the Hague Regulations. Article 43 of the Hague Regulations states: "The authority of the legitimate power

provisions enshrined in the Jordanian Constitution are: a) the budget should be encoded in a law and available to the public in published form; b) the state should not collect more revenue than is required for the needs of the state; and c) taxes should be imposed in accordance with principles of justice and equality, and should not exceed the taxpayers' ability to pay.

Throughout the years of occupation, the Israeli military authority has been showing bad faith and irresponsibility in their administration of taxes to the severe detriment of the Occupied Territories. They have refused to publish the budget of the Occupied Territories showing all sources of revenue and items of expenditure.[22] Contrary to the requirements of local and international law, they failed to follow minimum internationally accepted standards of due process in assessment and collection, and they have neglected the concerns of the local people that all revenue collected be invested for the benefit of the local Palestinian population. The sum of this long list of violations is that the military occupation authority has lost any legal basis for tax collection in the Occupied Territories.

The tax tables prove deep discrimination and injustice. Comparing a Palestinian and an Israeli, each married and having five children (the Palestinian wife not working, the Israeli wife working but receiving financial subsidy for children below age 18), the Palestinian starts paying income tax at 605 NIS income per month while the Israeli starts at 2,591 NIS.[23]

It is not difficult to see the difference in services offered to Palestinians in the Occupied Territories and the standard of living and services in Israel. If higher taxes are collected from Palestinians, why should we have less services? At least we should have the same services and the same facilities that exist in Israel.

having in fact passed into the hands of the occupant, the latter shall take all the measures in his power to restore, and ensure, as far as possible, public order and safety, while respecting, unless absolutely prevented, the laws in force in the country." Article 48 states: "If, in the territory occupied, the occupant collects taxes, dues and tolls imposed for the benefit of the state, he shall do so, as far as possible, in accordance with the rules of assessment and incidence in force, and shall in consequence be bound to defray the expenses of the administration of the occupied territory to the same extent as the legitimate government was so bound." (Quoted in Marc Stephens, *Taxation in the Occupied West Bank, 1967–1989* [Ramallah: Al-Haq, West Bank Affiliate of the International Commission of Jurists, 1990], pp. 5–7.)

22. The U.S. State Department, *Country Reports on Human Rights Practices for 1988*, states regarding deductions from wages, pp. 1272–74: "The same percentage is deducted from the pay of West Bank and Gaza Palestinians working legally in Israel as is deducted from the pay of Israeli workers for social contributions, and they receive equivalent pensions. However, they do not receive the same benefits from the National Insurance Institute (NII — similar to U.S. social security), because many NII benefits require residence in Israel. Thus, only 1.2 per cent of the pay of the workers from the West Bank and Gaza goes to the NII, compared to 5.35 per cent for an Israeli. The other 4.15 per cent is an equalization deduction to keep labor costs equivalent. It goes to a special Finance Ministry fund to be used only for social and development costs in the West Bank and Gaza. Palestinians estimate that this amounts to hundreds of millions of dollars since 1970 and complain that the Government of Israel has not accounted for whether or how the money has been spent in the territories. The Government of Israel says that these and other expenditures in the territories are accounted for internally, in the budget for the territories, but not made public."

23. The U.S. State Department, *Country Reports on Human Rights Practices for 1992*, states, Occupied Territories, Section 5: "Significant disparities exist between the personal income taxes levied on Palestinians as compared to the taxes levied on Israeli settlers. . . . [T]he minimum taxable income applied to Israelis and Palestinians differs markedly: while an Israeli pays no tax if his monthly income is below about $1,000, Palestinians pay taxes on any monthly income in excess of about $250."

The Israelis have taken over all of the West Bank resources including water resources. Remember, water is a very important and dangerous element. The water in Beit Sahour comes from wells a few miles away. (Digging artesian wells is strictly prohibited by military orders.) We pay 2.7 shekels for a cubic meter of water. There is a minimum charge of 27 shekels for ten cubic meters per month. Each additional cubic meter costs 2.7 shekels. Residents of Israel are paying 1.6 shekels per cubic meter. Newly settled Jews are paying 0.5 shekels for the same cubic meter. They are not only stealing our water, but also they are charging us twice as much as their citizens and five times more than settlers. Seventy-five per cent of our water is transferred to Israel and this constitutes 25 per cent of the total Israeli consumption of water.

In regard to health services on the West Bank, our hospitals are in a very miserable situation. You can visit the government hospital in Beit Jala and see what kind of hospitals we have. The equipment is terrible. Since 1967, the population has increased about 10 per cent but the number of beds in government hospitals has decreased almost 10 per cent from 2,300 to 2,100 beds. We have the highest infant mortality rate among all Middle Eastern countries.

More and more foreign aid to the Occupied Territories is relieving the occupation system of its obligations. The Italians and Germans are helping to build a sewage system in Beit Sahour, Bethlehem and Beit Jala. They offered $2 million for this. The Israelis are happy because it is their duty to do this and now somebody's doing it for them.

After the Israeli invasion of Lebanon in 1982, a new tax of 2 per cent was imposed on all importation to Israel. It applied to everything: medicines, merchandise, foodstocks. This meant that 2 per cent tax was paid on everything that was brought to the West Bank from Israeli ports, and it means that we still are supporting the Israelian army in its operation in the south of Lebanon. In what kind of law is this written?

During the Intifada, the Israelis have introduced new taxes especially on cars.[24] Until today, six new taxes have been imposed on car licensing. They started with names like rocks tax, glass tax, army tax, and the final tax which was the sixth tax was given the name of rocket tax. This was in response to the scud attacks in 1991. Israel officially declared that the losses caused by the scud attacks were $10 million. Israel got $14 billion from the West and, by

---

24. Marc Stephens writes in *Taxation in the West Bank, 1967–1989*, p. 34: "On 17 August 1988, a new tax was declared in M.O. [Military Order] 1249 Regarding Payment of a Special Fee (Vehicles) (Temporary Instructions). The tax was popularly dubbed the 'intifada tax.' The reasons stated in the preamble to the order for introducing the tax were, firstly, that 'due to the present circumstances there is a shortage of finances to cover vital services to the public,' and, secondly, the protection of public order. The order was temporary, effective for one year from 19 September 1988. The order was amended on 25 March 1989 by M.O. 1273, which made payment of the tax a condition for registering transfer of property in a vehicle, and extended the order to 31 March 1990." Stephens quotes numerous provisions of the order. Under Section 10 (ibid., p. 35): "(a) Any police officer or soldier authorised by the transportation officer has the right to seize a vehicle if he suspects that the owner has not paid the special fee. If the owner of the vehicle proves that he has paid the fee then the vehicle shall be released. (b) If a vehicle is in violation of this order it shall be seized by the police or transportation officer until the special fee is paid." And under Section 15: "A vehicle owner who refrains from paying the special fee shall face a sentence of two years in prison and shall be fined."

imposing the sixth tax on the car licensing, Israel got another $65 million. They lost $10 million and got $65 million. The Palestinians have to pay the price if anything goes wrong with them in the area.

We are like a milking cow for them. We are the markets for their products. We are supplying them with cheap labor. Millions of fees and taxes are collected at the bridges. If we can deprive the occupier from obtaining benefits from the occupied territory, then we can deprive him of the reasons for holding us.

The Struggle Continues

A friend of mine, a pharmacist in Bethlehem, wasn't paying taxes. He was taken from his pharmacy and he was forced to pay 5,000 shekels. He was then asked to pay 20,000 shekels to settle his tax problem. Later on he was requested to pay another 86,000 shekels. Even if you want to go and pay, the moment you start paying, they push you more. If you don't pay, you'll suffer.

My brother, who is an engineer living in Germany, came here to get married. When he wanted to go back, he had to get a travel document which needs an application with seven signatures: Income Tax, Value Added Tax, Intelligence Service, Police Department, Finance Department, Municipality, and the moukhtar. When he went to the Income Tax office, they said, "Ah, you are the brother of Elias and Risha Rishmawi. Your brothers haven't paid taxes. We are not going to give you a signature until your brothers come here and pay." This is highly illegal.

The authorities don't like to see other places follow the steps of Beit Sahour, so they black out all news coming out of the area. We might have an incident in Beit Sahour and no one would hear about it in Bethlehem because the authorities censor news about all kinds of incidents that might have incitement effect.

Israeli policy in the Occupied Territories makes life extremely difficult and insecure and brings Palestinians to the point where they want to leave the country. Statistics on Palestinian emigration out of Palestine are very high. We are coming to a very dangerous point because those who are leaving the country are the rich, the highly educated, the cream of our crop. Those who are staying supply Israel with cheap labor and keep the Occupied Territories a captive market for Israeli goods. The destruction of the Palestinian economic infrastructure deters investment. Palestinians in the Occupied Territories are deprived of economic power. Goading Palestinians to complete frustration and despair results in reactions which serve as an excuse to justify the Israeli policy of discrediting Palestinians and dehumanizing them.

Regarding my case together with the other three pharmacists, we have to face a very high sentence because we refused to make a deal with the military prosecutor. They asked us to plead and they would free us. We refused. We said, "We are going until the end. Legally, you have no right to collect taxes. You lost the legal basis for tax collection. We are not ready for any kind of compromise until the Hague regulations are applied."

On February 11, 1992, I succeeded in bringing one hundred taxpayers representing diverse sectors of the society to appeal to the Israeli High Court of Justice. The appeal was accepted and this was considered to be a preliminary success.

We have very limited trust in the Israeli courts, including the Israeli High Court, for these courts have proved during twenty-four years of occupation to be acting for the benefit of the occupying power. The Israeli courts together with the military system work in perfect harmony to enforce the elements of the Israeli ideology, to drive every Palestinian out of the country so as to fulfill the Zionist tragic dream: the promised land.

Hassan

"When I decided to go underground, I took my family's security, I took my own life and education, and I threw them against the wall."

I am twenty years old. I am in the military wing of one of the political organizations. My family became refugees in 1948.

My extended family is approximately fifty individuals. We have three martyrs. We have one person deported. I have four brothers in prison: one has been sentenced to sixteen and a half years; one to thirteen and a half years; one to four years; and one to five and a half years.

The first time I was arrested myself was in 1987 at the beginning of the Intifada. I was fifteen years old. I spent five months in a prison in the Negev Desert before Ansar 3 was opened.

The second time I was arrested I was held in administrative detention for three months in Ansar 3. Another time I was in interrogation for eighteen days. The last time, I was given a year and a half but I stayed only thirteen months; the first two months were in interrogation. Interrogation took place in the Central Gaza Prison.

This is what I went through personally in interrogation. Not to mention the hitting, my first nineteen days of the two months in interrogation were spent sitting on a very low chair with a bag of shit on my head, not allowed to sleep for nineteen days. I was poked. I had earphones put on me with an ear-piercing sound blasting.

The beatings and other methods were very scientific. If you had walked in and seen me under interrogation, you would have thought that nothing was wrong with me. But I went through severe beatings in very sensitive places where the bruises did not show. The worst I experienced was with electric shock. This was during the Gulf War.

We had a period of snow and we were put outside in solitary confinement facilities, one meter by one meter and a half. At any time of the night, they would come and take us, handcuff us, and tell us, "You are going to interrogation." It would never be on a routine basis. It was at any time. You do not know whether it is day and night when you are in solitary confinement. This is what we call "the slaughterhouse."

We did not have attorneys; we did not have a right to appeal; we did not even have a right to see a doctor.

I am a Rafah-born Palestinian. I have a family. When I decided to go underground, I took my family's security, I took my own life and education, and I threw them against the wall. I face martyrdom. It is not easy to do that. We are human also. But we are struggling for the security of the population and the security of the camp.

You must understand that all activists are wanted, whether we go underground or stay above ground. We are wanted at all times. Those of us who go underground have reached a level of desperation. We attempt to live as best we can under the circumstances, without thinking about how life was above ground, accepting our new condition and creating a new life. We see our family in the streets, or we make an appointment to meet them somewhere. If we enter a house to sleep, usually we do not go back for a period of time. When we do get together to meet, we have security shifts of our own people. We walk in the street and we speak to people in the street without a problem. But this is not a full life. We are confined to areas where we know we are safe.

We are convinced that if there is going to be a political solution in the future, it must be built on three pillars: the right of return, self-determination, and the independent Palestinian state with Jerusalem as its capital. The independent state with Jerusalem as its capital is not now being proposed. The right of Palestinians to return is not now being proposed. If autonomy is not to be self-determination — and it is not — what is left for us?

We will accept a comprehensive peace plan. Otherwise, we will struggle and struggle and struggle.

Riyad Malki

"There is another authority, the Palestinian popular authority."

I am a professor at Birzeit University. I have taught civil engineering since 1980. I have been involved for many years in the political activities here in the Occupied Territories. I used to be part of a Palestinian core delegation which meets with delegations coming from abroad. I met with almost, if not all, of the European foreign ministers who visited the area after the end of the Gulf War.

It is obvious that we Palestinians did not plan the Intifada. The Intifada is a reflection of how Palestinians perceive and react to the occupation. The occupation is not only military occupation. It is also economic, social, and cultural occupation. Since 1967 the Israelis have been occupying us totally, depriving us of our basic rights as Palestinians and as human beings.

Living in this way, the Palestinians had to explode one day, and they did on December 8, 1987. Why did that happen? Simply because of the accumulation of Israeli repressive measures over the previous twenty years.

First of all, there is the confiscation of Palestinian land. Right now close to 60 per cent of Palestinian land in the West Bank and the Gaza Strip has been confiscated by the Israelis. We need to understand and remember what land means for a Palestinian. The land is almost equal to the family and to life itself. So when you deprive the Palestinian of land you separate him from his beloved and from his life. When 60 per cent of the land has been confiscated, at least two-thirds of the families in Palestine have been affected by this Israeli policy of land confiscation.

Secondly, the Israelis try to create a *de facto* situation by confiscating land and immediately building settlements on that land. They bring settlers from Brooklyn, New York, settlers from Florida, settlers from California, settlers from South Africa, settlers from Argentina, and put them on confiscated lands in the West Bank and Gaza. As we speak there are more than 155 settlements in the West Bank and over 40 in the Gaza Strip. When you wake up in the morning and you look at your land that has been confiscated, and you not only cannot reach that land, but there are foreigners who are already living on that land, cultivating the land, the effect is doubled. You see the confiscator and you can do absolutely nothing about it.

Then we face the policy of deporting Palestinians. Every time the Israelis identify Palestinians who are community leaders or who have characteristics of leadership, who are beloved and have credibility among the Palestinian people, they are immediately jailed and deported. And yet Mr. Shamir and the Israeli officials come and say, "Bring me Palestinian leaders from the Occupied Territories and I will sit with them." How are they going to sit with these Palestinian leaders if they are going to put them in jail and deport them?

We should also speak about the demolishing of houses. This is a policy which was inherited by the Israelis from the British Mandate. When the British occupied Palestine, before 1947, they established emergency military laws. These emergency laws addressed the right of the occupier, or the forces in power, to detain persons without trial in administrative detention (for periods of at least six months, renewable every six months without any charges), to demolish houses, to impose prolonged curfews in large areas, to uproot trees, to confiscate land, etc., etc. These were the policies of the British in Palestine before 1947. The Israelis adopted the worst parts of the British Mandate law and are still applying them today. We not only suffered from these laws in the 1940s but we still suffer in the 1990s. Therefore, demolishing of homes is a current policy of the Israelis. They believe that this collective punishment will deter Palestinians from continuing violent actions against their occupiers.

Every time that your son, your brother, your father, whoever, has committed a crime in the eyes of the Israelis — "crime" means to be nationalist and to defy and resist the occupation — then not only is the individual punished by being put in prison for so many years, but his or her family is punished, too. When the Israelis entirely or partially demolish the family's house, or just seal the house, it is collective punishment. This is a policy which has been systematically applied against the Palestinians since 1967.

Another Israeli policy is that of uprooting trees. When the State of Israel was established, the Israelis began several campaigns to promote development within their state. One of these campaigns was to adopt and grow trees in Israel. They were successful in that campaign. But when it comes to a Palestinian tree — as if a tree can be identified as Israeli or Palestinian — then that Palestinian tree should be uprooted, whereas if a tree is an Israeli tree it should be nurtured and irrigated. This shows that the discrimination is not only against individual human beings, but is directed against everything Palestinian. If a house is Palestinian it should be demolished. If a tree is Palestinian it should be uprooted. If land is Palestinian it should be confiscated. If an individual is Palestinian he should be punished, either jailed, deported, or killed.

So this is the policy. It is a systematic policy. It did not start only yesterday or when we began the Intifada. It started the first day Israeli soldiers entered the Occupied Territories in 1967.

Now we come to another very important issue to us as Palestinians — education. When we lost our land in 1948, Palestinians found a new identity in education. We attempted to re-educate ourselves so as to overcome the tragedy that happened in 1948. As a result the Palestinian people became the most educated people in the Middle East. Palestinians have the highest percentage of educated persons vis-a-vis total population.

The Israelis saw this as a threat to their existence and to their survival. They wanted to punish the Palestinians where we have succeeded, in education. They decided to close all academic institutions: universities, community colleges, schools, and even kindergartens. When asked to justify the closure of kindergartens their answer was, "for security reasons." I cannot imagine how a child of two or three years can be a threat to Israeli security.

It is clear that when the Israelis closed kindergartens, schools, and universities, their actual policy was not revealed publicly but was demonstrated through their actions. The policy is to create a generation of ignorance, in the hope that this ignorant generation will accept being merely wage laborers for Israelis and not part of a people that yearns for freedom and independence.

This is very important. When you shoot a child and you kill that person, you terminate the person's life. But when you forbid a child to go to school you are killing the mind of that child. If you kill the mind, the consequence will be worse than killing the body. What the Israelis intend to do is to kill the mind of Palestinian society. You can imagine what type of leadership we will have and what type of future Palestinians will have if we are stripped of education.

Rehavam Ze'evi, who is the leader of an Israeli party represented in the Knesset, says very clearly that his objective is to force the Palestinians to leave. According to him, "We are not going to force them to transfer but we are going to make them leave voluntarily." At least he is frank in his aspirations.

The Israelis are implementing this policy but without saying so clearly. Their strategy is to do it little by little. When you close academic institutions, when you confiscate land, when you build settlements, when you uproot trees, when you demolish houses, when you detain and deport Palestinian people, etc., etc., you want the population to leave. They are creating a situation such that the Palestinians can no longer tolerate life. They want Palestinians to become convinced that their future has ended and that leaving is the only way to survive. In essence, they are forcing Palestinians to take a decision that has already been predetermined by the Israelis.

We Palestinians are aware of this master plan and have stated clearly that we are not leaving this land. We will not repeat what happened in 1947–48.

What happened on December 8, 1987, when the Intifada started, was the Palestinian response to all the above-mentioned policies. It's a Palestinian voice against the Israeli repression. It's a Palestinian voice against the international blindness. And it's a Palestinian voice which displays that we still have the will and desire to resist, and stay, and live in this land which is ours. This is why the Intifada started.

Our basic principles as Palestinians are first, that the Palestine Liberation Organization is our sole legitimate representative; second, our right of self-determination; third, our right to an independent Palestinian state with Jerusalem as its capital; and fourth, our right to return. We have no problem in recognizing Israel, but we cannot recognize Israel before getting our own independent Palestinian state.

The autonomy that is being offered is only an extension of the civil administration. The civil administration is directly controlled by the Israeli military officials. They are offering to transfer to us responsibility for the education system, health system, services rendered to the community, collecting taxes and that's it. Land will be in the hands of the Israelis. Water resources, which are going to be the threat for our existence in the future, will be in the hands of the Israelis. Security will be in the hands of the Israelis. Foreign relations will be in the hands of the Israelis. Law and order are and will be in the hands of the Israelis. Transportation and movement are in the hands of the Israelis. This is the autonomy that is being offered to us.

Dual authority is what is present here. The Israeli authority is here because they are present with their arms, by military means. But there is another authority, the Palestinian popular authority. You can see it in refugee camps. You can see it in villages. You can see it everywhere.

The Israelis were forced to accept this dual authority at certain times. When the Israelis closed our schools, the Palestinian authority promptly began to establish popular committees and created an alternative education to what the Israelis were offering. This program was extremely successful until the Israeli defense minister issued a statement, according to which anyone involved in popular education and popular committees was subject to ten years' imprisonment. As a result, Palestinians became careful about their involvement in such committees. But the Israelis cannot stop our offering alternative services to the population in the villages, camps and cities.

The Intifada is the first face-to-face Palestinian-Israeli confrontation. During past wars it was always Arab forces against Israel and Israel won. This time it's the Palestinian will, the Palestinian determination, the Palestinian individual living in the Occupied Territories against the Israeli army. The Israelis cannot defeat the will of the people. If we use firearms we will give the Israelis an excuse to eliminate us, an excuse to start massacres everywhere. We do have arms, but not enough to confront Israeli military might. But when we confront them with our will, our bodies, our stones, with alternative schools, with popular committees, etc., then this confrontation the Israelis cannot really defeat.

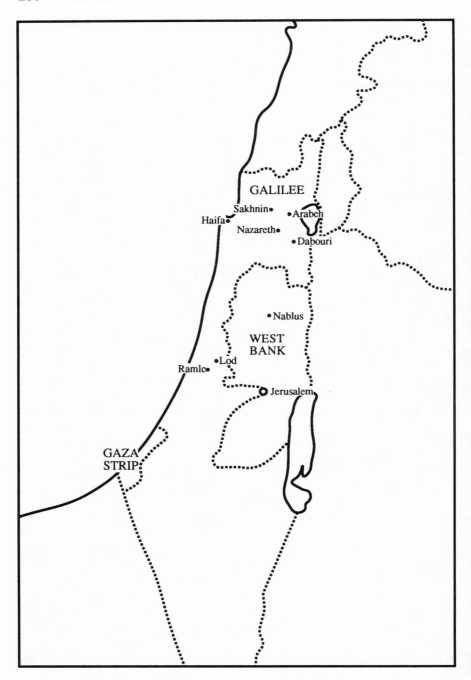

10

Resistance Behind the Green Line

Arabs who live within Israel are second-class citizens, and subject to the same process of land confiscation at work in the Occupied Territories.[1] As of 1985, title to 93 per cent of the land in Israel was claimed by the State or quasi-public organizations in trust for the Jewish people, and little of the remaining 7 per cent is ever on the market.[2]

In June 1987 the Palestinian community in Israel began a program for national and civic equality by holding a widely-observed one-day strike. The demands of that program are the demands of Palestinians everywhere:[3]

1. A complete withdrawal from the Occupied Territories and the establishment of an independent Palestinian state under the PLO.
2. Recognition of the refugee right of return, or to compensation.
3. Recognition of the Arab community in Israel as a national minority and as an indivisible part of the Palestinian Arab people, with full national and civil rights in complete equality with Jewish Israelis.
4. Repeal of land seizures and the return of confiscated land.
    . . .
8. Repeal of all discrimination against Arabs in the nationality law, in local government, employment, education and health.
9. Participation of the Arabs in central and local government on an equal footing.
10. The establishment of an Arab university in Nazareth, and the creation of an industrial plan for the Arab sector on an equal footing with the Jewish sector.

★   ★   ★

1. See, for example, John Quigley, *Palestine and Israel: A Challenge to Justice* (Durham: Duke University Press, 1990), pp. 97–150; David McDowall, *Palestine and Israel: The Uprising and Beyond* (Berkeley: University of California Press, 1989), pp. 123–45.
2. U.S. State Department, *Country Reports on Human Rights Practices for 1985*, p. 1264.
3. McDowall, op. cit., p. 238.

Ghanem Habib-Allah

"You want me to be a part of Israel only if you need me, but if I need you I am not an integral part of this state."

I was born in Ein Mahil village on the ninth of July, 1962. We are a big family. With all my brothers and sisters, we are eighteen. It is a family which grew for more than 400 years in our village. No one left the country after the massacre and the war in 1948.

My grandfather was a big leader in the village. All the people still remember Mohammed Ibrahim, my father's father. He has the reputation of a man who supported the people, who cared for all the village, not for himself. I still remember the stories that my mother and father and my big brother told me: that he always gave land to other people in the village who needed land to build houses and establish themselves; and that when someone wanted to take a loan from a wealthy man in Nazareth, they would take my grandfather to guarantee that the loan would be repaid. My grandfather didn't establish a big house for himself. Although he had much land, he didn't care for us more than he cared for all the people in the village. It's an integral part of our tradition that you can't be in a situation with a lot of land while your neighbor is living in a small area.

My mother said, "Your grandfather gave a gift of land to all these people and now you haven't any piece to establish a house for yourself." I said, "OK. I agree with him." Because I still hear the good reputation of my grandfather. I don't need land if the people hate me. I need the love of these people. I was arrested during the Gulf War in 1991 and when I came back home, all the village people came to shake hands and to say, "We support you and we hope that you will be like your grandfather."

Ein Mahil has had a bad relationship with Jewish settlements. Bet Qeshet was a Jewish settlement that tried to control Ein Mahil. Partition was established before 1948; there was a pact between Ein Mahil and Bet Qeshet. But in 1948 there was a battle in a small village less than two kilometers from Ein Mahil, and Ein Mahil lost eight men in this battle.

People from Ein Mahil, Kufr Kana, Reina, El Mashad, Dabouri and Aksal didn't leave, and many people from Nazareth didn't leave the country in 1948. I asked my parents why they didn't leave in 1948, and why in all this area people didn't leave. They said, "We understood that if we left, we would not find a place where we could live in freedom. All of us heard about many people who had lost their lives on the road between Palestine and Lebanon in 1948. There was no chance that we would be able to maintain our future in Lebanon or Jordan or Syria. Our decision was to stay here, in our homeland. If there was going to be a confrontation between us and the Jewish settlement, we had to be here. All of us agreed. We were going to continue to struggle here until the last man." This is what my parents said. I think that the battle between Ein Mahil and Bet Qeshet was what made them decide to stay here.

I still remember the lifestyle of my family. At five in the morning we would go to the fields together. We would take tomatoes and grapes and water. The fields were far away, about three kilometers from our house. We spent the time there working on our land because we were villagers and the land was our main resource. When we came back to our home at 6:00 or 6:30, we cooked some food. I still remember how we ate together, eighteen people in the same room. I still remember the traditional food. I still remember that in our home, my grandfather's house, we had two bedrooms and a big salon. The big salon was for the many visitors who came to my grandfather to talk about the issues in the village, about our problems and about our future. This style of life gave me a sense of belonging, that I am an integral part of this family.

I learned from my grandfather and after that from my father and mother, that we have to be together, we have to struggle, we have to love the people. We lived in my grandfather's home until he died and when they separated the land between the brothers, they gave this house to my father. When the land was separated between me and my brother, my brother gave me the house of my grandfather and of my father. I live, I sleep, I sit in the same house as my grandfather and my father. These things keep me believing that I have to continue in the same style of life, to struggle with my people. When I talk about land confiscations and about my village, it is not as a private case. I protest for all Ein Mahil villagers.

Land Confiscation

We have to look at the confiscations of land as a continuous process from 1948 to the present.

In 1948, land which had belonged to the British Mandate now belonged to Israel. The land of people who were "absent," who escaped or were forced to leave, was taken by the Israeli authority and given to the Jewish population. Other land was confiscated for a "public purpose."

They came to Ein Mahil and they said, "We want this land for a public purpose." They took many thousands of dunums from Ein Mahil and the surrounding villages, and they said they took it for a public purpose. While our population was increasing, they were taking the land.

Ein Mahil in 1948 had a population of 862 people with 14,000 dunums. The population increased up to 7,100 in 1992, and after all of the confiscation, we have only 4,100 dunums.

Take another example, Kufr Kana. In 1948, Kufr Kana had a population of 1,000 and 19,500 dunums. In 1992, there were 13,000 people and only 5,635 dunums.

Let's talk about Reina. The population in 1948 was 750; 15,777 dunums. The population has increased to 8,000 and in 1992 Reina has only 6,764 dunums.

El Mashad had a population of 823 people in 1948; in 1992, 7,000 or more. Land, in 1948, was 10,805 dunums; 5,420 in 1992.

The main issue is that there is an Arab majority in Nazareth and the surrounding villages, and the Israeli authority is trying to establish and maintain a Jewish majority and an Arab minority in the future. They can't maintain a Jewish majority if they don't have land for them.

From 1948 until 1964, the Israeli authority used military rule. If you wanted to move from Ein Mahil to Kufr Kana you had to have permission. If you wanted to buy anything in Nazareth, you had to have permission. The military situation made people more and more afraid and frustrated. People heard about the Deir Yassin massacre. People heard about the Sufsaf massacre. They heard what the Israeli authorities were doing to the Palestinian people and they were afraid that if they made any kind of protest, any kind of resistance, especially related to the land, the Israeli authority would take them outside the border. And who would care? The United Nations? No one would care. The people decided to be silent. You have to understand the frustration, the hopelessness.

After the 1967 war, after the abolition of military rule in Galilee and after connections were made with the West Bank and Gaza Strip, we had more and more students who finished secondary school, more students from the university, more understanding of what was going on, and more capacity to protest. We had parties. We had leadership. We had money. And we had resistance. We had the knowledge that we had to do something.

The First Land Day

In 1976, I remember the Land Day when the whole Palestinian population moved to the streets in Ein Mahil, in Kufr Kana, in Reina and Arabeh and all the villages, and I was one of them. We were protesting against the land confiscations and the Israeli policy of surrounding us. The West Bank and Gaza Strip supported us by protests on the same day.

Confiscation orders had been issued on March 9, 1976. It took us three weeks to organize everything with maps, with slogans, everything. It is my impression that the first Land Day was organized by two political movements, Sons of the Land, and the Democratic Front for Peace and Equal Rights, with the support of all the Palestinian population.

On March 30, 1976, all the people moved from Ein Mahil to Kufr Kana and in Kufr Kana there was a big protest. Then all the people moved from Kufr Kana to Arabeh, and to Sakhnin, and to other villages, to show that we were unified. It was not a case for Ein Mahil or for Reina or for Arabeh. It was a case of "to be or not to be." We had to fight against these confiscations of land.

In Sakhnin, I remember, we were in the protest and people began to say, "We'll sacrifice our blood in the name of Galilee." This meant, we'll not give you this land. We will not sit down and see you take this land.

Then the police began to shoot, to use force. I was not far away: I was here and the woman who was killed was there [about 30 yards]. The people were screaming, "Bring the ambulance! There is a woman killed." They took the woman to the hospital.

We didn't move. We stayed there. After an hour they said that she had died. Anyone could have been in the same situation. She was just part of the demonstration. Her name was Khledija. She was 23 years old.

The people were angry and they moved toward the police. The police began to use tear gas. And they arrested many people after that.

Until this day, the Israeli authorities say that they made a mistake to use force against this demonstration. It was a provocation to put themselves among the people when the people were angry and didn't want to see any symbol of Israeli authority.

After Land Day in 1976, the Israeli authority decided they would not go inside the village on Land Day. They would try to maintain security from outside the village. They understood the risk. On the thirtieth of March, 1992, they said, "You want Land Day? OK. You want to protest? You want to dance? OK. You are inside. We are outside. We will maintain the roads. We are not going to go inside the village." Because they understand that if they go inside the village, the same problem as in 1976 will happen again and again.

I think Land Day had an effect on the historical process. From 1948 until 1967, the Israeli authority tried to take the Palestinian people away from their political connection, from their social atmosphere, by confiscation of land, by taking them to work in the industrial area, by trying to move villagers to cities and to the Hebrew language and Hebrew culture. Go to Tel Aviv and you can see the lights, the cinema and everything.

They were successful with some people. Some say, "I am a Palestinian in Israel." Some say, "I am an Arab Israeli living in Israel." And some say, "I am not Palestinian. I am an Arab Israeli." Some of them work and support the Shin Bet activities.

After 1967, the border opened with the West Bank and Gaza Strip. There were many refugees who moved from here to the West Bank. We found our brothers there, we found ourselves there, and we began another historical process, which meant to come back to our roots. After Land Day in 1976, we came back to our roots more and more.

The Israeli authority had pushed this people to work in the cities without maintaining their social situation — no food, no house to sleep in, not enough money, no security. By land confiscation, they were surrounding us, and in 1976, the confiscation came to the borders of our homes.

Through Land Day and cultural activities and the connection with the West Bank and Gaza Strip, I think people now understand, without any hesitation, that they are Palestinian in their identity at the same time they are residents of Israel. Now, more and more people declare that we are Palestinian.

Student Activities

In 1979, I finished secondary school. I was investigated many times by the Shin Bet and the Israeli authority because I was very active as a student in secondary school. They came to my home to give me an order to come tomorrow to the investigator. When we decided to have Land Day, I tried to convince students to share in our struggle. The West Bank was having many, many struggles and we, myself and other students, tried to support our brothers in the West Bank and Gaza Strip. We organized cultural activities.

When I graduated from secondary school, my economic situation was not good enough to go to university. I had a brother who was studying at that time. In my house were me, my mother and father, and another brother and sister. It was my own decision that I had to work in a factory. From 1979 through October 1980, I did many kinds of work until I had a sum of money to support my academic studies.

In November 1980, I began my first academic year at the Hebrew University as a student of Hebrew language and the history of the Middle East. Why did I choose these subjects? I wanted to be a lawyer, but they didn't accept me. Then I decided to move to history because I love the subject, maybe because of the 1948 situation. I decided on Hebrew literature and language because I wanted to understand everything about the people who live with me. I wanted to understand their language, their literature, their style of life and everything. After three years I finished my B.A., and in June 1986 I finished my M.A. degree in the history of the Middle East.

I continued my struggle when I was at the university. I was a member of the Arab League committee from 1981–86. We tried to maintain our own Palestinian identity by inviting many researchers, many poets, many singers, to talk about Palestinian issues, Palestinian resistance, Palestinian culture, and Palestinian life. We organized visits to Deir Yassin village because we wanted students not to lose their history and to understand exactly what had happened to our people in 1948. I still remember our protest when bombs were placed in the cars of Bassam Shaka'a and other Palestinian leaders. [See above, Section 9, p. 256.]

All the time, we demanded an Israeli acceptance of the Palestinian ambition to establish their homeland, accepting negotiation with the PLO as the representative organization of our people, accepting the abolition of any kind of settlement, accepting the withdrawal from the West Bank, Gaza and East Jerusalem, and the right to return for the Palestinian people who were forced to leave this country in 1948.

While I was a student I was working with Arabic newspapers in Jerusalem as a researcher. I wrote about the Palestinian cause and about the conflict between Israel and the Palestinian people. Especially after I began the M.A. studies, I began to research and write essays about confiscations of land, about political issues, and about the situation in the West Bank.

After I finished my M.A. degree, I was thinking about continuing for a Ph.D. in the USA. But my father was sick, my brother was married and all of my brothers and sisters had moved from the village. There was no one in the house except my mother and father. I decided that I had to come back to my house because I had to be beside my father in this time. These things cut off my academic ambition.

Back to My Village

I came back to my village and I came back to my struggle against the land confiscations. I began to work in 1987 as a teacher of history in the Ein Mahil secondary school. At the same time I worked two days a week in Jerusalem at the Birzeit Institute of Research on the history of the Palestinian villages which were demolished in 1948. In 1988, I moved to work as a teacher in the secondary school of Nazareth.

In 1988, I established a council of professionals in my village. I was the general secretary or chairman. We began to discuss our part in Ein Mahil issues: land confiscations, political issues, economic problems, future development, the educational situation in the village, medical needs, issues dealing with our people. We understood that we had the capacity and the ability and we had to do something for the whole village.

In March 1989, the Israeli authority sent papers to the villagers saying they wanted the villagers to leave their land. The professional council began a protest. We began to send papers to a member of the Knesset, to the newspapers, to international committees, and we tried to convince all of these people that we were talking about discrimination against the Palestinian population inside Israel. We had details and documents.

After the Soviet Union opened its borders and new immigrants were coming to Israel from the Soviet Union, the Israeli authority declared that Upper Nazareth would be the target city for the new Jewish immigrants until Upper Nazareth grew to be the same in population with the Arab population.

Ein Mahil is now surrounded from all sides. In Ein Mahil, the new houses are right across the narrow street from ours. By surrounding the Arab village, they are making it a ghetto (like the Jewish lived in Poland and other places) with no option for the future.

By 1992, we needed hundreds of houses for our increasing population, but we were not allowed to build. In Upper Nazareth they have built 10,000 houses only for the Jewish. As an Ein Mahil villager, I can't go there to live. They will not give me permission. I am not acceptable there.

We haven't any factories and we need for our future to establish factories. If I wanted to be in a public relationship with Jews to establish a new factory, they would not support it. What about the future? We need another school. We need another area for our kids to play and to spend time.

October Protests

We organized a protest for the day the Israeli authority wanted us to leave the land, the eighteenth of October, 1989. And we made a decision that we were not going to take any money from the Israeli authority if they took our land. We were going to continue our struggle.

After this protest, the Israeli authority postponed the taking until March 1990. In March 1990, they sent the same people the same order, only they changed the date. They said the villagers had to leave the land by the twenty-third of October, 1990, and each one had to pay 450 shekels in administrative costs. For Ein Mahil the confiscation orders were for 1,500 dunum which belonged to 120 villagers. They were confiscating the land beside the homes.

We reacted by contacting the local councils around us, the Committee for

Land Defense, and the head of the local Arab Council. We decided to go to the High Court and try to convince the High Court that confiscations would be a disaster for the future of Ein Mahil.

We planned a protest for the twenty-third of October, with a press conference, radio and television. We invited Arab and Israeli television. We invited a member of the Knesset. We invited many land committees and local councils.

We had twenty minutes on Israeli television. Menachim Ariav, the head of the municipality of Upper Nazareth, said: "We need this land for the public purpose. We wonder why Ein Mahil villagers are against these confiscations, because we are going to establish factories where villagers of Ein Mahil can work."

He said one word and there was a confrontation between me and him. I said: "If you are talking about public purpose, what does this mean? Does it mean the public purpose for the whole population? Try to convince me! It means, for the sole benefit of the Jewish population."

I said: "You want public purpose? OK. Take your hands off of this land. Don't take my land and then say, 'I will establish factories.' Give me the opportunity, the permission, to establish *my* factories. You establish your houses and your swimming pool. Give me the opportunity to establish at least 300 houses for Ein Mahil villagers, to establish a swimming pool like the Jewish have, and to establish a new school. You think about your benefit, your sole benefit. Give me the chance to establish things for my village like what you have established for Upper Nazareth."

"No, no," he replied, "Public purpose. The government will decide what to do." And he said, "You are an integral part of this state. Then you have to be responsible and support the state which now needs this land for 400,000 people who came from the Soviet Union."

I said: "You don't give me the feeling that I am a part of this state. You want me to be a part of Israel only if you need me, but if I need you I am not an integral part of this state. I can't buy any house in Upper Nazareth because I am Arab. You will not allow me to live with you. And if you gave me the permission, I couldn't live with you because you don't give me the sense that I belong with this population. Equal rights? Just when you need me. When you need this land you say, 'public purpose.'

"Seven thousand people here don't have any factories. When we work in the Jewish factories, the salary is 1,500 shekels for the Arab worker who worked for a long time, maybe five years, and the Jewish come to work in this factory and they give him 2,000 shekels per month.

"Don't try to convince me about equal rights. You can convince yourself but you will not convince me. Never. Because I see facts in the area. I see that you try to surround us. You try to transfer our population, not by force like you did in 1948, but a transfer which we choose because we have no potential for the future."

After this protest, the Israeli authority decided again to postpone any activity against the farmers and the land.

During the Gulf War

In December 1990, I visited the USA. I returned two days before the Gulf War. At the beginning of the war they arrested me. They were accusing me of being a spy for Iraq about the scud missiles, and of having a connection with the PLO. They investigated me. There was no evidence. They said, "You are active in the land confiscations and other issues." We went to court and they had nothing against me except the activist things. I came back to my house. But they didn't allow me to travel outside the country.

The Gulf War began in January 1991. On February 19, 1991, while the war was still going on, the Minister of the Interior sent to Ein Mahil an order to take another 200 dunums for public purpose.

Justice

You can't talk about the High Court as separate from the Israeli authority. One supports the other. The Israeli authority went to the High Court and said, "We need this land for a public purpose. We are talking about 10,000 houses. We are going to establish houses and factories and all the needs for the new immigrants. We need this land."

Our advocate said to us that our case is not successful and we have to maintain, first of all, the public protest. There is no hope that we can obtain the restoration of our land. Now, we are trying to stop their activities on the land. Because we understand that the ambition of the Israeli authority is not only Ein Mahil, but will continue in Reina and Mashad and Kufr Kana.

We in Ein Mahil and the other villages understand and look at these confiscations as an integral part of Israeli policy from 1948, and maybe from 1881 when the Jewish immigrants began to come here and to confiscate this land. It is an integral part of the Zionist attitude that they came to a land without a people and they want this land for a people without land. They didn't accept the Palestinian existence and they continue in the same policy.

Their second ambition from this confiscation of land is to prevent any geographic connection between the Arab villages — between Ein Mahil and Mashad, between Ein Mahil and Reina, between Ein Mahil and Kufr Kana. They want to confiscate all the land between these villages. By confiscating this land, they can prevent any geographic connection in the future. They can fill this area with Jewish population and then they can control all these separate villages and then they can prevent any kind of public protest in the future.

The third reason for this confiscation, from my point of view as a man who is active in this issue, is that they want to maintain a Jewish majority in the future. There is now a Jewish majority in all of Galilee, but there is still a Palestinian majority in the Nazareth area. They declare that their ambition is that Upper Nazareth will have a Jewish majority by the year 2000.

The Israeli authority has begun to control the confiscated land. They cut our olive trees and they have begun to establish 10,000 houses at the edge of my village for the new immigrants. They established another three factories beside the houses.

If the farmer does not remove the trees from the confiscated land, he has to pay for the trees to be cut. It's about 2,000 shekels, depending upon how many cuts and what machine they use. Some of the farmers cut the trees because they have no money to pay. Some of the farmers refuse to cut the trees; it is difficult to order the farmer to cut his tree. If you will not pay, they are going to take you to jail. That's Israeli legitimacy. They confiscated the land and cut the trees and they try to force you to pay the money to the court. Justice!

Mohammed and Lawahez Burgal

"Wherever we are, as Palestinians, whether inside or outside Israel, we are a whole people."

Mohammed Burgal: My father and my grandfather and generations before them were here in Lod. Historically, we didn't come from some other place. This was our home. It seems that Lod is a very old city. No one knows when it was built. It was before the Assyrians and the Babylonians.

I remember, when I was a boy living in the slums of Lod in a section called "Mahatah." (In English, "the Station.") There was a certain holiday in Israel called Lag B'omer. They made fires everywhere and they would circle around the fires and dance. We saw them put a puppet of Gamel Abdul Nasser on the fire and, as children, we asked why they did that. We loved Gamel Abdul Nasser. His picture was in all of our homes because of what Nasser symbolized. As a response to that, I remember, we burned a puppet of Ben Gurion.

The Arab schools had classes on Saturdays. Every Saturday, when we would go to school, we would pass through the Israeli neighborhood where the Zionists were. (I say "Zionists," because not all Jews are Zionists.) They knew that we were Arab and they would attack us. Every Saturday we had a struggle with them. They threw stones at us and we responded. Our mother would try very hard to dress us well but when we arrived at school we no longer looked well dressed. That was life from the first to the eighth grade in school. Everywhere we went, we understood that we were Arab. There was tension and there could be a struggle or cursing. It would lead to conflicts.

We think about the reason why. At the beginning, I admit, we had just a general understanding: These are our enemies. They took our land, and they hate us. They don't try to let us live as human beings. They do not let us make progress as Arabs. They want us as just a lower class. They want to get more from us without giving us anything.

Also, we asked our mother and father. My father didn't want to speak about his experience. He fought in 1948 and was wounded in his thigh. He sold his horse to buy a weapon. He did not speak about that because he was afraid that if he said anything, it would make us more angry and we as young guys would try to do foolish things.

But we heard from my mother. For example, my brother came home from school and asked my mother, "Why do we think that Jews are not good, the Israelis are not good? Our teacher told us, they gave work to our father and now we have money and they protect us from burglars and enemies outside."

So my mother answered him. She felt she had to tell him the truth. I remember, she took him and sat with him and told him: "Look. If someone came now and took your house, this house over us, and then told us just to stay in the store; and he let your father work on the land that was his; and he killed your sister, which made your brother so afraid that he fled from the house; and then he told you, 'I am good enough to you to let you live here and you must accept the fact that you have to pay rent and you have to work and I will give you a little food.' Is that good enough for you?" my mother said. "Of course, it's not good. It's not fair." So, by that, she explained to him in a very simple way the whole Palestinian issue.

Before 1948, my family had a house and land. After 1948, they had no house and no land. The authorities confiscated the land and the house on it; it is now the property of a committee that is responsible for abandoned land. Even though we remained inside Israel, we are considered to be like those who left. It is ridiculous — we exist but we are considered as nonexistent — that is the law. Now my family pays rent to live in a house that belongs to them.

Little by little we came to understand that what we heard on the Israeli radio was false, that the state did not want anything for our benefit and that they were trying to cheat us. When we heard the Arabic stations, we heard very good songs about the necessity to liberate Palestine.

Where I lived, there were separate schools for Arab children through elementary school. In high school, I went to the Jewish school. Otherwise, I would have had to travel to Haifa and my parents would not accept that.

I had to enter into competition with pupils who had already studied in a Jewish elementary school. It was very hard for me to continue in high school with these students and subjects and with the program made for Jews. But it was the only opportunity I had to continue.

The official goal of Israeli education, according to the law of education, is to establish the culture of the people of Israel. The program of study includes the Holocaust, Israeli achievements in science, loyalty to the State of Israel and to the people of Israel, and there is no mention of another people who lives in this same land. You can see it in practice. What we are learning in the schools is without any mention of our history, without any mention of us as a nationality. It is systematically planned to diminish any feeling of our nationality or of our Arab minority inside Israel.

I had to study the Bible and Hebrew literature as if I were a Zionist student, not an Arab. In the schools for Arabs, they taught the Arabic language, grammar and literature, but they did not stress the history of our people.

The separation into Arab and Jewish schools was also discriminatory because the classroom hours that were given to the Arabs were two-thirds of those that were given to the Jews. So, the Israelis, the Zionists, had enough hours to be ready to succeed at the university examinations. They gave the

Arabs the same examination questions but they did not give us the same opportunity to prepare.

I had Arab teachers in the Arab school. But Arab teachers — and only Arab teachers — had to pass a Shin Bet security examination. The Shin Bet is the Israeli security service. A person could really want to teach and he could be qualified enough, but he could not teach if the Shin Bet would not accept him as a teacher. And every headmaster had to be approved by the Shin Bet.

The whole system makes it nearly impossible for the Arab students to achieve progress. You can see it also in the percentage of Palestinians in Israeli universities.[4] The percentage of Palestinians does not reflect their actual percentage in the whole society. It is much lower. In my pre-law year at the university, there were 360 students. Twenty were Arab students and I was one of two who succeeded and went to law school. Even though the requirements for Jews and Arabs to enter certain subjects are the same, it is much more difficult for Arabs to excel in the Israeli curriculum.

There is hard competition among Arabs. The academic fields for Arabs are mainly law and medicine, because nearly everything else is connected with security. If an Arab wanted to study electricity or electronics or engineering, as an Arab he would be regarded as too dangerous to be in such a sensitive position.

The only way that is open for an Arab is to go outside Israel. When a young adult sees how the world feels living in freedom, you can imagine that he is persuaded to live abroad. He thinks twice whether to come back or not. If he succeeds in his field abroad and has good conditions to work outside Israel, and if he finds a woman to share his life, then all of his life will be outside. But it is very hard for him to leave us and live abroad, because it will be difficult for him to continue living as an Arab.

Wherever we go, we have to understand our situation. It is part of our life. We are under the authority of a government and a law that is not serving us, an authority that is just capturing us in every facet of life.

Prison Was a School

I was a most polite and clever boy. But when I was about twenty years old, a friend and I started to ask ourselves, what could we do? Were we cowards? We started to share the struggle of our people including the struggle of Palestinians outside Palestine. But our situation was different from that of Palestinians in the occupied West Bank or Gaza or outside Palestine. We

---

4. The U.S. State Department, *Country Reports on Human Rights Practices for 1987*, p. 1187, states: "While Arabs make up about 16 per cent of the population of Israel, less than 2 per cent of the persons in senior government positions are Arabs, less than 3 per cent of Israeli judges are Arabs, and no large bank, industrial enterprise, or agricultural undertaking in Israel is headed by an Israeli Arab. Israeli Arabs make up 3 per cent of university students and less than 1 per cent of the academic positions in the universities." (The same paragraph also appears in previous *Country Reports*.) More recently, the State Department, *Country Reports on Human Rights Practices for 1991*, p. 1435, states: "Israeli Arabs have not received or attained the same quality of education, housing, or other services as Israeli Jews. Arab Israeli municipal officials state that the Government continues to underfund Arab municipalities. Relative to their numbers, Israeli Arabs are underrepresented in the student bodies of universities and in higher-level professional, academic, and business ranks."

needed to find what to do under our conditions.

First I reacted spontaneously to the situation. There was a "collaborator" that worked with me and my friend from the very beginning. He was my cousin from a refugee camp near Nablus and he collaborated with the authorities. They knew everything we did from the very beginning. He would lead us. He had the ideas. He tried to provoke us to catch soldiers and put them in houses, and to try to convince the authorities that the soldiers were being held outside the borders so the authorities had to release Kapuche or some young men. (Kapuche was a very famous religious man, a Christian man.) So they let us continue. As the expression says, they made the rope long but they held the end of the rope.

We were not members of a terrorist organization with weapons or anything like that. We simply tried to take an auto which was stopped and to take the soldiers and arrest them and then negotiate their release. That was the idea at that time. It was an idea that was not mature enough. It didn't take into consideration what was possible. It was reactive to the occupation in 1967. So that was my first arrest. It was in 1975. They put us in jail for four years. That was the maximum sentence. They wanted to make an example of us.

But inside the prison I met people who were thinking in a really deep way. It was my first opportunity to see and feel the Palestinian fedayin, not just as fighters who came to kill but in their humanitarian aspects. I was astonished to recognize and to meet these people and to understand the wider horizons of the Palestinian issue: it is not justified that people kill and be killed; it is a more complex problem. They explained how the Palestinian situation came into being. It was a school for us.

While I was in prison, I began to read and to study in many fields: sociology and political history. I made an appeal to the High Court to get books, and I also made an appeal to force the authorities in the prison to let a teacher come from the university and teach me mathematics. It was a struggle all the time. During that struggle we did make progress.

During my imprisonment, my father was working in construction. He continued to feed my family. After I came out from the prison I found that I had to find work without being in contact with the authorities. I decided that the best way was to buy a store. So my grandmother, who was like a mother to me, advanced a lot of money to me. I got loans from friends here or there. And with another friend, we together bought a grocery and started.

The grocery now belongs to my family. My father died four months before I bought the store. Now my mother and my little brother work in that grocery.

The Ghassan Kanafani Kindergarten

Lawahez Burgal: After I married Mohammed, I went to live inside the Green Line, in Lod. I felt that we were living under the same conditions as under occupation. The Israelis were saying that there was democracy, but the democracy was just for the Israelis. It is not true that the Arabs are living the same as the Jews inside Israel. There is a big, big gap between the Arabs and the Jews inside the Green Line.

I saw that my role, as a woman inside the Green Line, was to establish a women's committee. We established the Arab Progressive Women's Committee, and our first activity was to open a kindergarten. If we wanted women to go to work and to be independent, we had to offer them a place for their kids. In the early 1980s, when we started kindergartens for Arab children, there were approximately sixty kindergartens for Israeli Jews.

We opened kindergartens for about eighty-five children. Most of them were from poor families. Some of the fathers were dealing drugs. They didn't own houses. They didn't own lands even if they had title to their lands. They were living under bad conditions. We now have nine kindergartens inside the Green Line.

One of the kindergartens was named for Ghassan Kanafani,[5] not just because he was from the Green Line, but because he wrote about Palestinian children. We told the children, "Ghassan Kanafani wrote about you."

After three years, the Israeli authorities came: soldiers with journalists, with security men. They surrounded us in the kindergarten and they took the kids and their parents to interrogation. They asked one of the kids, "Who's Ghassan Kanafani? What do you know about Ghassan Kanafani?" And they asked the parents also.

They took pictures of the sign that said Ghassan Kanafani Kindergarten. All the neighbors could see that. They went to homes in the neighborhood and asked, "Did you see that sign?" "Yes." "What does that mean, Ghassan Kanafani?" They wanted to know whether the neighborhood knew about Ghassan Kanafani.

After that, they gave us an order that the Ghassan Kanafani Kindergarten was closed. They said the kindergarten was named for a "terrorist." We went to court and the lawyer said, "You talk about Ghassan Kanafani in the Hebrew University, and there are a lot of books by Ghassan Kanafani that were translated into Hebrew. If it is forbidden, why are you teaching Israeli students about Ghassan Kanafani?"

Finally they said, "OK, we're going to let you open a kindergarten, if you change the name, and if you build a new facility." That meant it would remain closed. We couldn't build because you needed a license from the municipality, and the municipality would not give us a license. And we didn't have money to rebuild.

Community Organizing

Mohammed: It is not so simple for Palestinians living inside Israel to think about how to continue our struggle. I think it would be fair enough for me and for other Palestinians who live inside Israel if we could live as human beings with equal rights — with democratic rights, with political rights, with national rights, and without racism. Wherever we are, as Palestinians,

5. Ghassan Kanafani was born in Acre in 1936. At the age of twelve he went into exile in Lebanon with his family. Kanafani became well known for his literary works including stories for children. He was also a spokesman for the Popular Front for the Liberation of Palestine. Kanafani was assassinated in Beirut in 1972.

whether inside or outside Israel, we are a whole people. Israel denies this and cannot accept it. Golda Meir said, "There is no Palestinian people." Now they speak other words, but the content has stayed the same.

We started a club in Lod, not just to support Palestinians in their struggle but to work on our own struggle and our suffering here. We put on educational activities to make people more conscious of belonging to their own Palestinian people.

We brought the Al-Hakawati Drama Group from Jerusalem. We were attacked in the main Israeli newspapers, saying that we were terrorists and that we wanted to "massacre the Jews." We never said that. They were trying to make people afraid of us. Even so, about 350 people came to the play and it was a success.

In remembrance of the Sabra and Shatila massacre, we decided to have a demonstration. We decided to go from the mosque, across a Jewish neighborhood, to a house where an Arab lived. We would be silent when we crossed the Israeli area. We measured every step in millimeters. We planned every step in that demonstration, because we didn't want people to have a hard experience that would make them feel put off by such an activity.

We started from the mosque. We bluffed the police. Someone had died in the Arab neighborhood so the police thought we would go to the cemetary. We changed direction in order not to get into a clash with them. It was a very responsible activity. At the end everyone knew what the effect and the importance of such an activity was.

After that, on the day of Palestine, the people of Lod and other places came together challenging the policy of the administration and demonstrating that we weren't afraid of the administration. There were women and children and all ages supporting that demonstration. One girl threw a stone at the police car. The police came and took an old woman and the girls and guys struggled with the policemen. The situation was like a scene from the West Bank or Gaza.

I, myself, was arrested while I was inside the market where the demonstration was. The only policeman that testified against me said, "I found him nearby, not shopping, not saying anything. I asked him to come to the police car and he entered and I took him to the police station."

After that testimony the judge, who was very "fond" of me and who knew my history, sentenced me to the hardest verdict of all, even more harshly than the guys who had struggled with the policemen. He gave me a fine, 2,000 shekels; the others were fined 70 or 700 and the highest was 1,000. Also he gave me six months probation: if I did any act under any chapter of the criminal law, I would be jailed for six months.

The authorities tried to make it impossible for us to continue our work and they put fear into the people: "These people will lead your sons to jail. They are extremists. Don't have anything to do with them." When the Ghassan Kanafani Kindergarten was closed, parents of children in the kindergarten were threatened with discharge or were fired by their employers. The authorities also went to parents to tell them not to have anything to do with us. I was jailed for 48 hours as a warning to them, to isolate me.

From the very beginning, they would put me and the others in jail for 48 hours simply like that. They claimed, "We were told that you have a connection with that bomb that we found in the market in Ramle." They knew that we had no connection, but they did it to show the people that, "You see? These people go to jail. Stay away from them. Keep your sons away from such people." They also put me under house arrest because of my political activity.

We had repeatedly to rent another house. Every time we rented a house — to teach people reading and writing, and we would have activities like folklore, dancing or plays or something like that — the authorities would pressure the owner of the house and he would say, "I can't continue to rent that house to you." Finally, a Palestinian American gave us enough money to buy a house.

It really affected our situation badly when they tried to convict me of a charge that I had information about someone who had committed a crime and I didn't tell the authorities. They put me in jail and I was released after three months: innocent. After that it was not convenient for me to continue this educational activity.

Becoming a Lawyer

There are not enough Arab lawyers inside Israel. Knowledge of the law is a tool; it is needed by my people. Every day there is someone that they put under arrest. It is not the main way of life, but for us in our political activity, this knowledge can help. I was accepted to the university to study law.

While I was a student, the authorities tried to charge that I was a member of a terrorist organization. One of my brothers was a very active young person and he thought, in literal ways, that he had to share the struggle of his people. He didn't know what fear was. He simply stepped in front of a bus and he threw a bomb against a military vehicle. It didn't burst but it scared the soldiers. The whole activity was not mature. The Israelis caught him and now he is in prison for life.

They put me in interrogation for forty days. Simply because he was my brother, they tried to make the connection to me. That was the very hardest experience that I passed through with the Shin Bet. I was released when they were not able to break me. Some of the Jewish students at the school of law came to see me after I had been under interrogation for two weeks. They cried when they heard what I went through in interrogation.

During the second year of the Intifada and during my second year in law school, I was put in administrative detention for six months. The authorities believed that I and eight of my comrades were so dangerous to the security of Israel that we had to be kept in prison.

In my last year in the school of law, after I finished the examination, they gave me house arrest for three months. I had been very busy studying. If I had done something that was illegal, they would have taken me to court and tried to sentence me. I do not understand why they found it proper to give me three months' house arrest.

The soldiers came with a paper from the judge. It said it was according to the emergency laws: Because of the fact that the Minister of Defense believes that Mohammed Burgal is dangerous to the security of Israel and there is no other way to defend that security but to put him under house arrest, it is necessary to the security of Israel that he be in the house one hour after sunset and he has to go to the police station three times a day and he has to accept every visit from the policemen to check up if he is really in his house, and he has to stay at this address and if he wants to change it he has to get permission from the authorities.

I had previously been under house arrest for one year. I had to go to the police station at 8:00, 12:00 and 4:00 every day, and I had to be in my home one hour after sunset. The police would come at any hour of the night to check that I was there. They would come at two or three in the morning and knock on the door.

This last time, they were very polite and very gentle soldiers. They searched every paper in my house. But they didn't bother my children. I began to feel the power of being a lawyer. They were simply afraid of me. They were up against a person who could teach them the law, so they felt that they were weak.

Now I am a man who knows the laws and I am qualified with a certificate but I am without permission to practice law. The only way to practice law is to be a member of the Israeli bar. There is no other bar. According to the law, you have to be admitted to the Israeli bar.

I can be barred from admission to the bar for having been convicted of a felony involving moral turpitude. However, I was a political prisoner. There is precedent. An anti-Zionist Jewish man was imprisoned fourteen years as a political prisoner. He was admitted to the Israeli bar and has been a lawyer for twelve years. I have to provide the papers to show that the accusations against me were political because, the judge told me, they destroyed the file in my 1975 case.

An Independent Minority

I am somewhat unusual among the Arabs inside Israel, because I acted as one that belonged to the community of the West Bank and Gaza Strip when I served in prison.

Our situation as Arabs inside Israel is different from the situation of Arabs in the West Bank and Gaza Strip. Leadership and organization developed there but not here. In the West Bank and Gaza, they are used to seeing soldiers and blood. Here they seldom even have smelled tear gas.

Arabs inside Israel ask, "Does the PLO consider us Palestinian or not?" There is no way for the PLO to give us any help at all. Everyone in the PLO says, "We want to help the Palestinians inside Israel," but there is not any mechanism to help us get a penny from any outside organization.

Palestinians in the West Bank and Gaza want their state now! I do not think Israel will let such a state come into being. But if there is a Palestinian state beside Israel, it will give us more cause to strive for our rights inside

Israel. It is the program of Ariel Sharon that if there is a Palestinian state outside Israel, "You Palestinians can go there and leave us here," as if this were really his land and not ours.

The authorities of Israel look at Palestinians as Israelis when it is a matter of not accepting us as Arabs and diminishing our national identity. Israeli identification was imposed on us and we have to accept it as Arabs. We, as a minority, need more civil rights.

Many of the top Israeli leadership admit the fact that there is discrimination against Arabs or, as they put it, a "gap" between the Israelis or the Zionists and the Arabs. But they want it both ways and they say of us, "They are Israelis. They don't have anything to fear. We are the State of Israel and we are responsible for them."

We need help from anywhere in the world that can give us help, especially from that part of the world that thinks Israel is a democracy. The help that has come to Israel through ordinary channels has been used to make parts of Israel very beautiful, but the Arab regions in Israel are poor. The mayor of Lod came here and saw how the house was leaning, and he got enough money but he didn't give any of it to the Arabs in order for us to better our living conditions.

We have to find the way to help our people to live as human beings, with all the opportunities and facilities of a community, and to achieve their progress as part of a Palestinian people who live inside Israel. For example, a project has been started with two ambulances in a clinic in the city of Shvaba, near Nazareth. It serves Shvaba and El Kaboul and other villages in that area. Within four minutes, the ambulance can be at the house of anyone who calls. Before, the Red Star of David ambulance service would take half or three-quarters of an hour to reach the sick person and sometimes the delay would cost a life. Now Palestinians have a very professional ambulance team with a doctor and nurses. The doctor is trained to care for people with heart attacks and they have very new equipment similar to the equipment Americans used in the Gulf. The people appreciate such activity very much. That is a project which works now. But money is needed to pay salaries, and sometimes the doctor works for as long as twenty-two to twenty-four hours.

Every project you want to start inside Israel is really hard, because the Israelis don't want to make it easy for any Arab to act independently from the Zionist committees or authorities.

Economic development by Arabs as a minority inside Israel is narrowly limited. Arabs work in factories canning and making pickles. They sell them very cheaply to a big company that exports them. We need a company that exports and imports. Little by little we need to develop an economic strategy.

We have to enter into every field of life of every Palestinian inside Israel, to help them to be what they are, not to lend them to the Israeli plan which would diminish them as a minority and create conditions to suggest they leave their lands. Strategic planning is very frightening. The needs for facilities and thinking are enormous and we are really poor in resources. But we accept the challenge.

It depends on us to build a new background of economic and educational and cultural activity and to develop as an independent minority in every field of life. We have to have our own institutions. There is no other answer to the needs of the people. If Palestinians inside Israel do not have minimal means of cultural and economic life, then it will be easy for the Israeli authorities to diminish them as a people.

We understand that our role is not just a political one. We are a people that wants to continue to live as human beings. Since the Intifada, in various places within the Green Line, Palestinians are ready to demonstrate or to sing about Palestine at their weddings. But why did that take twenty years?

If you just give the people political slogans they say, "OK, we understand we really are Palestinians. We want to do what you say. We appreciate you and we see that you are right. But, we also want to eat. We also want to live. We also want our students to study. We also want to attend to everything in life. And these things are under official policy." So we have to find the way to act as Palestinians, *and* to answer all of these needs.

I have anti-Zionist Jewish friends who understand the issues well and who work with us. We have to understand Jews as human beings. Some of them have been very good friends to me. It is harder and more artificial for a person from the West Bank to see a Jew as a human being.

We have to speak with Jews as human beings, not in a brutal way. We should behave the way we believe it is needed to be — to share our whole humanity.

If I were to leave here and find another way of life, I think it would be just an escape. I would only be solving the problem for myself. I could be another Palestinian in Europe — maybe I would have a life that was easier if I had the financial possibilities.

But I am part of a family and of a people. I think that I owe these people because of all the things that they gave me. I am conscious of their situation. I think it is not just my duty. I think it is my happiness as a human being to try to find the happiness of my people, and to make progress in this generation. Otherwise, I would be a miserable person. I act as a human being, and I struggle to make it better than it is now. This is the proper place for me to be: in my land, trying to make proper living conditions as a Palestinian Arab, in this land where I was born and my friends and neighbors — Jews and Arabs — are, and in Jerusalem perhaps to be in peace together. That is the dream of everyone who believes in peace.

Bibliography

Note: The following suggested readings are books that one or more of the editors have found particularly helpful. For a comprehensive bibliography, see David L. Williams, *The Palestinian/Israeli Conflict: A Select Bibliography*, published by the Chicago Public Library, Social Sciences and History Division.

Bennis, Phyllis. *From Stones to Statehood: The Palestinian Uprising*. New York: Olive Branch Press, 1990.

Brenner, Lenni. *Zionism in the Age of Dictators*. Westport, Connecticut: Lawrence Hill & Company, 1985.

Chacour, Elias. *Blood Brothers*. Tarrytown, New York: Chosen Books, 1984.

Cobban, Helena. *The Palestine Liberation Organisation: People, Power and Politics*. Cambridge: Cambridge University Press, 1984.

Cockburn, Andrew and Leslie. *Dangerous Liaison: The Inside Story of the US-Israeli Covert Relationship*. New York: HarperCollins Publishers, 1991.

Ellis, Marc H. *Beyond Innocence and Redemption: Confronting the Holocaust and Israeli Power*. San Francisco: Harper & Row, 1990.

Emerson, Gloria. *Gaza. A Year in the Intifada: A Personal Account from an Occupied Land*. New York: Atlantic Monthly Press, 1991.

Findley, Paul. *They Dare to Speak Out: People and Institutions Confront Israel's Lobby*. Chicago: Lawrence Hill Books, 1989.

Flapan, Simha. *The Birth of Israel: Myths and Realities*. New York: Pantheon Books, 1987.

Kanafani, Ghassan. *Men in the Sun and Other Palestinian Stories*. Washington, D.C.: Three Continents Press, 1984.

Khalidi, Walid. *All That Remains: The Palestinian Villages Occupied and Depopulated by Israel*. Washington, D.C.: Institute for Palestine Studies, 1992.

Khalidi, Walid. *Before Their Diaspora: A Photographic History of the Palestinians, 1876–1948*. Washington, D.C.: Institute for Palestine Studies, 1984.

Khalidi, Walid. *From Haven to Conquest: Readings in Zionism and the Pales-

tine Problem Until 1948. Washington, D.C.: Institute for Palestine Studies, 1987.

Najjar, Orayb Aref. *Portraits of Palestinian Women*. Salt Lake City: University of Utah Press, 1992.

Quigley, John. *Palestine and Israel: A Challenge to Justice*. Durham, North Carolina: Duke University Press, 1990.

Richards, Leila. *The Hills of Sidon: Journal from South Lebanon* 1983–1985. New York: Adama Books, 1988.

Said, Edward W. *The Question of Palestine*. New York: Times Books, 1980.

Timerman, Jacobo. *The Longest War: Israel in Lebanon*. New York: Vintage Books, 1982.

Turki, Fawaz. *The Disinherited: Journal of a Palestinian Exile*. New York: Monthly Review Press, 1972.

Wright, Clifford A. *Facts and Fables: The Arab-Israeli Conflict*. London: Kegan Paul, 1989.

The following organizations monitor human rights abuses in the Occupied Territories and publish a variety of books, documents and reports:

Al Haq, West Bank Affiliate
International Commission of Jurists
31 Main Street
P.O. Box 1413
Ramallah, West Bank

B'Tselem, the Israeli Information Center for Human
Rights in the Occupied Territories
18 Keren Hayesod Street
Jerusalem 92149

Palestine Human Rights Information Center
P.O. Box 20479
Jerusalem, via Israel
and

4201 Connecticut Avenue, N.W., Suite 500
Washington, D.C. 20008

Index

Of Related Interest

ORIGINAL SINS
Reflections on the History of Zionism and Israel
by Benjamin Beit-Hallahmi
ISBN 1–56656–131–0
paperback $14.95 (in Canada, $19.95)

"The book provides a very useful service to those interested in exploring the issues . . . from a fresh and challenging perspective. It has the potential to stimulate much necessary debate and reflection and hopefully it will do just that."
—*New Outlook*
"Its distinctive contribution is the insightful analysis of Israeli identity."
—*Middle East Report*

Many books on Zionism and Israel published in the West are limited to slogans and counter-slogans.
Original Sins goes beyond the accepted parameters by restating the terms of the debate. It provides a comprehensive overview of the origins, accomplishments, contradictions and betrayals of Zionism.
Starting from a non-idealizing, non-demonological review of Judaism, Jewish history and anti-Semitism, this book presents a sympathetic analysis of the development of political Zionism—and goes on to show how a dream became both a living reality and a nightmare. While Beit-Hallahmi does not fault the idea of a Jewish state in the abstract, he shows how Zionism in practice and in power becomes a kind of settler colonialism trying to ignore its victims—the Palestinians.
Benjamin Beit-Hallahmi is a noted Israeli scholar and author of *The Israeli Connection: Who Israel Arms and Why*. He teaches at Haifa University.

JERUSALEM IN HISTORY
edited by K.J. Asali
ISBN 0–940793–44–X
hardcover $16.95 (in Canada, $24.95)

The sanctity of Jerusalem has in many ways made its history. Loved and adored by hundreds of millions throughout the world and throughout the ages, Jerusalem has lived through times of glory in which it was built and embellished on a grand and impressive scale. Yet for the same reason of its unique place in the eyes of its faithful, Jerusalem was, in other times, to suffer terribly.
This important new book begins to provide a comprehensive outline of the amazing history of the city. *Jerusalem in History* moves from the Bronze Age to the tensions of present-day Jerusalem. It presents a balanced and authentic

picture, that helps to correct the often distorted images of the city presented over the last forty years.

The work represents a feat of international cooperation by eight eminent scholars from the Middle East, Europe and the U.S. They include K.J. Asali, also the editor, H.J. Franken, G.E. Mendenhall, John Wilkinson, Abdul Aziz Duri, Mustafa A. Hiyari, D.P. Little, A. Scholch, and M.C. Hudson.

BEHIND THE MYTH
Yasser Arafat and the Palestinian Revolution
by Andrew Gowers and Tony Walker
ISBN 0–940793–86–5
hardcover $24.95 (in Canada, $29.95)

"A first-rate biography . . ."
    —*Publishers Weekly*
" . . . [a] solid study informed by serious research and extensive interviews . . . Gowers and Walker trace his ascent with skill and dispassion; if you want to understand Mr. Arafat, they tell the story."
    —*The Wall Street Journal*
". . . impressive as narrative history and as political analysis. No single book does a better job of presenting the Palestinian movement as it presently exists, with a fair assessment of both achievements and failures."
    —*Foreign Affairs*
"The authors describe with great detail the internal dynamics of the PLO . . . up-to-date . . . Recommended . . ."
    —*Library Journal*

Behind the Myth is an inside account of one of the most controversial national movements of the modern era: of its origins, its armed struggle against Israel, its gradual shift from violence to diplomacy, and of the many pitfalls along the way. Based on hundreds of hours of exclusive interviews with senior PLO officials, including Arafat, as well as senior American, Arab, Israeli and European officials, it is a comprehensive portrait of the evolution of the Palestinian resistance from its earliest days as an unruly and little-noticed collection of guerrilla factions to its present international prominence. It also explores the many different roles Arafat has played during his 40-year career as a Palestinian leader.

For a complete catalog, please contact:

Interlink Publishing Group, Inc.
99 Seventh Avenue
Brooklyn, New York 11215